Kindling the

Celtic Spirit

Kindling the
Celtic Spirit

Ancient Traditions
to Illumine Your Life
Throughout the Seasons

Mara Freeman
Illustrations by Linda Carol Risso

HarperSanFrancisco
A Division of HarperCollinsPublishers

A portion of the proceeds from this book will be donated to Trees for Life, an organization that aims to restore the ancient Caledonian Forest of Scotland as well as many wild forests worldwide.

Permission acknowledgments are on page 402, which constitutes a continuation of this copyright page.

Library of Congress Cataloging-in-Publication Data
Freeman, Mara.
    Kindling the Celtic spirit : ancient traditions to illumine your life throughout the seasons / Mara Freeman ; illustrations by Linda Carol Risso.
      p.   cm.
    Includes bibliographical references and index.
    ISBN 0–06–251685–X (cloth)
    ISBN 0–06–251686–8 (pbk.)
    1. Celts—Religion. 2. Mythology, Celtic. 3. Spiritual life. I. Title.
BL900 . F74 2000
299.16—dc21   00–061443

06 07 08 RRD(H) 20 19 18 17 16 15 14 13 12 11

To the Dwellers of the Wildwood,
both seen and unseen,
and to DJW:
Cride hé
Daire cnó

Oh, the great gates of the mountains have opened once again,
And the sound of song and dancing falls upon the ears of men,
And the Land of Youth lies gleaming, flushed with rainbow light and mirth,
And the old enchantment lingers in the honey-heart of earth.

A. E.

CONTENTS

FOREWORD

Power of sea be yours,
Power of land be yours,
Power of heaven.
WEST HIGHLAND BLESSING

The great Celtic scholar Dr. Anne Ross once said, "Everyone with European roots can consider themselves of Celtic origin." People who are not directly descended from Irish, Welsh, or Scottish families tend to think they have no Celtic roots, but in reality so many different European tribes contributed to the creation of Celticism, and over thousands of years such a mixing of populations has occurred, that virtually anyone alive today with European ancestry can be said to have Celtic origins.

Nevertheless, over the centuries, the countries on the western seaboard of Europe—Ireland, Scotland, Wales, Cornwall, and Brittany—have become the guardians of Celtic culture, struggling to preserve their languages, and proud inheritors of a folklore and mythology replete with spiritual power.

This book is a celebration of those countries and those peoples who have managed to preserve such treasures for the world.

But this book is more than a celebration, because it is designed to make the treasures of Celtic culture and spirituality come alive and be of use to us in the midst of our modern and often busy lives.

Good books are like handfuls of seeds. They gift us with ideas, turns of phrase, images, and memories that grow with time to color our world and bring beauty and magic to our lives.

And the first step in discovering that beauty and that magic lies in the turning of a page. . . .

Philip Carr-Gomm
Chief of the Order of Bards,
Ovates and Druids
August 2000

Kindling the

Celtic Spirit

INTRODUCTION:
BURIED TREASURE

The old people had runes which they sang to the spirits dwelling in the sea and in the mountain, in the wind and in the whirlwind, in the lightning and in the thunder, in the sea and in the moon and in the stars of heaven. I was naught but a toddling child at the time, but I remember well the ways of the old people.

CARMINA GADELICA

In September 1868, young Jimmy Quin was digging potatoes in a ring-fort near the village of Ardagh in County Limerick. When he reached the bank close to a thorn tree he found the surface soft, and when he drove his spade down between the roots of the thorn, it struck something hard and metallic. He cleared away the earth and found a beautiful gold and silver cup now known as the Ardagh Chalice, considered by many to be the finest specimen of Celtic art ever found.

Like the Ardagh Chalice, the treasury of Celtic wisdom and lore lies not too far beneath the topsoil of memory. Digging through layers only a few generations deep, we can still uncover battered caskets of ancient customs and rituals that may reveal a shining hoard of story, prayer, and song. For the amazing thing is that despite a relentless tide of invasions, persecutions, and immigrations, there was enough gold in the storehouse of Celtic wisdom to survive the centuries of plunder.

Over two thousand years ago the first people that we call the Celts were a large group of tribal communities who inhabited much of the European continent. They were an energetic, intelligent, flamboyant people, whose passionate natures expressed themselves in heroic warfare, brilliant craftsmanship, and the worship of many gods and goddesses who dwelled in the earth below them and the sky above them. By the first century C.E., the Roman army had pushed them far into the northwestern hinterlands. Only Ireland and the most northern reaches of Scotland escaped being crushed by the military might of Rome.

In the fifth century Christian missionaries arrived in Ireland, and the old polytheistic religion gave way to the creed of the One God. Ireland became one of the greatest seats of the new religion in Europe and host to a golden age of learning and art, centered around the monastic settlements. In their turn, the monasteries were sacked by Viking invaders at the end of the eighth century, the monks were slaughtered, and most of the magnificent books and holy treasures were destroyed. The flower of this new manifestation of the Celtic spirit was bitten by the frost of successive invasions, first the Normans and then the English, and almost withered and died completely in the nineteenth century when systematic oppression drove thousands to the immigrant ships or to death by starvation in the Great Potato Famine. A similar story of almost total cultural annihilation played itself out in Scotland, Wales, and Cornwall, while on the continent Brittany was engulfed by France.

Yet in the past thirty or so years, many willing minds and hands have undertaken the task of rekindling the guttering flame of the Celtic spirit. Even as the languages began to die on the lips of a people forbidden to speak in their own tongue, a new generation has sprung up to reclaim its spiritual and cultural birthright. As we enter a new millennium, musicians are playing traditional melodies and songs; poets are writing and reciting in their mother tongue; while thousands of the descendants of the Celtic diaspora, chiefly from North America and Australia, are making pilgrimages to the homes of their great-grandparents and visiting the once-neglected sacred sites of their ancestral homes in Ireland, Scotland, or Wales.

Whether or not we have Celtic ancestry, many of us today are finding ourselves deeply attracted to Celtic spirituality, living as we do at a time when the sacred seems so absent from our world. There is a Welsh word, *hiraeth*, that roughly translates in English as a longing for what is absent, the yearning of the exile for the shores of home. Adrift without a living tradition today, as so many of us are, we behold the many-faceted jewel of Celtic spirituality sparkling like the sun on water, inviting us to set sail for those longed-for islands of the soul. To step ashore is to discover a world in which there is no separation between the visible and invisible, between spirit and nature, heaven and earth. Here we can embrace an awareness of the sacred in every moment and within all forms of life, for the pre-Christian Celts lived and worked in easy relationship with the unseen world. Sharing their lives in close-knit communities, they felt the protection of their tribal gods, while all around them the earth was alive with the spirits of rivers, rocks, and trees. At the coming of Christianity the world was viewed with love and respect since it was the divine creation of God. Old Irish scholar Robin Flower described the first Celtic Christians as regarding the world with "an eye washed miraculously clear with continuous spiritual exercises," which gave them "a strange vision of natural things in an almost unnatural purity."

Hundreds of years later in the nineteenth century, a customs and excise officer named Alexander Carmichael, while working in the Highlands and islands of northwestern Scotland, discovered ordinary farming and fishing families still living every day in close communion with the divine. Woven through their lives was a complex and beautiful tapestry of daily and seasonal prayers, rituals, and ceremonies, which Carmichael preserved in an extraordinary compilation called *Carmina Gadelica,* Gaelic songs. Whether sowing seed, spinning wool, or milking cows, these country dwellers carried out every task in the spirit of prayer, despite the poverty and hardships of subsistence living. Although they prayed to Christian saints and angels, these figures thinly veil the pagan gods and goddesses whose names they once bore. What is more, these invisible protectors were found not merely in church on Sundays or in a heavenly beyond; they attended everyday life in kitchen, field, and barn. As poet and mystic George Russell wrote, "During all these centuries the Celt has kept in his heart some affinity with the almighty beings ruling in the unseen, once so evident to the heroic races who preceded him. His legends and faery tales have connected his soul with the inner lives of air and water and earth, and they in turn have kept his heart sweet with hidden influence."[1]

If we put our ear to the cracks of silence within the roar of twenty-first-century life, we can still hear the echo of these ancestral voices and the sound of footsteps that have not yet quite faded upon the air. If we listen respectfully, they may teach us the songs and stories that can open the gates to the Many-Colored Land. If we walk with them along the windy shore or up onto the heather-scented moors, we can rediscover our connection with the natural world and take our rightful place in the great circle of life. And if we follow them home, they may invite us into their houses and teach us how to kindle the flame of Spirit within our hearths and our hearts.

A FEW NOTES

Because this book is mostly concerned with old traditions, I use the past tense when referring to the Celtic peoples. But it is important to recognize that the convenient ethnic and cultural term *Celtic* refers not only to the tribal Celts of Iron Age Europe but also to the modern peoples of Alba (Scotland), Breizh (Brittany), Cymru (Wales), Éire (Ireland), Kernow (Cornwall), and Mannin (Isle of Man). There is also a case to be made for Galicia, a region of northwest Spain, being the seventh Celtic nation. Both because of space limitations and my personal background, this book deals only with the "insular Celts" of the British Isles and Ireland, with an emphasis on the latter.

The stories in the book are retellings of myths and folktales, and in some cases I have adapted them slightly for modern audiences. To read more literal translations of some of the early tales, you may want to refer to more scholarly works, such as *Early Irish Myths and Sagas,* by Jeffrey Gantz (London: Penguin, 1981), and *Ancient Irish Tales,* by Tom Peete Cross and Clark Harris Slover (New York: Barnes & Noble, 1969).

THE SPIRAL DANCE OF THE YEAR:
UNDERSTANDING SACRED TIME

*Nothing perisheth, but (as the Sun and Year) every Thing goes in a Circle,
lesser or greater, and is renewed and refreshed in its Revolutions. . . .*
ROBERT KIRK, *The Secret Commonwealth*

Everywhere we look, we see that life moves in a spiral motion. From snail shell to sunflower, from the invisible coils of the DNA molecule to the boundless whirling galaxies, life unfolds as a spiral. This simple pattern holds the secret to the whole universe, for within its form lies the feminine circle and the masculine line. Without these two movements, there would be no motion and consequently no life in this world of opposites. Spirals swirl through the art of the early Celts as they swirl on the stone walls of the burial chambers of their European Neolithic predecessors. In Celtic countries people have danced in spirals since time began. Even today the people of Brittany dance in all-night festivals where the music of bagpipe and hurdy-gurdy never stops. Slowly and rhythmically, they move into the center and out again in huge spirals. Arms closely linked, bodies swaying, they stamp the earth, mimicking the sowing of seeds and other farming tasks. Their dance reflects their participation in Earth's mysteries of blossom and leaf fall, the ebb and flow of the circling year.

The early Celts divided their year into halves, called in Old Celtic *gam*, winter, and *sam*, summer. These words also have deeper resonances of meaning as dark/light, female/male, rest/work. *Samhain* at the end of October and beginning of November marked the start of winter, and evidence suggests it may also have been the Celtic New Year, for the Celts reckoned the birth of the year from the darkening months, and, likewise, their days began at dusk. *Beltaine*, at the end of April and beginning of May, marked the beginning of the light half of the year and was the gateway into summer.

The light and dark halves of the year were themselves divided into two by *Imbolc* at the beginning of February and *Lughnasadh* at the beginning of August, giving a fourfold division of the year:

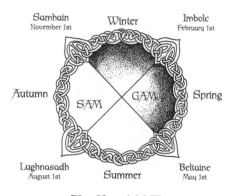

The Fourfold Year

The Celtic Wheel of the Year

The story of the people and the land revolved around this wheel:

Samhain (*sow*-ihn) was the time when the last crops and fruits had been gathered in and the livestock were taken into the byres for their winter quartering, while some were slaughtered for their meat. It was a time of death but also a time of rest, both for the land and for the hardworking people. Faeries roamed abroad, and the ghosts of the dead returned to their old homes on Earth.

At Imbolc (*im*-bolc) new life began as lambs were born, fishermen could once more put out to sea, and the ground became soft enough for seeds to be sown. The name originally referred to the milking of the ewes. The days grew longer, and spring's return was heralded by the goddess Brigit, or Bride, as a young maiden.

Beltaine (*byel*-tin-yuh) ushered in the light half of the year, when the livestock were driven outside to graze on the hills, crops and fruits flourished in the heat of the sun, and both the human and animal kingdoms celebrated the return of summer with unbridled sexuality.

Lughnasadh (*loo*-nuh-suh) marked the coming to maturity of the year's yield. Earth's bounty was put on display at huge trading fairs named after the culture god, Lugh, the "many-skilled." Produce and livestock were exchanged, while all kinds of arts, entertainment, and sporting events celebrated the fruits of human creativity.

Originally, these great turning points of the year were not precisely marked on a calendar but reckoned from the careful observation of star, sun, and moon. Wind and weather, the movements of animals and birds, and the voice of the Earth would have yielded more vital information. Although we do not know for sure, it is also likely the druid astronomers understood how to reckon time from the magnificent stone circle observatories left by the megalith engineers.

According to the Law of Three, the festival days traditionally lasted three days before and three days after the dates shown earlier. But it is also important to note that these were not the original dates. To begin with, the ancient Celts had a complex lunar and solar calendar, called the Coligny calendar, after the French town where it was discovered in 1897 engraved on fragmented bronze plates. After the Roman invasion, the Celtic world conformed to the Julian calendar, but through the centuries this proved to be highly inaccurate and led to the adoption of the Gregorian calendar by the mid—eighteenth century. This put everything eleven days before the old reckoning, and there was quite an outcry in many areas against what seemed like an arbi-

trary rearrangement of sacred time. Even up to the present century, many considered January 6 to be the true "Old" Christmas Day and continued to hold Lughnasadh fairs in the middle of August.

The original festivals, at least Samhain, Beltaine, and Lughnasadh, were great tribal gatherings to enact religious rites involving prayers, offerings, and sacrifices designed to ensure the continuing fertility of the earth and well-being of the clan. On a social level, festivals were times to renew old relationships and establish new ones, make important legal decisions and judgments, and enact new laws. But above all, these were high-spirited communal celebrations with feasting and drinking on a lavish scale, entertainment by master poets and musicians, games, dances, and sporting contests. Only Imbolc seems to have been a quieter, more local affair, held mostly indoors.

If we place the solstices and equinoxes on the Wheel of the Year, a figure emerges with eight spokes, where the Celtic festivals fall between the arms of the solar cross. This is why they are sometimes referred to as the cross-quarter days or simply quarter days. At least two of the solar festivals, Summer Solstice (Midsummer, the Feast of St. John) and Winter Solstice (Yule, Christmas, Hogmanay),

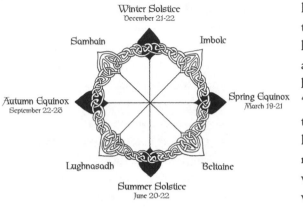

Winter Solstice
December 21-22

Samhain · Imbolc

Autumn Equinox
September 22-23

Spring Equinox
March 19-21

Lughnasadh · Beltaine

Summer Solstice
June 20-22

The Eightfold Year

were celebrated by the people of the British Isles and Ireland in a similar way to the quarter days. We do not know for sure whether the early Celts celebrated the equinoxes; Easter may have replaced a pre-Christian spring festival, while the festival of Michelmas clearly overlaid a harvest celebration. Yet long before the Celtic tribes came to these islands, the great turning points of the solar year were indicated by megalithic temples such as Stonehenge and Newgrange, built by an earlier race.

The Celtic festivals mark powerful nodes of the year, often termed *liminal* by scholars, from the Latin word *limen,* meaning "threshold." The four quarter days, along with the Winter and Summer Solstices, are particu-

larly potent. (Each day has threshold points, too; dawn and dusk are the twin thresholds between night and day, as to a lesser extent are noon and midnight: faery funerals are held at noon, while we are all familiar with "the witching hour"!) They were in-between times when the seen and unseen worlds collided and everyday rules were suspended. The normal world was turned upside down, giving way to a brief period of anarchy and misrule, with the seeds of chaos being sown by masked and costumed players and musicians:

> *Mollie-men and mummers and the*
> *Old Gray Mare,*
> *A ragtag procession bound for heaven knows*
> *where,*
> *with bagpipe and small pipe and hurdy-*
> *gurdy man,*
> *and the devil take the hindmost if he can!*

The crack in time also enabled seers and diviners to see into the future and give oracles. Celebrations involved feasting, plays and processions in costume, music and dancing, and the all-around suspension of everyday rules. These were delicious but also dangerous times, when the gates of the Otherworld opened wide, faery hosts roamed abroad, and the adventurous—or foolhardy—could slip into their magic realms. The unwary traveler could be "taken" by the faery host, his cows bewitched and their milk soured, or a burning coal stolen from his hearth-fire, a theft bound to bring great misfortune.

Fire was one of the strongest protective forces, and, with the exception of Imbolc, which was more of an indoor festival, communities gathered at huge bonfires on the hills, which is why the quarter days are sometimes called "fire festivals." Bonfires are also a main feature at Summer Solstice celebrations, while the Yule log performs that function at Winter Solstice. The fire brought the life-giving power of the sun down to combat the dark, and both the flames and ashes were used to purify evil influences. Under the influence of the Church, the festivals were reassigned to Christian feast days, and instead of pagan deities, saints became the focus of the rituals. But the old festivals continued to be observed throughout the centuries, especially in rural areas, in a typically Celtic interweaving of pagan and Christian beliefs and practices.

Awareness of life as an unfolding spiral is something that, sadly, we have lost today. In the modern world progress is seen as a linear upward march. If we do not consistently improve and achieve, we think there is something wrong. But through consciously aligning ourselves with sacred time by attuning our lives to the spiral of the Celtic year, we are accepting the invitation to the grand dance of the universe, in which our partners are the sun, moon, and stars and every living thing. With this greater sense of connection to the flow of the cosmos, we find a greater appreciation of the present moment and can now enjoy the journey instead of grimly fixing our sights toward a distant goal on an ever-receding horizon. By embracing a "spiral attitude" toward life, we can gracefully take each step of the dance as we are led joyfully along by what the great Irish hero Fionn McCumhaill once called "the music of what happens."

THE WELCOME OF THE DOOR

I pray for a house roofed, sheltered, shining
a house wherein is honor and welcome.

IRISH, SEVENTH CENTURY

Step over the threshold into an old-style Irish house, and imagine this is your home. You find yourself in a simple, one-room dwelling with a hole in the middle of the roof. Here you gather with family and friends around the fire in the center of the room, which reminds you of the light and warmth of the sun. In the older, round house, you feel safe within the compass of the circle. In the later, rectangular house, the four corners stand about you like guardian angels. Benevolent household spirits weave an unseen mantle of protection about you.

The earthen floor just inside the threshold of old cottages in the south and west of Ireland was known as the "welcome of the door." Upon entering, a visitor would stand here and say a blessing for the household.

This was holy ground, and dirt scraped from it was good for curing a number of ills. An in-between place, it was sacred because it marked the boundary between the life of the family within and the wide world without. It was neither "here" nor "there," and so it allowed a crack to open between the worlds where the power of the Otherworld could flow into our own.

The month of January finds us standing on the threshold of a new year, and an invitation awaits us: to create a space in our lives where we can begin to live in a sacred manner. Celtic spirituality teaches us that we do not have to go further than our own homes in order to begin.

THE FIRST CELTIC HOUSES

Celtic people of the Iron Age lived in isolated farmsteads scattered throughout the countryside. These were known as ring-forts (in Irish: *rath, dún,* or *lios*), but they were not really designed for defense. A ring-fort consisted of a circular bank of earth or stone, possibly topped by a wooden fence and in some cases surrounded by a ditch. In the center stood the house, farm buildings, and granaries: circular structures made from wooden posts, clay, and wattles, with a high, conical thatched roof.

The hearth-fire was kindled in the center of the floor, and the smoke escaped through a hole in the roof. They had little furniture apart from a few wooden trestles, stools, and cooking pots, and at night they slept on beds of straw and rushes, covered with rugs and animal skins.

Nowadays all that remains of the first Celtic homes are circles of earth and stone, places of mystery long thought to be the haunts of faery folk.

SACRED HEARTH

Until quite recently in Ireland, nobody built a house before consulting the spirits of the land. Four piles of rocks or four rods were set up in the chosen location the night before. If they were found to be undisturbed in the morning, building could proceed, but if they were fallen or scattered, a new place had to be found, for this was faery ground. It would not do to build on the path to a *lios*, or faery fort, or on the *lios* itself, on the site of a forge, or on a height. When the foundation stone was laid, an offering—a silver coin or an animal skull—was deposited beneath it, to invite prosperity into the new house.

Old rectangular Irish houses were oriented according to the passage of the sun. The most auspicious place for the front door was facing east or south, where the sun is strongest. The room facing west was associated with sunset and death and was reserved for family mementos, old people, and the dead, who were laid out for their wake, after which they left the house for the last time through the back door. In the center of the house stood the sacred shrine of domestic life: the hearth-fire.

The sacred design of four quarters surrounding a center is a template of cosmic harmony. In many ancient cultures, cities and temples were built according to this pattern.

Archaeological excavations show that late Iron Age Celtic sanctuaries were usually oriented to the four directions. Ireland itself was divided into four provinces, with a fifth one representing the center. In the central province, called Meath, meaning "middle," rose the hill at the sacred heart of the land: Tara, seat of the high kings. Scotland and Wales may have been divided up in the same way.[1]

The old Irish house brought sacred space into everyday life. No matter how poor or oppressed, families were from birth to death encircled by this protective fourfold pattern. Their lives revolved around the fire as the life-giving sun of their universe.

The house also connected the family with the invisible abodes of the gods above and below. Like other Indo-European peoples, the Celts viewed the physical world as situated between an Underworld and an Upperworld, with a vertical *axis mundi,* or World Tree, joining all three worlds together. In some western cottages, pots were buried in the earth in front of the hearth-fire for good luck. This was, perhaps, a memory of the marvelous cauldron of the Underworld gods, which was always full of delicious food. The Upperworld was represented by the roof and smoke hole in the thatch above the fire. Even though most houses did not have a central support, the ridgepole that runs along the top is still called a "roof-tree" and is considered one of the parts of the house most vital to the family's well-being, spiritual as well as physical. In Scotland, a common toast was "To your roof-tree!" The smoke hole was the door through which the gods sometimes descended when they wished to enter the human world.

Tús agus deireadh an duine tarraingt ar an tine.
The beginning and end of one's life is to draw
closer to the fire.
IRISH PROVERB

Until recent centuries the hearth was built on stones in the middle of the floor, where it became the heart of the home. Fire not only provided the vital means for keeping warm, cooking food, heating water, drying clothes, and giving light; it also acted as a conduit for spiritual energy to flow into the house, symbolizing the power of the sun brought down to the human domain. By the fire's light, the family spent the long northern winters at household chores and domestic crafts: spinning, weaving, knitting, making brooms and baskets, or carving wood. Here they gathered in a circle to enjoy the *craic* (an untranslat-

able Irish word roughly meaning "good company and conversation"), listen to the old tales, tell jokes, and ask riddles. Visitors, whether friends or strangers, were never asked their business at the door; that could wait until they were comfortably seated by the hearth.

In fact, the old Irish word for hearth, *teallach,* has always been associated with *teaghlach,* "household" and "family."[2] The same goes for the Welsh word *aelwyd,* which not only means "hearth" but is almost synonymous with "home" and "family."[3] The words *heart* and *hearth* are almost identical, as are their Anglo-Saxon root words, *heort* and *heorth.* The hearth also functioned as a point of connection with the ancestors; in medieval Wales, the right to occupy and hold land owned by one's father was called *dachannud,* "uncovering the fire," and involved lighting a fire in the old fireplace. As late as the twentieth century, Welsh squatters' rights determined that if someone built enough of a cottage in one night so that the smoke could be seen rising out of the chimney the following morning, he could call it his own.

For centuries Scottish and Irish fires have been made out of turf or peat, cut from the bogs that blanket so much of the land. Although it does not make a spectacular blaze like wood, peat is sweetly scented, and, most important, the fire made from it will last for three days or more if properly laid. The hearth-fire was never allowed to go out, even at night. This served the practical purpose of keeping the sods and thatch dry as well as potently symbolizing the strength of family continuity. In Ireland it was said the faeries would be displeased if there was no fire for them during the night.

Fire dispelled evil spirits; in the days when an Irish family shared its cabin with the farm animals, it was thought to be unlucky if the cow could not get a glimpse of the fire. When a person was sick, extra care was taken to make sure the fire burned brightly, for the patient's health was bound up with the vital life force of the flames. In Wales some people in isolated mountain areas were still practicing pagan fire rituals in the early twentieth century. When they were experiencing a problem, they touched the stone over the chimney piece, then threw a handful of dry earth into the fire. As it burned, they whispered the cause of their trouble to the flames, believing that the power of fire could heal the situation.

In some areas the fire was ritually extinguished and renewed at special times. On May Eve, the festival of Beltaine, households in the Scottish Highlands put out their hearth-fires while a huge central bonfire was lit ceremonially on the nearby sacred hill in a ceremony known as "kindling the need-fire" (see May). When the night was over members of each household took a brand from the new fire to rekindle their own. Only at one other time might the hearth-fire be extinguished. In the event of the most terrible misfortune that could befall a pastoral people—a murrain on their cattle—every fire in the district was put out, for fire represented the source of life, which had somehow been polluted. A new, pure fire had to be obtained through prayer and ceremony. In Ireland the fire was completely put out on Candlemas Day, the old feast of Brigit, goddess of fire. Before it was extinguished a special candle was lit from it. The woman of the house swept the hearth, laid a new fire, and used the blessed candle to light it. It was kept ablaze until the next Candlemas Day. In Wales, too, there were houses where the fires blazed continuously all the way down to the nineteenth century.

Tending the fire, morning and night, was the task of the woman of the house. In Scotland, Highland women invoked the presence of Brigit, who was a Celtic goddess of fire before the Church made her a Celtic saint (see February). Before going to bed, the woman spread the embers with reverence and care over the hearth and divided them into three equal sections, leaving a small heap in the middle. She laid a peat between the sections, each one touching the central mound. The first peat was laid down in the name of the God of Life, the second in the name of the God of Peace, and the third in the name of the God of Grace. She then covered the circle with ashes, a process known as "smooring" or "smothering," taking care not to put out the fire, in the name of the Three of Light. The heap of ashes, slightly raised in the center, was called *Tula nan Tri,* the Hearth of the Three. When the smooring was complete, the woman closed her eyes, stretched out her hand, and softly intoned this lovely invocation:

I will build the hearth
As Mary would build it.
The encirclement of Bride and of Mary
Guarding the hearth, guarding the floor,
Guarding the household all . . . [4]

The next morning the woman performed the ceremony of "lifting" the fire by removing the ashes and kindling the flame while softly intoning a prayer to Saint Brigit, the "radiant flame" herself. This ceremony was performed every day without fail, catching her up in the divine dance of the constant renewal of the flame of life.

Even in later times, when the fireplace was no longer built in the center of the house, the hearth remained at the heart of the home. Folklorist Henry Glassie, who studied an obscure Irish community called Ballymenone near the border between North and South Ireland, witnessed its vital function as late as the 1970s:

Light flickers at the heart of Bally-menone's culture. The fire on the hearth burns in the middle of daily existence. The food on which life depends is cooked there. Children's games and adult conversations curl around it. The ancient märchen told to children are called "fireside tales"; the ceili's talk is called "fireside chat"; the community's unwritten, yet formal laws pertaining to rights of land use and access are called "fireside law." The house with a cold hearth is considered dead: soon its thatch will fall, its walls will tumble. [5]

CREATING A SACRED HEARTH

In his book *Irish Country Households,* Kevin Danaher talks about how the open hearth and its tradition remains part of Irish consciousness, even while it is a thing of the past: "We sit facing the hearth, even in suburban drawing rooms when the summer evening is too warm for a fire. A misguided person who turned his chair around and sat with his back to the fireplace, even when empty, was regarded as an untimely joker or as not being 'all there.' "6

So where now is your sacred hearth? Where do you come together with your family or friends, not necessarily to participate in some activity or to hold a meeting, but to pass the time together in the evening? For many of us in today's work-driven society, this may be hard to imagine outside of Christmas or other special occasions. With modern transportation and artificial lighting, we can carry on work or play far from home without thought for the cycles of sun and moon. The evenings when we do relax at home are more likely to be spent in front of the electronic glow of the television, which, unlike the hearth-fire, takes us away from, not toward, the center of our lives together.

Here are some ideas for creating a sacred hearth in your home:

1. If you have an open fireplace, wood-burning stove, or even gas logs, you are already halfway there. The next step is to establish your hearth-fire as the family gathering place, and if you have children this will be easier when they are young. The first time you do this, you might want to ask the children what gives us light and warmth and makes us feel good by day. Then lead them to make the connection with the fire as the "indoors sun."

2. Activities around the hearth can include talking about your day; telling stories (see November), riddles, and jokes; singing or playing music; playing word games; working on crafts individually or together.

3. There will also be times when you just want to sit around the fire and be together without structured activity. We are so used to being "human doings" instead of "human beings," this may be more challenging than you think! Let go, breathe, enjoy the conversation—and also the silences in between.

4. Involve older children in making the fire. In the Celtic ritual manner, make a circle of kindling going from left to right in multiples of three. (See February, "The Sacred Three.") As you put down the pieces, recite the following:

I (We) lay this wood in the name of the Sacred
  Three:
Giver of Life,
Bringer of Peace,
Bestower of Grace.

5. For most of us today it is not practical to keep the fire alight throughout the night, but it is important to end the evening with a simple ceremony of closure. As the flames die down, or as you turn off the gas, you might say something like,

May the flame in our hearth be relit in our
    hearts,
and keep us safe and warm all night.

6. The Triple Candle. If you do not have any kind of fire, a large candle with a triple wick placed on a central coffee table can work just as well. In my home I alternate between the fireplace and the candle when it's too warm for a fire. I like to change the color of the candle according to the time of year:

Winter (Samhain to Imbolc)	Red
Spring (Imbolc to Brigit)	White
Summer (Brigit to Lughnasadh)	Green
Autumn (Lughnasadh to Samhain)	Gold

You can use the same invocations and blessings for the hearth-fire as you light or extinguish each wick in turn, again in a sun-wise direction.

THE LUCK OF THE HOUSE

The most important areas of the house—the threshold and the hearth—held the luck of the house, and it was important to protect them with special talismans. Often these were made from the wood of the rowan, a tree that has always been revered for its powers of protection. In Scotland carpenters often made the beam that ran over the fireplace from rowan wood. This is where the cooking pots were hung, and the rowan served to keep evil influences away from the hearth-fire and out of the food. Rowan was the best choice for roof supports also: an old Scots word for the crossbeam was *rantree*, a variation of *rowan tree.*

Sprigs or crosses made of rowan were hung above the front door along with horseshoes, points upward to hold the luck. In Ireland the crosses were more often made from straw or rushes and dedicated to Saint Brigit. There is a link between these two kinds of threshold talismans: rowan was revered because its bright red berries suggest fire, while Brigit was associated with fire. Fire, symbolizing the light and warmth of the sun, always offered the most powerful protection throughout the Celtic world.

Sweeping the threshold then sprinkling it lightly with ashes from the hearth-fire was another way to make sure no evil influences entered the house.

If you are lucky enough to have access to a rowan tree—in North America more often known as the mountain ash—you can make traditional rowan crosses to hang above your door or hearth by tying two twigs together crosswise with red thread. If you can't find rowan you can use birch, another tree used for this purpose (see "The Sacred Grove: Birch," on the next page), or make a Saint Brigit's cross as shown in February.

AN OLD WOMAN OF THE ROADS

O, to have a little house!
To own the hearth and stool and all!
The heaped up sods upon the fire,
The pile of turf against the wall!

To have a clock with weights and chains
And pendulum swinging up and down!
A dresser filled with shining delph,
Speckled and white and blue and brown!

I could be busy all the day
Clearing and sweeping hearth and floor,
And fixing on their shelf again
My white and blue and speckled store!

I could be quiet there at night
Beside the fire and by myself,
Sure of a bed and loath to leave
The ticking clock and the shining delph!

Och! but I'm weary of mist and dark,
And roads where there's never a house nor bush,
And tired I am of bog and road,
And the crying wind and the lonesome hush!

And I am praying to God on high,
And I am praying Him night and day,
For a little house—a house of my own—
Out of the wind's and the rain's way.
Padraic Colum

BIRCH

⊕HE SACRED ⊕ROVE

The pale, slender trunks of birches stand out against the darker trees of the wood, shining like candles amid the winter's gloom. Birch is the tree of beginnings, one of the first to grow on bare soil and so give birth to the entire forest. In Scotland "birch of the waterfalls" was among the nine sacred woods that kindled the festival fires. In Ireland it was one of the "seven noble ones" of the high sacred grove. Birch gave its name, *beth*, to the first letter in the ancient ogham alphabet, which was carved on wood and stone. According to legend, the first thing ever written in ogham was carved on a birch rod.

The white bark suggests cleansing and purification, and since it periodically peels

away it also symbolizes renewal and regeneration. No wonder birch was used in many parts of the British Isles to ritualistically beat out the old year and beat in the new. Traditional besoms—brooms made out of twigs—are made from birch.

To make either a hand brush or full-sized broom, gather equal-sized twigs of birch. Make a handle from the branch of an ash tree, about four feet for a full-sized besom or smaller for a hand brush. Lay the handle on your working surface, and lay the twigs along its length, starting from about three inches from the bottom. When you have enough to completely surround the handle, bind them securely with willow withes (the flexible twigs of willow). Continue adding as many layers as you wish, depending on how thick you want the besom to be.

On New Year's morning, or as close to January 1 as possible, arise at dawn and open your front door to admit the first light of the day and year into your house. Take your besom, and sweep your threshold from the inside out so that the cleansing energy of birch will purify your house or apartment of old or unwanted energy. You can also lightly sprinkle the threshold with ashes from the fire or holy water to protect your home.

PURIFYING THE HOUSE

The New Year was one of the special times of the year when the house was *sained*, ritually purified and blessed with holy water and incense. The evening before January 1, bands of young men brought branches of juniper down from the hills and spread them around the fire to dry. Another member of the household fetched a pitcher of "magic water" from the "dead and living ford." This was a ford over which funeral processions passed. A ford was thought to be a special in-between place: neither river nor dry land, a threshold between the worlds, full of numinous power.

The next morning the household came together, and the pitcher was passed around for each to take a drink. The head of the house went from room to room with some assistants, sprinkling water in the four corners, on the beds, and on anyone not present at the main gathering. Then doors, windows, keyholes, and other openings were sealed off, and the juniper branches were set alight and carried throughout the house as incense. If smoke from the more enthusiastic conflagrations resulted in bouts of coughing, all the better, for it showed that people were ridding themselves of disease! Afterward, everyone recovered with a drink of whiskey followed by a hearty New Year's breakfast.

To Purify and Bless Your Home

1. To purify your house at the beginning of the New Year or at any other time, use water that has been collected in a sacred manner (see April). If you live with other people, form a circle around the hearth or central candle. Pass the water in a sunwise (clockwise) direction for everyone to drink, then take it around the house and sprinkle some in the four corners of each room.

2. A *saining* can be done by water alone. But if you also want to use juniper incense, it is not difficult to obtain, being a popular garden plant as well as one that grows wild in many parts of North America. Cut a few sprigs the night before, and put them on the hearth or other warm place to dry out a little. (For a better burn, dry the juniper by the hearth, on layers of newspaper, or hang it in a dry place for a few days or weeks.) When you light the sprigs, hold a small bowl or abalone shell to catch any ash or sparks that might fall. Using either your hand or a long feather, fan the smoke around each member of the household in turn, then take it to each room and blow some into the four corners.

3. An even simpler house blessing from Ireland involves lighting a candle and taking

the flame around to the threshold, the
hearth, and four corners of each room
while reciting this blessing from the
Hebrides:

May Brigit give blessing
To the house that is here . . .
Both crest and frame,
Both stone and beam;

Both clay and wattle;
Both summit and foundation;

Both window and timber;
Both foot and head;

Both man and woman;
Both wife and children;

Both young and old;
Both maiden and youth . . .

Plenty of laughter,
Plenty of wealth,
Plenty of people,
Plenty of health,
Be always here.

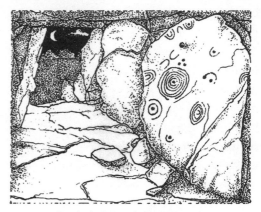

Inside the Mound of the Hostages

HOLY GROUND
TARA
(COUNTY MEATH, IRELAND)

. . . No keep like Temair could be found;
she was the secret place on the road of life.
Irish, tenth century

Tara, seat of the High Kings, lies in the
ancient province of Meath and is the royal
center of Ireland. At first sight, the low green
hill with its scattered earthworks seems unpre-
possessing, rather like the poets' image of Ireland as a poor old woman whose shabby
mantle conceals her faded glory. But Tara's
outer garment of mounds, ditches, and stones
barely conceals layer after layer of the richest

mythology and history of any one place in Ireland. We can still peer into the Mound of the Hostages, built five thousand years ago by a Neolithic people who decorated its stones and aligned its entrance to the movements of the sun at Imbolc and Samhain. The Lia Fáil (*lee*-uh *fawl*), or Stone of Destiny, which cried out at the touch of a rightful heir to the throne, is still standing on the Ráth na Ríogh (*rah* nuh *ree*), the Fort of the Kings.

And what we can no longer see we can imagine: the five ancient roads that linked Tara to the rest of Ireland; the sacred fires kindled on the summit by successive waves of invaders; the splendid Samhain feasts; the ritual mating of the prospective king with the goddess of the land. This goddess may have been Tea, who, according to tradition, gave her name to Tara (originally Teamhair or Teamair), or Queen Maeve, whose "palace" is a nearby ring-fort.

In later centuries Tara became a rallying place for the United Irishmen's rebellion of 1798, while thousands gathered to hear Daniel O'Connell, "The Liberator," in 1843. Even a small group of Irish Volunteers assembled there before the 1916 Easter Uprising. As writer and local resident Michael Slavin writes, "In some mysterious way, Tara touches the very soul of Ireland."[7]

CELTIC HOSPITALITY

O King of the starry sky,
Lest Thou from me withdraw Thy light—
Whether my house be dark or bright,
My door shall close on none tonight.
MEDIEVAL IRISH

Celtic people are renowned throughout the world for the friendliness and hospitality they show to their guests, a tradition that has its roots in earliest times. The Greek writer Diodorus Siculus said of the Celts in the first century B.C.E., "They also invite strangers to their banquets and only after the meal do they ask who they are, and of what they stand in need."

This attitude has persisted throughout hundreds of years. In some parts of Ireland today, it is traditional to welcome the visitor in and give him or her a good seat by the fire before asking the reason for the visit.

In early Ireland every free man was expected to offer food and shelter to a visitor, whether noble or low born; to do otherwise was to break an ancient law. The royal courts laid on sumptuous banquets and rivers of mead and ale, especially to visiting poets, who might sing their hosts' praises in return. Particular cuts of meat were reserved for certain chiefs and professional men according to rank, and these were written into the laws of the time: "A thigh for a king and a poet; a chine for a literary sage; a leg for a young lord; heads for charioteers; a haunch for queens."[8]

In medieval times travelers in Ireland could also rely on the hospitality of the monasteries. The monks might have lived frugally, but their guests enjoyed as much fish, flesh, and fowl as they could eat. Saint Brigit personifies the spirit of hospitality, as the many tales about her relate (see February). In this wonderful poem, she dreams of holding a feast for the heavenly family:

I would wish a great lake of ale for the King of
*   Kings;*
I would wish the family of Heaven to be drinking
*   it throughout life and time.*
I would wish the men of Heaven in my own
*   house;*
I would wish vessels of peace to be given to them.
I would wish joy to be in their drinking;
I would wish Jesu to be here among them.
I would wish the three Marys of great name;
I would wish the people of Heaven from every side.[9]

The tradition of caring for the visitor was unfailing even in the "dark days" of Ireland, when country people were forced to live in direst poverty. The vagrant at the door was still welcomed in and given the shelter of an already overcrowded dwelling, a share of a meager supper, and bed with the rest of the family around the hearth, feet toward the fire.

RUNE OF HOSPITALITY

I saw a stranger yestreen;
I put the food in the eating place,
Drink in the drinking place,
Music in the listening place;
And, in the sacred name of the Triune,
He blessed myself and my house,
My cattle and my dear ones.

And the lark said in her song,
*   Often, often, often,*
Goes the Christ in the stranger's guise;
*   Often, often, often,*
Goes the Christ in the stranger's guise.
                          SCOTTISH GAELIC[10]

GREETINGS AT THE DOOR

Here are some Celtic phrases of welcome that are used today:

Language		Pronunciation	Meaning
Irish Gaelic	*Céad Míle Fáilte!*	kyayd *meel*-uh *fawl*-chuh	One hundred thousand welcomes!
	Dia dhuit!	*jee*-uh ghitch	Hello! (literally, "God to you")
Scottish Gaelic	*Fàilte!*	*fwaal*-chuh	Welcome!
	Ciamar a tha sibh?	*kee*-mur uh haa sheev	Hello! ("How are you?")
Welsh	*Croeso!*	*croy*-so	Welcome!
	Shw mae!	shoo mie	Hello! ("How is it?")
Manx	*Failt ort!*	Filch ort	Welcome!
	Laa mie	Laa mie	Hello! ("Good day!")
Cornish	*Dynnargh*	Din-arh	Welcome!
	Dydh da	Dith dah	Hello! ("Good day!")
Breton	*Deuet-mat oc'h!*	Duh-it *mahd* okh	Welcome!
	Demat!	Dey-*mahd*	Hello! ("Good day!")

GODS OF THE CELTS:
THE DAGDA

Celtic hospitality was personified by the Dagda (*dagh*-thuh), the father of the Tuatha Dé Danann (*too*-u-huh *jey don*-unn), the race of gods who were the early inhabitants of Ireland. His name means the "Good God," in the sense that he was "good at everything." He had a magic cauldron "from which no company ever went away unsatisfied," two marvelous pigs (one always cooking and one alive), and trees full of ripe fruit, for he was a lord of the Otherworld, the realm of never-ending abundance. He could also control the weather and the crops. The Dagda had a "great weakness for porridge." The Tuatha Dé Danann were preparing for war with the Fomorians, their one-eyed monstrous enemies, and he visited their camp to get the lay of the land. To mock him, they dug a great pit in the ground and poured eighty gallons of milk and the same amount of flour and fat, added some whole goats, sheep, and pigs, and told him he must eat it or be killed. The Dagda ate it with a spoon wide enough for a man and woman to lie in side by side, then scraped out the rest with his finger.

His other famous possession was a huge magical club. With a single blow from one end of it, he could kill nine men, then bring them back to life with the other end of it. Behind the medieval burlesque stands an ancestral deity of abundance and fertility who could wield the power of life and death.

THE HOSPITALITY OF CUANNA'S HOUSE

The following story is a version of a well-known Irish folktale featuring the Irish hero Fionn McCumhaill (fin muck koo-wil) and his warrior band known collectively as the Fianna (fee-an-uh). As well as being a wonderful wisdom tale, it illustrates the importance to the Celts of hospitality.

One day Fionn was up on the hill of Cahernarry in County Limerick with his companions, Caoilte (*kweel*-chuh) and Diarmaid (*jee*-ur-mwij), his son Oisín (ush-*een*), and Mac Lugaidh (muck *loo*-ee).

Their five dogs, led by Fionn's favorites, Bran (*bron*) and Sceolan (*shkyoh*-luhn), frolicked around their heels and rolled in the sweet-scented heather.

Suddenly a huge figure loomed before them on the road ahead. It was a coarse and hairy giant, and he carried a pitchfork with a squealing pig between its prongs. Behind him, a beautiful young girl kept shoving him forward as fast as she could. Fionn and his companions jumped to their feet to meet the strange pair, but a dark druidic mist rose up before them and the road was hidden from view.

When the mist cleared, the Fianna were astonished to find themselves in front of a fine thatched house at the edge of a ford. In front of the house was a green lawn with two wells. On the edge of one was a rusty iron pot and on the other a beautiful copper bowl. The door of the house was open, so they walked inside, and there they saw a very old white-haired man standing to the right of the door, while next to him sat the beautiful young girl. Beside the fire sat the hairy giant, boiling the pig in a cauldron. On the other side of the fire sat a gray-haired peasant with twelve gleaming eyes all over his body. A huge ram with a black head, a white chest, blue horns, and green feet trotted around the fire, while at the very end of the house huddled an old hag wearing an ash gray cloak.

The old man at the door gave them a hearty welcome, as if he had been expecting them, the girl arose and curtsied, and the five companions all sat down on the floor around the hearth, their dogs at their side. The old man glared at the giant, who went on cooking the pig.

"Get up and show some respect for Fionn, son of Cumhaill, and his people, you great lout!" he ordered.

The giant rose heavily to his feet, grumbling to himself, "Always must I give and never do I get." But all the same, he gave Fionn a rough bow.

Presently, a strange thirst came over Fionn so that he could hardly speak, and his words came out in a croak. Nobody in the house seemed to notice, so, highly annoyed at this breach of hospitality, Caoilte sprang up and demanded a drink for his chief.

"Why, Caoilte," said the old man at the door, "you have only to get a drink for Fionn at one of our wells outside."

Off strode Caoilte and returned in a trice with the copper bowl filled to the brim. Fionn drank it down and it tasted like honey, but no sooner had he wiped his mouth with a satisfied sigh than terrible pains wracked his whole body and he doubled up in agony. The rest of the household ignored the man who was rolling around in what appeared to be the throes of death, until Caoilte leaped to his feet in angry alarm and demanded the old man's help.

"Why, Caoilte," said the old man mildly, "you have only to bring him a drink from the other well."

In great haste, Caoilte filled the iron pot and poured the water down Fionn's throat. It tasted terrible—bitter as gall—but the moment Fionn had drained the last drop, he felt better than he had ever felt in his life.

Then the man of the house asked if the pig was ready to be eaten.

"Indeed, it is ready," said the giant. "And I will have the dividing of it."

"And how will that be?" asked the old man.

"One hindquarter to Fionn and his dogs, the other to his four companions," replied the giant. "The forequarter for me, the chine and rump to the man by the fire and the hag in the corner. The entrails to you and the young girl beside ye."

"A fair division!" cried the old man.

But at that moment the ram reared up on its hind legs and in a loud bleating voice cried, "I never heard of a worse division in my life. You have entirely forgotten me-e-e-e-e-!"

The ram charged, scattering Fionn, his men, and the dogs, seized their half of the pig, and proceeded to guzzle it in a corner. The furious

Fianna drew their swords and beat the ram, who ignored the blows and went steadily on champing.

The man with the twelve eyes got to his feet.

"Never have I seen a band of warriors let a sheep take their food," he muttered, lightly seizing the ram by the hind legs and tossing him out the door.

The Fianna had hardly opened their mouths to protest when the old hag in the corner suddenly rose up with a shriek of laughter and threw her gray gown over Fionn's four companions. Instantly they became as four weak and withered old men, bent double with age. Fionn gazed at these proceedings in horror, but as he took a step forward he fell into a dead sleep.

When he awoke, it was to see the four back in their old shapes again and the old man standing before him.

"Is there wonder on you at the ways of this house?" asked his host with a smile.

"I never wondered more at anything I saw!" gasped Fionn.

"Then I will tell you the meaning of them," said the old one.

"The name of the giant is Sloth and the girl is called Intellect, for nothing is swifter than thought. The old man with the twelve eyes is Time, and he is stronger than any other. The ram he threw out is Desire, who must have whatever he wants, but in the end Time puts an end to all Desire. The hag is Old Age, whose gown withered your four comrades, and although they are now young again, yet by and by they will not escape her ragged gift. And the two wells you drank from are Lying and Truth, for although it tastes sweet at first to tell a lie, it is bitter in the end.

"And as to myself," he finished, "I am Cuanna (*koo*-un-nuh) from Innistuil, and I have always wanted to meet you and see if you were really as clever as people say you are. And the hospitality of Cuanna's house to Fionn will be the name of this story to the end of the world.

"And now let us gather round the fire and sleep until morning, for indeed you must be tired."

And so they did, but when they awoke, they found themselves alone on top of Carn Ferghal, with no house in sight, and only their dogs fast asleep in the heather beside them.

DOG

A CELTIC BESTIARY

Three glories of a gathering: a beautiful wife,
a good horse, and a swift hound.
IRISH TRIAD

Dogs have always held a special place in the human world, and this was as true among the early Celts as it is today. Revered for their strength, courage, and loyalty, they gave their names to heroes and kings. The great Ulster warrior Cúchulainn (*koo-khul*-in) was "the hound of Cullan," while the Irish king CúRoi (*koo ree*) was "the hound of Roí." In Britain the name of the chieftain Cunobelinus—familiar to most of us as Shakespeare's Cymbeline—means "hound of the god Belinos."

Dogs were invaluable for hunting deer, boar, hares, and other animals for food and also for killing predators. On the farm they herded sheep and cattle and stood on guard against intruders. In medieval Ireland the watchdog was sometimes called the "dog of four doors," for it guarded the house, the sheepfold, and the byres of calves and oxen. As they do today, dogs made favorite pets. In medieval Ireland children were given puppies to play with, while it was considered proper for a pet dog to accompany a physician, a harpist, a queen, or a hospitaler. Small lap-dogs were popular with women of all ranks, not only as companions but also as protectors against evil spirits. When a woman was in childbirth, her dog kept guard by her side.

Fionn's favorite dogs, Bran and Sceolan, accompanied him on the hunt and in battle, but they were also intelligent advisers and faithful companions. Like many legendary Celtic animals, they were originally human, being the children of Fionn's sister, who had been turned into a dog by the magic of a jealous woman. Bran was "a ferocious, small-headed, white-breasted, sleek-haunched hound; having the eyes of a dragon, the claws of a wolf, the vigor of a lion, and the venom of a serpent." He often warned Fionn of approaching danger, and once, when the Fianna lost a battle, he lay down by his master, shed tears, and howled in sorrow.

In the Celtic world dogs were particularly associated with nurturing and healing. Many Celtic goddesses from the Roman-Celtic era are portrayed holding a lapdog or with a large, guardian animal standing benevolently by their sides. Images of dogs are also found in the healing temple of the god Nodens, in Gloucestershire, England. It seems that Celtic wisdom is being rediscovered today, as recent studies have shown that owning a dog can actually help us live longer and healthier lives.

HOGMANAY

Get up, goodwife, and shake your feathers,
And dinna think that we are beggars;
For we are bairns come out to play,
Get up and gie's our Hogmanay!
SCOTTISH RHYME

Although it will never been known for certain, the ancient Celts most likely held a twelve-day or longer midwinter feast, along with the rest of pagan Europe. Historian Ronald Hutton believes that "the highly charged atmosphere which still prevails upon the British New Year's Eve is a faithful reflection of one of the oldest festivals of the island."[11]

In most parts of the British Isles and Ireland, January 1 was significant only as the latter part of the midwinter celebrations, because up until 1751 the legal date of the New Year was March 25, close to the Spring Equinox. But in Scotland, it was, and still is, the more important feast—and for good reason. At the Reformation, the Scottish Kirk banned the usual high-spirited Yuletide festivities because they smacked too much of paganism and—even worse!—popery. Over the centuries, the old customs and rituals were moved forward to January 1, called Hogmanay.

Hogmanay means both the New Year's celebration and a gift given at this time. Nobody knows for sure where the word came from, but it most likely derives from the Norman-French *hoguinané*. This in turn came from the medieval French word *aguillanneuf,* which may refer to the New Year's gift. Or perhaps it originated with the Gaelic phrase *oge maidne,* "new morning."

In some areas of Wales, the New Year's gift was called the *callennig*. Children went around the neighborhood houses singing songs and bearing an apple or an orange studded with oats and raisins and decorated with nuts and evergreens as a symbol of prosperity. In return, they were given gifts of food or money.

But whatever its origins, Hogmanay was charged with magical significance, being the threshold to a new solar cycle. Just as the sun was reborn in the depths of winter, it offered an opportunity for both closure and renewal. It was a time to forgive and forget old debts and grievances and heal any rifts among family and friends. Old failures could be allowed to fade into the past while the new gateway opened up vistas of hope for the future.

It was important to bring to a close all the business of the year gone by. Debts had to be paid and borrowed items returned to their owners. Everything in the house was given a good scrubbing—the children included!—brass and silverware polished till they gleamed, clocks wound up, and musical instruments tuned.

New Year's Day was regarded as a template for the year to come, for whatever happened on that day would be reflected in the months ahead. So people ate sumptuous meals to make sure they would have plenty to eat all year, and they filled their pockets with coins to ensure wealth.

Above all, it was important that the first person to enter the house on New Year's Day brought good luck. Rather than leave this to chance, a handsome young man or woman was chosen to be first over the threshold after midnight. The "first-foot" had to be healthy and cheerful and come from a good family. Children were especially popular when they arrived at their grandparents' houses.

As ambassadors of the year ahead, the first people over the threshold brought with them gifts: whiskey, oranges, shortbread, oatcakes, salt, and most important, a piece of fuel for the hearth-fire. This might be a peat, small log, or lump of coal, which they brought in with ritual solemnity and silence and set on the fire to burn. Sometimes they also placed an evergreen branch or sprig of sacred mistletoe over the fireplace to symbolize the spirit of growth. Then, bending down, they stoked up the fire to a roaring blaze, turned around to the silent, waiting company, and wished them all a happy and prosperous New Year, while cheers broke out all around.[12]

Another rite undoubtedly of ancient origin was fetching the "flower" or "cream" of the well. This was the first water of the New Year, and it brought great good fortune. The young girls of the village vied with one another to be first at the well, and they had to draw the water in silence and without letting the pail touch the ground. In South Wales children fetched the water before dawn and went about the neighborhood sprinkling it on

anyone they met with a sprig of evergreen, as they wished them a Happy New Year. They also sang a curious old carol whose meaning lies shrouded in mystery but whose jumbled words appear to refer to an ancient ritual involving the coming of the New Year as a young maiden:

Here we bring new water from the well so clear,
For to worship God with, this happy New Year.
Sing levy-dew, sing levy-dew, the water and the wine;
With seven bright gold wires, the bugles they
* do shine.*

Sing reign of Fair Maid, with gold upon her toe,
Open you the West Door, and turn the Old
* Year go:*
Sing reign of Fair Maid, with gold upon her chin,
Open you the East Door, and let the New Year in.

CELTIC WAYS TO SAY "HAPPY NEW YEAR!"

Language		Pronunciation
Irish Gaelic	*Athbhliain faoi Mhaise!*	*ah*-vlee-ihn fwee *wah*-shuh
Scottish Gaelic	*Bliadhna Mhath Ùr dhuit!*	*blee*-ah-nuh vah oor ghoot
Welsh	*Blwyddyn Newydd Dda!*	*bloo*-thin *neh*-with thah
Manx	*Blein Vie Noa!*	blehn vee no-uh
Cornish	*Blydhen Nowydh Da!*	*Blith*-en *now*-ith dah
Breton	*Bloavezh Nevez Mat!*	*Blwah*-vez *neh*-vez mahd

This connection between the New Year and the divine feminine is also found in Ireland, where Epiphany (January 6) was often referred to as the Women's Christmas. Cakes and wine were served, and a circle of white candles was lit—a design often associated with a female bringer of light, such as Saint Brigit in Ireland and Saint Lucy in Sweden. At midnight, as the Twelve Days came to an end, three miracles occurred: water in the well became wine, rushes became silk, and sandstone turned into pure gold.

HOGMANAY SHORTBREAD AND WASSAIL BOWL

Ho ri vi o
This is the night of the cakes!
HEBRIDEAN RHYME

Hogmanay was sometimes called *oidhche nam Bonnag* (*uh*-ee-hyuh num *bon*-nuck), Cake Night. Bands of young people paraded from house to house with the hide of a bull, an ancient symbol of fertility and good luck. In exchange they received "hogmanays," New Year's gifts of cakes and drink. One of the most delicious was a special round shortbread cookie made with crimped edges to represent the rays of the sun, which is reborn at midwinter.

Before leaving the house, the little band walked three times sunwise around the hearthfire and chanted this blessing:

Great good luck to the house
Good luck to the family,
Good luck to every rafter of it,
And to every worthy thing in it.

Good luck to horses and cattle,
Good luck to the sheep,
Good luck to everything,
And good luck to all your means.

Good luck to the good-wife,
Good luck to the children,
Good luck to every friend,
Great good luck and health to all.

Ingredients
1 pound butter, softened
1 cup packed light brown sugar
4 cups unbleached all-purpose flour

Method
1. Cream butter and sugar until pale and fluffy.
2. Mix in about 3¼ cups flour to form a soft, nonsticky dough. Don't overknead, or it will become tough.

3. Turn onto a floured surface and roll out lightly to about ½-inch thickness. Use a 3-inch cutter to stamp out rounds, crimp the edges to make "sun rays," and cut a hole in the middle with an apple corer or similar.
4. Place on a greased baking sheet. Prick each round with a fork.
5. Bake at 325 degrees for 20 minutes, or until shortbread is pale golden brown.
6. Dust cookies with sugar while still warm, then carefully place on a cooling rack to crisp up.

Makes about 18

WASSAIL BOWL

In those parts of Britain where there are many apple orchards—mostly Wales and the West Country—Twelfth Night was the time to go wassailing. *Wassail* comes from the Old English *was hel*, "be whole," and was a very old drinking toast. A wassail bowl is made from warmed spiced ale or cider with roasted apples floating in it, and it was often served in a special ornately decorated bowl.

In Cornwall farmers and their workers took the bowl to the orchard and sang a toast to each of the trees in turn. After the bowl was enthusiastically passed around, they poured the rest of its contents over the roots of the tree as a libation. This was done to ensure a bumper crop of apples next autumn.

The wassail bowl was sometimes called "lambswool" because of the fleecy appearance of the baked apple pulp:

Next crowne the bowle full
With gentle lamb's wooll;
Adde sugar, nutmeg and ginger,
With store of ale too;
And thus ye must doe
To make our Wassaile a swinger.
ROBERT HERRICK, SIXTEENTH CENTURY

Ingredients
6 baking apples
12 cups good brown ale or apple cider (traditionally "hard" or alcoholic cider, but you can also use nonalcoholic apple cider)
1 cup sweet sherry
4 ounces sugar
1 teaspoon grated nutmeg
1 teaspoon ground ginger
3 whole cloves

Method
1. Core and prick the apples, then bake until the flesh is very soft and oozes out of the skins.
2. Pour all ingredients except the apples into a large pan, and simmer until the sugar

"TO YOUR HEALTH!"—SOME CELTIC TOASTS

Language		Pronunciation
Irish Gaelic	*Sláinte!*	*slawn*-chuh
Scottish Gaelic	*Slàinte!*	*slawn*-chuh
Welsh	*Lechyd da!*	*yekh*-id *dah*
Manx	*Shoh slaynt!*	show slainch
Cornish	*Yeghes da!*	*yeh*-hez dah
Breton	*Yec'hed mat!*	*yekh*-ed mahd

More Toasts

From Scotland:

Long may your lum reek (Long may your chimney smoke),
may your porridge never sour,
and may a wee mouse never leave your larder hungry.

From Ireland:

May the roof above us never fall in, and may we friends gathered below never
*   fall out.*

May you have warm words on a cold evening, a full moon on a dark night, and
*   the road downhill all the way to your door.*

Here's that we may always have a clean shirt, a clean conscience, and a guinea
*   in our pockets.*

May you live to be a hundred years with one extra year to repent.

May you live as long as you want
*   and never want as long as you live.*

dissolves (about 10 minutes). If using alcoholic ingredients, do not boil.

3. Pour into a warmed bowl and float the apples on top. Serve in individual mugs or tankards with spoons to scoop up the apples.

4. For a richer variation, spoon whipped cream on top.

Serves 6

CREATING SACRED SPACE

Thresholds between the physical and spiritual planes exist throughout the Celtic world. Sometimes called "thin" places, they can be found at the riverbank and shoreline, where land and water meet; where two or three streams converge; at fords and crossroads; by faery forts, trees, and standing stones. These are places where people came to perform rituals, create poetry, and make magic or pray because the power of the spirit world was palpably close.

It is also possible to create a threshold place in our own homes where we can go to journey into both our personal inner world and also the Celtic Otherworld, which lies beyond the boundaries of the personal. In our own sacred space we can meditate, write in a journal, reflect, or perform simple rituals and journey to those hidden realms and bring back some of its treasures to enrich our spiritual lives.

1. Choose a place that will not be used for any other purpose. It should be kept clear of everyday objects and be a haven of quiet where you can be completely private. This is your sacred space, or *temenos,* which divides the world of time and busyness from the timeless world.

2. Use a low table, piece of wood, shelf, or other surface to create your altar. Unless it is naturally attractive, cover it with a cloth, either plain or with a Celtic design.

3. Make a seat, preferably with pillows or a backrest, but a chair will do if you have difficulty sitting on the floor. You may find it more comfortable to do some of the inner journeying in this book lying down, so give yourself that option, too, with more pillows, a rug, or blankets.

The Celtic Mandala

To create sacred space in a Celtic way, you need to locate the four cardinal directions by using a compass or by noticing the passage of the sun. Each direction has a number of symbolic meanings.

In Scottish tradition the circle of time is superimposed on the circle of space. East equals spring, south is summer, west is autumn, and north equals winter. This may have come

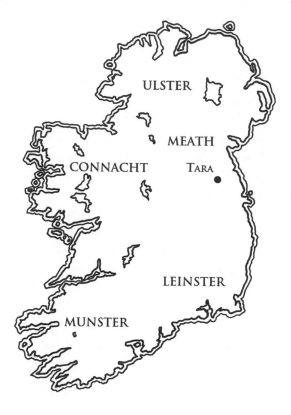

ULSTER

MEATH

CONNACHT

TARA

LEINSTER

MUNSTER

The winds that blew from each direction had a particular color and quality. The most fortunate wind blew from the east and was the royal color of purple. The south wind also brought good luck and was white. From the west blew the ill wind that was a dun color like the setting sun, while the cold north wind was black. The direction of the wind at birth could determine a child's fate.

As described earlier, Ireland was divided into four provinces around a fifth central one. Each province had its own symbolic resonance: Leinster in the east was associated with prosperity, *Bláth;* Munster in the south was associated with music, *Séis;* Connacht in the west with learning, *Fis;* Ulster in the north with battle, *Cath.* The central province, Meath, the ruling center, was associated with kingship.

The pattern of four quadrants surrounding a center is often termed a *mandala,* a visual tool for the spiritual journey. We see it in works of religious art throughout the world, from the *yantras* of Eastern religions to the Native American medicine wheel; it is there in medieval European illustrations of Christ surrounded by the four evangelists and in the Aztec calendar stone in Mexico. Although our modern culture reserves no place for it in art or architecture, this sacred symbol fre-

about from early astronomers' observations of the constellation of Ursa Major, the Great Bear, which contains two stars in the cup of its Big Dipper that line up with Polaris, the Pole Star. They point eastward in spring, southward in summer, and so on around the circle, which is why the Scots used to call the Great Bear the "Farmer's Clock."

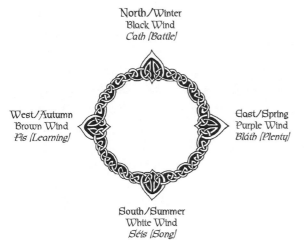

North/Winter
Black Wind
Cath [Battle]

West/Autumn
Brown Wind
Fis [Learning]

East/Spring
Purple Wind
Bláth [Plenty]

South/Summer
White Wind
Séis [Song]

quently appears in dreams and visions within the landscape of our own psyches, especially when we tap into the transpersonal dimensions of life. As a founding father of modern psychology, C. G. Jung rediscovered that this ancient image is not only a symbol of the outer world but also the primary symbol of integration within the human psyche. To create the Celtic mandala upon our altar makes it a template of the sacred Celtic universe and a powerful spiritual center for the creative journey of our soul.

Decorating the Altar

EAST: This is the place of dawn, springtime and growth, and plenty and prosperity.

Consider what truly enriches your life, and place symbols of these things on the east side. These might be photos and pictures of your partner, children, grandchildren, or pets or any other people, places, or things that enrich your life. If you feel poor in certain areas, put a symbol of what you lack here also, as a witness of what you'd like to have increased, such as a coin for money, heart for love.

SOUTH: This is the place of noon, midsummer, song, and poetry—in Celtic tradition brought about by the fire of *imbas,* or inspiration. What do you feel passionate about? How do you express your creativity? Put symbols of your inspiration on the south side of your altar. If this is an area of your life you neglect, add something to bring it into your life. If you aspire to athletics, place a picture of an athlete here, or if you've always wanted to play a harp, find a model of that instrument, and so on.

WEST: This is the place of dusk and autumn. Where the sun (everyday consciousness) dips into the darkness of the Underworld, inner wisdom becomes available. Spend some time thinking of the wisdom you have learned on your journey through life so far. Place suitable symbols for this in the west. If there's an area in your life where you would like to have more understanding, place a symbol for that here, such as a photo of a loving couple to invoke more understanding about relationships.

NORTH: This is the place of midnight, winter, and the battlefield. All challenges and the strength to deal with them appropriately have their place in the north, where the dark is dominant. What are the recurring conflicts and challenges in your life? Where do you most need to have the warrior's alertness and courage? Place here symbols of the qualities you need to face these issues, such as a rock for endurance, a crystal for clarity, a model spear for battle.

THE CENTER: In pre-Christian sanctuaries, the sacred center was represented by a well, a fire, a mound, a pillar stone, a tree, or a post. It was the *omphalos,* the navel of the world, which connected the tribe with the Upperworld and the Underworld, a direct line to the gods. On your altar, you can place here a chalice or bowl (for the well); a leafy or flowering plant or vase of flowers (for the tree); or a candle (for the fire). As we arrive at each of the four great festivals of the year, you will be given suggestions as to other suitable objects to place in the center for that season.

Visit your altar at the liminal times of dawn or dusk, or both if you choose. As the Celts knew, it is much easier to enter the Oth-erworld at these in-between times. Under the light of the sun we tend to feel drawn into the outside world, while late at night our consciousness tends to sink too deep and it can be difficult to stay awake. At dawn and dusk we are in the ideal state of balance between the outer and inner planes so that the inner realms are available to us and our conscious minds can be aware of what we experience.

If you spend time on a regular basis in your sacred space, you will be building an energy field that forms an inner threshold between the worlds, which will make it easier for you to move in and out at will. You will be able to drop into a meditative state much faster, and your meditations and inner journeys will become deeper and more vivid.

CIRCLE OF THE SUN

The Celtic circle is always traced in a sunwise (clockwise) direction, *deiseal* in Irish Gaelic. Rituals of all kinds begin facing east, where the sun rises, and moving toward the south, west, and north in turn. This sacred way of orienting the self in the world in accordance with the sun's movement is reflected in both Welsh and Gaelic: the word for north also means the left-hand side, south means the right-hand side, east means front, and west means back. An Irish king set out southward from Tara to make a ritual circuit of the land, always with the sea "at his left shoulder," in a sunwise direction. In early times warriors approaching a fort indicated whether they were friend or foe by advancing either clockwise, *deosil* (*jesh*-el), or counterclockwise, *tuaitheal* (*too*-hil), the direction used for cursing. To take the left-hand path against the sun has been considered unlucky or evil in many traditions: our word *sinister* comes from the Latin word for "left."

Until quite recently in Ireland and Scotland, expectant mothers walked around a church three times sunwise to ensure an easy delivery; fishing boats rowed in three circles before putting out to sea for a good catch; wedding processions circled the house three times before entering; and pilgrims still circumambulate holy wells and other shrines in this way. To make the sunwise circle is to align oneself with everything in nature, to trace the primary steps of the dance of life, which

THE SACRED CIRCLE

The circle is perhaps the most sacred figure in primal cultures, including the pre-Celtic and early Celtic worlds. The Celts grew up in natural surroundings, watching the sun, the moon, and the wheeling stars and the round rim of the horizon. They lived in circular houses and danced in rings at the circles of stone built by the original inhabitants of those islands. The Celtic cross, found in so many early churchyards, town centers, and crossroads, existed before Christianity came to these isles and is basically a cross within a circle: a worldwide symbol of cosmic order and harmony. The cross symbolizes the manifest world, while the unbroken circle reminds us that the oneness of spirit underlies all forms.

Celtic cross at Kilree, County Tipperary, Ireland

moves continually and inexorably from birth to growth to maturity to death. In many primal cultures this is the natural way to move. Sioux medicine man Black Elk explains why his tribe enters the sacred tipi in this way:

> Is not the south the source of life, and does not the flowering stick truly come from there? And does not man advance from there toward the setting sun of his life? Then does he not approach the colder north where the white hairs are? And does he not arrive, if he lives, at the source of light and understanding, which is the east?[13]

When you lay your fire or light your triple candle—or even when you stir batter, plant a garden, or walk around a supermarket—do it in a sunwise direction! A simple awareness of moving the way the sun does, even in the most mundane situation, can subtly yet noticeably help you feel more connected with the circle of life as you tune in to the daily and yearly cycles of the Earth.

DEISEAL

Siúlaim deiseal
ar lia, tobar is bile.
Siúlaim deiseal
ar shliabh, loch is coill.
Siúlaim deiseal
ar shlí na bíse
ar shlí na físe
ar shlí na fírinne.

SUNWISE

I walk sunwise
around standing stone,
*   well, and sacred tree.*
I walk sunwise
around mountain, lake,
*   and wood.*
I walk sunwise
on the path of the spiral
on the path of the vision
on the path of the truth.
DENNIS KING

The Caim: Ring of Protection

Healers throughout the Celtic countries used the circle in their practices, and in Scotland ordinary people performed a ritual known as the *caim* (*kime*) or "encircling," when they felt in need of divine protection. To make the *caim*, stretch out your right arm, point the index finger toward the floor, and turn around slowly three times in a sunwise direction to describe a circle around yourself. As you do so, invoke the divine presence in a prayer, such as the one following. This is adapted from traditional prayers and draws upon the power of the sacred numbers of the Celtic cosmos, three and four. Make the *caim* three times, one for each of the first three verses, then face the four directions specified in each line of the last verse, with arms outstretched.

Encircle me, Giver of Life,
Keep safety in, keep danger out.

Encircle me, Giver of Light,
Keep brightness in, keep darkness out.

Encircle me, Giver of Grace,
Keep peace within, keep conflict out.

May You be a bright flame before me,
May You be a guiding star above me,
May You be a smooth path below me,
And a loving Guide behind me,
Today, tonight, and forever.

THE INNER CAULDRON
VISIONING

Now sit before your altar for a meditation that will prepare you for the New Year.

At the start of a new year we have an opportunity to create a new vision for the future. As we stand on the threshold, we can close the door on any aspects of the past that we wish to leave behind, and we can also take with us those successes that have helped us build a good, solid foundation for the coming

cycle. Our future lies before us beyond the open door, an adventure that will be shaped partly by our own imagination and creativity, partly by the great Weaver of our lives.

Meditation: The Dolmen Gate
Close your eyes and take a few deep breaths. See before you an ancient dolmen of stone. Two giant pillars support a massive capstone. The stones are formed from gray rock, yet the one to your left is flecked with gold, while the right-hand pillar is of a greenish cast.

Walk toward this stone gateway and stand between the pillars, turning to face back toward the direction from which you came. Raise your arms so that each hand touches the stone on either side, and look back. Look at the landscape of the year gone by. Is it green and lush, stony and barren, or dirty and polluted? Do different parts of it display different qualities? See the road that led you to the place you stand today. Is it straight or winding, smooth or rocky?

Notice in particular any landmarks along the road. (Just let the images form without trying to remember with your conscious mind.) You may be surprised at what images emerge that symbolize people, places, or events of significance. If you had to choose one word to describe the landscape or any prominent feature in it, what would that be?

Now scan this landscape one more time. Decide what you wish to leave behind and what you would like to take with you into the new cycle. Then turn around, facing into the stone gateway, touching the pillars as before. See the road stretching before you, smooth and untrodden. What are the features of the landscape of the year that is about to begin? Using your imagination, place in the land-scape those things from the past you want to bring with you.

Ask yourself what you would most like to create this year, from the deepest part of yourself. This might be a quality, like love, beauty, or peace, or something very specific, like bringing harmony to a difficult family situation, creating a work of art, establishing a relationship, or becoming involved in a community project. Let an image emerge of whatever it is. (You may either see a realistic picture of your project or a symbol of it.) Look at it from all sides, and see what it has to tell you. When you are complete with this process, take a deep breath, walk beyond the twin pillars, and step into the New Year.

When you open your eyes, write down or draw your image, and keep it in a prominent place to remind you of your vision for the coming year.

HOUSE BLESSING

Peace of God and peace of man,
*Peace of God on Columb-Killey**
On each window and each door,
On every hole admitting moonlight,
On the four corners of the house,
On the place of rest,
And peace of God on myself.
                    TRADITIONAL MANX

---

*[Saint Columcille].

THE FESTIVAL OF BRIGIT

Radiant flame of gold . . . beloved Bride . . .
CARMINA GADELICA

I n the dim winter days of the early year there grows within all of us a longing for more light. In old Scotland February fell in the middle of the period known as *Faoilleach,* the wolf month; it was also known as *a' marbh mhiòs,* the dead month. But although this season was so cold and drear, small signs of new life began to appear: lambs were born, and soft rain brought new grass. Ravens began to build their nests, and larks were said to sing with a clearer voice. The Cailleach (*kal*-yukh), Old Woman of Winter, was transformed into Bride, the Fair Woman of February, fragile yet growing stronger each day as the sun rekindled its fire. As Alexander Carmichael writes in *Carmina Gadelica,* "Bride with her white wand is said to breathe life into the mouth of the dead Winter and to bring him to open his eyes to the tears and the smiles, the sighs and the laughter of Spring. The venom of the cold is said to tremble for its safety on Bride's Day, and to flee for its life on Patrick's Day."[1]

Bride's Day is February 1, one of the four great festivals that are gateways into the seasons of the turning year. In early Ireland her festival was known as Imbolc, or Óimelc, a name that probably refers to the first milk of the year as ewes birthed their lambs, heralding the return of new life. In later centuries it came to be known as Brigit's Feast Day, but in the Christian calendar the festival was replaced by Candlemas Day on February 2, dedicated to the Virgin Mary and featuring candlelight processions. A powerful female figure of light hovers over both celebrations, and indeed, Brigit was often called Mary of the Gael.

WOMAN OF WISDOM

Who was Brigit? That is not an easy question to answer, for her origins are lost to our view, and in later years it is hard to tell the Celtic goddess apart from the Christian saint of the same name. And yet, perhaps it is a quality of Brigit herself that she cannot be readily categorized. For in the lore of both goddess and saint she seems to have been the overarching benefactor of every aspect of the life of

FESTIVAL NAMES

Language	Name	Pronunciation
Irish Gaelic	Imbolc (Old Irish)	imb-*olc* or im-*molc*
	Lá Fhéile Bríde (Modern Irish)	*law* ayl-uh *breej*-uh
Scottish Gaelic	Là Fhèill Brìghde	*lah* ayl *breej*-uh
Manx	Laa'l Vreeshey	*lal* bree-zhuh

(There is no trace of a festival of Brigit in Wales or Cornwall. Wales once celebrated the Gwyl Fair y Canhwyllau, Mary's Festival of the Candles, when a candle was lit in every farmhouse window.)

the people and the land. In fact, it might be said that Brigit is the nearest thing we have to a Great Mother of the Celts.

There are many variants on her name, including *Brigid, Brighid, Bríd* in Ireland, *Bhrighde* and *Bride* in Scotland, *Ffraid* in Wales, and *Breeshey* in the Isle of Man. It may originally have been a title rather than a personal name. Some scholars believe it originated with the Sanskrit root *brihati*, which means "high" or "exalted one," giving us words such as the *brig* of a ship today. A tenth-century Irish glossary describes the goddess Brigit as one of the Tuatha Dé Danann, the daughter of the Dagda, yet she was also known as the mother of the three gods of Danu, which perhaps reflects an earlier matrifocal, or woman-centered, tradition. The writer, a Christian monk of Cashel, Cormac, calls her a "woman of wisdom . . . a goddess whom poets adored, because her protection was very great and very famous."[2] Since the discipline of poetry, *filidecht*, was interwoven with seership, Brigit was seen as the great inspiration behind divination and prophecy, the source of oracles. Cormac mac Cuillenáin goes on to say that she had two sisters—Brigit the Physician and Brigit the Smith—but it is generally thought that all three were aspects of a triple goddess of poetry, healing,

and smithcraft, all magical arts of transformation. Elsewhere Brigit is described as the patroness of other vital crafts of early Celtic society—dyeing, weaving, and brewing—and she was a guardian of farm animals, especially cows.

Brigit is deeply associated with the country of Ireland, where to this day some Irish rivers bear her name. She had two oxen, called Fea and Feimhean, who gave their names to a plain in County Carlow and one in Tipperary. She was also the guardian of Torc Triath, king of the wild boar, whose name was given to Treithirne, a plain in West Tipperary. These three totem animals used to raise a warning cry if Ireland was in danger. In the mythic history of the Tuatha Dé Danann, she was both the daughter of the Dagda and wife of his enemy, the Fomorian king, Bres. Celtic scholar Miranda Green sees her as "an ancestor-deity, a mother-goddess whose main concern was the future well-being of Ireland."[3] But perhaps the simplest illustration of her guardianship of the land comes from the folk tradition, which tells how Brigit spread out her green mantle over all of her beloved country and made it the Emerald Isle.

SAINT BRIGIT

With the coming of Christianity, the powerful energy of the goddess was transmuted into Ireland's much-loved saint, second only to Patrick himself. This happened almost literally in Drumeague, County Cavan, at a place called the Mountain of the Three Gods. Here a stone head of Brigit as the triple goddess had been worshiped for centuries, but in the Christian era it was hidden away in a Neolithic tomb. Later it was recovered from its burial place and mounted on a local church, where it was popularly canonized as Saint Bride of Knockbridge.

Saint Brigit was supposedly born in the year 453 C.E., about twelve years before the death of Saint Patrick. She was the daughter of a druid who had a vision that she was to be named after a great goddess. She was born at sunrise while her mother was walking over a threshold and so "was neither within nor without." As we saw in January, dawn is both a liminal time and place, when the doors between the worlds are open and magical events can occur. Another legend tells how her mother was carrying a pitcher of milk at the time, with which she bathed her newborn child. As a child, Brigit was unable to eat ordinary food and was reared on the milk of a special white, red-eared cow. White animals with red ears are beasts of the Otherworld. Like her pagan predecessor, Saint Brigit was closely associated with livestock in general and dairy cows in particular. As an adult, she was accompanied by a white cow who supplied her with all the milk she needed. In Scotland she was invoked as Milkmaid Bride or Golden-Haired Bride of the Kine.

THE FULL POT

The original goddess of increase and plenty shines through the legends of the gentle saint who fed poor people, animals, and birds with an open heart and hand. One day, while she was helping to prepare a feast in honor of her father's guests, a starving dog limped into the kitchen, drawn by the fragrance of cooking bacon. Brigit couldn't resist giving the wretched animal a piece of meat, and then another, and another, till she realized with horror that the pot was empty. At that moment, her father came into the kitchen to see if dinner was ready.

"Go look in the pot," said Brigit, praying very hard.

The pot was full.

THE LAKE OF MILK

When seven bishops paid a surprise visit to Kildare Abbey, Brigit went straightaway to the kitchens but found her cook, Blathnet, was completely out of food. Knowing that it would be shameful not to feed the holy visitors, she knelt down and began to pray for a solution. A band of angels appeared to her and told her to milk the cows again, even though they had already been milked three times earlier that day. Brigit hurried off to the byre, and the cows gave her so much milk it not only filled the pails, it overflowed Leinster's green fields until it made a lake that is called the Lake of Milk to this day.

FIERY ARROW

Brigit, excellent woman,
Flame golden, sparkling,
May she bear us to the eternal kingdom,
She the sun, fiery, radiant!
SEVENTH-CENTURY HYMN TO SAINT BRIGIT

Early writers believed Brigit's name stemmed from *breo-aigit*, "fiery arrow," a fitting name for a goddess of the hearth, the forge, and the flame that burns within the hearts of poets. She was also guardian of an eternal flame that burned within a sacred enclosure at her abbey in Kildare. Gerald of Wales, a twelfth-century traveler, described this as a hallowed precinct surrounded by a protective hedge of interwoven willow branches that only women were allowed to enter. Stories about the flame's miraculous properties tell how it stayed alight through the grace of God, while the ashes from the burned wood never increased even though it burned for a thousand years, from the fifth to the sixteenth centuries. During Brigit's lifetime twenty nuns kept watch over the flame. When she died the nineteen took turns guarding the fire each night, and when the twentieth night came, the last nun put the logs beside the fire and said, "Brigit, guard your fire. This is your night."

In the morning the wood was found burned and the fire still alight. Originally, this may have been the pagan sanctuary of the Brigantes tribe, presided over by the high priestess of Brigantia.

In 1993 Brigit's sacred flame was relit after four hundred years by the ancient order of Brigidine Sisters. In the heart of Kildare, the sisters have set up a community to carry forward the spirit of Brigit in our time. By 2002 the flame will be on view in a special vessel and kept burning in the center of Kildare's town square for all to see.

Beyond the many wonderful legends about Saint Brigit, there is little evidence of her as a historical figure, which prompted Sir James Frazer, author of *The Golden Bough*, to call her "a goddess in a threadbare cloak." Yet the power of Brigit has been carried down through time in the hearts of the Celtic people, particularly in Ireland and Scotland. As we saw in the previous chapter, the hearth fire was kindled with her blessing. As a bringer of life, she was called upon by mothers at childbirth, and she was invoked whenever protection was needed. People prayed for her healing power in times of sickness, for it was said she wove healing threads into the first piece of cloth ever made in Ireland. She presided over water as well as fire and is the guardian spirit of many sacred springs throughout the British Isles and Ireland. Even today, pilgrims still flock to the holy wells dedicated to her in order to drink or bathe in the water she has blessed. And like the perpetual flame she once guarded, she burns as bright as ever in the spiritual lives of many today.

SAINT BRIGIT AND THE SUNBEAM

When Brigit was a young woman her early miracles drew the attention of the famous Saint Brendan, who stopped by her farm one day unannounced. She had been out working in the fields on a rainy day and was so surprised to see the great man in her house that she flung off her rain cloak without bothering to hang it up. The cloak caught on a sunbeam and, to Brendan's astonishment, hung there till it dried.

THE SACRED THREE

Many Celtic deities had three aspects, for three and its multiple, nine, are the most magically charged numbers in Celtic tradition. Brigit is a triple goddess, and so is the Mórrígan (see November), while Ériu, Banba, Fótla (*ey*-ryuh, *bahn*-wuh, *foh*-luh) are female personifications of Ireland. A number of statues and reliefs from Romano-Celtic times show gods and goddesses either in threes or with three faces. The most serious oath was sworn by land, sea, and sky.

The number three can signify many aspects of life: beginning, middle, and end; mother, father, and child; past, present, and future; the Underworld, Middle World, and Upperworld. A number of proverbs and sayings come in sets of three, known as triads. Many of these appear to be mnemonic devices, which helped the druids, poets, and storytellers to memorize the huge amount of information they learned as "living libraries" of an oral culture.

Three slender things that best support the world:
the slender stream of milk from the cow's udder into the pail,
the slender blade of green corn upon the earth,
the slender thread in the hand of a skilled woman.

Three sounds of increase:
the lowing of a cow in milk,
the din of a smithy,
the swish of a plow.

Three candles that illumine every darkness:
Truth, nature, knowledge.

As the Celts were already familiar with the sacred power of the number three, they readily received the Christian teaching of the Holy Trinity. The Sacred Three is invoked in many Scottish and Irish prayers, charms, and incantations, some of which are so clearly pagan in origin that we can only wonder who the original triune divine power could have been. From now on, whenever it is suggested that you invoke the Sacred Three in this book in blessings, prayers, or rituals, you can insert whichever trinity is most meaningful according to your own spiritual tradition. Examples of your own Sacred Three might be:

Brigit, the Triple Goddess of poetry, smithcraft, and healing
A threefold power of nature, such as sun, moon, and stars or the traditional Irish land, sea, and sky
The divine Father, Mother, and Child

The Sacred Three are invoked in this beautiful night blessing from Scotland:

The Sacred Three
To save,
To shield,
To surround
The hearth,
The house,
The household,

This eve,
This night,
Oh! This eve,
This night,
And every night,
Each single night.
CARMINA GADELICA

BRIGIT'S BLESSING

I am under the shielding
of good Brigit each day:
I am under the shielding
Of good Brigit each night.

I am under the keeping
Of the nurse of Mary,
Each early and late,
Every dark, every light.

Brigit is my comrade-woman,
Brigit is my maker of song,
Brigit is my helping-woman,
My choicest of women,
my woman of guidance.

CARMINA GADELICA

THE TRISKELE

The triskele is an ancient triune symbol
meaning "three legs,"
which may represent the threefold Celtic
universe in motion.

GODS OF THE CELTS: BRIGANTIA

Brigantia was the ancestral goddess of a group
of European tribes known as the Brigantes and
may be equated with Brigit herself. A branch of
this tribe lived in County Kildare, where a high
priestess presided over her cult center. This
was probably the origin of Saint Brigit's association with this area. The Brigantes were the
most powerful and widespread tribe of Iron
Age Britain, holding sway throughout the
north. Under the Romans, Queen Carti-
mandua ruled the tribe and may have also per-

formed the role of Brigantia's high priestess and mortal representative of the goddess.[4] A stone relief of Brigantia from southern Scotland portrays her as a strong and warlike protector bearing a globe and spear, showing similarities to the Roman goddesses Victory and Minerva, who, like Brigit, were also associated with crafts and healing. Places as far apart as Brechin in Scotland and Bregenz in Austria, once the center of the Brigantes, all reflect her presence on the land, while the rivers Brent in England and Braint in Wales were named after her.

*Stone relief of Brigantia
from Birrens, Scotland*

COW

A CELTIC BESTIARY

In early Celtic society cattle were the most highly valued of all animals, revered as symbols of plenty as they were in ancient Egypt, India, and other Indo-European cultures. The cow was associated with Brigit and other divine women in Celtic myth and legend, including Boand, the goddess of the River Boyne, whose name means "white cow." Even the country of Ireland itself was given the poetic name of Druimin Donn Dílis (*drihm-*een *donn jee-*lish), the Faithful Brown, White-Backed Cow. In many ways the cow symbolizes the life-giving fertile goddess of the land. At Beltaine, when the people hoped for plenty of milk, butter, and cheese, Irish farmers watched for a sacred, snow white cow to appear among their cattle—a sign of the greatest good luck. An old Irish song that may allude to this cow—or, perhaps, to the goddess herself—goes:

There is a cow on the mountain,
A fair white cow;
She goes East and she goes West,
And my senses have gone for love of her;
She goes with the sun and he forgets to burn,
And the moon turns her face with love to her,
My fair white cow of the mountain.

SAINT BRIDE OF SCOTLAND

Bride put her finger in the river
On the Feast Day of Bride
And away went the hatching mother of the cold.
CARMINA GADELICA

In Scotland Saint Brigit was known as Bride, and like the goddess, she reigned over fire, over art, and over beauty. As she presided over the birth of spring, legends tell that she was the midwife at Christ's birth. She was called Muime Chriosda (*mwim*-yuh *khrees*-tuh), Foster Mother of Christ, and her presence was invoked at childbirth, as Alexander Carmichael recounts in *Carmina Gadelica:*

When a woman is in labor the midwife . . . goes to the door of the house, and standing on the door-step, softly beseeches Bride to come in:

"Bride, Bride, come in!
Thy welcome is truly made,
Give thou relief to the woman,
And give thou the conception to the Trinity."

As Bride looked after women in childbirth and presided over the hearth-fire, so Là Fhéill Bhrìghde (Bride's Feast Day) was primarily a women's festival, celebrated with heartfelt prayers and songs. On Bride's Eve, the girls made a female figure from a sheaf of corn and decorated her with colored shells and sparkling crystals, together with snowdrops and primroses and other early spring flowers and greenery. An especially bright shell or crystal, symbol of the return of light, was placed over its heart, as the "guiding star of Bride." The doll was called the *brìdeag* (*bree*-jag), little Bride, and was carried about the town in procession by young girls known as the *banal Bride,* the Bride maiden band, dressed all in white and wearing their hair down, personifying the spirit of purity and youth.

Everyone they visited had to pay homage to Bride and give her a gift, such as a flower or a crystal, while the mothers gave bannocks, cheese, or butter, in thanksgiving for Bride's lavish gifts of food. When they had finished their rounds, the girls spent the night at a house where the brìdeag sat in state while they prepared the Bride feast for the next day. The young men of the town soon came knocking at the door and were let in to pay tribute to Bride, after which there were songs, dancing, and much merrymaking until the break of day. At first light, they all joined hands and sang a hymn to Bride and shared the remains of the feast among the poor women of the town.

The older women also conducted a ceremony on the Eve of Bride. They, too, made a doll representing Brigit out of oats, lovingly decorated it, and prepared for her a basket called *leaba Bride*, Bride's bed.

One woman stood at the door of the house and called softly into the darkness: "Bride's bed is ready."

Another woman behind echoed: "Let Bride come in. Bride is welcome."

The woman at the door called again: "Bride, Bride, come thou in, thy bed is made. Preserve the house for the Trinity."

The women then placed the doll with great ceremony into her waiting bed, and in her hand they placed a wand made of willow, birch, or other white wood.

Even today, there are places in Scotland where Saint Bride's Day is still very much alive. For example, Canon Angus MacQueen on the Isle of South Uist celebrates all the Celtic feast days with his parishioners, especially the Day of Bride, when the *brìdeag* is still borne around in procession to every house on the island.

Brigit of the mantles,
Brigit of the peat heap,
Brigit of the twining hair,
Brigit of the augury,

Brigit of the white palms,
Brigit of the calmness,
Brigit of the kindness,
Brigit of the kine.

CARMINA GADELICA

A brìdeag

GROUNDHOG DAY

Groundhog Day, February 2, has its origins in the ancient festival of Brigit. If it's a fine morning and the groundhog sees his shadow, it means there will be six more weeks of winter. The custom comes directly from Europe, and Scotland in particular, where an old couplet warns:

If Candlemas Day is bright and clear,
there'll be two winters in the year.

A Scottish verse about the Feast Day of Bride begins:

This is the day of Bride,
The queen will come from the mound . . .

Irish scholar Séamus Ó Cáthain believes this rhyme has its roots in northern traditions concerning the reappearance of the hibernating bear. For this is the time when the animal world begins to stir from its winter sleep in the depths of the earth, and life and light is ushered in by Brigit, the Queen.

WELCOMING BRIDE: A RITUAL

In the following ritual we can invoke Brigit's blessing on all that we wish to give birth to in the coming year.

Cover your altar with a white cloth. Place white candles in a semicircle, open at the front, and surround them with whatever greenery you can find (traditionally, branches of the box tree; holly or Christmas boughs must not be used). If you can find early spring flowers, put them in a vase of water on the altar, too, especially the snowdrop, called in Wales the Fair Maid of February.

Within the circle of candles, place a wicker basket on the altar with a little straw or similar padding inside. This is Bride's bed.

If you have the time and materials, take or make out of straw a small figure dressed in white to be the *brìdeag*, the Bride doll. Or choose something to symbolize her, such as a bag of grain or packet of seeds, a beautiful white shell or crystal.

Sit (facing east if possible) and hold your symbol of Bride, then close your eyes. Take a few deep breaths, and let your mind become quiet and centered. Say the following words:

"Bride, Bride, come thou in, thy bed is made."

Then say three times: "Let Bride come in. Bride is welcome."

Wait until you feel a shift of energy that signals her presence has entered the house.

Now place the straw figure or symbol of Bride in the basket and say:

"I welcome you, Bride, to this my house. Protect and keep me/us safe throughout the coming year."

Place the symbol of Bride in the basket. Meditate for a few moments on what you would like to see begin, or grow, this spring time: for yourself, your family, your community, for the Earth. Get a clear picture of what each new beginning will look like, and ask Bride to bless the vision.

Sing or recite the following invocation for her threefold blessing:

INVOCATION TO BRIGIT AT IMBOLC
(to the tune of the English folksong "All Things Are Quite Silent")

We welcome you, Brigit, on Candlemas Eve,
We pray for your blessing, new life to receive,
O Mother of Poetry, teach us your art,
That your inspiration may enter each heart.

O Mistress of Magic that stands by the fire
And shapes the bright metal to the form you desire;
O Mother of Smithcraft, please teach us your art,
That the power of changing may enter each heart.

You kindle the springtime to quicken the earth,
From under your mantle the old has new birth,
O Mother of Healing, please teach us your art,
That peace and contentment may enter each heart.
         M. F.

choices for the *brìdeag* doll in Scotland. Like Brigit herself, willow brings good luck at childbirth, and perhaps the mysterious allusion in a medieval Irish poem to it being "sacred to poems" points to another connection with Brigit, the "goddess whom poets adore."

In Ireland, it was a tree of protection: travelers carried a willow rod on journeys, and farmers wrapped the butter churn with willow to keep evil spirits away. Perhaps this was because of willow's healing properties: white willow bark contains salicin, the active ingredient in aspirin, and was traditionally used for rheumatism, arthritis, and all damp diseases.

WHITE WILLOW TEA

Collect the bark of white willow in the springtime. Soak 1–2 teaspoons of the bark in 1 cup of cold water for 2–5 hours. Bring to a boil, then allow to steep for an hour or longer. Drink up to 5 cups a day.

THE SACRED GROVE

The noble willow . . . a tree
sacred to poems . . .
MEDIEVAL IRISH

Willow is a tree of the early spring, when rain swells the rivers. In Scotland, it was one of the nine sacred woods used to kindle the Beltaine fires. A watery, feminine tree, "willow of the streams" is ruled by the moon and so is naturally associated with women's ceremonies at Imbolc. A peeled willow wand was one of the

THE RETURN OF BRIDE

The Cailleach Bheur (*kal*-yakh veer) was the Old Woman of Winter in Scotland. She was very tall and very old, and everyone was afraid of her. Her face was blue, and she only had one eye. Her teeth were red as rust and her long hair as white as an aspen covered with snow. When she was angry she was as fierce as the biting north wind, and she roared like the sea in storm. Every autumn she struck the ground with her magic hammer and turned the grass into blades of ice.

All winter long, the Cailleach kept captive a beautiful young princess named Bride. She was jealous of her beauty and gave her ragged clothes to wear and made her work in the kitchen of her castle in the mountains. The young girl had to perform the meanest tasks, and the Cailleach scolded her constantly. Bride's life was wretched indeed.

Now the reason the Cailleach Bheur kept Bride a prisoner was because her favorite son, whose name was Angus-the-Ever-Young, had fallen in love with her. Angus lived on the Green Isle of the West, which is also called the Land of Youth, and he never grew any older. The Cailleach knew that if he ever married Bride, he would be able to take his place as the Summer King and Bride would be his queen. Then the Cailleach's reign would be over.

Angus gazed into the Well of Youth that lies at the heart of the Green Isle. He saw storms and he saw winds—and he saw Bride all alone weeping in her castle prison. Straightaway, he went to the King of the Green Isle and said, "I must go to her at once and set her free!"

But the King of the Green Isle said, "You cannot go now, Angus, for February, the month of the wolf, has come, and uncertain is the temper of the wolf. Wait a while until the grass begins to grow and flowers start to bloom, and then you shall set Bride free."

But Angus said, "I shall cast a spell on the sea and a spell on the land, and borrow for February three days from August."

And so he borrowed three days from August, and the sun came out and shone like pale gold over mountain and glen, while the sea lay smooth as buttermilk. Angus mounted his white horse and rode eastward to Scotland over the isles and over the Minch by day and by night, and he reached the Grampian Mountains just as the dawn was breaking. As he rode, his royal robe of crimson streamed from his shoulders, and his cloak of shining gold spread out around him, setting the mountains ablaze with light.

For three days Angus rode up and down the land, but he could not find Bride anywhere. Then one day, as he rode through a thick and tangled forest, he heard a soft sad voice singing among distant trees. It was Bride in the woods near the castle, where the Cailleach had sent her to gather logs for the fire. Angus gazed upon the living girl whom he had only seen in a vision, and he called her name. When she looked up and saw him, it was as if the sun itself pierced the ice around her frozen heart. She warmed at his gaze, and his words of love melted all her sorrow.

Said Angus, "I have come to rescue you from the Cailleach Bheur, who has held you prisoner all winter long."

Bride replied, "For me this is a day of great joy."

Said Angus, "From this time forth it will be a day of great joy to all of Scotland, as well."

For the day on which Angus found Bride was the first visit of spring, which ever after was called "Bride's Day." The hard earth began to thaw, and blades of new grass pierced the softening soil. Pale yellow primroses glowed in the woods, and young leaves unfurled on branches, green and tender.

Yet the Cailleach's reign was not yet over. When she found out what had happened, she and her eight hag-servants mounted their shaggy black goats and rode out of the mountain to wage war upon Angus and Bride. First she raised the wind called the Whistle, which blew high and shrill, and brought down showers of cold hailstones. It lasted for three days and killed the sheep and their newborn lambs upon the moors. Then she raised the Sharp-Billed Wind, which lasted for nine days and pierced the land to its core, pecking and biting like a sharp-billed bird. Finally, she raised the eddy wind that is called the Sweeper, whose whirling gusts tore branches from the budding trees and bright flowers from their stalks. Angus was moved with pity for the people, whose horses and cattle died for want of food. He drove the hags back to the far north, where they fretted and fumed in a fury.

But that night, the Cailleach Bheur borrowed three days from Winter that had not been used, because Angus had borrowed three days from August. The three days of Winter were spirits of the storm, and the Cailleach let them loose upon the land, riding on the backs of black hogs. They summoned the snow to the newly plowed fields and breathed the winds of death into cottage window and stable door. The rivers rose in flood, and many were drowned. The days on which this happened were called the Three Hog Days.

Then one bright morning at the beginning of March, the Cailleach saw Angus riding boldly over the hills on his white horse, scattering her hag-servants before him. She felt the unmistakable tide of life rising through the veins of the land and knew it was too strong for her. She flung down her magic hammer and turned into a large gray stone on the slopes of the mountain, where she was forced to stay until wintertime returned.

Angus and Bride were married, and wherever they stepped dandelions sprang up beneath their feet, and people called them the "little notched ones of Bride." As they rode throughout the land, the linnet sang of Bride's beauty, and so she was known ever after as the "Bird of Bride." When they came to the seashore, the first bird that chirped with joy was the oystercatcher, and so he is known as the "Page of Bride."

Spring had come at last.

BRIGIT IN IRELAND

On the eve of Brigit's feast day, known as Oíche Fhéile Bríde in Ireland, bands of boys and girls went around the houses with a *brídeog* doll to announce Brigit's return to her people. Every farmer's wife made a special cake, the ale was brought out, the neighbors came round, and a festive evening was had by all. Fresh butter was churned and always formed part of the meal. The more wealthy farmers gave gifts of butter to poorer neighbors, along with some roast meat, to celebrate the return of the bountiful saint.[5]

At this time, Brigit herself was believed to travel about the countryside with her white cow, blessing the people and the farm animals. In some parts, women would place a piece of cloth outside on a bush on Saint Brigit's Eve. They believed that during the night the saint would pass by and touch the cloth, imbuing it with healing properties. It had magically turned into the *brat Bríde*, Brigit's mantle, which could bestow an easy labor and healthy babies on both women and animals giving birth.

It was important to leave an offering of food on the windowsill for Brigit as she visited each house. Sometimes they left also a sheaf of corn for her cow to eat. A bundle of straw or fresh rushes were laid on the threshold for her to kneel upon to bless the house, or possibly so she—or the cow!—could wipe her feet before entering. The food was usually a round, unleavened oat bread called a *strone* in Ireland and called in Scotland *bonnach Bride*, Bride's bannock. The family was sure to eat one, too, piping hot and spread with lashings of homemade butter. Because of Brigit's associations with the dairy, this was essential.

Samhain Eve without food,
Christmas Night without bread,
Saint Brigit's Eve without butter,
That is a sorry complaint.

BRIDE'S BANNOCK

Celtic breads were traditionally baked on a griddle (Gaelic *greadal*). Originally a hot stone suspended over a fire, it was one of the oldest cooking methods known. Today a cast-iron skillet or barbecue grill can be used, or a heavy frying pan will work just fine. Here is a traditional recipe:

Ingredients
6 ounces oatmeal
2 ounces all-purpose flour
1 ounce butter
1 teaspoon salt
1 pinch baking soda
10 ounces water

Method

1. Sift the flour, salt, and baking soda into the oatmeal.
2. Boil the water, add the butter until melted, then pour into the dry ingredients. Mix until the mixture is a spongy dough. (A little extra water can be used if necessary.)
3. Turn mixture onto a surface covered with plenty of dry oatmeal, and scatter more on top. Flatten the dough and roll out to ¼-inch thickness, then place a dinner plate on top and trim into a neat circle. Scatter on more oatmeal, and rub it in all over the surface.
4. Score the top in the shape of Brigit's Cross.
5. Lift carefully onto a greased, preheated griddle or pan. Cook on medium heat till the bottom is golden brown and the sides are beginning to dry out and curl.
6. Place under the broiler to toast the top.
7. Serve hot and crisp.

BRIGIT'S CROSSES

People made special Brigit's crosses out of rushes and hung them high in house and byre to honor the saint and win her protection. Rushes are traditionally laid down in the birthing place, so they may carry the symbolism of new life.[6] The *cros Bríde* came in many different shapes, some of which resemble

A triskele cross

symbols of the sun in cultures throughout the world. One kind was actually not a cross at all but a figure with three legs, recalling the threefold nature of Brigit. It is, in fact, an ancient symbol known as the triskele and is still being made in some parts of western Ireland.

Another kind of cross was the *crios Bríde*, Saint Brigit's girdle, made from braided straw, which people carried around the neighborhood with a *brídeag* doll. Members of each household took turns jumping through the large straw hoop to ensure Brigit's protection and good health in the coming year, while the bearers chanted:

Crios Bríde

Brigit's girdle is my girdle,
The girdle with the four crosses,
Arise, housewife,
And go out three times.
May whoever goes through my girdle
Be seven times better a year from now.

Brigit's girdle can be easily made by braiding together three long ropes and joining them in a circle big enough for people to step through. Attach four Brigit's crosses as shown in the illustration. Each person steps through the circle three times sunwise, right foot first, then passes the circle three times around the waist while all present chant the verse.

The combination of the three and the four in this ritual recalls the structure of the Celtic universe, with its three worlds and four directions. Together, three and four make seven, another sacred number in Celtic lore. To step *idir na fáinna* (between the rings) is to move between this world and the Otherworld.

How to Make a Brigit's Cross

Gather together

3 dozen wheat straws, grasses, reeds, or rushes of the same length

String for tying ends

A clothespin for holding the center of the weaving together while working (optional)

Method

1. Soak your weaving materials in hot water about thirty minutes or until they are flexible. Various materials may require longer soaking times. Remove the straws from the water and wrap them in a damp cloth to keep them flexible while weaving.

2. Imagine the face of a clock measuring the year of time. Following the progression of the circle will assist you in weaving the cross. Place one straw vertically pointing toward twelve o'clock (north, winter) and six o'clock (south, summer). Fold a second straw in half around the center of the first, pointing toward three o'clock (east, spring). Fold the next straw in half and place it over the second straw pointing toward six o'clock (south, summer). Fold the next straw over straw one and three pointing toward nine o'clock (west, autumn). Continue to work in a circular pattern of folded straws, progressing outward, carefully weaving straws side by side. Tighten straws and reposition to fill in gaps when needed.

| STEP 1 | STEP 2 | STEP 3 | STEP 4 | STEP 4, COMPLETED |

3. As you move around the circular pattern, meditate on the progression of the woven events in the seasons of your life, past and present. Visualize what you want to manifest in the coming year as each straw weaves a dream for the future.

4. When at least twenty-eight straws have been woven for the center of the cross, tie off each arm of the cross, leaving about three inches of straw to create the arm. Trim ends evenly.

The traditional time to make Brigit's Crosses is after the evening meal on the eve of February 1. In Ireland, all the members of the household made the crosses together, so try it with your family or a group of friends. They are simple enough for children to make, too, and it's a wonderful thing to do while one person tells stories.

If you are doing this in a group, it is traditional for a young girl representing Brigit to bring the materials into the house. She should go outside and knock three times. After each knock, she must say: "Go down on your knees, do homage, and let Blessed Brigit enter the house."

After the third time, all inside respond: "Oh, come in, Brigit, you are a hundred times welcome!"

Hang the crosses over your front door, and leave them there to protect the house with Brigit's blessing until the following year. Children's crosses are traditionally hung above their beds so that Brigit will protect them through the night.

Other Simple Ways to Celebrate Brigit's Day

- As this is traditionally a time of purification, clean your house! If you have any Christmas greenery lingering, burn it now.
- If dandelions grow wild in your area, gather the leaves, wash them thoroughly, and eat them in your salad. These plants, whose golden faces remind us of the sun's return, are sacred to Brigit.
- Measure a colored ribbon, then put it out on your doorstep or on a bush in the yard for Brigit to bless as she comes by tonight. In the morning, pull it tight and measure it again to see if it has grown. (This is fun for children to do.) You now have Brigit's Mantle, which can be used for healing.
- In the evening, fill your house with lighted candles, especially white and green ones. If there are small children or animals in the house that you are concerned about, float special water candles in bowls, pans, or your bathtub.

Faoi bhrat Bhríde sinn!
(fwee *vrat vree*-juh shin)
May you be under Brigit's mantle!
Irish blessing

HOLY GROUND
KILDARE

Saint Brigit founded her abbey at Kildare, a small town in County Kildare southwest of Dublin. Its name was originally Cille Daire, Church of the Oak, for legend says that Brigit loved a great oak that grew here and held it so sacred that no one dared harm a leaf of it. Under its shade she built her church, at what once might have been the pagan sanctuary dedicated to the goddess Brigit of the Brigantes. The thirteenth-century cathedral that stands here today was built on the site of the original sixth-century church. The foundations of the fire temple where Brigit and her sisters tended the sacred flame still exist. A mile or so away in a quiet country lane stands Saint Brigit's Well, an ancient place of prayer and pilgrimage.

The town lies on the edge of the plain known as the Curragh of Kildare, now a famous racecourse. Saint Brigit once asked a miserly king for a contribution to her charities. He grudgingly told her she could have as much of the Curragh as her cloak would cover. Brigit laid out her mantle on the ground, and the king watched in horror as it began to spread rapidly over the plain for miles and miles. It had almost covered the whole country by the time he begged her to stop. Perhaps this story holds the memory of the time when all of Ireland was held within the folds of Brigit's green mantle.

At St. Brigit's Well, Kildare, the water runs through two stone tubes, bringing to mind the breasts of the life-giving mother.

THE INNER CAULDRON
INSPIRATION

With the growing need in the world to honor the feminine aspect of the divine, Brigit's spirit is very much alive today. Part of her enormous appeal is that as both goddess and saint, she crosses the borders of religion. On the same day that the Brigidine Sisters relit Brigit's sacred flame at Kildare (Lá Fhéile Bríde, 1993), a group of women calling themselves the Daughters of the Flame lit one in Canada—an event of extraordinary synchronicity. Members of this latter group take turns looking after the flame in their own homes on the traditional twenty-day rotation, although they live in different parts of the globe. Other groups that include men have since formed throughout the world, so instead of burning in one temple alone, Brigit's flame now burns on personal altars, garden tables, and even computer desks in more than ten countries throughout the world. (See "Resources" at the end of the book for how to contact these groups.)

Brigit's appeal to a new generation of spiritual seekers has a lot to do with the way she shows us how to embody Spirit in the world. At a time when we can no longer afford to keep our spirituality separate from everyday life, she teaches us about the power of committed action on behalf of those in need, in both the human kingdom and the natural world. As the personification of the sun and fire, she continually affirms life, light, and growth, recharging our often-flickering candles of faith with hope and belief in our visions for a better world.

And yet hers is not just the strength of one who has never known sorrow. As patroness of childbirth, she witnessed the struggle to bring life into the world again and again, and she experienced the grief of its loss firsthand. When her son Ruadhán (*roo*-an) died in battle, she rushed to the battlefield and, cradling his dead body in her arms, cried out her agony in the first *keening* Ireland ever heard.

As goddess, she kindles the flame of inspiration for works of beauty and wisdom, setting our minds ablaze with the passion to create. Being the patroness of smithcraft, she teaches us about the mysteries of art, how to transmute the dull metal of the mundane into something splendid through the skillful wielding of the creative fire. Like the sun, her bright spirit brings an awareness of the possible into our lives and gives us the courage to act upon our dreams.

Meditation: The Forge in the Forest

For the season from Imbolc to Beltaine, place a big white candle upon your altar, preferably with a triple wick for Brigit's three aspects. This symbolizes the growing light that she brings to our lives in the early spring and the loving brightness and warmth of her presence. A pillar was often used by the ancient Celts to symbolize the sun. The following meditation takes you to her forge to gain inspiration for the vision you birthed in January.

Light your candle. Gaze into the flame for a few moments, then close your eyes. You will still see the image of the flame against your eyelids. Now imagine it is growing brighter and brighter, and see yourself standing in a place filled with the warmth and red gold light of leaping flames. . . . Imagine, in fact, that you are standing in the entrance to a forge in a forest, where a blazing fire is roaring, and in front of it stands a woman. Thick, auburn hair is tied back, but a few rippling curls have escaped around her face. She is dressed in dark green with sleeves rolled up to the elbows, revealing strong white arms. Brigit, for of course it is she, stands over a large anvil, beating a sheet of soft gleaming bronze with a great hammer. . . . At last she looks up and smiles at you warmly. She has finished her creation and holds it up to the light of the fire for you to see. As you look at it, it appears to continually change shape: first it seems to be a leaf, then a globe . . . and now it has become a star. Brigit laughs deeply, musically, and tosses the star into the air, where it sails into the night sky and takes its place among the glittering constellations. . . .

And now Brigit turns toward you and asks, What have you come here to create? . . . You tell her of your vision, whether great or small, personal or for the wider community . . . and she beckons you over to the fire. As you look into the flames, pictures start to move and you see yourself at work, filled with enthusiasm and passion as you make your vision a reality. . . . You and your creation are surrounded and shot through with the golden light of inspiration. Brigit is there, too, watching over you with love as you work, encouraging you and filling you with confidence and creativity. . . . If any self-doubt or fears start to arise, see Brigit surrounding you with her mantle of protection: a warm soft cloak of green that makes you feel safe and inviolable. . . . Now see yourself with your vision turned into reality, feeling a sense of accomplishment and pride. . . . Thank Brigit for showing you this vision, and ask her to tell you what your first step should be toward bringing it into reality. . . . When you have finished the conversation with her, see the forge suddenly glow even more brightly so that all forms and shapes, including that of Brigit herself, melt into a suffusion of golden light. . . . And now see that the light is just the candle flame reflected on your eyelids. . . . Slowly come back to the room. Open your eyes and write down what she has suggested. In the coming weeks, call upon Brigit to help keep your inspiration alight.

BRIGIT SPEAKS

I am older than Brigit of the Mantle,
I put songs and music on the wind
before ever the bells of the chapels
were rung in the West
or heard in the East.

I am Brighid-nam-Bratta: Brigit of the Mantle,
but I am also Brighid-Muirghin-na-tuinne: Brigit, Conception of the Waves,
and Brighid-sluagh, Brigit of the Faery Host,
Brighid-nan-sitheachseang, Brigit of the Slim Faery Folk,
and Brighid-Binne-Bheule-lhuchd-nan-trusganan-uaine,
Brigit the Melodious Mouthed of the Tribe of the Green Mantles.

And I am older than Aone [Friday],
and as old as Luan [Monday],
and in Tir-na-h'oige my name is Suibhal-bheann: Mountain Traveler,
and in Tir-fo-thuinn, Country of the Waves, it is Cú-gorm: Gray hound,
and in Tir-na-h'oise, Country of Ancient Years, it is Sireadh-thall: Seek Beyond.

And I have been a breath in your heart,
and the day has its feet to it
that will see me coming into the hearts of men and women
like a flame upon dry grass,
like a flame of wind in a great wood.

FIONA MacLEOD

THE WELL OF WISDOM

Running water is a holy thing.
<small>OLD SOMERSET SAYING</small>

March is the second month of Spring, according to the Celtic calendar. Brigit's flame is growing in strength, and around March 21 daylight is at last equal to the hours of darkness. Spring Equinox has arrived.

In Wales this time marked the end of the *amser gwylad* (*ahm*-sair *goo*-uh-lahd), the indoor winter period that began around the Autumn Equinox. In some places households held a ritual of closure, as the maid ceremonially handed back to her mistress the candle that had lit their winter evenings. From now on the household would go to bed at dark and rise at the break of day. In the Gwaun Valley in Dyfed, a wooden candle was put in the place of the wax candle on the table as a reminder that it was no longer needed at suppertime. This took place

on Old Saint David's Day, March 12, hence
the rhyme:

Nos Wyl Ddewi fe gaiff Ben
Fwyta'i swper wrth ganwyll bren.

Saint David's Eve and Ben shall
Eat his supper by a wooden candle.[1]

In most parts of the British Isles and Ireland
the lengthening days and warmer weather
meant that it was time to plow and sow. The
staple crops were usually oats, barley, rye, and,
from the seventeenth century onward, potatoes. Up until modern times in Ireland the
whole family assembled in one of the fields for
the ritual turning the sod, accompanied by
prayers. Now the plowing could begin, preferably on the lucky day of Friday or, best of all,
on Good Friday. The plowman led his horses in
a sunwise direction, to invoke the sun's blessing
on his work. When he yoked and unyoked his
team, he made sure their heads faced south.
The sower began his work with the solemn
words "In the name of God," and his first job
was to give the horses a handful of seed from
his bag and throw a clod of earth upon their
rumps. Mixed in with the seeds were ashes
from the hearth-fire or, better still, ashes from
the midsummer bonfire, for the protection
and luck of sacred fire.

In Scotland the farmer prepared the seed
three days before sowing time by sprinkling it
with water in the name of the Sacred Three
as he walked around it sunwise. As he sowed
this first consecrated seed, he chanted the
invocation:

I will go out to sow the seed,
In the name of Him who gave it growth;
I will place my front in the wind,
And throw a gracious handful on high . . .
Every seed will take root in the earth,
As the King of the Elements desired . . .[2]

PREPARING THE GROUND

A seed will remain forever dormant unless it is
planted in earth that has been well prepared
for it. What groundwork do you need to do
before you can give expression to your soul?

As the plow may encounter hard, stony
soil, we may allow all sorts of things to get in
the way of making changes. Take a look at
any resistance you may have to working
toward your most important goals.

In the modern world we are continually
bombarded with distracting stimuli. The
straight, orderly furrows of a plowed field
remind us of the need to focus on our own
projects. Look at ways in which you can clear
space and time for cultivating the soul.

TWO MARCH SAINTS

Two of the most important Celtic saints have their feast days in March: Saint David in Wales and Saint Patrick in Ireland.

Saint David's Day is March 1, Gwyl Dewi (*gooil deh*-wee). David, or Dewi Sant, as he is known in Wales, was a sixth-century monk who became a bishop. Before he was born his father, a prince of Ceredigion, had a dream in which an angel told him that if he went down to the River Teifi he would discover three treasures that would foretell the life of his unborn son: a stag, a salmon, and a swarm of bees. These three are sacred creatures of the Celtic animal kingdom, and they bring the gifts of spiritual power, wisdom, and sweetness.

Despite his high rank in the Church, David and his monks lived a life of voluntary simplicity in West Wales, wearing nothing but animal skins, laboring in the fields, cultivating bees, and caring for the poor and sick. The last advice he gave his followers before his death was to pay attention to the "little things" in life rather than get caught up in the illusion of grand gestures. His saying, "*Gwnewch y pethau bychain,*" "Do the little things," is today a well-known phrase in Welsh and has proved a timeless inspiration and a recipe for peace of mind.

Saint David's Day is a day of Welsh national and cultural pride all over the world. The flag of Y Ddraig Goch, the Red Dragon, flies high, and festivities begin with dancing, singing, poetry, and, of course, the wearing of the national symbol, the leek.

Saint Patrick's Day is March 17, Lá Fhéile Pádraig (*law eyl*-uh *paw*-rick). Saint Patrick was also born in Wales around 390 C.E. but was captured by pirates and taken to be a slave in Ireland. He managed to escape but later returned as a missionary. Patrick announced his presence in Ireland by kindling a sacred fire at Slane, near Tara, the seat of sacred power, as all conquerors of that land did before him. When the king and his druids climbed the hill to challenge him, Patrick acted like a druid himself by calling up a cloud of darkness and an earthquake to rout them.

The defeated king pretended to submit and invited Patrick and his monks to his palace, planning to set an ambush for them en route. But God informed Patrick of the plan, and the little band of men, followed by their young servant lad, passed through safely in the shape of a herd of deer with a little fawn bringing up the rear.

Saint Patrick's Day is to this day one of the most important holidays in Ireland—and a glorious day of cultural pride for Irish-Americans. The original popularity of the feast day may have had something to do with its date, which was a welcome oasis of conviviality, food, and drink in the middle of the Lenten fast. At the end of the day came the time-honored custom of "drowning the shamrock" that had been worn in coat or hat all day. The leaf was put into the final glass of grog or punch for the last toast, after which it was tossed over the left shoulder for luck.

THE SHAMROCK

The Irish word *seamrog* means "clover" and refers not to one but to a whole variety of related clovers and trefoils. Saint Patrick was said to have used its leaf to explain the three-in-one, one-in-three nature of the Holy Trinity, but this saying was not heard before the eighteenth century. Be sure to avoid "shamrock tea"; it's what the Northern Irish call tea that tastes so weak it must have been brewed with only three leaves!

HEALING WATERS

March can be a wet and blustery month in the Celtic lands. Yet Brigit is as much a guardian spirit of water as she is keeper of the sacred fire. Many parts of the British Isles, but particularly Ireland, are dotted with holy wells dedicated to Saint Brigit, and these wells most likely were once sacred to the goddess. Flowing water, which emerged miraculously from the invisible realms underground and could heal and cleanse and fertilize the earth, was associated with the nurturing milk flowing from the breast of the Great Mother of Ireland.[3] Pilgrims have visited these wells for centuries to ask Brigit for healing or to ask her to grant them a wish, foretell the future, or help them conceive a child if they were barren. Many wells are still visited today, such as Brighid's Well at Liscannor, near the cliffs of Moher in County Clare, whose underground chamber is filled with candles and prayers written on paper, tucked in wherever there is room on the crowded walls. In the early twentieth century an old woman recounted her experiences at Liscannor:

I had a pearl in my eye [probably a cataract] one time, and I went to Saint Brigit's well on the cliffs. Scores of people there were in it, looking for cures, and some got them and some did not get them. And I went down the four steps to the well and I was looking into it, and I saw a little fish no longer than your finger coming from a stone under the water. Three spots it had on the one side and three on the other side, red spots and a little green with the red, and it was very civil coming hither to me and very pleasant wagging its tail. And it stopped and looked up at me and gave three wags of its back, and walked off again and went in under the stone. . . . And in three days I had the sight of my eye again. It was surely Saint Brigit I saw that time; who else would it be?[4]

It is an extraordinary thing to consider that there are still literally thousands of holy wells in the British Isles and Ireland. Most of these are natural springs; some are covered with stone edifices, others are simply open pools. The majority, however, are in ruins, overgrown and no longer visited. Some have been desecrated by cattle or human presence. Posies of flowers, white stones, silver coins, and pieces of cloth tied to nearby trees are testimony that pilgrims still follow the old tracks that lead to the mysterious water

beckoning with its magical promise. From
kings to peasants they came, seeking relief for
a variety of ills from rheumatism to scurvy,
broken bones to leprosy. They washed sore or
blind eyes because of the magical connection
between the shining well that reflects the sun
as the eye of a god.

It was always the custom to walk sunwise
around the well before taking the water. In
the Christian era these rounds became known
as a "pattern" or "patron" where prayers were
made at the Stations of the Cross. Pilgrims
tied rags from their clothing on nearby
bushes or trees so that the spirit of the well
would know who to work on. In Scotland
these became known as "clootie wells" from
the word for cloth. They cast offerings into
the well to "silver the water"—a coin if they
could afford it, a bent pin if not. These
humble gifts were faint shadows of the
great treasures discovered at the bottom of
early Celtic and Roman Britain wells. At
Coventina's well in Carrowbaugh, Northumberland, more than fourteen thousand coins
as well as bronze figurines, jewelry, glass, pot-
tery, and a human skull were discovered in
the shaft.

Pilgrims came to dream at wells. Dream
incubation was a form of healing practiced by
the ancient Greeks at temples beside sacred
springs. Here the sick would fast and take
part in rituals designed to induce the healing
dream. In Roman Britain, a dream temple was
built at Lydney Park in Gloucestershire over
several springs, and centuries later we hear of
Saint Madron's Well in Cornwall being used
likewise. Madron Well, as it is often called
(possibly from *Madron,* meaning "Mother"),
is hidden away in a bluebell wood, a sacred,
mysterious spot near Land's End. Here a
severely crippled man, John Trelille, "upon
three several admonitions in his dreams,
washing in St. Madern's Well and sleeping
afterwards in what was called St. Madern's
bed, was suddenly and perfectly cured."[5]

Recent researchers have studied this connection between wells and dreams. Paul
Devereux, coordinator of the Dragon Project, which researches the effect of sacred
sites on human consciousness, has found that
people today often become unaccountably
drowsy and fall asleep at holy wells, a phe-
nomenon he correlates with the mildly
radioactive properties found at many of the
well sites. In his book, *Re-Visioning the
Earth,* he describes his own experience at
Madron Well:

It was a warm, drowsy summer afternoon, and I fell deeply asleep on the

ledge on the north wall of the little ruined medieval chapel, with the springwater rushing and gurgling in the stone reservoir in the southwest corner as background sound. I awoke suddenly about ten minutes later and sat bolt upright. I had seen two feminine hands dipping into water; they came up dripping and massaged the muscles around my eyes in a specific way. I immediately went over to the water . . . and acted out the procedure the hands had demonstrated in the dream, using my fingers to massage the edges of my eye sockets with the ice-cold water.[6]

Waters of Vision

The early Celts viewed all forms of water as sacred—rivers, streams, lakes, and ocean. In Scotland the place where three streams meet was considered a potent place. People came to drink the water, which was thought to have magical properties, and courts of justice were often set up nearby. On the island of Anglesey, North Wales, 175 pieces of Celtic metalwork were recently recovered from the lake, Llyn Cerrig Bach. Among them were spears, swords, shields, cauldrons, complete two-wheeled chariots, and a curved bronze trumpet—all from the second century B.C.E.

They were offerings to the deities, cast into their underworld realms.

Dreaming with Water

To spend time by water is to stand on the threshold between the worlds. Whether you take a walk along a beach, sit by a stream, or soak in a natural hot spring in the forest, you are at the meeting place of two elements, earth and water as well as at a traditional Celtic entrance to the Underworld. Most of us can recall at least one peaceful timeless experience of bathing in or simply staring at flowing water, even if we have to think far back into childhood.

Find a place by water, preferably a stream, waterfall, or the sea, where you can spend some time uninterrupted.

Sit or lie in a comfortable position and see whether you can follow the water's flow. At the same time, listen to its sound. The continual sound of water can have the same effect on the brain as drumming, which has been found to alter consciousness.

Relax into the sound, soften your gaze, and allow any images to appear *just below the surface of the water.* You may see faces, figures, or scenes. Using your imagination, talk to the figures, walk into the scenes, and just see what happens.

You can also let yourself fall asleep to the sound of the water, and see what kind of dream it brings you. It's a good idea to bring a journal with you so you can jot down the dream afterward.

An important note about the imagination: We are brought up to believe that to imagine something means that we do not perceive the truth. "It's all in your imagination!" is the ultimate devaluing remark. In fact, *imagination is the language of the soul.* The images that appear during reverie, dream, and vision are the interface between ourselves and the invisible inhabitants of the world that lies beyond the five senses. So don't be concerned that you're "making it all up." The more you give free rein to your imagination in these exercises, the more you will get out of them.

At Coventina's Well, Carrawburgh, Northumberland, the goddess reclines on a lily leaf.

The Voices of the Wells

Flowing water is a feminine element. In Ireland almost all the rivers are named after goddesses. In Wales, faery women live in the lakes. At Bath the local native goddess Sul gave her name to the Roman hot springs, Aquae Sulis, while in Carrowbaugh a ruined temple lies over the well dedicated to Coventina, the Romanized name of another native deity. A votive tablet shows her floating on a water-lily leaf; while a relief depicts three of her female attendants bearing goblets; out of one pours a stream of water. In Christian times pagan wells were rededicated to saints, many of them female: to Saint Anne, Saint Catherine, and Saint Mary as well as to Brigit or Bride. In some places a ghostly White Lady is seen haunting an ancient well. In many urban districts the wells have disappeared altogether, leaving only an echo of her name: Brideswell, Marywell, Ladywell.

From the beginning of civilization, water has been considered the "home of wisdom," and prophecy and wisdom went hand in hand in the ancient world. In classical Greece priestesses took up residence within a nearby grotto or cave and drank the water before going into trance for oracular knowledge. Traces of a well priestess tradition survived into the seventeenth century in west Cornwall. An old woman looked after Gulval Well

and broadcast the "virtues and divine qualities of those waters"[7] in return for a fee. She
gave oracles to strangers and revealed the
whereabouts of lost and stolen objects,
including local cattle. For miles around she
was highly regarded as the "priestess of the
well," probably the last in Britain.

Once, so the legend goes, every well had its
attendant priestess. These were the mysterious "damsels of the wells" described in a
medieval Grail text. The story goes that long
ago in the rich country of Logres (an archaic
term for Britain), tired hunters or travelers
found refreshment at sacred grottos where a
spring gushed out. Here they were given food
and drink by the "damsels of the wells,"
maidens who were the guardians—or perhaps
the spirits—of these holy places. But one day
an evil king raped one of them and stole her
golden cup, and his followers treated the
other maidens likewise. After this the grottos
were empty, the wells dried up, and the countryside was stricken with drought:

The land was dead and desert . . .
So that they lost the voices of the wells,
And the maidens who were in them.

The "voices of the wells" suggests that the
maidens were also oracles. Like the priestesses
of ancient Greece, they sat at the entrance to
a sacred well, one of the gates into the Otherworld, where they had a direct line to the
spirit within the earth. When the Damsels of
the Wells were violated, the channels to the
Otherworld were severed, leaving the world
cut off from its wisdom. Its spiritual riches,
once so accessible to humankind, were withdrawn:

> And since then the court of the Rich
> Fisher which made the land to shine
> with gold and silver, with furs and pre-
> cious stuffs, with food of all kinds, with
> falcons, hawks and sparrow-hawks could
> no longer be found. In those days when
> the court could still be found, there
> were riches and abundance everywhere.
> But now all these were lost to the land
> of Logres.[8]

This extraordinary little tale makes the
point clearly that violence done to women is
violence done to the Earth—and to the feminine within each one of us, be we man or
woman. Living in a world that constantly
devalues the feminine principle—that which
is oriented to intuition, feeling, art, relationship, and process—it is no wonder that the
image of the Wasteland is as fresh today as it

was seven hundred years ago. T. S. Eliot sounded the anguished note of the modern age with his great poem of the same name, where dryness becomes a metaphor for spiritual bankruptcy:

What are the roots that clutch, what branches
    grow
Out of this stony rubbish? Son of man,
You cannot say or guess, for you know only
A heap of broken images, where the sun beats,
And the dead tree gives no shelter, the cricket no
    relief,
And the dry stone no sound of water.[9]

A good exercise to help you garner inspiration and ideas for your spiritual goals in the coming months is to sit before your altar and light a candle so that it shines over the bowl or chalice filled with water. Gaze at the patterns of light on water, letting your focus go soft and your mind relax into a dreamy state. Notice what images and ideas arise for you, and jot them down.

Collecting Sacred Water

The water from a sacred spring may be drunk or used for bathing or fully immersing oneself in to take advantage of its healing properties. In Irish mythology there was a magic well called the Well of Sláine, which could bring the dead back to life. Dian Cécht, his two sons, Octriuil and Míach, and his daughter, Airmid, who were the healer gods of the Tuatha Dé Danann, stood and chanted spells over the well as mortally wounded warriors were thrown into it during battle. Thanks to their magic and the powers of the well, the soldiers emerged fully alive. Pilgrims still bathe in holy wells today, such as in the pool at the lovely shrine of Saint Winifred's Well in North Wales, although the waters have not proven quite as miraculous as in the days of the Tuatha Dé Danann.

If you want to take water from a healing well in a Celtic country or from one of the many sacred springs or pools in America, there are certain traditional rites to observe.

Visit the site between midnight and dawn and preferably toward the end of the first quarter of the moon. Bring a bottle or other container.

Approaching from the east, walk around it three or seven times in a sunwise direction.

Make an offering of silver to the spirit of the well or pool.

Cup your hands, and drink three times in

silence. You can make a wish at this point, but it must not be revealed.

Carry the water home in complete silence. Do not allow the container to touch the ground.

Use the water on an area that needs healing or on something from which you want to remove negative energy. Sprinkle it three times over the affected person, animal, or object in the name of the Sacred Three. It can also be sprinkled over the threshold to protect the house.

Water from streams and rivers that have a numinous quality can also be used in this way. Traditionally, boundary and south-running streams are very fortunate because they "flow to meet the sun."[10]

Holy water can also transfer its healing power to certain objects, such as a silver coin, crystal, or gemstone. This is useful to know if you wish to use the healing properties of water but cannot carry it away with you. Just make sure you bring one of these items in your backpack or pocket when you go for a hike. A famous crystal used by a whole community in this way was the Keppoch Charm Stone owned by a local family, the Macdonnells, near Keppoch, in the Scottish Highlands.

This was a large oval quartz crystal set in a bird's claw of silver, and it was used in conjunction with a well dedicated to Saint Bride. For healing purposes, it was dipped into the well water to "charge" it with Saint Brigit's power, while the following incantation was recited:

Let me dip thee in the water,
Thou yellow beautiful gem of power!
In water of purest wave,
Which pure was kept by Brigit.

. . . A blessing on the gem,
A blessing on the water,
And a healing of all bodily ailments
To each suffering creature![11]

An important note about the use of crystals: There are plenty of recorded instances of the Celts using crystals in their rituals, but for the most part these were white quartz stones easily accessible in the landscape. The crystals sold in shops today are mostly mined in huge quantities by heavy machinery that devastates the environment. To show your respect for the living Earth, use stones you find on the ground or beach or in a river. White stones and stones with holes are traditionally suitable for ritual work.

RUNE OF THE WELL

The shelter of Mary Mother
Be nigh my hands and my feet,
To go out to the well
And to bring me safely home,
And to bring me safely home.

May warrior Michael aid me,
May Brigit calm preserve me,
May sweet Brianag give me light,
And Mary pure be near me,
And Mary pure be near me.

TRADITIONAL SCOTTISH

GODS OF THE CELTS: DANU

In the pagan Celtic world, rivers, streams, and springs were the abode of local female deities and water spirits. Some of these bequeathed their names to their waters for all time. Among them were:

Boann	River Boyne, Ireland
Sinann	River Shannon, Ireland
Sequana	River Seine, France
Matrona	River Marne, France
Sabrina	River Severn, Western England
Verbeia	River Wharfe, Yorkshire, England

There may also have been one great goddess of the waters who gave her name to many waterways across Europe and Russia, including the Don, the Dneiper, the Danube. Some believe she originated with the goddess Dānu of ancient India, whose name means "Stream" and "Waters of Heaven." In Ireland Danu (*don*-uh) was the mother of the Tuatha Dé Danann, whose name means "People of

WATERS OF LOVE

In Scotland lovers plighted their troth by standing on opposite sides of a stream, dipping their fingers in the water, and clasping their hands across the stream. The water acted as the "sacred witness" to their vows. This is the way Robert Burns exchanged vows with his beloved, Highland Mary, on the banks of the Fail, a tributary of the River Ayr.

the Goddess Danu," while in Wales she became Dôn, the divine mother of a magical family whose exploits are related in the collection of Welsh medieval tales known as the *Mabinogi* (mah-bee-*nog*-ee). She may also be equated with the goddess Anu, who gives her name to the twin hills in Kerry, Dá Chích Anann (*daw kheekh on*-unn), or Paps of Anu, which rise like breasts from the body of the Earth.

WATERS OF LIFE

When a baby was born in the Scottish Highlands and islands, the midwife sprinkled nine drops of water upon its forehead in the name of the Sacred Three and sang the following blessing to "the sweetest music that ever ear heard on earth":

> *A small wave for thy form,*
> *A small wave for thy voice,*
> *A small wave for thy sweet speech;*
>
> *A small wave for thy luck,*
> *A small wave for thy good,*
> *A small wave for thy health;*
>
> *A small wave for thy throat,*
> *A small wave for thy pluck,*
> *A small wave for thy graciousness;*
> *Nine waves for thy graciousness.*[12]

ASH

ᚦHE SACRED ᚷROVE

May your footfall be by the root of an ash!
<small>OLD YORKSHIRE BLESSING</small>

The ash is a tree powerful in healing and magic and is often found growing beside holy wells. At the division of Ireland, five sacred trees were planted at the center of each province. Three of these were ash, named the Tree of Tortu, the Tree of Daithi, and the Branching Tree of Uisnech. In Scotland the ash was one of the trees by which oaths were sworn along with the oak and thorn, and it was one of the nine sacred woods used in kindling the Beltaine fires.

An ash of great size and beauty used to shade Saint Kieran's well near the River Boyne in Ireland. Several trout, held in great veneration, swam in the well and were said to have been there since the beginning of time. Once, a rumor spread that the old tree was bleeding, and people flocked in thousands to see it, bearing away in vessels the miraculous liquid said to cure the incurable.

People visited ash trees for healing, particularly for children's ailments. They hung locks of a baby's hair upon the tree to prevent whooping cough. For infant hernia, the child was passed three times through a cleft in an ash at sunrise. The ash has a reputation for healing adults, too, and has been found to be especially helpful against warts.

This extraordinary figure presides over the old Roman temple at Aquae Sulis. Archaeologists have widely differing theories as to its identity: it might be a sun god, a sea god, the Gorgon's head, or perhaps even King Bladud, the legendary founder of the baths.

HOLY GROUND
BATH
(AVON, ENGLAND)

The only hot springs in Britain flow into the city of Bath in the southwest of England. The Romans named the town Aquae Sulis, the Waters of Sul, after a Celtic goddess whom they identified with Minerva. But excavations have revealed that human use of the springs began at least ten thousand years ago.

We know very little about Sul herself, although she has been called "the most impor-tant of the British water-deities."[13] Her name may derive from root words associated with the sun, referring to the hot water, and also the eye. In the Romano-Celtic era, her sanctuary was transformed into a sumptuous temple complex for bathing, drinking the mineral-rich waters, performing rituals, and receiving oracles. Doctors, priests, and diviners were on site to attend to the pilgrims who flocked daily to the temple and whose offerings—of coins, brooches, pins, shoes, and spindle whorls— have been recovered from her sacred spring.

Sul was an avenger as well as a healer, and among the offerings cast into her waters were lead "cursing tablets" on which angry peti-tioners wrote the name of an offender, a description of the crime, and graphic details of the punishment they hoped the goddess would administer. The criminals were mostly thieves who specialized in removing the clothes of bathing pilgrims!

The baths continued to be used throughout the Middle Ages, although the splendid build-ings fell into disrepair and were covered with a succession of churches, culminating in the magnificent Bath Abbey. Only in the eigh-teenth century were the baths rebuilt in grand classical style when the city became a fashion-able resort. To wander through the baths today and explore their multilayered history is

THE CELTIC SWEAT HOUSE

Like Scandinavians and Native Americans, the early inhabitants of the British Isles and Ireland believed in the power of fire and water to cure disease. In Ireland they built small beehive-shaped huts out of stone, roofed with heather and turfs. They kindled a fire of turf inside until it was as hot as an oven. Then they swept out the embers and ashes and splashed water on the stones until it filled up with steam. The patient, who may have been suffering from rheumatism or a chest complaint, crawled in covered with a blanket and sweated for an hour or so. Afterward, he or she crept out and plunged into a nearby pool and was rubbed dry until warm again.

At a number of Bronze Age "burnt mound" sites in Scotland, which may once have been sweat houses, white quartz stones have been found. Quartz has always been revered as a magical healing stone in the Celtic countries and was used in sweat house ceremonies on the Isle of Skye, according to a rare seventeenth-century eyewitness account. The tradition was to dig a hole in the earthen floor and fill it with hazel sticks and rushes. Hazel, the tree that grows by the Well of Wisdom in the Celtic Otherworld, was one of the most treasured trees of the Sacred Grove. It was famous for protecting against disease and was a potent magical remedy as well. A red hot quartz rock was placed in the hole and water poured over it. The patient held the affected part of his body over the steam for the cure.[14]

In some places in the north of Ireland an old sweat house, known as the *tigh 'n alluis* (*tee*-nollish), can still be seen and was probably put into use within living memory.

to experience the evanescent river of time. The only thing that has not changed is Sul's sacred spring. Its bubbling green waters, wreathed in steam, continue to gush at the rate of 250,000 gallons a day from their mysterious source in the Underworld.

KING BLADUD OF BATH

> A fethered King that practisde
> for to flye and soare . . .
> HARDYNGE'S CHRONICLE, 1543

If you visit the Roman Baths today, you will see the small statue of a regal figure in a niche overlooking the King's Bath. The inscription reads: "Bladud, son of Lud Hudibras, 8th King of the Britons, first discoverer and founder of these baths." A shadowy figure from mythical British history, Bladud (*bla-dith*) was the father of a much more famous monarch, Shakespeare's King Lear. Like his famous son, Bladud also came to a tragic end. Legend has it that he was an ingenious inventor who soared through the skies on artificial wings. But he met his death when he fell onto the Temple of Apollo in London, where he was dashed to pieces.

Long before the Roman infantry marched over Salisbury Plain, Lud Hudibras, King of Britain, held his court near Stonehenge. His oldest son was Bladud, the flower of British manhood and a brilliant scholar besides. He was due to return from eleven years' study at the Academy of Athens, and a royal welcome had been prepared for his return, with all kinds of feasting, music, and games.

But instead of seeing his son ride triumphantly home through the castle gates, the king was horrified to see a thin figure covered with sores walking slowly toward him, followed at a distance by a small, glum-faced retinue of servants. Bladud had contracted leprosy while in Greece and was a wretched figure, no longer fit to be the next king of Britain.

The king's subjects were stricken with panic and demanded his banishment from the court. Lud Hudibras had no choice but to obey, and he stood silently with his weeping queen as Bladud took leave of the castle and made his way westward over the plain with nothing but an ash staff, a few coins, and a pack of food upon his back. But before he had gone out of sight, the queen impulsively lifted up her skirts and ran after him. When she had almost caught up with him, she pulled her chased gold ring from her finger and threw it on the ground toward him.

"Take it," she cried. "And should the gods ever see fit to restore you to health again, show this ring as proof that you are my beloved son!"

Bladud slowly knelt and picked up the ring. He threaded it on a leather thong and carried it next to his heart. Then he turned toward the downs and wandered along their chalky paths, drinking from dewponds and sleeping beneath the hedgerows that provided him with berries and nuts. He roved through the great oak forests that sloped down to the River Avon, until an old farmer took pity on him and gave him a job as a swineherd. One day Bladud drove his pigs to graze upon the acorns that studded the forest floor until he came at last to a deep valley whose slopes were clothed in ancient mossy oaks. The ground beneath them was thick with acorns, so Bladud set up camp here for the winter, which was fast approaching. It was a sheltered spot, under the lee of Solsbury Hill, a sacred seat of the druids. Later it would be called Swineswick, and then Swainswick, after the encampment of Bladud's pigs.

But one winter's morning, when the hoarfrost lay in white tracery over the silent trees, Bladud awoke to find his herd missing. He leaped up from his warm bed of animal skins and cast about frantically for them, crunching through the brittle leaves. He blew blast after blast on his antler horn, but all he heard was its mournful echo from the impassive hill. At

last he came upon fresh tracks leading away down the valley to where the Avon made a wide loop. And there were his pigs, wallowing in a muddy swamp overhung with alder trees, grunting and squealing with delight. At first Bladud was surprised to see them bathing on such a cold morning, but as he drew near he saw clouds of steam rising up from the bubbling mire. He knelt down, and to his amazement his hand came away smeared with warm, soft mud.

It took some time, but at last Bladud lured the pigs away from their muddy playground by dropping acorns from his satchel as he walked toward a shallow part of the river, where he planned to see they had a good washing. The second surprise of the day came when they were dripping clean and he saw that the various blemishes, scars, and sores sustained by the pigs in their wild habitat were completely healed over.

It wouldn't hurt to try, he thought.

Slowly, the young man turned and walked back to the pool, removed his ragged swineherd's clothes, and lowered himself into the silky dark morass. The warmth seeped into his frozen bones . . . and he felt something else, too. Parts of his body where the leprosy had indifferently eaten his flesh for the last three years tingled into life. With a cry, Bladud leaped trembling from the pool and examined his body through its glistening coat of mud. It was true—he was completely healed.

Overflowing with joy, he gathered his herd together and drove them back to the old farmer, who hugged him tearfully. Then he hastened back to his father's court, where a great feast was in progress. But despite his protestations, the guards would not let the ragged, sunburned swineherd put one foot inside the castle gates. Bladud paced up and down outside in frustration, until a servant passed him on his way to deliver more barrels of mead. The drink gave Bladud an idea: he showed the man the queen's ring and persuaded him to drop it secretly into her cup. When the queen saw the ring she cried out, "Bladud—my son—he is here! Bring him to me at once!"

There was a joyful reunion, and Bladud was restored to his place of honor as the next heir to the throne. And when he was king, the first thing he did was to return to the scene of his miraculous healing and dedicate a shrine to Sul, goddess of the healing waters. Here he lit a perpetual flame in her honor, and about her shrine he founded the city that later became known as Bath. Neither did he forget the kindness of the old farmer who had given him work when the whole world shunned him as a leper. He made him lord of a nearby village, which has been known throughout the centuries as—Hogs Norton.

It would be hard to find a life more brimming with magical Celtic elements than Bladud's. The motifs of the oak forest, the druids' hill, the pigs—Underworld animals—who find a healing spring, together with the implied connection between Bladud and the sun god, Apollo, all perhaps hint of a forgotten myth of the Underworld goddess and the god of the sun.

ATHOLL BROSE

Aye since he wore the tartan trews,
He dearly lo'ed the Atholl Brose.
NEIL GOW

One man who had cause to regret a visit to a well was John, Lord of the Isles, in the Highland Rebellion of 1475. He had fled to the hills, but his enemy, the Earl of Atholl, discovered where he was drawing water and ordered the well to be filled with a mixture of whisky, honey, and oatmeal. Lord John lingered too long over the delicious brew and so was captured. Since then, atholl brose has become a popular luxury drink in Scotland, made even more mellow with the addition of cream.

Here is a modern dessert version, an extravagant ending to dinner on a cold night.

Ingredients

1¼ cups heavy cream

¼ cup whisky

3–5 tablespoons liquid honey, heather if possible

2 tablespoons oats, ground in blender or food processor

fresh raspberries, about 6 ounces

Method

1. Spread the oats on a baking sheet, and toast them in a broiler or toaster oven until lightly browned and giving off a nutty fragrance.

2. Whip the cream until thick. Fold in the honey, whiskey, and all the oats except for two teaspoons.

3. Chill.

4. When ready to serve, divide raspberries among four dessert glasses, spoon the cream mixture over the fruit, and sprinkle the remaining oats on top.

Serves 4

HOW CORMAC MAC ART WENT TO FAERIE

Cormac, son of Art, son of Conn the Hundred-Fighter, stood on the high walls of his castle in the silence before the sun. Over the Hill of Tara a long wind was blowing, and out of the wind came a man: a young warrior wearing a shirt of woven gold with a purple fringed mantle about him. Upon his feet were blunt-toed shoes of white bronze, in his hand a branch of silver from which hung three golden apples.

The warrior came to the castle gate and, looking up, smiled at the king and gently shook the silver branch. The golden apples chimed out music so sweet that all want and woe and weariness of the soul melted away, and the sick were lulled to sleep.

As the notes died away, the warrior greeted Cormac with light and pleasant words, but his eyes were as deep as forest pools and his face as old as the wildwood. Cormac saluted him. "Where have you come from, O warrior?"

"I come from a land," said he, "where only Truth dwells. There is neither age nor decay there, gloom nor sadness, envy nor jealousy, hatred nor haughtiness."

"It is not so with us," replied Cormac, unable to take his eyes off the apple branch.

By now, the sun was rising over Tara's Hill, making the golden apples gleam. And Cormac was filled with a desire so deep to possess them that he quite forgot to show the proper courtesies to a visitor at the gate but asked him abruptly if he would be willing to sell the magical branch.

The warrior smiled slowly. "It is yours in exchange for three boons you must grant me when next I return to Tara."

"Whatever you want will be yours!" cried the king, barely able to conceal his excitement, and the warrior bound him to his promise, laid the branch carefully in his arms, and turned his back on Tara, seeming to disappear into the beams of the rising sun.

Cormac almost ran back into the castle. The household was just waking up. Men hewing wood, women drawing water, children and dogs tumbling about all looked up with astonishment to see their king standing in the middle of the courtyard waving a silver apple branch. But when they heard the sweet chimes of the apples, ah, then all lines and furrows smoothed away on the foreheads of the careworn. The harried housekeeper forgot to scold the servants and sweetly smiled, and inside the hospice the battle-wounded ceased their tossing and turning, sighed, and fell dreamlessly asleep.

And so did the silver branch soothe and bring solace, sweetness, and comfort to all at Tara for one whole year. But at the end of that time, at another day's dawning, the gray-haired warrior returned and demanded his first payment: Cormac's young daughter, Ailbe (*al*-vuh). The king was stunned but had no choice but to hand over the girl, who in no time at all disappeared with the man as if into the beams of the rising sun. Cormac's wife and the women of Tara were beside themselves with grief; but Cormac snatched up the branch and waved it over them, and their grief left them as quickly as a dream vanishes upon waking.

A month later the warrior returned, and this time he took with him Cormac's fine young son, Cairbre (*kar*-buh-ruh). Weeping and sorrow filled the halls of Tara, and that night no one ate or slept, such was the darkness of grief that hung over them all. But Cormac shook the branch above them all, and once again their sorrow faded away into forgetfulness.

At the same time the next month, the gray-haired warrior returned for his third and last payment: Cormac's beloved wife, Ethne (*eth*-nyuh). But this time Cormac gave a roar of anger and refusal. He called for his guards, and they rushed forward to seize the man as he walked toward his wife's chamber. But he merely looked at them with his ancient eyes, and they all froze on the spot like statues. Calmly he walked into Ethne's chamber and took her by the hand. Impelled by a great will, she rose and followed her captor out of Tara, casting one anguished glance at her spellbound husband as she went.

They were far beyond the gates before the spell lifted, and Cormac and his men rushed out after them. But a great mist descended all about them, and the king was separated from the rest. For many hours it seemed he wandered lost and alone, calling in vain for his wife and his companions, unable to find his way home again. Then after what could have been a short time or a long time or no time at all, the mist unfurled like a curtain, and Cormac found himself standing on a wide grassy plain, with the wind blowing through the long grass and a cloudless blue sky overhead.

Ahead of him, Cormac saw buildings and people moving among them. He drew near and came to a large fortress with walls of bronze. Inside was a house of silver, half thatched with the feathers of white birds. A host of faery people on horseback were carrying armfuls of feathers for the thatching, but every time the roof was covered, a great gust of wind blew up and carried the feathers away. A little farther on, Cormac saw a giant man engaged in making a fire. On top of the kindling he threw down a huge log of oak, and Cormac watched it blaze up merrily. The giant gave a grunt of satisfaction and turned to add another log, but as soon as he turned back, the first log was burned to ashes and he had to start all over again. This happened many times. Cormac was bursting with questions about these wonders, but when he tried to speak no sound came out of his mouth.

At last he came to what must surely be the royal center of this land: a great rampart of bronze with four palaces within. The gate was wide open, and Cormac boldly walked inside. In the center of the enclosure was a huge hall with silver walls and beams of bronze, thatched with the wings of white birds. But the greatest marvel of all was in the courtyard. Here stood a magnificent well, a fountain of water bubbling up from its center, which overflowed into five channels cut in the stone paving and streamed out to join five great rivers beyond the palace walls. Around the well grew nine hazel trees, laden with purple nuts that every now and then dropped into the water. To Cormac's astonishment, five huge gleaming salmon leaped up out of the well and cracked the nuts in their jaws, sending the shells flowing away down the streams. A host of people of all ages, dressed in strange garments as if they were pilgrims from many lands, knelt in turn at the well to take its waters. As they arose, each appeared to glow with an inner radiance, as if refreshed by the water of life itself. But the loveliest thing of all in this strange and lovely place was the music of those streams, which was so sweet it would break your heart to hear it.

Cormac stood for a while, mesmerized by the heavenly sound, all his own sorrows forgotten for a while. But he was brought back to himself by a deep voice that called out to him words of welcome. Looking up, he saw standing in the arched doorway two who were surely the lord and lady of this place: a tall handsome warrior with a wise and merry face, and a yellow-haired woman wearing a gold crown, the loveliest of all women in the world. With great courtesy, the lady led Cormac to a bath, where invisible hands placed hot stones in the water to heat it and afterward dried him with soft towels.

Then at the exact hour of nine, the lady came for him again and, smiling, led him into the feasting hall. As he took his place on the couch between his host and hostess, there came a loud scuffling from without, the skin curtains parted, and in walked a huge man bearing an ax, a bundle of firewood, and a live and squealing pig.

"Prepare the feast," cried the lord, "for we have a noble guest with us tonight!"

The man dealt the pig one blow with the ax and struck it dead. He blew up a fire with the wood beneath the great cauldron that hung in the middle of the hall and cast the pig into the pot. After a while, the lord inquired, "Is it not time to give it a turn?"

But the kitchener solemnly shook his head.

"That would be useless," he growled. "For never will the pig be boiled until a true story is told for each quarter of it."

"Then be the first to tell us one, good fellow!" cried the lord with a roar of laughter.

"Here's a true story, then," said the kitchener, squatting on his haunches by the cauldron. "This here pig is a magical beast. For every night I throw him into the pot, but every morning I find him in his sty alive and well again."

And because this was indeed true, the pig was turned and they found one quarter of it cooked.

"Another tale of truth!" cried the lady.

"I will tell one," said the lord. He took up a loaf of bread from the table and held it in both hands. "Last spring when it came time to plow the field, we went outside and found it already plowed, harrowed, and sown with wheat. When we desired to reap it, we found the crop stacked in the field. When we desired to store it, we found it already in the barn. We've been eating it from that day to this, and it never grows any the less."

Then the pig was turned in the cauldron, and another quarter had cooked.

"It is now my turn," said the lady. "I have seven cows and seven sheep. The milk of the cows is enough for all the people in the Land of Faerie, and the wool from the sheep makes all the clothing they desire."

At this story, the third quarter of the pig was boiled.

"And now," said the lord, turning to Cormac, "it is your turn!"

So Cormac related how his wife and his son and his daughter had been taken from him and how he had pursued them and arrived at last in this very hall.

And with that, the whole pig was boiled.

The meat was carved and a portion placed before Cormac. But, hungry though he was, the king pushed it away. "I will eat no food until I have found my family again!" he declared, and he rose to his feet as if to leave. But in that moment, the lord began to sing a strange and haunting song. It was the song of the silver apple branch and the song of the streams, and it stole Cormac's soul away so that he fell down into a deep sleep. The music wove its unearthly beauty through his dreams and seemed to carry him away on rivers of light, but now another voice joined the song: a well-loved, familiar voice, calling him to return from the waters of sleep.

The voice of Ethne, his wife.

He opened his eyes, and there she was smiling down at him, and his son and daughter on either side of her. And behind them, fifty of his band of men from Tara. Great and joyous was their reunion, and they celebrated with a great ale feast, liberally supplied by the lord and lady with much merriment. The warrior himself drank from a splendid cup of gold, and Cormac remarked on the strange and intricate shapes carved upon it.

"There is something even more strange about it," said the lord. "Let three falsehoods be spoken under it, and it will break into three. Then speak three truths under it, and it will unite again." He placed the cup in Cormac's hands.

"Soon you may return home with your family, and you may take also the cup. It will help you discern the true from the false. And you shall also have the silver apple branch for music and delight. But on the day you die they will disappear once more from the world. I am Manannán mac Lir (*mon*-un-awn muck *lihr*), King of the Land of Faerie; I it was who brought the silver branch to Tara and took your family so that you would follow me here."

And before all retired to sleep that night, Manannán explained the meaning of the strange sights Cormac had seen in that land.

"The horsemen you saw thatching the house of silver are the Irishmen who live only to collect horses and wealth, which passes away into nothing. The man who tried in vain to light a fire is the thriftless young chief whose extravagance consumes all he has earned. Remember these lessons, Cormac, for there is much that needs setting to rights in your land. And above all, you must remember the well of the five streams. For that is the Well of Wisdom, and the streams are the five senses through which knowledge is attained. But no one will have wisdom unless they drink both from the streams and the wellspring itself. The people of many arts are those that drink from both."

These were the last words Cormac heard before he fell asleep. When he awoke the next morning, he found himself on the green of Tara with his wife and his children, and in his hands the silver branch and golden cup of truth.

SALMON

Salmon actually do make awe-inspiring journeys between river and sea. They leave the river pools where they are born and swim sometimes hundreds of miles to the ocean. When they are fully grown, they swim upriver again to lay their eggs in the very same pool in which they were born, often making prodigious leaps over waterfalls on the way. Their strength and agility inspired Celtic warriors like Cúchulainn to make the "salmon leap" in combat, a great spring that astounded their opponents.

A CELTIC BESTIARY

In both Irish and Welsh tradition, the salmon was considered one of the Oldest Animals of Celtic tradition, and the most wise. The greatest desire of poets and wisdom seekers was to find and eat either the hazelnuts that dropped into the Well of Wisdom or the salmon who ate them, for then they would be filled with *imbas* (*im*-bus), divine illumination. The salmon swam from the Well of Wisdom down into the rivers of Ireland, which is why poets believed that poetry was revealed upon the brink of water. In other versions, the well is located at the bottom of the sea, so salmon is a creature who brings the wisdom of the Underworld into our own, a messenger of two worlds.

RETURN TO THE SOURCE

Am I not a candidate for fame,
to be heard in song
In the four-cornered castle,
four times revolving?
TALIESIN

The holy well in the Celtic landscape is a reflection of the wellspring of spiritual wisdom located at the heart of the Otherworld. It was known by many names: the Well of Segais, Connla's Well, or the Well of Wisdom. Throughout the ages, seekers of truth have made the perilous journey to the well, and for us today it is one of the central symbols of Celtic spirituality, offering wisdom, healing, and renewal.

The Three Worlds

tions and the three realms, often referred to as Sky, Land, and Sea.

In Welsh literature this Otherworld castle is called Caer Sidi, the Castle of the *Sídhe* (shee), or faery folk. In an early Welsh poem, "The Spoils of Annwn," King Arthur makes a perilous sea voyage to a four-cornered castle, which contains a wonder-working cauldron, clearly the Welsh equivalent of Manannán's abode. The great Welsh bard, Taliesin, sings of his sojourn there:

Perfect is my seat in Caer Sidi . . .
Neither plague nor age harms him who dwells
     therein.
Manawydan and Pryderi know it . . .
And around its corners are ocean's currents,
And the fruitful spring is above it.
Sweeter than white wine is the drink in it.[15]

Manawydan (mah-nah-*wuth*-an) is the Welsh Manannán, and the "fruitful spring," whose water is "sweeter than white wine," is clearly the Well of Wisdom. In the later Middle Ages, the Otherworld castle became the home of the Holy Grail, when wandering troubadours spread the old Celtic tales throughout the courts of Europe, adapting their themes to the times. In the French story *Perlesvaus*, the Grail knight sails to a castle on an island in the sea.

In the story of Cormac mac Art, this sacred center of the spirit world is found in the castle of Manannán mac Lir, an Otherworld king. Within a wall of gleaming bronze—probably circular, like the typical Irish hill fort—stand four palaces, with the Well of Wisdom and the sacred trees in the center, representing the Underworld and the Upperworld, respectively. The Otherworld castle conforms to the pattern of the perfectly ordered Celtic cosmos. Once again, we encounter the sacred design of the four direc-

As the ship draws near, four horns sound at the four corners of the walls. Within the lovely castle grounds is a beautiful tree and "the fairest fountain." Another Grail romance, *Sone de Nausay,* describes a square island castle with four palaces at the four corners of its walls, where a fountain gushes out of the center through a horn of gilded copper. The Grail chalice is, of course, a later version of Cormac's cup of truth.

At the center of the castle lie the well and the trees. Together they form a pair of opposites that represent the two dynamic forces of the universe—the well as the receptive feminine principle, and the Underworld; the trees as the creative, masculine principle and the Upperworld. At the cosmic center (the third principle, making the Sacred Three), Cormac learns the most fundamental lesson of living as a spiritual being in a human body. To truly realize our potential in life, whether as a leader, healer, artist, parent, teacher, or whatever we know in our heart of hearts to be our true calling, we must continually connect back with that source of our inspiration, the spiritual wellspring that ever bubbles below the surface of the outer life. Because Cormac has taken the journey to the sacred center, he regains all he has lost and returns with the cup of truth and the silver branch, emblems of well and tree, the worlds below and above, to become a wise leader of his people.

THE INNER CAULDRON
REFLECTION

Within each of us is a well of wisdom, yet we rarely stop to drink from its waters. We live in a time that values constant action and busyness over contemplation and reflection. Taking time for reflection gives us access to our intuition, which is the voice of the soul. Intuition speaks to us in a number of ways. It may come as a sense of knowing, the "still small voice within," as a gut feeling, or in images. Through listening to the soul, we learn how to find the answers within ourselves rather than seeking them constantly from the outside.

The Well of Wisdom is sometimes described in Irish stories as being "at the bottom of the sea." This may be hard to imagine until we realize it is a symbolic map of different layers of consciousness. The well itself is the soul, which is individual to each of us; the sea is beyond personal consciousness and represents the Celtic Underworld, the home of the deities of the lower world. In modern psychological terms, we might regard the well as the place of the personal unconscious and the sea as the realm of the transpersonal unconscious.

At night we go down to the well to dream, and occasionally we may even swim in the boundless sea beyond. But to infuse our everyday lives with the streams of spirit, we must also go to the well when we are awake to gaze into the depths of our own soul and draw its wisdom up to the light to nourish our family, our community, and ourselves.

The element of water is also important in the creative process of our lives. Irish druidic lore tells us that within water is a radiant essence called *imbas forosnai*, "the wisdom that illuminates." When we drink from the inner waters of the soul, we may experience "flashes" of inspiration, "illuminating" ideas, "brilliant" thoughts. At first we may have to sit by the well in a state of receptivity and allow images and ideas to bubble up from within. Then we can interpret them as faithfully as possible in the outer world. There may be a lot of sitting still and waiting for the inspiration to arise, and sometimes it requires a

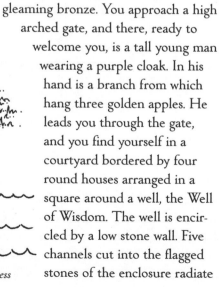

Three Layers of Consciousness

great deal of trust in the creative process, for it cannot be forced. But without this stage, our efforts will be dry, brittle, and lifeless.

In the following meditation, we go to the sacred well to replenish the thirsty soul.

Meditation: The Well at the World's End
Sit before your altar, close your eyes, take a few deep breaths, and begin to relax. Let the breath carry you away to another place, another time, before the beginning of time. . . . You are standing on a plain in bright sunlight, and before you towers a great circular wall of gleaming bronze. You approach a high arched gate, and there, ready to welcome you, is a tall young man wearing a purple cloak. In his hand is a branch from which hang three golden apples. He leads you through the gate, and you find yourself in a courtyard bordered by four round houses arranged in a square around a well, the Well of Wisdom. The well is encircled by a low stone wall. Five channels cut into the flagged stones of the enclosure radiate

out from the well and carry the overflow beyond the courtyard to join other streams. Over the well stand nine trees, their branches swaying like hair in invisible currents of air. Every now and then, purple-husked nuts are shaken loose into the water below. A flash of light—and a fish with glittering scales leaps up and catches one in its jaws. Now and then the discarded husks can be seen floating away down the streams.

The world is more alive here than you have ever imagined it could be: colors burn and flicker; sounds vibrate like plucked strings, and each breath you draw makes you feel a little giddy and light-headed, as if you are inhaling a purer element. . . . You are not alone. . . . A procession of pilgrims approaches the well in silence. Their sandaled feet make no noise. One by one, they stoop and drink the water in cupped hands. . . . When each arises, they appear to glow with an inner radiance, as if refreshed by the water of life itself. . . .

And now it is your turn to approach the well. As you step toward it, you are no longer aware of those who have gone before you or those who wait behind. . . . You are alone with a deep Presence, immensely quiet, pregnant with life. Stooping down, you gaze into a serene pool glowing with a gentle blue-green light, reflecting the overhanging

trees. A fish glides like a shadow just beneath the surface. . . . But as you continue to look into the water, the reflection of the trees slowly dissolves, and you are now gazing into waters as dark and deep as midnight. . . . From its depths emerge images, messages from the soul bubbling up from deep within. . . . You may also receive a gift that floats to the surface for you to take. . . . (long pause)

You may also ask questions of the well . . . and listen as the answers emerge from the deep. . . . They may come as images swirling up out of the well . . . or through an inner voice or a sense of knowing. . . . Let yourself receive the answers. . . . (long pause)

Thank the well for its gifts, and now cup your hands and drink. . . . It is like drinking light itself. . . . A feeling of deep, quiet well-being spreads through you as the water washes away the wounds of the past and purifies your heart and mind. In forgotten dry ditches, seeds begin to grow, and luxuriant growth greens the bare earth. . . . Before you leave, you throw into the waters an offering to the spirit of the well . . . and the waters bear your offering away. . . . And now it is time for you to go. . . . You step beyond the well and walk toward the gate of the courtyard. As you approach the arch, you turn to say farewell to the young guide who brought you here. He is standing by the great wooden door that leads into the castle, but he is no longer the lad that first came to you. He is now a grown man: a bearded king wearing a crown made of apple branches, and in his hand he bears a branch on which are both blossoms and fruit. . . . His wise and kindly face smiles at you, and you bow your head to him, knowing that he is the guardian of this place: Manannán, King of the Otherworld.

You walk through the gate, and after a short while the magical mist swirls up around you again. . . . Soon all has disappeared from view, and as the mist begins to clear you become more and more aware that you are sitting in this room, in this place, in this time, and it *is* time to return.

FIRE IN WATER

I have been told,
"The sun on deep waves is beautiful."
And have dreamed on those words.
I will dive down to the edge of darkness,
to see where fire is drowned
in understanding.
FIONA DAVIDSON

APRIL

THE TREE OF LIFE

Where the forest murmurs there is music: ancient, everlasting.
Fiona MacLeod

The spirit of Spring is abroad in April and declares itself in the quickening wood, the new yellow buds of gorse upon the moorland, and the song of birds returned from southern shores. Throughout the Celtic countries, the church festival of Easter has long since been the established way to welcome back the spirit of renewal through the celebration of Christ's resurrection. Yet it is named after an Anglo-Saxon goddess of spring, Eastre (or Eostre), whose sacred animal was the hare—the original Easter bunny! Many believe that the determined efforts of the early church to institute a separate date for Easter point to a popular pagan rite of spring, long since forgotten.

We can only imagine that in those times there was singing and dancing, fertility rituals and offerings made to the gods to ensure a prosperous harvest, for we catch the faint echoes of these ancient rites in isolated pockets of the Celtic lands. In the thirteenth century a parish priest of Fife, Scotland, was brought before the bishop for having celebrated Easter week "according to the rites of Priapus." Apparently he had gathered together the young women of the town and encouraged them to dance around an unambiguously phallic standing stone, singing all the while. On Maundy Thursday (the day before Good Friday), farming families living on the coast of western Scotland and the Hebrides made offerings to the gods of the sea to send them seaweed, a vital fertilizer for their crops. At midnight a chosen man walked into the sea up to his waist and poured out a dish of specially prepared porridge, chanting:

O God of the Sea,
Put weed in the drawing wave
To enrich the ground,
To shower on us food!

Behind him on the darkened shore, the huddled crowd took up the chant, and their prayers drifted out over the waves of the listening sea. Alexander Carmichael found this custom still alive on the Isle of Lewis in the late nineteenth century:

There was a winter during which little seaweed came ashore, and full time for Spring work had come without relief. A large dish of porridge, made with butter and other good ingredients, was poured into the sea on every headland where wrack used to come. Next day the harbors were full.[1]

On the borders of Wales families used to go out into the fields on Easter Sunday to call on the Corn Spirit for a good harvest. They picnicked on a meal of plum cake and cider then solemnly poured a libation on the earth and buried a piece of the cake while saying prayers for the farmer and for a good crop. After the feast they joined hands and danced across the field. A West Country spring blessing captures this spirit:

Good luck to the hoof and horn
Good luck to the flock and fleece
Good luck to the growers of corn
With blessings of plenty and peace!

EASTER EGGS AND CAPERING CAKES

Eggs have always symbolized the mystery and wonder of birth. They played a part in the springtime festivals of ancient China, Egypt, Greece, and Persia long before the early Christians saw them as emblems of the resurrection. In Scotland Easter eggs are called "peace" or "pace" eggs from the Hebrew word *Pasch* or *Paschal,* meaning "Passover," and they were forbidden food throughout Lent in Catholic areas. When the Easter feast came around, they were enthusiastically welcomed back:

When Yule comes, dule comes,
Cauld feet and legs;
When Pasch comes, grace comes,
Butter, milk, and eggs.
OLD SCOTS RHYME

Throughout Easter week in Ireland and Scotland, boys and girls collected every egg they could lay their hands on and secretly stashed them away in the thatch of the house, a hole in the ground, or a crevice in the peat stack. On Easter Day they hauled their cache to a secret spot in the woods, made a fire, and cooked up a feast of roasted eggs, which they ate with gusto from spoons made from ash or oak boughs.

Eggs were also whipped up into cakes for the traditional Easter Sunday cake dance at the crossroads. The cake, known in some places as a *prioncam* cake, from *princeam,* "capering," was often decorated with animals, birds, and mythical beasts and enthroned in the middle of a garland of wildflowers. Around this symbol of spring's abundance, dancers whirled in a ring to the music of fiddle and pipe. The best dancer won the prize, hence the old saying: "That takes the cake!"

Raisin Spice Cake

This moist, delicious cake is easy to make and a good choice to take on spring picnics.

Ingredients
2¼ cups water
3 cups raisins
1 stick (8 tablespoons) butter
1 cup sugar
3 cups unbleached, all-purpose flour
1 teaspoon salt
2 teaspoons baking soda
1 egg
½ teaspoon cinnamon
½ teaspoon ginger
½ teaspoon allspice
½ teaspoon coriander
1 teaspoon nutmeg
¼ teaspoon cloves

Method

1. The day before you want the cake, combine the water, raisins, butter, and sugar in a medium saucepan. Add the spices. Bring to a boil and simmer for 20 minutes. Remove from heat, let cool, and refrigerate overnight.

2. Next day, remove the raisin mixture from the refrigerator and allow to come to room temperature. (You could also put this on a very low heat to warm slightly.)

3. Preheat oven to 350 degrees.

4. Sift flour, salt, and baking soda. Combine with raisin mixture. Add egg and mix until well blended.

5. Pour into greased 9-inch-by-2-inch round cake pan.

6. Bake 1 hour or until lightly browned.

7. Optional glaze: Melt 3 tablespoons sugar in $\frac{1}{4}$ cup water and pour over warm cake.

DECORATING EGGS

Easter eggs were made more festive by being boiled with natural dyes from plants and vegetables or whatever was on hand in the kitchen.

Method

1. Before you begin, use wax crayons to draw symbols on your egg, such as spirals, triskeles, concentric circles, and flowers.

2. Dye eggs using the methods below. The shades will be subtle. (If you want brighter hues you will have to use special fixatives or watercolors.)

3. After your eggs dry, use a vegetable oil and soft cloth to polish them.

4. You can eat the hard-boiled eggs on Easter Day, but be sure to make some for decorating a special May bough, as Irish families did. As these eggs will be threaded onto the branches, blow the raw eggs before dyeing by gently inserting a pin into both ends and blowing the liquid out into a dish.

Plant	Dye	Method
Onion skins	Bright yellow to reddish brown	After ten minutes, eggs will be bright yellow, and the color will darken the longer you leave them in.

Plant	Dye	Method
Blueberries	Pale lavender	Boil the eggs directly in a packet of frozen berries for at least a half hour. Stand eggs in blueberries overnight to darken.
Raspberries	Pale pink	Follow directions for blueberries.
Red cabbage	Pale blue	Boil cabbage and remove leaves. Cool. Boil eggs in another pot. Set boiled eggs in cold cabbage water overnight in refrigerator.

THE ENCHANTED FOREST

In April a ripple of green fire spreads through the woods, as the spirits of the trees awaken from their winter rest. Even in the most developed urban areas today the sight of a flowering cherry in a park or the leafing out of pale green willows along a city river uplifts the heart with the fresh promise of spring. We can only imagine what it must have been like for the early Celts, whose lives were spent in the cradle of the great forests that once clothed all northern Europe. It was said that in those days a squirrel could hop from branch to branch from one end of a country to the other without touching the ground. In the Iron Age Scotland was clothed with the magnificent Wood of Caledon; Ireland was covered with oak woods and Brittany with the magical forest of Brocéliande, whose remaining groves are haunted still by Merlin's ghost.

In this environment it is no wonder the forest was perceived as the source of a tribe's sustenance, culture, and spirituality. A food store of nuts, berries, and game, a pharmacopoeia of medicines, a wood supply for shelter and the kindling of sacred fire—the forest was all of these and more to the early Celts. Trees not only provided earthly sustenance; they were also regarded as living, magical beings who bestowed spiritual blessings. With their roots stretching down to the Underworld and branches reaching to the Upperworld, they connected the powers above and below with the physical world. In

Ireland an individual tree of power was known as a *bile* (*bill*-eh) and was regarded with great reverence. The Bile Tartain, a giant ash that grew in County Meath, was said to have existed since the beginning of the world. The names of trees formed the letters of the ogham alphabet and made potent spells when carved on staves of yew; scarlet-berried rowan protected the byre; strong ash lent power to the spear's flight. The first man was an alder and the first woman a rowan tree.

When a tribe cleared the land for a settlement in Ireland, they always left a great tree in the middle, known as the *crann bethadh* (*krawn ba*-huh), or Tree of Life, as the spiritual focus and source of well-being. They held assemblies and inaugurated their chieftains beneath it so that they could absorb power from above and below. One of the greatest triumphs a tribe could achieve over its enemies was to cut down their sacred tree, their foundation of strength and support.

In the mythical history of Ireland, a giant "as high as a wood" with yellow hair down to his thighs and surrounded by a shining crystal veil once came out of the setting sun bearing a golden branch. On the branch grew apples, nuts, and acorns at the same time, and he gave some of the fruit to be planted in the five provinces of Ireland, where they grew

into five sacred trees: the Ash of Tortu, the Yew of Ross, the Oak of Mugna, the Bough of Daithi (also an ash), and the branching Ash of Uisnech, which stood next to the Stone of Divisions, the sacred navel of the country.[2] Here they grew to great height and girth as guardians of the land until they fell in the seventh century.

THE TREE OF PLENTY

A tree of gold on the field free from battle,
its crown reached the cloudy welkin;
thence the music of the men of the world
was heard from the tree's crown.

Whenever the violent wind would beat
on the soft fresh foliage of the tree
there would be vast plenty, O men!
of its fruits on the soil of the earth.

Every fruit the hosts would choose,
from east, from south, and from north,
like the flood-tide of the lazy sea,
would come from the top of that one tree.
IRISH, TWELFTH CENTURY[3]

THE WISE ONES OF THE OAK WOODS

Reaching into both earth and sky, trees are doorways into the unseen. That most magical of Celtic trees, the oak, derives its old name (Old Irish *dair*, Welsh *derw*) from the Indo-European root word *deru*, "strong, hard like wood," which also gives us *door*. In folk etymology the druids are believed to have derived their name from this word, which, combined with the Indo-European root *wid*, "to know," makes them the "wise ones of the oak wood." Today linguists consider it more likely the word means "great knowledge," for the druids were the learned class of the ancient Celts: the judges, philosophers, teachers, astrologers, healers, magicians, and priests. They held important assemblies and performed their rites in a forest clearing called a *nemeton*, a Gaulish word that became *nemed* in Ireland. In Scotland they were called *neimheadh* (*nev*-eh), which survives in many place-names such as Navity or those ending with *-neve* or *-nevyth*. On the island of Anglesey, the druids' stronghold in Wales, dense woods of oak and hazel formed their forest sanctuaries until the Romans desecrated them in 60 C.E. Within the nemeton there might have been a stone shrine, a central tree or mound, and frequently a well.

In ancient Britain Queen Boudicca performed rites to the goddess Andraste (Victory) in a sacred grove so that she might defeat the Romans in battle. There was also a Goddess of the Grove called Nemetona, who was worshiped by tribes in Switzerland and also at Bath in England. Heroes in Irish mythology were sometimes named after trees: Mac-Cairthin was the Son of Rowan Tree and Mac-Daire, Son of Oak, perhaps because they had dedicated themselves to that particular tree, as the hero MacCuill held sacred the hazel (*coll*) from which he took his name. There were even entire tribes named after trees, such as the Eburones, the People of the Yew, and the Lemovices, the People of the Elm, in Gaul.

As doorways out of time, trees aided the druids in divination. Slips of hazel, yew, birch, and other sacred woods were inscribed with ogham letters and cast upon the ground. The way they fell predicted future events.

Woe your woods are withering away.
AODHAGAN O'RATHAILLE

Sadly, the ancient forests of northern Europe have now mostly disappeared. First agriculture replaced hunting and gathering, which meant the forest no longer represented the primary sustainer of life. Then the early Church fathers prohibited worship in the old sacred groves, and when the five guardian trees of Ireland finally fell, this was seen as a triumph of Christianity over the old religion. Yet seventh-century Irish law protected certain trees because they were the "seven noble ones of the high sacred grove." These were the oak, holly, hazel, apple, birch, alder, and willow. The fine for cutting down any one of them was a cow, while to destroy the sacred grove itself merited a fine of three cows.

Under Celtic Christianity, nature continued to be revered as an expression of God, and many of the early saints were connected with sacred trees. In February we saw how Saint Brigit founded her abbey at Kildare (Cille Daire, the Church of the Oak) beneath a sacred tree that may once have been a pagan shrine. Saint Patrick founded a church near the great Ash of Tortu, and Saint Columcille founded monasteries at Durrow (Daire Maugh, Plain of the Oaks) and in what was probably once a pagan sanctuary at Derry (Daire Calgaich, the oak grove of Calgaich). Columcille loved this grove so much that he built his oratory facing north-south instead of the usual Christian orientation of east-west so none of the trees would be disturbed. When he went into exile on the Isle of Iona in Scotland, he ordered his successors not to touch any tree that might fall but to let it lie for nine days, the sacred Celtic number, before cutting it up and distributing the wood. Of all his concerns about what he was leaving behind, none worried the saint so much as the fate of these trees. He wrote:

Though I am affrighted, truly,
By death and by Hell;
I am more affrighted, frankly,
By the sound of an axe in Derry . . . [4]

But in later centuries the two-headed Leviathan of capitalism and imperialism gobbled up the last of the great forests for house building, shipbuilding, and charcoal for smelting iron. Today, after the further ravages of two world wars, only fragments of the Celtic forests remain, and they continue to be threatened by road construction and development in a world that no longer recognizes the sanctity of trees. Now that we are finally becoming aware of the vital role played by trees in the ecosystem of our planet, it is time to get to know our trees once again, to replant the sacred groves, and to rediscover the wisdom and healing power they can bring to our lives.

STAG

A CELTIC BESTIARY

The stag embodies the mysteries of the forest. Its fleetness of foot, its branching antlers, and its aggression during the rutting season all suggest untamed beauty, power, and sexuality. In springtime the treelike antlers grow, and in autumn they are shed, following the cycle of growth and decay throughout the year and reminding us of the continual regeneration of life.

The Celts regarded the stag as the King of the Woodland, and, like the salmon and eagle, it was one of the Oldest Animals. Celtic stories tell of wild men who lived in the forest, mysterious figures akin to the shaman and the poet who dwelt in close communion with the animals. In the Caledonian Forest, Merlin led a herd of deer, riding on a stag. In Ireland the mad king Suibhne Geilt (*swiv*-nyuh *gyelt*) fled the horrors of war "to turn his back on mankind, to herd with deer, run along with the showers, flee with the birds, and to feast in wildernesses."[5] To inhabit the forest was to live between the worlds, and the stag shows the way through the unmarked paths and perilous ways of the Otherworld. In many tales a beautiful white stag appears to lure the hunter away into that enchanted land, a symbol, perhaps, of the longing for our original wild nature, which runs free only in the forest of our dreams.

MERLYN IN CALYDON

If you sit still long enough
on the forest floor,
the universe will approach you
like a shy animal.

Breathe softly and don't move:
If encouraged it will nuzzle your open hand.

Open more!
Open your heart   your head   your soul
all doors   all bars

that catch and trap and bind
the wild and dreaming beast
that sleeps
in you.

M. F.

THE GROVE OF HEAVEN:
A STORY FROM WALES

There was once a pious monk of Clynnog Fawr on the Lleyn Peninsula who went walking one evening through the little grove by the monastery. Deep in meditation, he slowly made his way down past the stream that tumbles swiftly over the rocks in its hurry to reach the sea. Suddenly, a bird on the branch above him burst into song. The monk was stopped in his tracks by the beauty of the heavenly music, which flowed through the air like a torrent of liquid sound. The golden notes rippled through every pore of his body, filling him with ecstasy. He was so enchanted by the unearthly melodies that streamed from the bird's throat that he lost all track of the time and stood there entranced for hours. When the last notes finally died away, the cleric came to his senses and stumbled back through the darkening wood to the monastery.

To his surprise, all the monks were strangers, and they wore outlandish garb. They crowded around him in wonder as he told them what had happened. Then, bemused by these mysterious events, he asked to be led to a cell where he could pray. After a while one of the brothers went to see how he was and found only a heap of ashes on the floor. On consulting an ancient monastic chronicle, the brothers learned of a monk who had disappeared when he went for a walk in the grove hundreds of years before. From this time on, the place was called the Grove of Heaven.

GODS OF THE CELTS: CERNUNNOS

The Old God sleeps
down in the dark, moist,
odorous underfoot,
Waiting for us
To put down our roots.
HUE WALKER

On the famous silver cauldron found in a peat bog in Gundestrup, Denmark, a male figure wearing antlers sits in ecstatic trance surrounded by a menagerie of wild animals. In his left hand he holds a curious creature: a snake with ram's horns. In his right he bears a *torc*, the neck ring worn by royalty. A stag stands next to him so close that their antlers touch, their branches hinting, perhaps, of the forest in which these creatures run free.

Is he a god, a priest, or a shaman? He is most likely Cernunnos (kair-*noon*-oss), the Lord of the Animals, a god of fertility, abundance, and regeneration, whose name means the "Horned One." Although he is not mentioned in literature, there are many images of this god in metal and stone throughout Europe. Some images show Cernunnos with symbols of abundance; in one he holds a great sack out of which coins or grain come

pouring, while in others he offers the cornucopia, or horn of plenty. On a stone relief from France he is depicted feeding two ram-horned snakes from a heap of fruit and a bowl of porridge on his lap. There are sockets in the god's head for antlers, which were possibly inserted or removed at seasonal rituals. Both the cycle of the stag's antlers and the shedding of the snake's skin symbolize regeneration, while both creatures have connotations of virility, as does the ram. In other images, Cernunnos also sports the ears and hooves of the stag, or his legs turn into the snakes themselves. Part man, part beast, he embodies the wisdom of deep communion with the wildness of the world.

The antlered figure on the famous Iron Age silver cauldron found in a peat bog in Gundestrup, Denmark, may be the horned god, Cernunnos.

THE WISDOM OF TREES

Imitate the magnificent trees that speak no
words of their rapture, but only breathe
largely the luminous breeze.
D. H. LAWRENCE

One of the most essential teachings of Celtic
spirituality is that the natural world is radi-
antly alive and sentient. Learning to perceive
trees as conscious, living members of our
planetary community opens the way for the
next step in the evolution of modern Western
consciousness—to realize that members of
what ecopsychologist David Abram calls the
"more-than-human" world are as conscious in
their own way as the human race. When this
is fully realized, it opens up entirely new possibilities of relationship, a subject we will
explore more in the next chapter as the
lengthening days coax us out to spend more
time in the Green World, to use Scottish poet
Fiona MacLeod's term for nature. We can
start by getting to know these great wise
beings whom the modern world has regarded
merely as providers of timber or as decorative
props on the human stage.

To walk among trees is to reconnect with
our deep ancestral roots in the forest. To
look through the spiraling branches of a
giant redwood is to contemplate a living
mandala; to gaze at the colors of a maple in
autumn is to witness the ever-changing
canvas of a sublime artist. To inhale the fragrance of pine and cedar is to absorb the
essences of nature. Trees can help clear our
minds from the frenzy of our fast-track lives,
inspire our thoughts, calm our emotions, and
fill us with serenity. They are elders on this
planet who embody an ineffable wisdom that
they will share with us if we but seek it out. I
have found that just a short while spent in
the presence of certain trees can make me
feel soothed and relaxed, as if the tree itself
is gently helping me put my fears and anxi-
eties into a broader perspective. Recent scientific studies have confirmed what many of
us know intuitively—that trees can reduce
the stress in our lives. My own research has
shown that trees not only take in carbon
dioxide and give out oxygen; they also act as
purifiers by absorbing the negative emotional energy given off by human beings and
transmuting it into healthy positive energy.
They breathe in noise and breathe out
silence; they inhale our pain and exhale
peace. They take into themselves all the
cacophony of the world of humans and
machines and turn it into a dance of wind on
branches, the swaying of green canopies, sun

dapple on leaves, and all the joyous movement of light.

Connecting with Trees

In order to make a connection with the Tree
Kingdom, begin by taking notice of the trees
in your neighborhood or nearby park. When
you take a walk, look at them and greet them
warmly as you would a beautiful dog or cat
you chanced to meet. (You can do this
silently if there are people about.) Each time
you go by, notice the changes in the growth
and color of their branches, leaves, flowers,
and fruit as the year turns. Also notice more
subtle changes of mood and energy. Smile at
them and touch them as you pass. Sit beneath
a tree to eat your lunch, have an afternoon
nap, or relax after work. Let the lives of trees
become part of your experience of your
immediate world.

To deepen your relationship with trees, go
to a park or wilderness area or to any woods
where you will not be disturbed.

1. Wander through different groups of trees,
   quiet your mind, and practice tuning into
   their energy. In some parts of the forest
   the trees may seem more "awake" than in
   others. Some may appear to exude
   warmth and friendliness, while others
   remain aloof. Notice how different species
   emanate different kinds of energy.

2. Let yourself be drawn toward one tree in
   particular, and move closer to it. Observe
   every part of it from root to top. Every
   tree has an energy field, an aura. See if
   you can detect where the aura begins by
   walking toward and away from the tree
   and using the palms of your hands to
   sense its energy.

3. Send warm energy toward the tree from
   your heart, and ask if it will allow you to
   draw closer and spend some time with it. If
   it is granted, walk closer to the tree and
   circle it slowly in a sunwise direction. Then
   put both your hands and your body against
   the trunk and tune into its consciousness.
   Notice how the tree looks close up, how it
   smells, and how it feels against your skin.

4. Rub a fresh leaf or needle between your
   fingers and inhale the fragrance.

5. Now sit down against the trunk and open
   yourself to the power of the tree. Let it
   take you into a deep state of meditation.
   You don't have to do anything other than
   stay relaxed and present and let the tree
   calm your thoughts and gently cleanse
   your mind of all the agitation of modern
   living. Enjoy this state of peace for as
   long as you want.

6. When you are ready, stand up and place your hands on its trunk again, sending it thanks from your heart. Cultivating an attitude of gratitude toward trees is an important part of building a relationship with them. We have received their gifts for many millions of years and given so little back in return. On page 125, in the "How to Plant a Tree" section, you will find some practical ways to give back to the Kingdom of the Trees.

They are beautiful in their peace,
They are wise in their silence.
They will stand after we are dust.
They teach us, and we tend them.
G. MacDunelmor

A Reverence for Trees

Trees provided people of the Celtic lands with countless precious gifts of food, drink, dyes, and herbal medicine. They were an invaluable source of fuel and material for houses, furniture, vessels, tools, and all manner of farming implements. Reverence for their power and gratitude for their gifts continued to live in the hearts and minds of country people well into the modern age, and many would have been horrified to see the way trees are treated merely as inanimate objects—"timber"—today. Centuries of living in the presence of trees led to an intimate knowledge of their spiritual nature above and beyond their physical properties and uses. Trees were considered to be alive, ensouled. A sacred tree that was wrongfully cut or felled might bleed or scream. As late as the seventeenth century, antiquarian John Aubrey wrote, "When an oake is falling, before it falls it gives a kind of shriekes or groanes that may be heard a mile off, as it were the genus of the oake lamenting. E. Wyld, Esq. hath heard it severall times."[6]

To harm a sacred tree was to invite disaster. Sickness, death, or financial loss could attend those foolhardy enough to disturb a faery hawthorn, if only by picking a leaf or plucking a switch. Even hanging out your washing on a thorn was ill advised, as it might cover up the faeries' clothes already spread out there. If you are out for a drive in the Irish countryside, it can be quite disconcerting when the road makes a sudden sharp bend around a faery tree, which the road builders had refused to move. As recently as the 1980s, workers in the DeLorean car plant in Northern Ireland claimed that one of the reasons the business had so many problems was because a faery thorn bush had been cut down during the construction of the plant. The management took this so seriously that they planted a replacement with all due ceremony!

Country people continued to make offerings to sacred trees throughout the centuries. In nineteenth-century Scotland fishermen in the Cromarty area would visit a rowan tree before setting out to sea. They placed small white stones in a hollow of its trunk so that the spirit would protect them and ensure a good catch. As we saw in the last chapter, pilgrims continue to visit holy wells and tie wool, ribbons, or rags to the nearby "clootie" tree in hopes of receiving a cure. Driving on the main road through Black Isle near Inverness in Northern Scotland, motorists today can see the extraordinary sight of a clootie well whose trees bend under the weight of thousands of knotted rags from shirts and towels to handkerchiefs, baby clothes, and even sneakers.

In return, trees offered their branches and berries for healing, protection, and good luck. Sprigs of holly worn on the coat protected the wearer from evil. Farmers hung crosses of rowan above stables and barns to protect their livestock. Drivers of hearses carried whip handles made of elder to keep spirits at bay. Like the druids, people turned to trees to learn about the future; an ash leaf placed under the pillow at night would bring dreams of a future lover. They knew when to gather the wood for protective crosses, wands, or amulets—at dusk, dawn, or midnight and in accord with the phases of the moon. They were careful to ask permission from the spirit of the tree. For example, one asked the Elder Mother who lived inside the elder tree by saying, "Old Woman, give me some of thy wood and I will give thee some of mine when I grow into a tree." This old invocation points to another folk belief that centuries of Christianity did little to alter—that humans spirits could reside within a tree. Ancient stories and ballads describe trees that grow from the graves of lovers and entwine together in loving embrace. In the tragic Irish tale of Baile and Ailinn, Baile (*bwa*-lyuh) died of grief for the beautiful Ailinn (*ah*-lin). When he was buried, a yew tree grew out of his grave and "the likeness of his head was in the branches." After seven years poets cut down the yew and made writing tablets out of it; perhaps Baile's great love inspired their compositions.

Bark, flowers, leaves, berries, and nuts—herbalists past and present have used all the different parts of the tree. Yet people also recognized that the real healer was the spirit of the tree itself. In some places the oak tree was considered so powerful that healing could occur simply by walking around the tree and wishing the ailment to be carried off by the first bird alighting on its branches. In Wales rubbing the oak with the palm of your left hand on Midsummer's Day kept you healthy all year. Tree spirit medicine was at work a couple of years ago when a woman stood between two ancient yew trees at a sacred center in North Wales. The woman had breast cancer and was taken there by healers who had discovered the curative power of these trees. As she stood between the trees, she felt an enormous bolt of energy course through her body, and from that moment on she was cancer free. Interestingly enough, yew contains a substance called taxol, which is used in the treatment of breast cancer.

Recently, a few people on the cutting edge of alternative medicine have rediscovered the ancient art of tree spirit medicine based on Celtic tree lore. (See "Resources" for how to contact them and obtain the tree essences they distill.)

A WOODLAND POTPOURRI

Bring the scent of the forest into your home by making a potpourri with found ingredients from trees and shrubs and essential tree oils. It can also be used as a form of aromatherapy. Aromatic tree oils can be obtained from herbal suppliers and include birch, bay, cedar, cypress, eucalyptus, juniper, pine, sandalwood, and tea tree.

Collect from a forest, garden, or park a mixture of

bark peelings
oak moss
lichens
fibrous leaves, such as bay, manzanita, huckleberry
twigs
seed pods
eucalyptus bells
pine needles
small cones, such as cedar, fir, spruce, redwood
berries, such as juniper, bay
acorns and other nuts

Everything should be as small as possible. If you prefer, these items can also be purchased at herbal crafts suppliers.

Optional: Add cinnamon sticks, sliced ginger root, orange peel, or chili peppers for a spicy scent.

Let everything dry in a warm dark place, such as an airing cupboard.

When the ingredients are completely dry, mix them together in a bowl. Add 20 drops of essential tree oils and 2 teaspoons of orris root powder to every couple of handfuls of the dried mixture. (This does not have to be too exact.) You can also substitute 1 cup of oak moss or Icelandic moss for the orris root. Experiment with the fragrance by using single essences or blends of two or more tree oils, depending on personal preference or the spiritual qualities of the trees you would like to bring into your room.

Mix well and store in an airtight container for a week to allow the fragrances to blend together. Shake the container now and then.

If you are not using the potpourri right away, seal in glass containers. As well as placing bowls or baskets of the mixture around your house, you can make small sachets to carry with you for their qualities, such as rowan for protection, hazel for wisdom. (See "Resources" at the end of the book for how to obtain the oils.)

TALKING WITH TREES

With a finer acuity than our own, the people who lived on the land were fully aware of the spirits of trees. Our notion of reality is conditioned by the culture we live in. If we are no longer able to see the invisible inhabitants of the living universe, it is we and not they who have closed the doors of perception. To open them again, we have to unlearn the scientific materialism that pervades the modern worldview. The best way I have found to do this is to cultivate a childlike openness and willingness to embrace a reality beyond our five senses.

There are two kinds of tree spirits in the forest, the spirits of individual trees, which reside within and around the physical trees, and a huge ethereal being that dwells around and above a grove or copse of trees. Recently, some people have given the latter spirit the Indian name of deva; others, including me, prefer to use the ancient Greek name of dryad, to which the spirit seems to respond more readily.[7] The two spirits might be compared to the individual personality and the higher self of a human being. The dryad is the overlighting spirit for an entire species and sometimes an entire forest. In a wood, park, or arboretum with many kinds of trees, there can be quite a few spirits hovering around each species.

If you want to experience a dryad, you must have a sincere desire to get to know it, just as you would want to get to know a person or an animal—not for what you can get out of it but for the delight of relating to one of the many other-than-human expressions of life. Ella Young, Irish mystic, storyteller, and friend of W. B. Yeats, was strongly against merely looking for phenomena when communicating with the natural world. She said, "You have to be content to know that you love that tree, and you want to love it more, and you know it's alive and you want to come closer to it."[8]

1. To connect with a Dryad, you need to spend some time with a tree in the meditative state described on pages 115–16. When you are ready, send a feeling of love toward the tree, and tell it in your own words that you would like to get to know it better. I like to softly sing or chant to the tree, which also helps put me quickly and easily into a meditative state of mind. Be receptive to the tree's response. Most often you will feel a subtle shift of consciousness and sometimes even a change in your surroundings, such as a sudden ray of sunlight or breeze.
2. Open up a dialogue with the dryad. You can ask questions about it or about

yourself, and you can request guidance on any problems. Sit in the silence and wait for a response, which usually comes as a sense of inner knowing.

(Note the difference between water wisdom and tree wisdom. At the holy well, one enters into the Otherworld to gain its wisdom through dreams, but the tree, whose trunk stands firmly in Middle Earth, speaks to us while we are awake. But it does require a special kind of listening. This may take you a while to learn, not because it is difficult but because it requires us to trust and be receptive, which most of us are not used to being.)

3. Because the imagination is the universal language of the inner worlds, use your inner eyes to see the spirits of trees. There are two ways I have found useful to practice this:

- Take drawing materials and a pad of paper with you to the tree. With your eyes closed, tune in to the dryad and get an image of what it looks like. Open your eyes and draw what you see.
- With eyes open or closed, look at an individual tree or group of trees with whom you have made a connection.

Imagine the tree spirit walking toward you from out of, or from behind, the tree. Use your imagination to fill in all the details from top to bottom of the being you see. This will work only if you ignore the critical adult part of you that says you're making it all up.

Remember: the imagination is what gives the invisible world form, like a suit of clothes, so that we can interact with it. Open up to a childlike sense of play, and have fun! Subsequent visits and continued practice will strengthen the reality of your experiences, but it does take time, patience, and a lot of faith because you are swimming against the tide of the modern materialistic construct of reality.

The Green Man, foliage sprouting from his head, peers like a tree spirit from hidden corners in medieval churches. This one is from the church at Old Radnor, Powys, Wales.

WOOD FOR THE FIRE

The lore of sacred woods is preserved in a number of old rhymes. The one below contains good practical advice for the homesteader who has to feed the family fire, but it is also full of hidden wisdom. Triadic in form, it consists of three verses, each containing three rhyming couplets plus a final couplet that is repeated three times. Could "the Queen" be the Triple Goddess in her aspect of the Three Norns, or Fates, who sat enthroned beneath the great ash, Yggdrasil, the World Tree of Scandinavia? Or perhaps she was Mary, Queen of Heaven, who bathed the baby Jesus by a fire of ash logs, according to Scottish legend.

Beech-wood fires are bright and clear
If the logs are kept a year.
Oaken logs burn steadily
If the wood is old and dry.
Chestnut's only good, they say,
If for long it's laid away.
But Ash new or Ash old
Is fit for a Queen with a crown of gold.

Birch and fir-logs burn too fast—
Blaze up bright, but do not last.
Make a fire of Elder-tree,
Death within your house you'll see.
It is by the Irish said,
Hawthorn bakes the sweetest bread.
But Ash green or Ash brown
Is fit for a Queen with a golden crown.

Elm wood burns like churchyard
mold—
E'en the very flames are cold.
Poplar gives a bitter smoke:
Fills your eyes and makes you choke.
Apple wood will scent your room
With an incense-like perfume.
But Ash wet or Ash dry—
For a Queen to warm her slippers by.

HAZEL

☫HE SACRED ☫ROVE

I went out to the hazel wood
Because a fire was in my head . . .
W. B. YEATS

Growing ninefold at the heart of the Other-world, the hazel might be said to be the quintessential Celtic tree. The hazels drop their purple nuts into the Well of Wisdom, fertilizing its waters with the tree's potency. In "How Cormac mac Art Went to Faerie," in the previous chapter, the salmon eat the nuts and send the husks floating downstream; in other versions, the hazelnuts cause bubbles of "mystic inspiration" to form on the surface of the water. The goal of Irish poets and seers

was to "gain the nuts of wisdom," most likely a metaphor for the heightened state of awareness and inspiration sometimes referred to as "fire in the head," although the more literally minded have argued that this might refer to a potent brew made from hazels that could alter consciousness. Actually, there are a number of references in early Irish literature to drinking hazel mead, while Scottish druids were said to gain their prophetic powers from eating hazelnuts.

In the Celtic landscape hazels grew in "thin" places where wisdom might be found. The Gaelic word for hazel is *calltuinn* (*kawl-tin*), and a number of places called Calton or Carlton are associated with entrances to the Otherworld, one being the famous Calton Hill near Edinburgh, which was still used for magical gatherings in the seventeenth century. The great monastery of Clonard in Belfast was established in the pagan grove, Ross-Finnchuill, the Wood of the White Hazel. Tara, the royal seat of kingship in Ireland, was built close by a hazel grove. The druid's wand was made of hazel, as the diviner's dowsing rod is to this day. As the rod bends to reveal the water within the earth, perhaps it is straining to reconnect with its ancestors, the nine sacred trees deep within the memory of the land.

HOLY GROUND
LOCH MAREE
(ROSS AND CROMARTY, SCOTLAND)

An ancient forest of Scots pine at Loch Maree in northwest Scotland is one of the rare surviving fragments of the Great Wood of Caledon, which once clothed most of the Highlands. On the lake itself are small wooded islands, and one, Isle Maree, still bears the sacred oaks of a druid grove. One of these was known as the Wishing Tree, and its remnants still stand over a healing well, famed for curing mental disorders. For centuries the sick were brought to the island by a boat that circled it three times sunwise before landing. When the patient had drunk from the well, a coin was driven into the bark of the tree as an offering. Queen Victoria once visited the island and is said to have left her own coin there.

In the seventh century, Maelrubha, an Irish saint, built a chapel on the island whose ruins can still be seen. But he probably took over the cult of a pagan forest god, for even in the nineteenth century locals still called the island by its old name: Eilean-a-Mhor-Righ (*el-yun uh voar-ree*), the Island of the Great King. As late as the seventeenth century, four men sacrificed a bull to the old god, "Mourie," for the sake of a wife who was sick, but the church outlawed the practice shortly afterward.

Due to centuries of clearing, only 1 percent of the Caledonian Forest now remains, but the Scottish environmental organization Trees for Life is working toward restoring the forest to its original wild state. (See "Resources" for how you can help.)

REPLANTING THE SACRED GROVE

Love and respect for trees must translate into practical action in a world where ancient forests are disappearing at unprecedented rates, contributing to worldwide ecological degradation. In the U.S. alone, only 5 percent of our old-growth forest remains. Replanting trees can help provide vital habitats for wildlife, clean the air of pollutants, increase oxygen, fight global climate change, and restore topsoil and rivers. Plant a tree in your yard, your neighborhood, or your children's school. If you are unable to plant one yourself, have an organization such as American Forests plant one on your behalf as part of their Global ReLeaf Project. Some organizations will give away tree seedlings for free. (See "Resources" for details.) If you plant thirty trees a year, you will be paying your annual "carbon debt," the amount of carbon the average American releases into the atmosphere.

How to Plant a Tree

1. Choose a native species or one that's well adapted to your area. A seedling in a one-gallon container will establish itself quicker than a larger size.
2. Plant between the last frost and up to four weeks before the first frost. In Celtic tradition, Friday is a good day to choose, especially when the moon is waxing.
3. Select a site where the seedling will have adequate space to grow into a full-sized tree both above and below the ground. (Pay special attention to utility wires.)
4. Prepare a planting area as deep as the root ball and three to five times its diameter by loosening the soil. Dig a hole in the middle of the area, and set the root ball even with the ground level.
5. Water thoroughly to settle the soil and remove air pockets in the planting area.
6. Spread a two- to three-inch layer of mulch over the entire area, but not within six inches of the trunk.
7. Protect your seedling from damage caused by feet, lawnmowers, and pets. Water it generously every week or two during the first year.

Following is a blessing that can be recited at a tree-planting ceremony or simply used to invoke protective energy toward trees locally or worldwide.

A DRUID BLESSING FOR THE TREES

A ninefold blessing of the sacred grove
Now be upon all forests of Earth:

For willow of the streams,
Hazel of the rocks,
Alder of the marshes,
Birch of the waterfalls,
Ash of the shade,
Yew of resilience,
Elm of the brae,
Oak of the sun,
And all the trees that live and grow
On hill and brake and glen:

No ax, no saw, no fire shall harm you,
No mind of ownership shall seize you,
No hand of greed or profit claim you.

But grace of the stepping deer among you,
Strength of the rooting boar beneath you,
Power of the gliding hawk above you.

Deep peace of the running stream through
   your roots,
Deep peace of the flowing air in your boughs,
Deep peace of the shining stars on your leaves,

That the harp of the woods be heard once more
Throughout the green and living Earth.
            —M. F.

THE WORLD TREE

People in the ancient world viewed the Tree of Life as an *axis mundi*, or World Tree: a cosmic pillar that upholds the universe. A Sumerian cup from the second millennium B.C.E. is inscribed with a dedication to the Lord of the Tree of Truth, long before the author of Genesis described the Tree of Knowledge in the Garden of Eden. In India the Buddha sat beneath the bodhi tree to attain enlightenment.

Those who have journeyed to the Otherworld have caught glimpses of its marvelous trees. They could be made of crystal or covered with white blossom or bearing blossom, fruit, and nuts at the same time:

At the doorway to the east,
Three trees of brilliant crystal,
Whence a gentle flock of birds calls
To the children of the royal fort.

A tree at the doorway to the court,
Fair its harmony;
A tree of silver before the setting sun,
Its brightness like that of gold.

Three score trees there
Whose crowns are meetings that do not meet,
Each tree bears ripe fruit,
For three hundred men.[9]

AN ACT OF GRATITUDE

A very old man went out one day on the land beside his house, and began planting fruit trees.

A young man walked by. "What are you doing?" the young man asked.

"Planting fruit trees," the old man replied.

"But you will not see fruit in your lifetime," the youth said.

"The fruit that I have enjoyed in my lifetime," the old man answered, "has been from trees that people before me have planted. So to express my gratitude of them, I am planting trees to give fruit to those who come after me."

MEDIEVAL IRISH[10]

In "How Cormac mac Art Went to Faerie," in the previous chapter, there are nine hazels, rather than a single tree, growing by the Well of Wisdom. Nine, being three times three, is a most sacred Celtic number and one associated with shamanic spirit journeys to the Upperworld in a number of cultures from Siberia to Nepal. For example, in one Siberian community the initiate is carried in trance on a mat along a row of birch trees nine times, after which he or she climbs each tree, circling it nine times, calling the spirits from the top.[11]

Where the Well of Wisdom is the receptive feminine principle that connects us with the Underworld, the Tree of Life thrusts skyward to the Upperworld, symbolizing the expressive masculine principle. In Celtic mythology the old Irish word for a sacred tree, *bile*, comes from the same Indo-European root that gives us *phallus*. And yet the Tree of Life belongs to both god and goddess, and from its tangle of roots burrowing into the secrets of the Earth to its topmost leaves, which sparkle with the stars, the tree forms a bridge between the worlds.

THE SILVER BRANCH

In some Irish tales the Otherworld tree is an apple tree that grows in the heart of an island ruled by faery women. When the hero is given an apple or a silver branch from this tree, he has the key that will take him to her kingdom. On the tree sit many birds whose song fills the air with sweet sounds, and they can still be heard singing in the silver branch. Early poets carried branches of bronze, silver, and gold hung with chiming bells according to their grade, for a poet also is a frequent voyager to that country. This tale is taken from "The Voyage of Bran," one of a class of medieval Irish stories about sea journeys known as imrama.

As Bran mac Febal (*bron* muck *fyev*-ul) went walking on the shore near his royal *dún* (fortress), sweet music drifted by upon the breeze. It seemed to come from behind, but when he looked there was no one there, and whichever way he turned the music was always at his back. The haunting melody and gentle rhythms made him so drowsy that he sank to the ground and surrendered to sleep. When he awoke the music had faded away, but in his hand was a silver apple branch covered with glistening white blossoms.

Bran returned home in a daze, looking so unlike himself that his men wondered what had happened. That night in the feasting hall, a beautiful woman appeared in their midst, dressed in strange, shining garments. She began to sing, and this was her song:

> *I bring an apple branch from the Isle of Emhain*
> *From the far island around which*
> *are the shining horses of the sons of Lir.*

Curling waves about her shores,
Brightness falling from their hair,
Sun and sea mist intermingle
Every shining color there.

Four columns of white bronze beneath her,
White rock and white sea shine together,
Where coracle races against chariot
In the silver plain to the south.

Melody of birds on the tree of flowers,
Calling in sweet harmony,
Songs of delight and enchantment
Drop like blossoms on the Silver Cloud Plain.

There is no sorrow there or mourning,
Health and strength are there unweakening,
None are wounded on the plain of kindness,
No malediction or dark treason.

And though all men can hear my song,
These words, Bran, are for your ears alone!
Set sail, Bran, on the shining sea,
And I will meet you in the Land of Women.

The moment she finished her song, the silver branch of apple blossom sprang from Bran's hand to her own, and she disappeared.

The next day Bran put out to sea with three companies of nine men in leather coracles, and after two days and two nights on the restless waves he met Manannán mac Lir driving his two-wheeled chariot over the water. Manannán sang:

Bran sails his coracle across the watery main,
But I ride a chariot over a flowery plain.

Bran sees countless waves glittering on the sea
But I see scarlet blossoms waving languidly.

Sea-horses glisten in summer, the speckled salmon leaps
These are my herds, Bran, that I tend like sheep.

And your coracle sails over forests of trees:
The bountiful orchards of the Land-under-Seas.

"Row steadily on, Bran, and you will reach the Isle of Women before the setting sun!"

And so they journeyed on till they came to an island that was called the Isle of Joy. As they rowed alongside the shore, they saw a multitude of people, all laughing away fit to burst. When they caught sight of Bran and the fleet of coracles their laughter redoubled, yet they said not a word. Bran sent one of his men to go ashore and learn about these people, but as soon as this man landed he, too, joined the crowd and began to laugh uproariously with them. Bran and the others rowed right around the island, and whenever they caught sight of their companion they shouted to him, begging him to return. But he paid no heed to their call, only looked at them and doubled up with laughter, till at last they had to sail away and leave him there.

At last they reached the Land of Women at the setting of the sun. And there stood the queen at the head of the port, her arms raised to him in welcome. But Bran suddenly became seized with fear and could not bring himself to go ashore. So the queen threw a ball of thread toward him, and when he caught it in his hand, it stuck fast.

And she reeled him in to shore.

The queen and her maidens led the men to a great house, beautifully furnished, with tables groaning under a sumptuous feast and thrice nine couches there, large enough for two. The food was what each one loved most, and the more they ate and drank, the dishes and goblets remained full and overflowing. The queen took Bran to be her lover, and each of his men lay with her maidens, and there they stayed for what seemed but a year and a day under the spreading branches of the silver apple tree.

But by this time, despite the many pleasures of the Land of Women, some of Bran's men grew homesick and begged their chief to let them return to Ireland, just to see their families and their native land for one more time. The queen was not pleased at this but let them go with this warning: not to set foot on dry land, or all would not go well for them.

And so Bran and his company sailed back to Erin and at last drew near to the shore. There they saw a band of people gathered on the beach, and Bran called out to them to see if he was known in these parts. But the crowd drew back in fear. Only one very old man quavered, "Yes, we have heard tell of Bran mac Febal, but that was hundreds of years ago and is now but a tale that is told at the fireside."

At this, one of the crew, Nechtan, leaped from the boat in a panic, but no sooner did his feet touch the shore than he crumbled into a heap of ashes. So from his coracle, Bran told the story of his wanderings to the people and wrote in ogham the songs he had learned there. He bade them farewell and pushed off from the shore, and after that time his wanderings are not known.

ᵺHE INNER CAULDRON
CENTERING

Beloved, gaze in thine own heart,
The holy tree is growing there.
                    W. B. YEATS

The Tree of Life can teach us about turning our visions into reality. When a tree grows, its first task is to establish a root system, to create a foundation that will support its upward growth. The future success of our ideas and visions depends on the way in which we set realistic goals and make careful preparations. Unless we are "grounded" at the beginning, it will be impossible to soar ahead at a later stage. The tree develops as a result of the myriad complex interchanges that take place among its roots, branches, and leaves and with nutrients in the soil and air. A tremendous amount of energy goes into its growth. We, too, need to let the seed of our creativity take root, grow, and bloom, as we align ourselves with the natural energies of the universe. This means we have to be willing to work hard, stay focused, and be totally determined to bring our dreams into the world, to see them blossom and bear fruit.

As the tree brings up nutrients through its roots to nourish its visible portion, we draw the inspiration from the soul into our everyday lives. But the growth of the tree also depends on the sun, rain, and air. So our dreams must also be exposed to the analytical scrutiny of the mind, which helps us figure out ways and means and solve problems; to discriminate between what can and can't be done, what is and is not working. The following meditation will help you feel grounded, filled with energy, and as strong and centered as a tree so that you can move ahead with your work. It can be done sitting before your altar but also works well standing up, especially outdoors in a natural setting.

Meditation: Tree of Life

Close your eyes. Take a deep breath, and as you let it out, send the breath down into your feet and imagine that you are a tree sending a taproot deep down into the Earth. . . . Now begin to feel the feeder roots growing outward, spreading all around, their tips pushing between and all around the particles of soil and stones . . . anchoring you to your home in the Earth. . . . Every time you exhale, send more and more energy down into those roots, until your legs and feet feel really rooted to the ground where you sit. Feel the stability and strength of being a tree, so firmly anchored in the ground, established in your own place on the planet. . . . Be aware of the cavernous Underworld kingdoms below you, where underground rivers seep through the unutterable darkness—the womb of the goddess of the land.

Now feel your thousands of rootlets absorbing the water and nutrients in the soil. As you breathe in, breathe the energy of the Earth up through your roots into your toes, feet, and legs. Breathe it in through your hips, abdomen, stomach, and chest. Feel your spine as the heartwood that supports the structure of your trunk. . . . Be aware of the bark, the skin that protects your living tissues. All around you there is grass and flowers at your feet, animals brushing past, resting beneath you, or climbing into the hollows of your trunk to sleep or store their food.

Now as you breathe even deeper, experience the energy of the sap rising up your trunk. . . . Feel it flow along your branches to every twig and leaf. . . . Let it pour through your arms and hands . . . and circulate through your whole body. . . . Breathe it up into your neck and head, and let it flow out through the top like a fountain of light. . . .

Feel your branches reach up and outward into the air, and notice how the smaller branches and twigs sway in the breeze. . . . Become aware of your green leaves and how they turn toward the sun to receive its warmth and light. . . . Feel the energy of the light charging the chlorophyll—the green blood—in your leaves, and the pores opening to breathe in the carbon dioxide and exhale the oxygen as your gift to the animal kingdom. Notice the airy freedom of the Upperworld, home of the sky god, where birds soar and the wind dances . . . the ecstasy of the sun's golden fire drenching every vein of your leaves by day, the play of the silky cool white moonlight by night . . . the rain that washes you clean and the soft cold snow that blankets you in winter. . . . Feel the turning of the seasons, the slow cycling of the centuries as you live, breathe, and grow in your forest home.

When you are ready to end the meditation, bring your awareness back down through your head and arms, becoming aware of your human body, down through your chest, stomach, and abdomen, and last through your legs and feet. Now you are firmly rooted in the center of your world, held in the embrace of earth and sky. You are filled with the creative power to bring your dreams into the world.

A DRUID BLESSING OF
THE SACRED GROVE

May Rowan of the scarlet berries shield you,
and Ash protect you from the lightning flash.

May Oak be a door of strength for your departing,
and Willow weave a green bower for your returning.

May the Apple-branch of longing bear you to the Blessed Isles,
and the Birds of Rhiannon sing for you
where blossoms fall forever on the silver-cloud plain.

May Hawthorn flowers fill your heart
with the green fire of love in the wildwood.

May the Hazels of Wisdom drop their nuts in Connla's Well for you,
and may you glimpse the Salmon in its depths.

May slender Birch celebrate all your bright beginnings,
and Yew of Darkness fold you into the gathering dusk.

M. F.

THE FESTIVAL OF BELTAINE

Welcome, with your lovely greenwood choir,
summery month of May for which I long!
WELSH, FOURTEENTH CENTURY

When the gates of Beltaine swing open on May 1, sunlight and blossom welcome the procession of the year into the green halls of summer. At Imbolc we rejoiced at the return of light; now we celebrate life, growth, love, and sexuality: "the force that drives the green fuse through the flower," in the words of Welsh poet Dylan Thomas.

While the second part of Irish *Beltaine* and Scottish *Bealtuinn* clearly means "fire," from the old Celtic word *tene*, linguists are uncertain as to whether *Bel* refers to Belenos, the Gaulish Apollo, or is simply derived from *bel*, meaning "brilliant." It might even derive from *bil tene*, or "lucky fire," because to jump between two Beltaine fires was sure to bring good fortune, health to your livestock, and prosperity.

FESTIVAL NAMES

Language	Name	Pronunciation
Irish Gaelic	Beltaine	*byel*-tin-yuh
Scottish Gaelic	Bealltainn	*byahl*-tin
Manx	Boaldyn	*bole*-dun
Welsh	Calan Mai, Calan Haf (First of May, First of Summer)	*cal*-ahn mie, *cal*-ahn hawv
Cornish	Kalann-Me	*ka*-lunn mey
Breton	Kala-Mae	*kah*-la may

In Irish mythology events that mark the end of an old order and the beginning of a new frequently take place at Beltaine. The mythical history of Ireland consists of a series of invasions by different races who in turn became the ruling class. One of these was the race of gods, the Tuatha Dé Danann, who arrived in Ireland one Beltaine riding through the air on dark clouds. After they had reigned for centuries the next invaders, the sons of Míl (meel), the supposed ancestors of the Irish, arrived on the west coast of Ireland by ship and defeated the Tuatha Dé in battle to become the new rulers. Finally, according to some legends, Saint Patrick lit a fire on the Hill of Slane near Tara at Beltaine to pro-claim the triumph of Christianity over the old religion. In later centuries ordinary country people experienced the strong tide of change from winter to summer and, to ensure a smooth passage, performed many rites and ceremonies that we will explore below.

GODS OF THE CELTS: BELENOS

Belenos (Beh-*ley*-noss) was a sun god who may have been connected with the festival of Beltaine. His name means "bright" or "bril-liant." The Romans called him Apollo Belenos, after their god of the sun, but he seems to have existed as a Celtic god in his own right before this period. His cult extended from northern Italy and up through Austria and Gaul, where there were sanctuaries dedicated to him at healing springs, for the sun was believed to have marvelous curative properties when associated with water.[1] A shrine to Belenos may still stand at Paimpont in the old forest of Brocéliande in Brittany, the traditional heart of the Celtic mysteries in Gaul. In the clearing, the sacred well known as the Fountain of Barenton bubbles up near an ancient dolmen stone. The old name of the sacred well was Belenton, probably a contraction of *Bel-Nemeton*, the sacred grove of Belenos.

In the British Isles a shrine to him bearing a Roman inscription was discovered in Scotland. In Wales he may be equated with the ancestral figure, Beli Mawr (*beh*-lee *mah*-oor), but one searches in vain for his name in Ireland. Yet he may appear in veiled form in a story about Diarmaid, one of Fionn McCumhaill's warriors. Diarmaid is walking over a beautiful plain when he comes upon a sacred sanctuary: a tall, fruit-laden tree surrounded by a circle of stones. By the tree in the center stands a stone where a crystal clear spring bubbles up. Diarmaid is thirsty and drinks from the well, but his action summons the well's guardian, an enormous giant clad in armor and wearing a golden crown, who

strides out of the east. He challenges Diarmaid to a fight, which lasts for three days. Every evening the giant disappears down the well, but on the fourth evening Diarmaid follows him down and finds himself in the Land Under Wave. The giant was surely none other than Belenos, coming out of the east crowned with gold like the newly risen sun and disappearing into the Underworld each evening.

THE BLESSING OF FIRE

> *I'll tell you of a special festival,*
> *The glorious dues of May-day;*
> *Ale, roots, sweet whey,*
> *And fresh curds to the fire.*
> EARLY IRISH CALENDAR POEM

On Beltaine Eve the druids and their successors assembled on high hills with a view of the rising sun. They came to raise the great fires that would bring the power of the sun to Earth and to sanctify and purify the whole community and their livestock in readiness for the new cycle. Fire was an interface between the human race and the divine, in particular, the elemental powers of the Upperworld who would determine the fate of the herds, the flocks, and the growing harvest. Sacrificial offerings were cast into the fire to gain their goodwill, borne skyward on flames like hands uplifted in prayer.

In later centuries the Beltaine fires continued to blaze in Scotland and Ireland. An eighteenth-century account from the Scottish Highlands describes how every fire in the household was put out, and on the hill the fire for the great bonfires, known as the "need-fire," was kindled with the wood of nine sacred trees. Only the best men were fit to kindle the sacred fire. If any were guilty of murder, adultery, theft, or other major crime, the fire would not kindle or else it would lack its usual virtues. Three times three, three times nine, or even nine times nine men took turns twirling the stick, or "windle" of oak, which fitted snugly inside a hole bored in a well-seasoned plank of oak, the tree of the sun. As soon as sparks began to appear, they applied a piece of agaric, a fungus that grows on old birch trees and is very combustible. Birch, as we have seen, is a tree associated with new beginnings, purification, and the spirit world.

The fire came like a blessing from the gods. From this magical flame the great bonfire was lit, and now shadowy figures emerged from their darkened homesteads below the hill, driving their cattle before them. They also carried provisions—a custard of eggs, butter, oatmeal,

and milk, and plenty of beer and whiskey. Some of the custard was poured on the ground as an offering to the gods and the sacred land. There was also an oatmeal bannock upon which were raised nine square knobs, one each for a god or saint who protected their flocks and herds, and also for the particular animals that preyed on them. Turning to the fire, each person broke off a knob and threw it over his or her shoulder, saying, "This I give to thee, preserve thou my horses; this to thee, preserve thou my sheep." And to the predators: "This I give to thee, O Fox! Spare thou my lambs. This to thee, O hooded Crow! This to thee, O Eagle!" When the ceremony was over they ate the rest of the food.

A nineteenth-century account from Ireland gives us a glimpse of the scenes that might have followed. The whole hillside came alive as the boys thrust brands of dried sedge and heather into the newly roaring flames and whirled them about their heads in imitation of the circling sun. Dancers spun in a ring. Young men leaped through the flames to *sain*, or protect, themselves and their livestock, while old folk slowly walked around the fire, muttering prayers. A man about to embark on a long journey or a dangerous undertaking—or to do both by getting married—leaped backward and forward three times through the flames for luck. In some places two fires were built and the livestock driven between them to purify them from disease after the long winter inside. As the fire sunk low, the girls jumped across it to procure good husbands; pregnant women stepped through it to ensure an easy birth; and mothers carried their children across the smoldering ashes. All celebrated the power of the sacred fire to purify the air of demon and disease, thunder and lightning, and anything else that might harm their hopes for the unborn child of the year's harvest. When the fire died down the embers were thrown among the sprouting crops for good luck, while each household carried some back to kindle a new fire in their hearth. When the sun rose those who had stayed up to watch it might see it dance for joy three times upon the horizon before leaping up in all its summer glory.

THE NINE SACRED WOODS

An old Scottish rhyme preserves the lore of the wood used in kindling the Beltaine fire. Notice, however, that only eight trees are mentioned; the ninth will always remain a mystery.

> *Choose the willow of the streams,*
> *Choose the hazel of the rocks,*
> *Choose the alder of the marshes,*
> *Choose the birch of the waterfalls.*
> *Choose the ash of the shade,*
> *Choose the yew of resilience,*
> *Choose the elm of the brae,*
> *Choose the oak of the sun.*

In some parts of Ireland and Scotland people still use the expression "between two Beltaine fires," meaning to be in a dilemma.

EAGLE

A CELTIC BESTIARY

I wonder, seeing I am a bard,
On the top of the oak and its branches on high
What the vision of an eagle, what the illusion.
THE DIALOGUE OF ARTHUR AND ELIWLOD

The eagle is the supreme creature of the Upperworld, for its ability to soar to great heights gives it the power of clear vision and prophecy. Where the salmon purveys the mysteries of the watery depths of the Underworld, the eagle brings the wisdom of the skies.

Sacred eagles built their nests on the crags of all the great mountains in Wales, while the highest one, Mount Snowdon, was called Caer Eryri, the stronghold of the eagle. Here the birds were snow white and revered as oracles. In ancient days the druids watched their flight before battle: if they soared and circled high in the air victory was certain, but if they swooped to earth all would be lost. In North Wales it used to be said that the beating of eagles' wings caused high winds over Wales, so that in windy weather people would say, "The eagles are breeding whirlwinds on Snowdon!"

Like the salmon, the eagle is one of the Oldest Animals of Celtic tradition. In the story of Culwch and Olwen, from the *Mabinogi*, a giant sets King Arthur some near-impossible tasks, so he sends his messenger to seek the aid of the wise old Eagle of Gwernabwy, who tells him of his great age.

"I came here," said the eagle, "a long time ago. And when I first came here, I had a stone. From the top of that stone I could peck the stars each night; now it is but the size of a fist in height."

And when Arthur himself was buried deep in a cavern under Mount Snowdon, two eagles stood guard by his tomb, where they will remain until the time comes for him to awaken and bring a new golden age to Britain.

THE BLESSING OF WATER

The fair maid who, the first of May,
Goes to the fields at break of day
And washes in dew from the hawthorn tree,
Will ever after handsome be.

Young girls who rose before dawn to bathe in the dew were assured of a beautiful complexion, according to the old custom. But to the early Celts, May dew had even more powerful effects than the purely cosmetic. Dew was regarded as having magical, life-giving properties that brought fertility to the fields. Corn and milk, the basic foods, were sometimes referred to poetically as *druchta Déa*, the dew of a goddess.

The magic of dew remained part of folk tradition throughout the centuries. Walking in May dew kept feet from becoming sore. Men who washed their hands in it became skilled in making knots and nets. In Scotland mothers wrapped their sick children in cloths soaked in the dew for its healing effect. Dew collected in the cups of hawthorn flowers or in the trunk of the tree was especially potent, as hawthorn is sacred to May. In Ireland a hawthorn hung over Saint Patrick's Stone on an island in the River Shannon and filled its hollow with dew, which had great healing powers. The waters of a Saint Bride's Well in Cork were made more potent by the dew that dripped into it from an ancient faery thorn.

A number of May Day customs involved sprinkling people with water from holy wells and pools or other sources of water. This often happened in the course of ritual processions; in nineteenth-century southern Ireland, a band of May Day mummers included a masked clown who carried a pole covered at one end with shreds of cloth, rather like a mop. This he would dip into a convenient pool or puddle and liberally anoint the shrieking crowds that lined the route.[2]

In Cornwall, May 1 was known as Ducking Day or Dipping Day because young lads claimed the right to splash water over anyone they met in the streets who was not wearing a sprig of hawthorn. In the east of the peninsula it was customary to bathe in the sea on the first three Sunday mornings in May, and pilgrimages were made to Cornwall's many holy wells. Saint Madron's well was a popular destination for parents hoping to cure their children of rickets and other childhood ailments. A piece of the child's clothing was torn—not cut, as iron repels the spirits—and fixed to the boughs of a hawthorn tree. The parents undressed the child and dipped him or her three times in the well, while they faced toward the sun. Next the child was passed around the well nine times in a sunwise direction and laid on a specially created mound of earth to sleep in the sun. If the water bubbled up as the child slept, it was considered a good sign. Silence was observed throughout the whole ritual in order not to break the spell.

For at Beltaine it was as important to be *sained* by water as by fire. The element of fire belongs to the realm of Sky, the Upperworld, for it represents the sun; it is kindled with wood from sacred trees and its energy rises upward. Water belongs to the realm of Sea, the Underworld, for it lives within the depths of Earth, and its energy moves downward. These two elements are associated with the *sam* and *gam* of Celtic cosmology, and at the beginning of summer their power unites in a divine marriage that results in the fertility of all living beings on Earth, the "middle" kingdom.

The three most powerful divinations are by fire,
*   by water, and by clay.*
These are the three great powers:
the power that ascends, which is fire;
the power that falls, which is water;
and the power that lies level on the earth,
and has the mystery of the dead,
which is clay.

IRISH TRIAD

GATHERING MAY DEW

On Beltaine morning, collect water for use in ritual and healing by one of two ways.

Collect dew before dawn, as it loses its potency after the sun has risen. Gather it from grass growing in a pesticide-free area, from hawthorn flowers or branches, or the hollow of a rock. Wash your face, hands, or feet in it, and if you feel brave take off all your clothes and roll in the dew for a truly refreshing start to the summer!

Go to a special spring, pool, or stream just before sunrise. Fill a bowl or chalice—preferably the one from your altar—and hold it up so that the first rays of the sun fall upon the water, charging it with the power of fire. Containing the virtues of both the upper and lower worlds, this water is considered very potent.

It is also traditional at this time of the year to bless the spirits of rivers and wells. If you live near water, make a garland or posy of spring flowers and cast it into the water with your thanks.

THE GAY SHEILINGS

Summer's return called the country people out from the dark and smoky interiors of their farmsteads where they had worked, played, eaten, and slept in close community with one another—and many of their ani-

mals—all winter through. They tumbled outdoors into the spacious freedom and long
hours of daylight of the northern summer.
Now it was time to lead their cattle, sheep,
horses, and goats to their summer grazing
grounds on the hill pastures known as the
sheilings. Each household divided into two
groups: young people and children, together
with most of the women, stayed on the hills
all summer with the animals, while the men
returned to the farms to tend the crops.

In Scotland all the families of the townland
gathered together with their animals and
started up the hills in a long procession. The
men carried spades, sticks, pins, and ropes for
repairing the summer huts, while the women
carried blankets, meal, churns, dishes, and
dairy utensils. Creels full of domestic gear
were slung over the horses' backs. Wealthier
people had carts, which they loaded to the
brim, with the old women and spinning
wheels perched on top.

Alexander Carmichael describes the festive
atmosphere of this special day in *Carmina
Gadelica:*

When the people meet, they greet each
other with great cordiality as if they had
not seen one another for months or
even years, instead of probably only a

few days before. There are endless
noises in the herd: sheep bleat for their
lambs, lambs for their mothers, cows low
for their calves, and their calves
respond, mares neigh for their foals, and
foals whinny in reply to their dams as
they lightly skip and scamper, curveting
in and out, little dreaming of coming
work and hard fare. The men give directions, several at a time; the women knit
their stockings and sing their songs,
walking free and erect as if there were
no burdens on their backs or on their
hearts, nor any sin or sorrow in the
world as far as they are concerned.

Ranged along on either side of the
procession are barefooted, bareheaded,
comely girls and sturdy boys, and saga-
cious dogs who every now and then, and
every here and there, have a neck-and-
neck race with some perverse young
beast, unwillingly driven from his home,
for, unlike his elders, the animal does
not know or does not remember the
pleasures of the heathery knoll, the
grassy dell or fronded glen, and the
joyous freedom of the summer sheiling.[3]

As the procession wound up the hill, the villagers sang and chanted prayers of protection

on their herds. They invoked Bride, the "beauteous shepherdess of the flocks," and the great archangel, "Michael of the white steeds," to spread his wing over them all. On the island of South Uist they recited the lovely Beltaine Blessing:

Bless, O Threefold true and bountiful,
Myself, my spouse and my children,
My tender children and their beloved mother at
 their head,
On the fragrant plain, at the gay mountain
 sheiling,
On the fragrant plain, at the gay mountain
 sheiling . . .

       Carmina Gadelica

In at least one place, people still remembered the old gods who had looked after the mountain people since the dawn of time. In a Perthshire valley, the road to the sheilings passed the Tigh na Cailliche, the Cailleach's house. This was a rocky shrine perched above a little stream, the Allt na Cailliche. From its recesses were brought three large stones strangely shaped like squat figures. These were the Cailleach, the Old Woman, the Bodach (*bod*-ukh), the Old Man, and the Nighean

(*nee*-un), the Daughter. They were carefully carried to the stream to be washed and given offerings of the special Beltaine bannock, while their little "house" was reroofed with thatch. At the end of summer the family of stones was put back inside and their house winterproofed with moss to keep them warm and dry in the coming season. These rites ensured the Cailleach's protection of their livestock and crops. Even though the time of the sheilings is long past, the Cailleach's house and the family of stone is there to this day. A solitary shepherd still tends the little shrine.

When they reached the sheilings, the men repaired the summer bothies, while the women kindled fires and prepared a special feast of a male lamb, "without spot or blemish," that had been killed earlier that day as a ritual sacrifice. Now their summer home was ready. By day they watched the flocks, milked the cows, churned butter and made cheese, spun, and cooked. In the evenings the men walked up the hillside after work to join their families and tell stories, play music, and sing. The young men came to court the girls and dance with them beneath the summer stars, and this season was looked upon as "the happiest and best of the entire year."[4]

BLESSING FOR CLIPPING THE SHEEP

Go shorn and come woolly,
Bear the Beltaine female lamb,
Be the lovely Bride thee endowing,
And the fair Mary thee sustaining,
The fair Mary sustaining thee.
CARMINA GADELICA

SYLLABUB

In parts of Ireland the first milk of Beltaine was poured on the ground as an offering for the faeries. Next, for a real treat, the cow was milked straight into a bowl of whiskey, sherry, or mead for the frothy concoction known as syllabub—a breakfast that assured a merry start to May festivities! Here is a version that doesn't require access to a cow:

Ingredients
⅓ cup sherry
½ teaspoon amaretto liqueur (can substitute almond extract)
Juice and zest of 1 lemon
6 tablespoons sugar
2 cups heavy cream
12–18 amaretti cookies
6 wine or sundae glasses

Method
1. Put the sherry, liqueur or extract, lemon juice, zest, and sugar into a large mixing bowl.
2. Add the cream and whip until the mixture stands in soft peaks.
3. Crumble 2 or 3 cookies at the bottom of each glass. Spoon cream mixture on top.
4. Chill for several hours before serving.

Serves 6

BRINGING IN THE MAY

Summer! Summer! The milk of the calves,
And ourselves brought the summer with us,
The yellow summer, and the white daisy,
And ourselves brought the summer with us.
IRISH MAY SONG
(TRANSLATION FROM GAELIC)

May Flowers

Between sunset and sunrise at Beltaine, Irish children took to the fields to gather flowers as golden as the sun: primroses and cowslips, buttercups and furze blossoms, and above all, the luckiest plant of Beltaine, the marsh marigold. Yellow flowers were not just for decoration: as symbols of the life-giving sun, they were made into posies and tied to doors and windows, or their petals were scattered over the thresholds of house and byre as protection against the faeries, who were out in force at this turning point of the year. Some were kept for fragrant baskets that the children brought to the sick and elderly. In many parts of southwest Ireland, leafy branches of sacred trees were brought home from the woods, to the old rhyme:

Cuileann agus coll,
Trom agus cárthan,
Agus fuinseóg gheal,
Ó bhéal an átha.

Holly and hazel,
Elder and rowan,
and bright ash from beside the ford.[5]

Like the flowers, the boughs were hung around the house in profusion, making wood and stone appear to melt into the gold and green of a forest arbor, stirring memories of the first homes in the greenwood. Flowers were also for lovers, who wove them into wreaths to exchange as gifts. In Wales and Cornwall young men made posies and garlands and left them secretly on their girlfriends' doorsteps at night. Hawthorn and birch, both trees associated with love and sexuality, were favorites that would not fail to get the message across.

Creating a Fresh Flower Garland

This is a garland you can wear around your head at Beltaine celebrations or hang on a door to announce the arrival of summer.

Gather together

3 or 4 lengths of round reed (or any flexible natural material such as willow switches), 36 inches long

Natural raffia in 4-foot lengths

Ribbons, assorted colors: 1/8 inch wide, 8 feet long

A large bouquet of colorful spring flowers

Scissors

Method

Form reed or willow switches into a 6½-inch diameter circle. Secure the reed garland base by tying strands of raffia every three inches to create a sturdy, circular form.

1. Wrap the circle with a bundle of 4 strands of natural raffia.
2. To attach flowers: Cut flowers, leaving 2–3 inches of stem. Twine 2 strands of raffia around the circular base, overlapping the flower stems securely. Continue to overlap the flowers and wrapping the stems with raffia around the circle.
3. Fasten long strands of multicolored ribbon to the garland by folding them in half and tying them to the garland so that they hang down your back.

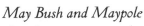

May Bush and Maypole

Another reason to gather branches was to make the May bush. A bough or clump of the tree, hawthorn being the most popular, was decorated with flowers, ribbons, paper streamers, and other bright scraps of material. Colored eggshells, carefully saved by the children from the Easter festivities, were threaded on string, and sometimes a golden ball was hung from the bush, perhaps representing the sun. Candles or rushlights were attached to it, and it was lit with all due ceremony at dusk on Beltaine Eve.

The family hung the May bush in a prominent position outside the house, but a bush for the whole community was set up at the crossroads. People also decorated a living tree if it grew in a central place. That evening everyone turned out in their finest to dance around the glowing bush or tree. Boys carrying green boughs and girls wearing garlands of flowers held hands and took part in a long serpentine dance around the May bush, as once their ancestors had circled around the Tree of Life at the center of an Iron Age settlement.

The maypole, that primary symbol of the returning growth and strength of the summer, was popular in the more English-influenced parts of Ireland and the British Isles, especially Wales and Cornwall. On May Eve in Wales, country people of all ages headed for the woods singing songs of May time and blowing loud horns. They felled a tall birch tree and hauled it back to the village on a wagon drawn by oxen. At sunrise, the young people decked their houses with the branches of May and the maypole was set up on the village green, bright with garlands of flowers and colored bows, rosettes, and ribbons. Now it was time for the *dawns y fedwen,* the "dance of the birch," to begin. The master of ceremonies tied a long streamer to the pole, and the dancers added theirs in turn. A fiddler or harper, who sat on a nearby mound or stone garlanded with oak boughs, struck up the tune, and the dancers began weaving in and out the age-old measure of "threading the needle." The day was given over to games, feasting, and revelry that lasted into the night, while spirits were kept merry with mead or the spiced honey wine known as *metheglin.* There were also plenty of ales and homemade elderberry and rhubarb wines, while a May drink of mead flavored with woodruff was a special treat. Here is a version made with wine:

May Cup

Woodruff is one of the sweetest smelling herbs; its scent is reminiscent of freshly mowed grass. As well as imparting a delicious flavor to drinks, it can be taken as a tea that has a reputation for dispelling "fits of melancholy."

Ingredients

1 bottle of white wine (nonalcoholic wine works fine)
Juice and grated rind of 1 lemon
Fresh organic strawberries, preferably wild
Bunch of fresh woodruff (dried for two days in a well-covered china bowl) or green-dried, whole woodruff leaves

Method

1. Add ⅓ bottle wine to the woodruff leaves.
2. Allow to steep for 1 hour.
3. Filter and add remaining wine. Flavor with lemon juice and rind.
4. Add sliced strawberries.
5. If you have fresh woodruff flowers, float them on top.

Mayers and Mummers

For we are up, as soon as it is day-o,
For to fetch the summer home,
the summer and the May-o,
For summer is a-coming in
and winter is a-gone.
CORNISH MAY SONG

An ancient rite of May throughout Europe is the welcoming of summer with processions through town and village streets. Bands of "Mayers" used to go to the woods and bring home flowers and leafy boughs to show the rest of the community that summer had indeed arrived. In return they received gifts of food or money. Those who failed to reward these messengers of summer were warned that their crops might fail and their animals sicken, for miserliness was dangerous to the well-being of the community: food, the substance of life, had to be circulated generously within the community so the circuit of life could be kept flowing. What was more, the Mayers were performing an important ceremony for their community and deserved to be rewarded: "the group *sees* spring before anyone else, *brings* it to the village, *shows* it to the others and *hastens* its coming with song, dance and ritual."[6]

As the primal energies of song, dance, and ritual hasten the passage of summer into the human community, processions in many parts featured musicians, dancers, and the masked characters known as mummers, or guisers. In Ireland girls and boys in colorful dress marched with a May bush, along with a terrifying-looking Fool and his wife; in North Wales an elaborate garland, the *cangen haf* (summer branch), was carried in procession by a character called the Cadi, a buffoon who was dressed as part male, part female and wore a hideous mask.[7]

But perhaps the most exciting May procession is associated with the fishing village of Padstow, Cornwall, because it still goes on every year, unadulterated by the modern world. The festival is dominated by a hobby-horse, known as the Obby Oss, a spectacular creature who looks more like a mythical beast than a horse, decorated in the Otherworld colors of black, red, and white. His "rider" wears a great hoop covered with a skirt of black

The Obby Oss cavorts through
the streets of Padstow on May Day.

tarpaulin and a ferocious mask over his face. He is led capering and cavorting through the streets to the pulsating rhythm of a huge drum, while Mayers dressed in white play music and dance through narrow streets thronged with hundreds of local people and tourists. Occasionally the Oss lunges into the crowd and captures a young girl beneath his skirt, guaranteed to get her either a husband or a baby in the coming year. Every now and then the Oss sinks to the ground in a ritual death, and the victorious song of summer that has made the town's rooftops echo dies into a mournful dirge. The next moment he has revived—the Earth is reborn after winter's death—and the procession surges on into the night. The relentless hypnotic drumbeat, the continual cycling of the horse's death and resurrection, the revelry and carousing in the pubs, which stay open all day, all combine to sweep us off our feet and plunge us into that swift-coursing current until we are no longer separate from the river of life:

Unite and unite and let us all unite
for summer is i-cumen today,
And whither we are going, we all will unite
in the merry morning of May.

MAKING A MAY BOUGH

Make this on May Eve and place on your altar, or use as a table centerpiece in your home.

Cut a small budding branch with a number of twigs from any of the Beltaine trees mentioned in the rhyme on page 139. Other flowering trees can be substituted according to what's available in your area, for example, hawthorn, crab apple, cherry, lemon, forsythia, or dogwood. Crush the bottom so that it will absorb water properly, and anchor it in water in a vase, using stones if necessary.

Take the blown colored eggs left over from Easter, or prepare some new ones with vegetable dye or paint. Double a thread the length you want to hang each egg, knot the ends, dab the knot with some glue, and thread through the hole at the small end of the egg. Let it dry, and hang the loop over a branch.

Make a wish, and tie a colored ribbon on the branch or twig for the spirit of Beltaine to work upon. If you are doing this with children, lay out a selection of colored ribbons and scissors for them to choose, and let each child make a wish and tie the ribbon on the bough by themselves.

May day! Delightful day!
Bright colors play the vale along.
Now wakes at morning's slender ray
Wild and gay the blackbird's song.

Now comes the bird of dusty hue,
The loud cuckoo, the summer-lover;
Branchy trees are thick with leaves;
The bitter, evil time is over . . .

Loaded bees with puny power
Goodly flower-harvest win;
Cattle roam with muddy flanks;
Busy ants go out and in.

Through the wild harp of the wood
Making music roars the gale—
Now it settles without motion,
On the ocean sleeps the sail.

Men grow mighty in the May,
Proud and gay the maidens grow;
Fair is every wooded heights;
Fair and bright the plain below . . .

Loudly carols the lark on high,
Small and shy his tireless lay,
Singing in wildest, merriest mood,
Delicate-hued, delightful May.

Irish, ninth century, translated
by T. W. Rolleston

HAWTHORN

⑥HE SACRED ⑥ROVE

A hundred years I slept beneath a thorn,
Until the tree was root and branches
of my thought,
Until white petals blossomed in my crown.
KATHLEEN RAINE

The hawthorn, once known simply as "May," is, naturally enough, the tree most associated with this month in many parts of the British Isles and Ireland. When we read of medieval knights and ladies riding out "a-maying" on May morning, this refers to the flowering hawthorn boughs they gathered rather than the month itself. For on this day the woods and hedges are alight with its glistening white blossoms—at least, this was usually the case before the calendar change, when May Day fell on May 13 or 14. Hawthorn is often found linked with lovemaking. In ancient Greece the wood was used for the marriage torch, and girls wore hawthorn crowns at weddings. Some find the sweet, musky scent from the flowers suggestive of sex.

Hawthorns are also sacred to the faeries who ride out into the human world when the gates of Beltaine open. Beltaine is known in Ireland as one of the three spirit nights of the year (the other two being the eves of Midsummer and Samhain, or Halloween). In Ireland hawthorns were known as the faeries' Trysting Trees and frequently grew on burial mounds or at crossroads and other thresholds to the Otherworld. An old woman from southwest Scotland recalled witnessing the Faery Ride when she was a girl in the eighteenth century, as she sat with a friend under a hawthorn bush at dusk on Beltaine Eve:

We had not been sitting long beneath the hawthorn-bush when we heard the loud laugh of people riding, with the jingling of bridles and the drumming of hoofs. We jumped up, thinking they would ride over us. We thought it must be drunk people riding to the fair in the evening. We gazed around, and saw it was the Faerie Ride. We cowered down till they passed by. A beam of light was dancing over them more bonny than moonshine. They were a wee wee folk with green scarves on, except for the one that rode in front, and that one was a good deal larger than the rest, with bonnie long hair bound about with a band that glittered like stars. They rode on lovely little white horses, with great long sweeping tails, and manes hung with bells that the wind played on. . . . Marion and me were in a broad meadow when they came past; a high hedge of hawthorn trees kept them from going through Johnnie Corrie's corn, but they leapt over it like sparrows, and galloped into the green meadow beyond.[8]

May brandy, said by some to be more delicious than the best cherry brandy, can be made with hawthorn flowers. Simply fill a wide-mouthed jar with hawthorn flowers, cover with brandy, and infuse for 2–3 months. Strain and rebottle.

THOMAS THE RHYMER

A famous ballad from Scotland tells the story of a poet who sat by a hawthorn known as the Eildon Tree and met the Queen of Elfland. Thomas the Rhymer, as he was known, actually lived in Earlston, a village near Berwick-on-Tweed, in the thirteenth century. His May-time encounter with the Otherworld brought him the gift of seership, which earned him a new name: True Thomas.

One bright morning in May Thomas the Rhymer took his harp to the Eildon Hills and sat beneath the flowering thorn. Sometimes he played and sometimes he slept, but always a queen came riding through his dreams. Between sleep and waking he saw her now, as she rode her white horse over the ferny brae:

> *Her skirt was of the grass-green silk,*
> *Her mantle of the velvet fine,*
> *And at every lock of her horse's mane*
> *Hung fifty silver bells and nine.*

Only this time, instead of vanishing when he rubbed his eyes, she was still there, looking up at him with a face like the hawthorn flower.

Thomas leaped to his feet, pulled off his cap, and made a deep bow.

"Hail, Lady, Queen of Heaven. Unworthy am I to look upon your beauty!"

A laugh like silver bells.

"That name does not belong to me, Thomas. I am queen of another country, and your music and your longing called me here. Play to me, Thomas, but be warned: if you kiss my lips, your body will belong to me alone."

A caution wasted on one who longed for her white blossom body and lips like hawthorn berries.

> *"Betide me well, betide me woe,*
> *That weird shall never daunt me."*
> *And he has kissed her rosy lips,*
> *All underneath the Eildon Tree.*

But in that moment her beauty withered like a winter leaf, and out of her shriveled face sprang teeth like thorns. Her gray eyes merged and became a dark pool in the center of her head. Her white body bent like a twisted tree, and the scent of hawthorn flowers, which smell of sex and death, smothered him so that he could not scream. Gnarled hands like ancient branches held him fast, and a dry voice creaked,

> "Now, you must go with me," she said,
> "True Thomas, you must go with me,
> And you must serve me seven years,
> Through weal and woe, as may chance to be."

> She mounted on her milk-white steed,
> She's ta'en True Thomas up behind,
> And aye, whene'er her bridle rang
> The steed flew swifter than the wind.

The Night Mare rode toward the hill, and Earth's body parted like a mist to let her mistress through. For three days and nights they waded through a river of blood without light from sun or moon. Bitter black it was, and all the time there was a roaring like the sea.

But at long last came daylight and cool sweet air and an orchard where fruit hung fragrant on the trees—apples, pears, damsons, and figs. Thomas, half dead and faint from hunger, reached a hand toward the brimming trees, but the Lady said, "Not one fruit may you eat in this land, Thomas, or you will never go home again. See here: I have brought you wholesome bread and wine from Middle Earth. Take your fill."

And as he ate, she sang to him of the way ahead:

> "Oh see you not yon narrow road,
> So thick beset with thorns and briers?
> That is the road to righteousness,
> Though after it but few enquires.

And see you not yon broad, broad road,
That runs across that lily leven?
That is the road to wickedness,
Though some call it the road to heaven.

And see you not that bonny bonny road
That winds across the ferny brae?
That is the road to fair Elfland
Where you and I this night must gae."

And off they set on the bonny, bonny road, and as soon as they entered the gates of her country the lady once more became a radiant beauty, richly dressed. But when Thomas started to speak she put her finger on his lips.

"Not one word must you speak in my land, Thomas," she said, "or never will you go home again."

But her last words were drowned by the river of music and dancers that flowed from the castle to greet them. Harp and lute, fiddle and psaltery swept them into the merry dance, and all the bright company whirled like stars in the summer night. Thomas found himself dressed head to toe in elfin clothes of velvet green, and for what seemed like three days and three nights there was minstrelsy and revelry and feasting without end. But suddenly the queen pulled Thomas away from the dance and spoke to him gravely.

"Thomas, it is time for you to leave."

"But I have been here only three days!" cried the rhymer.

"Yet three years have gone by on Earth," said the queen. "And tomorrow the devil will come for his fee, and I fear he means to take you! But because you have journeyed to the land where no time dwells, I give to you this gift: a tongue that can never lie."

Thomas looked alarmed:

"My tongue's my own," True Thomas said;
"A goodly gift you'd give to me!
I'll neither dare to buy nor sell,
At fair or tryst where I may be."

But his words rang hollow on a cold hillside, and Thomas found himself standing alone in a gray dawn beside an old thorn tree. And in that moment past, present, and future came rushing in toward him from all sides, and infinity made a home in his head. Thomas found himself running toward Earlston in green velvet shoes to tell what he had seen.

THE GREENWOOD MARRIAGE

Fosterer of tender lovers is May . . .
DAFYDD AP GWILYM

May has always been a merry month for lovers, when the swift current of the erotic impulse courses through leaf and vein. Fourteenth-century poet Dafydd ap Gwilym (*dah*-vith ahp *gwil*-im) wrote many poems in praise of the season of love, and the girls he wished to share it with, including a young nun:

Is it true, the girl that I love,
That you do not desire birch, the strong growth
*   of summer?*
Be not a nun in spring,

Asceticism is not as good as a bush.
As for the warrant of ring and habit,
A green dress would ordain better.
Come to the spreading birch,
To the religion of the trees and the cuckoo . . .[9]

For as well as supplying the village maypole, the birch woods became lovers' bowers, the setting for the "greenwood marriages" that so horrified the Puritans:

It was lovely, girl, for a moment
Leading our lives beneath the birch.
Fondling each other, more pleasurable it was,
sheltered together in the secluded wood,
co-mingling like sands of the sea . . .[10]

Every May Day, an age-old love triangle played out as the King of Summer fought the King of Winter for the hand of the May Queen. An old Welsh tale describes how Gwynn ap Nudd (*gwin* ahp *neeth*), King of Annwn (*ahn*-noon), the Welsh Underworld, fought Gwythyr son of Greidawl (*gwooi*-thur *gry*-dawl) for the hand of a beautiful maiden, Creiddylad (kry-*thuh*-lahd), every Calen Mai (May 1) until the day of doom. This cosmic battle used to be reenacted every year in parts of Wales and the Isle of Man. In Wales the men and young boys of the village formed two teams. The team representing winter was led by a captain dressed in a long coat and hat trimmed with fur. He carried a stout black-thorn stick and a shield studded with tufts of wool to represent snow, while his companions wore waistcoats of fur decorated with balls of white wool. The summer captain wore a white smock decorated with garlands of flowers and ribbons and a broad-brimmed hat trimmed with flowers and ribbons. He bore a willow wand wreathed with spring flowers and tied with ribbons. The mock battle commenced with the winter team flinging straw and wood at their opponents, who used birch branches, willow wands, and young ferns to beat them off. After a lot of horseplay, summer finally won the day. The victorious captain chose a man to be the May King, and the people nominated a May Queen, who was crowned and led back in triumph to the village.

The rivalry between an old man and a young for the hand of a summer-fair maiden has given rise to a number of beautiful Celtic love tales. One of the finest renditions of this ancient drama is a Welsh version of the romance of Tristan and Isolde.

HOW TRISTAN WON ESYLLT

Esyllt (*ess*-ihlt) had run away from her old graybeard husband, March ap Meirchion (*markh* ahp *mire*-khyon), to be with her beloved, young Tristan ap Trallwch (*truss*-tahn ahp *tra*-hlookh). The lovers wandered together as outlaws in the wood of Caledon all summer long. By day they learned the songs of the blackbird, and at night they slept upon a mossy bed in a house made of leaves, their arms and legs intertwined like the branches of the white birch trees. They were unaware that in his fury March had paid a visit to his cousin King Arthur, demanding vengeance for Tristan's insult and the return of his wife.

King Arthur consented and rode north at once with March and a company of armed men. They found the wood where the lovers lay and surrounded them, weapons at the ready. Esyllt heard the sound of trampling feet and loud voices and trembled in Tristan's arms till her lover awoke and asked her what was amiss.

"I hear the sound of my husband's voice and many men on horseback. I see the flash of sword and shield and fear it will be the end for you!" she wept.

Tristan arose, threw on his clothes, and went to meet March, sword in hand. Now Tristan had magic protection, for whoever drew blood from him was bound to die, and whomever he drew blood from was also doomed to death. March refused to fight him hand to hand for fear of losing his own life, and, seeing his cowardice, Arthur's men refused to lift their swords on his behalf. For now the lovers were safe, but March was beside himself with rage and demanded more effective action from the king. This time Arthur counseled March to send harpers and poets to play sweet music and sing Tristan's praises from afar. The beauty of their songs softened Tristan, and he agreed to accompany Arthur's chief peacemaker, Gwalchmai ap Gwyar (*gwalkh*-my ahp *gooy*-ahr), to the king's court to make a truce with March.

Arthur spoke to the old man and the young for many hours, but neither of them would agree to live without Esyllt. At last Arthur made his judgment:

"One of you shall have her while the leaves are on the trees, but when the leaves fall she must go with the other. And because you are her lawful husband, March ap Meirchion, you will have the choice."

March scratched his beard a moment and thought. His eyes gleamed lasciviously.

"Then I shall have her when the leaves have fallen, for it is then the nights are longest."

At that, Esyllt gave a broad smile and sang this *englyn:*

There are three fine trees in the greenwood,
The holly and ivy and yew;
they put forth leaves every season,
So Tristan shall have me the whole year through!

And so March ap Meirchion lost Esyllt for good, and the lovers fled back into the greenwood.

THE MANY LOVERS OF QUEEN MAEVE

Queen Medb (Maeve) was a strong-willed, independent woman who was the warrior-queen of Connacht. Dramatically beautiful, with a long pale face and flowing hair, she dressed in a red cloak and went about with a pet bird perched on one shoulder and a pet squirrel on the other. She was famed for her insatiable sexuality, being known as "Medb of the friendly thighs," and claimed that it took thirty-two men to satisfy her. She had countless lovers and boasted that she was "never without one man in the shadow of another." But she would only take a husband on three conditions—that he be without stinginess, without jealousy, and without fear. One of her husbands, Ailill, was continually coming upon Medb in compromising positions with her lover Fergus MacRoy—origi-nally Fergus Ro-ech (Great Horse)—who had enormous genitals. Finally, the cuckolded husband could stand no more. When he saw the lovers in a lake, and Medb sitting on Fergus's breast with her legs entwined around him, he had one of his warriors shoot Fergus through the heart with his spear.

Medb's name means "she who intoxicates" and is related to *mead,* which gives us a clue to her original identity. She is actually a humanized version of the Celtic goddess known as Sovereignty, who conferred upon a king the right to rule. She was an aspect of the land and its fertility, and to ensure the prosperity of the tribe, an Irish king had to ritually mate with her in a sacred marriage before he could be inaugurated. In stories connected with this rite, the Sovereignty goddess gave the king a special drink of red ale as a token of her acceptance of him as her consort. Medb was the wife of nine kings in succession, and no king was allowed to rule at Tara without mating with her first. Her promiscuity was not of the human variety, but a symbol of the fecund Earth itself.

The three with the lightest hearts:
a student after reading his psalms,
a young lad who has left off his boy's
clothes for good,
a maid who has been made a woman.

IRISH TRIAD

The fire of Beltaine brings the sleeping senses of winter to life. This is the time to celebrate your sensuality. On May Eve, whether you have a sexual partner or not, honor your body and delight your senses by filling the house with fragrant flowers and branches and enjoying sensual food and drink such as syllabub and May wine (recipe on page 145). Wear a May garland. Take a bath by candlelight and scent the water with essential oils.

Read love poetry out loud. Here are some Irish poems, ancient and modern. With the exception of the poem by Yeats, all the others are translations from the Gaelic, and it is highly worthwhile to learn to read them in the original language. (See "Resources" at the end of the book for learning Gaelic.)

LOVE EPIGRAM

The son of the king of the River Muad,
in midsummer,
found a maiden in a greenwood:
she gave him blackberries
from the bushes,
and as a love-token,
strawberries on a rush-tip.

TRANSLATED BY SEÁN O' FAOLÁIN[11]

SHE'S THE BLACKBERRY-FLOWER

She's the blackberry-flower,
the fine raspberry-flower,
she's the plant of best breeding
your eyes could behold;
she's my darling and dear,
my fresh apple-tree flower,
she is Summer in the cold
between Christmas and Easter.

ANONYMOUS

THE BLACKTHORN BUSH

*A hundred men think I am theirs
When I drink wine;
But they go away when I start to think
On your talk and mine.
Slieve O'Flynn is quiet, silent
With snowdrift's hush,
And my love is like sloe-blossom
On the blackthorn bush.*

TRADITIONAL IRISH SONG,
TRANSLATED BY JAMES CARNEY[12]

HE WISHES FOR THE CLOTHS OF HEAVEN

*Had I the heavens' embroidered cloths,
Enwrought with golden and silver light,
The blue and the dim and the dark cloths
Of night and light and the half-light,
I would spread the cloths under your feet:
But I, being poor, have only my dreams;
I have spread my dreams under your feet;
Tread softly for you tread on my dreams.*

W. B. YEATS[13]

DEAR BLACK HEAD

*Put your head, darling, darling, darling,
Your darling black head my heart above;
Oh, mouth of honey, with the thyme for fragrance,
Who, with heart in breast, could deny you love?
Oh, many and many a young girl for me is
      pining,
Letting her locks of gold to the cold wind free,
For me, the foremost of our gay young fellows;
But I'd leave a hundred, pure love, for thee!
Then put your head, darling, darling, darling,
Your darling black head my heart above;
Oh, mouth of honey, with the thyme for fragrance,
Who, with heart in breast, could deny you love?*

VERSION BY SAMUEL FERGUSON

MY HOPE, MY LOVE

*My hope, my love, we will go
Into the woods, scattering the dews,
Where we will behold the salmon, and the ousel in
      its nest,
The deer and the roe-buck calling,
The sweetest bird on the branches warbling,
The cuckoo on the summit of the green hill;
And death shall never approach us
In the bosom of the fragrant wood!*

ANONYMOUS (EIGHTEENTH CENTURY?),
TRANSLATED BY EDWARD WALSH[14]

GRVSTNVSHICIACIT
CVNOWORIFILIVS

HOLY GROUND
THE TRISTAN STONE
(CORNWALL, ENGLAND)

Iseult and Tristram—
. . . names of dust and fire!
CYRIL EMRA

The Arthurian romance of Tristan and
Esyllt has captured the imagination of
writers and artists for centuries, but fasci-
nating clues in the Cornish landscape suggest
there may be more truth to the old legends
than might be supposed. King March, or
Mark, had his royal court at Castle Dore
near the small riverside town of Fowey on
the south coast. Excavations of this small hill
fort, which stands on a ridge by an ancient
track leading to the sea, have revealed
timber structures dating from the fifth or
sixth centuries, showing it was the headquar-
ters of a significant chieftain. Within walking
distance stands the peaceful old church and
holy well of Saint Samson, originally built
over a sixth-century hermitage on the banks
of the River Fowey. Here Esyllt and Mark
came to make their devotions, and the queen
laid her gold silk gown upon the altar as an
offering.

Three miles from Castle Dore stands
Tristan's Stone, a seven-foot-high grave marker
set in a circular base. On one of its sides faint
letters can be discerned that read in Latin:
"Here lies Drustan son of Cunomorus."
Cunomorus is thought to be Kynvawr, a sixth-
century Cornish king who is identified with
King Mark. The inscription suggests that
Drustan (Tristan) was his son rather than his
nephew, as in the romance, so the theme of
the original story may have concerned the
classic triangle between father and son over

the father's second and younger wife, a theme well known in Greek tragedy.

The happiness of Tristan and Esyllt was short-lived. Fate decreed their separation from each another, and this stone seems to stand as mute witness to Tristan's lonely end, although in some versions of the tale the lovers were buried in one grave. Against the constant play of light and shadow over the Cornish coastline, the centuries dissolve, and it is easy to imagine the vague shapes of these tragic figures walking the land as they continue to play out the oldest story at love's command.

THE INNER CAULDRON
COMMUNION

Have not all nations had their first unity
from a mythology that marries them
to rock and hill?
W. B. YEATS

When we talk of love, our imagination usually stops short at romantic and sexual love between human beings. Because our lives are so cut off from the natural world, it is hard for us to experience a genuine connection with nonhuman forms of life, as our Celtic ancestors did. Nowhere is this tragic, self-

limiting tendency more eloquently expressed than by D. H. Lawrence:

Oh, what a catastrophe, what a maiming of love when it was made a personal, merely personal feeling, taken away from the rising and setting of the sun, and cut off from the magic connection of the solstice and equinox! This is what is the matter with us, we are bleeding at the roots, because we are cut off from the earth and sun and stars, and love is a grinning mockery, because, poor blossom, we plucked it from its stem on the tree of Life, and expected it to keep on blooming in our civilized vase on the table.

The love of all life has been termed *biophilia* by Pulitzer Prize–winning biologist Edward O. Wilson, who believes that human beings have an innate sensitivity to and need for other living things because we have coexisted in the closest relationship with the natural world for so many millennia. He defines biophilia as "the connections that human beings subconsciously seek with the rest of life."[15]

A beautiful Celtic image of deep connection with nature emerges from a story about

Fionn McCumhaill known as "The Man in the Tree." Fionn has gone in search of his mysterious servant, Dearg Corra (*jyar*-ug *kor*-ruh). He finds him at last sitting in a tree surrounded by creatures, engaged in what we would call today "interspecies communication." He has

> a blackbird on his right shoulder and in his left hand a white vessel of bronze, filled with water in which was a skittish trout and a stag at the foot of a tree. And this was the practice of the man, cracking nuts; and he would give half the kernel of a nut to the blackbird that was on his right shoulder while he would himself eat the other half; and he would take an apple out of the bronze vessel that was in his left hand, divide it in two, throw one half to the stag that was at the foot of the tree and then eat the other half himself. And on it he would drink a sip of the bronze vessel that was in his hand so that he and the trout and the stag and the blackbird drank together.[16]

This image with the tree, salmon, and cup bears some similarities to the scene at the center of the Otherworld in "How Cormac mac Art Went to Faerie." Here, at the spiritual heart of the Celtic cosmos, the source of all life is found in the ecology of water and trees: the Well of Wisdom and the Trees of Life. No static image here, the deepest Mystery dances with life and motion, and many interchanges take place: water flows, nuts fall, the salmon leap in a dynamic interplay. The well depends on the trees, and the trees must have the water of the well to survive.

A walk in any forest reveals the archetypal pattern of trees and water made palpable in the natural world, where they are partners linked in the dance of life. Streams and rivers are primary carriers of seeds, while flood and rain soften the earth for their bed. Water moistens the seed case then unlocks the dormant powers of growth within so that it unfurls into sprouts. Swirling rivers carry minerals down from mountains to nourish its roots. One tree in full foliage may consume a ton of water a day. Likewise, trees are guardians of water and soil. Their roots ensure that water from rain or snow is allowed to seep gradually into the earth to prevent erosion.

The ecology at the heart of the Otherworld is in perfect balance, but in our world, where we have ignored the importance of living in harmony with the life around us, our lack of biophilia is destroying the natural world and will ultimately destroy ourselves. To take just the example of trees and water: on deforested land, storms create terrible damage as they wash away topsoil, choke watersheds, and cause floods. Paradoxically, this can create water shortages later in the drier season, because there is often insufficient groundwater storage to keep springs, streams, and rivers supplied. Wildlife, of course, suffer, too: the clear-cutting of forests in the Pacific Northwest is destroying salmon and bird and animal habitats, and where the trees no longer form a shady canopy, water temperatures are rising and killing fish and insects in the rivers.

The early Celts held a profound awareness of kinship with the living world. We can learn from them how to return to a mutually beneficial relationship with the many forms of life that hover about us, pressing against the windows of our dreams, waiting patiently for the simple act of recognition: that we are here to share this planet in harmony together.

In Celtic tradition the poet-shamans were able to shape-shift into other forms of life to expand their consciousness. Amergin (*ah*-vir-gin), the poet of the Sons of Míl in Ireland, describes his experience in a famous incantation:

I am the wind that blows on the sea,
And I am the wave of the ocean,
I am the sound the sea makes,
I am the stag of seven tines,
I am the bull of seven fights,
I am the hawk upon the rock,
I am a teardrop of the sun.

I am the fairest of flowers,
I am the boar of boldness,
I am the salmon in the pool,
And I am the lake in the plain,
I am the word of skill,
I am the spear-point of battle.

I am the god who kindles fire in the head.
Who makes wise the company on the mountain?
Who foretells the ages of the moon?
Who knows the secret resting-place of the sun?

Amergin is describing the experience of a visionary ablaze with the ecstasy of inspiration. He is in the full throes of *imbas*, the "fire in the head," given to those who drink the waters of the Well of Wisdom or eat the hazelnuts of the Trees of Life. Like metal in the blacksmith's forge, his identity has become molten and is able to flow into many different forms. The following meditation shows us a way in which we can begin to feel more connected with other aspects of creation.

Meditation: Shape-Shifting

First, place your May bough in the center of your altar to symbolize the Tree of Life and the blossoming season of summer that Beltaine ushers in. A flowering plant or simply a vase of flowers is an alternative.

Close your eyes, and send your consciousness down through the room, down through the floor of the building, and down, deep down, into the earth. Be aware of the mass of rock that lies beneath the soil—shale, quartz, sandstone, granite; the black, white, and red—shot through with bands of minerals, darkly glittering; crystals that shine like stars within the stones.... Let your consciousness become one with the mineral kingdom. You might choose to become a mountain as old as the planet itself, once part of the seabed, thrown up by unspeakable forces now stilled, enormously, timelessly rooted in the earth, its head in the stars ... or a minute grain of sand, one among trillions and trillions, endlessly shifting, sifting, with the ocean tides ... or become a stone ... the stone people are alive, it's just that their hearts beat slower than ours....

Now become aware of the plant kingdom: algae and seaweed, forests of kelp, grasses blowing in a savanna wind, yellow and orange lichens on a rock in a wood, prickly pears, an oak wood, a rain forest blooming with delicate orchids, vines hanging with fruit.... Become one with the plant kingdom now—soft green moss on a rock by a stream, a mountain strawberry, a wild rose.... What does it feel like to be blown softly by the wind ... or to split your husk and feel your seeds fall to the ground?

And now become aware of the animal kingdom.... Listen to the voices of the wild: the roar of the tiger, the belling of the stag, the howl of the wolf; the cries of owls, and the tapping of woodpeckers, the whirring of birds' wings, the padding of soft paws.... Become one now with the animal kingdom, with the salmon leaping upstream, the fox gliding through the night, or the snake shedding its skin.... Feel what your new body is like and what it feels like to creep, walk, climb, run, or fly in free motion....

And now become aware of the human kingdom.... You are standing on two feet.... Notice how different that feels: you can stand like a stone, grow like a plant, move like an animal, but you can now create with your mind and your hands, and you can sing and dance and dream in your heart and make that dream real upon the earth. . . . And when you are ready, slowly open your eyes and come back to the room.

The next time you take a walk in nature, practice this "floating your consciousness" into the different life forms you encounter, from a blade of grass to a cloud in the sky. You will find this not only increases your appreciation and gratitude for the extraordinary universe we live in but also gives you a sense of belonging, which acts as a wonderful antidote to the loneliness that often accompanies urban life.

WINTER AND SUMMER

All the sweetness of nature was buried in black winter's grave,
and the wind sings a sad lament with its cold plaintive cry;
but oh, the teeming summer will come bringing life in its arms,
and will strew rosy flowers on the face of hill and dale.

In lovely harmony the wood has put on its green mantle,
and summer is on its throne, playing its string-music;
the willow, whose harp hung silent when it was withered in winter,
now gives forth its melody.
Hush! Listen! The world is alive!

THOMAS TELYNOG EVANS

MIDSUMMER MAGIC

Gay are the hills with song: earth's faery children leave,
More dim abodes to roam the primrose-hearted eve.
A. E.

At Summer Solstice light suffuses the northern lands as the sun reaches the height of its strength. In some parts of Scotland it is barely dark at midnight. Yet at the crowning point of light the seed of darkness is born, and from now on the nights will grow longer. The sun has touched the northernmost point along the horizon and is about to embark upon the long journey back south, ending at the Winter Solstice in mid-December.

Solstice means "standstill" and refers to the way that the sun appears to rise and set in the same place for a few days around June 20 and 21. In most parts of Europe the festival is celebrated on June 24 due to calendar changes and is known as the feast day of Saint John the Baptist.

Saint John was born six months before Christ, so his feast day is set exactly six months before Christmas. Before that, we have no name for this festival, which was clearly so important to the ancient inhabitants of the British Isles and Ireland. In the Celtic year it is almost as important as the four quarter days and is celebrated very much like an extension of Beltaine into the summer months.

The magical power of fire was especially important at midsummer. People lit bonfires to celebrate the sun at its height of power and implore it not to withdraw into winter's darkness. Fires ritually strengthened the sun to swell fruits and ripen grain, and it protected both humans and livestock from insect-borne disease. The festival began the night before Midsummer Day, according to the Celtic custom of starting a new day at dusk, hence the title of Shakespeare's magical play, *A Midsummer Night's Dream.*

When the festival began on Midsummer Eve, the countryside of Cornwall was covered with a spangled net of light that shone from bonfires on every peak and hilltop. Old people would count the distant fires and tell the future from the number they saw and the brightness of the blaze. Up on the hills dancers adorned with garlands and posies of flowers spun around the fire, and young men performed feats of daring such as jumping through the tall flames—perhaps to encourage the crops to leap up, too. When the flames died down to glowing embers, chains of dancers skipped through them, being careful not to break the chain, which would bring bad luck. In Penzance boys paraded through the town with blazing torches, whirling them in circles around their heads like wheels of fire. Beyond the town farmers carried bunches of burning gorse sunwise around the cattle folds, passing the smoke over the cows. Embers or charred fragments of wood were brought home and placed on the hearth. Some people kept the cinders or ashes in the house to bring good luck. Others believed they would ensure a peaceful death to ailing old people. They also mixed them with water for a medicinal drink. The next day was a holiday celebrated with fireworks and other amusements.

After it was almost extinct, Cornwall's midsummer bonfire tradition was successfully revived during the 1920s, and it continues to be a popular festival. Music is often provided by the local brass band, who haul their instruments up the winding paths to celebrate the sun's power with the blare of trumpets and saxophones.

The long evenings brought people out to dance in the streets. Girls put on their white dresses and decorated them with laurel leaves before setting forth to dance with brothers or lovers. In some towns people joined hands and wove through the streets in long, serpentine dances with names like Threading the Needle and the Snail Creep. This latter dance involved the leader taking the linked dancers around and around into an ever-decreasing spiral, ending with everyone bunched together in the middle. When the leader was the brass band in its entirety, this was quite an experience! At this point, the dance was unwound all the way out again, guided by boys who directed the traffic by waving green leafy boughs. The spiral is a symbol particularly associated with the solstices, and it may be that these ancient dances mimic the pattern of the sun as it continually moves from its point of contraction at the center of the spiral at Winter Solstice to its point of expansion at Summer Solstice and back again.

In Wales and the west country groups gathered to perform the ancient ritual of rolling a blazing wheel down a hillside to emulate the journey of the sun. In the vale of Glamorgan, in southern Wales, a cartwheel was covered with straw and set on fire. The crowds watched anxiously as the wheel hurtled down to the bottom of the hill. If the flames went out, there would be a poor harvest ahead, but if it continued to burn vigorously, cheers broke out because this guaranteed an excellent yield. There are many examples of the spoked wheel as a symbol of the sun in early European art.

In Ireland there were similar solstice fire customs and perhaps an even greater awareness of the supernatural aspect of this time. Midsummer Eve was known as one of the three spirit nights of the year, the other two being at Beltaine and Samhain. In places where the faery faith was strong, people saw faeries joining in the festivities, mingling with the human revelers. At Cnoc Áine (now Knockainey), County Limerick, the sacred hill of the faery queen Áine, faeries were said to emerge from every *lios* and *rath* throughout Ireland bearing lighted torches in her honor. Faeries and humans walked in procession up the hill to light a huge bonfire. At the end of the festivities Áine herself emerged from the dying flames bearing a blazing torch and led the way back down to the village with the villagers behind her.

GODS OF THE CELTS: ÁINE

Áine (*aw*-nyuh), whose name means "Brightness," may have been a goddess of the sun, for her funeral was said to be at midsummer, the date that marks the decline of the sun's power. In Gaelic the word for sun is *grian* (*gree*-un), a feminine noun. In the nineteenth century many families living around Cnoc Áine claimed direct descent from the faery queen. They spoke of her in near-human terms as "the best-hearted woman that ever lived."

One midsummer in the nineteenth century, no torches were lit on the way up the hill out of respect for a local man who had just died. But the villagers noticed that the faeries' torches burned with exceptional brightness as if to compensate, while Áine herself led the way directing the whole proceedings. On another occasion a number of girls had stayed late on the hill, playing and generally having fun, when suddenly Áine appeared among them. She thanked them for honoring her but said she now wished them to go home since her Otherworld friends wanted the hill to themselves. As a favor, she let some of them look through her ring, through which the entire hill could be seen thronged with the faery host. Áine is also found in other regions of Ireland, for example, at Dún Áine, now Dunany, in Louth, and Lissan in Derry. Within another hill called Cnoc Áine, at Teelin, Donegal, she has a beautiful faery palace in which she passes her time "spinning the sunbeams and making gold cloth of the thread."[1]

HOLY GROUND
CALLANISH
(LEWIS, OUTER HEBRIDES, SCOTLAND)

The magnificent standing stones of Callanish stand on the bleak moorlands of the Hebridean island of Lewis. Four rows of stones lead into a circle from the four directions, forming a Celtic cross in the landscape. Like both Stonehenge and the Ring of Brodgar on

Orkney, Callanish is a megalithic astronomical observatory aligned to the solstice sunrises and sunsets as well as to the sun's equinoctial movements. It is an evocative place to spend Midsummer Eve when the sun sets late into the night, and the jagged stones look like frozen dancers silhouetted against an endless red sky.

The stones are steeped in a legendary history, which may hold tantalizing pieces of the truth. In the seventeenth century locals told a travel writer that it was a temple for "heathenism," where the chief druid stood at a large central stone and addressed the assembled people. One legend tells that the stones were brought to Callanish in many ships, accompanied by priests, a priest-king, and a gang of black men who erected the stones. The priests wore cloaks of colored feathers, and the chief priest always appeared with wrens flying around him. (The wren was traditionally the druids' bird.) As late as the nineteenth century certain local families were said to be "of the stones." Though ministers expressly forbade visits to old stones on old festival days, they went in secret, "for it would not do to neglect the stones."[2]

The cuckoo is said to perch on one of the Callanish stones at Beltaine and call the people to celebrate summer's return. At sunrise on Summer Solstice, she returns to be the herald of the "Shining One" who walks up the long stone avenue—the beams of the midsummer sun.

CALLANISH

Callanish, I saw you standing 'gainst the sky
Where the shores of lost Atlantis once rose high,
Where the embers of the sunset glow and die.

Ancient race of frozen dancers, worn and thin,
Waiting always for the music to begin,
Hearing only seagulls' voices in the wind.

On Beltaine Eve the villagers would stand,
And watch the cuckoo fly between your span,
To welcome back the summer to the land.

Are the old ones' superstitions really true?
Are you here to let the life-force be renewed?
Can the night fall on such shining ones as you?
M. F.

THE MAGIC OF HERBS

I have gathered luss
At the wane of the moon,
And sucked its sap
With a yewen spoon.
The Herb Leech, JOSEPH CAMPBELL

The sky over Land's End is streaked with red, and in the graying dusk the surrounding hills come alive with flickering points of orange light. It was a steep climb through grass and heather wet with yesterday's rain. You are grateful for your seat on one of the big gray boulders. Before you looms the jagged silhouette of the waiting stack of brushwood, gorse, and empty cardboard boxes. But before it can be lit, one more thing has to be done. Out of the shadows steps a figure in white bearing a huge sheaf of herbs and flowers, tied with ribbons of many colors. It is the Lady of the Flowers. First in English, then in the ancient Cornish tongue, she recites the blessing:

In one bunch together bound
Flowers for burning here are found
Both good and ill.
Thousandfold let good seed spring
Wicked weeds, fast withering,
Let this fire kill!

The flowers are tossed onto the waiting pyre. The flames roar into life and greedily devour their sacrifice. You cannot help but rise to your feet and add your voice to the great cheer that goes up all around. It feels good to be part of a chain of light that links you both to the land and to the people of an almost-forgotten past.

The Lady of the Flowers plays a vital part in the modern Cornish midsummer bonfire celebrations. We don't know how traditional this figure is, but similar customs have taken place in many areas of the British Isles and Ireland for centuries. In nineteenth-century Wales girls with bunches of three or nine different kinds of flowers joined hands with boys who wore flowers in their buttonholes and hats. Together they jumped over the midsummer fire, then threw all their flowers into the heart of the flame for good luck and to honor the sun, symbolized by the fire itself. A woman who longed for a husband made a wreath of nine different kinds of flowers. Walking backward, she threw it behind her, hoping it would catch on the branch of a tree. The number of times it fell to ground showed the years she would be unmarried.

Midsummer was the traditional time to cull magical plants and healing herbs, which were at their most potent at this time of the year. Although herbalists used countless herbs for medicinal purposes, ordinary people swore by a particular five or seven, which differed according to region. Here are five of the most common Celtic sacred plants associated with midsummer:

St. John's Wort

This golden, star-shaped flower was first of all herbs to be gathered on Saint John's Eve. Called the "blessed plant" in Wales, it was renowned throughout the Celtic lands for bringing peace and prosperity to the house, health to the animals, and a bountiful harvest. It was cast into the midsummer bonfires in Scotland and placed over the doors of houses and farm buildings for protection. Saint Columba himself used it for healing, applying it in the armpit, where its properties could be absorbed into the skin. This is probably why Highland men and women wore it in their undershirts on Midsummer Eve to keep evil faeries away. It was most efficacious if gathered at midnight and plucked in a ritual manner with an incantation:

St. John's Wort, St. John's Wort,
. . . I will pluck thee with my right hand,
I will preserve thee with my left hand.
Whoso findeth thee in the cattle-fold
Shall never be without kine.[3]

Vervain

Vervain is more commonly known as verbena, a slender plant with spikes of tiny blue flowers. Called the "holy herb" or "enchanter's plant," it enjoyed a reputation as one of the greatest sacred plants of the druids, who used it to foretell the future. In Wales it was traditionally gathered at the rising of the Dog-star, "without having been looked upon by the sun or moon."[4] A libation of honey was poured on the ground all around. Only the left hand was to be used in digging it up, and the plant was immediately waved above the head of the digger. An infusion of vervain in water was sprinkled over the tables and floors of the banqueting halls and upon the cushions of royal apartments. Ordinary people hung it in the house and sewed it inside their babies' clothes to keep evil spirits away. Vervain and St. John's wort worn together provided infallible protection on Midsummer Eve. In a Scottish ballad, a demon lover pleaded in vain with a young girl to lay aside her protective garland and go with him:

If thou hope to be a Lemman of mine
Lay aside the St. John's grass and the Vervine.

Yarrow

In Ireland yarrow with its creamy white umbrels of tiny flowers was known as "the herb of seven cures." It was another plant dedicated to Saint John that was hung up in the house on Midsummer Eve. In Scotland women picked it to the following incantation, translated from the Gaelic: "I will pick the smooth yarrow that my figure may be sweeter, that my lips may be warmer, that my voice may be gladder. May my voice be like a sunbeam, may my lips be like the juice of the strawberry. . . ."[5]

When Irish women went on a journey they would pick ten stalks of yarrow, throw one away as a tithe for the faeries, and put the other nine in their stockings, under the heel of the right foot, for protection.

Yarrow was also used in divination. At midsummer girls danced around it singing,

Good morrow, good yarrow, good morrow to thee,
Send me this night my true love to see.
The clothes that he'll wear, the color of his hair,
and if he'll wed me.

In the Hebrides people believed it could bestow *an dà shealladh*, the "sight of two worlds" or "second sight," when held over the eyes.

Fern

Fern was a bridge between the human and faery kingdoms. A Cornish folktale describes how a young woman was listlessly pulling fronds of fern as she sat resting by the wayside. Suddenly a faery appeared and told her that his wife had just died and he was searching for someone to look after his little son. She consented to come with him to faeryland, and the contract was sealed when she kissed a fern leaf. Fern seed had special properties when gathered on Midsummer Eve. If it was culled before it touched the ground, it could make you invisible.

Mugwort

Mugwort, an undistinguished-looking plant with small brown flowers, is as famous for its healing properties as St. John's wort throughout the British Isles and Ireland. In fact, its Welsh name is *llysiau Ieuan*, "John's herb." After it was picked it was purified and strengthened in the smoke of midsummer bonfires. Then it was hung up over the doors of house and barn and also made into garlands. Those who had sick family members at home singed it in the flames and took it back for the patient to inhale the smoke. A legend from southwest Scotland tells of a young man who sat by the shore lamenting his sweetheart who was almost dead of consumption. A mermaid appeared and sang to him:

Wad ye let the bonnie May die in your hand,
And the mugwort flowering i' the land?

He gave her the juice of the mugwort, and
she recovered.

A Midsummer Herbal Bouquet

1. Choose any *nine* of the following sacred
   plants and leaves, as availability allows:

roses	fennel	rowan leaves
foxgloves	clover	mistletoe
St. John's wort	oak leaves	vervain
elderflowers	broom	valerian
wild hops	meadowsweet	sage
agrimony	wormwood	mallow
rue	hedge mustard	elecampane
mugwort	yarrow	

2. Don't let them come into contact with iron.
3. Tie them with ribbons of the following
   colors and symbolism:

Color	Symbolism	Cornish
White	strength	*nerth*
Green	wisdom	*skyans*
Blue	love	*kerensa*
Red	sacrifice	*sacryfys*
Yellow	the sun	*an howl*

4. Give them to friends, display them on
   your altar, or hang them over the door.

5. If you have a garden, tie them together
   with samples of weeds that cause you the
   most trouble, and burn the whole sheaf
   ceremonially in a bonfire while chanting
   the rhyme on page 174.

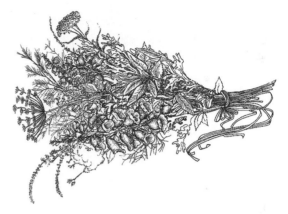

An Herbal Amulet

To make a protective herbal amulet to wear
or carry with you, gather three or nine of the
following before sunrise on Midsummer Day:

lavender	nettle	thyme
chamomile	ground ivy	rue
St. John's wort	comfrey	mugwort
vervain	clover	rose petals
yarrow	woodruff	plantain

Hang or spread out to dry in a cool dark
place. When they are dry, crumble them and
fill a small cloth pouch. Tie with a red thread.

AIRMID'S CLOAK

An early Irish story tells how the ancient knowledge of herbal medicine was lost. When Núadu (*noo*-uh-thuh), the king of the Tuatha Dé Danann, lost his hand in battle, Dían Cécht (*jee*-un *kyaykht*), the gods' physician, fashioned a new one from him out of silver. But Dían Cécht's son, Míach (*mee*-ukh), was more skilled than his father. He made Núadu a hand of flesh so that he was made whole. In a jealous fury, Dían Cécht struck his son three times with his sword; but three times Míach healed himself. The fourth time, Dían Cécht sliced through his brain, and he died. When he was buried, three hundred and sixty-five herbs grew from his grave, corresponding to the number of his joints and sinews. Míach's sister, Airmid (*ar*-i-vith), uprooted them carefully and spread them out on her cloak according to their properties. But Dían Cécht came along, and mixed them all up "so that no one knows their proper healing qualities unless the Holy Spirit taught them afterwards."

Mise Miach, mac an athar
a mharaigh mé agus
a mhill an cnuasach
a rinne Airmhidh.
Tá beatha agus sláinte
i ngach ball de mo chorp,
scaipthe anois, ag fás
ar fud gleannta is sléibhte.
Is méanar don té
a chuirfeas in ord
is in eagar mé.

I am Miach, son of the father
that killed me and
ruined the gathering
that Airmid made.
Life and health
are in every part of my body,
scattered now, growing
across valleys and mountains.
Fortunate the one
who can put me
to rights again.

DENNIS KING

BLODEUWEDD

In a Welsh tale from the *Mabinogi*, the magician Gwydion (*gwuh*-dyon) makes a wife for the hero, Lleu (*hluh*-ee), out of flowers. She is named Blodeuwedd (blo-*duh*-ee-weyth), Flower Face. Welsh poet Robert Graves reconstructed a medieval poem to tell her tale:

Not of father nor of mother
Was my blood, was my body.
I was spellbound by Gwydion,
Prime enchanter of the Britons,
When he formed me from nine
    blossoms,
Nine buds of various kind:
From primrose of the mountain,
Broom, meadow-sweet and cockle,
Together intertwined,

From the bean in its shade bearing
A white spectral army
Of earth, of earthly kind,
From blossoms of the nettle,
Oak, thorn and bashful chestnut—
Nine powers of nine flowers,
Nine powers in me combined,
Nine buds of plant and tree.
Long and white are my fingers
As the ninth wave of the sea.[6]

Blodeuwedd

MORE USES FOR HERBS

Faery doctors and herbalists used plants and herbs to treat a vast array of physical and psychological disorders. Herbs proved invaluable in many other areas of everyday life, too, from early times onward. Here are some examples:

Floor coverings: Sweet-scented herbs were strewn over floors, creating far more fragrant and hygienic carpeting than we have today! Woodruff and sweet flag were favorites among the early Celts, who also sprinkled infusions of flower-scented water over rushes on the floor. In the Hebrides, meadowsweet, bogmyrtle, and fleabane were used until quite recently on croft floors.

Dyes: The flowers, stems, leaves, and roots of native plants and trees were used in dyeing cloth. Among these were:

bracken	yellow-green
sorrel	red
agrimony	fawn
heather tops	bright yellow
madder root	bright red

The early tribes in Ireland and Britain also cultivated woad, whose leaves yield an indigo dye that was used both for cloth and for tattooing the body. The early tribes of Scotland, the Picts (from Latin *Picti*, Painted Ones), painted their bodies with fierce animal designs in woad to appear more terrifying in battle.

Flavorings for food and drink: Mead and beer were spiced with many combinations of sweet briar petals, violet flowers, sweet marjoram, agrimony, bugloss, fennel, and caraway. Saffron, the blue crocus that gives a deep yellow dye, was used both for the traditional Irish saffron tunic and for coloring food. It still grows wild in parts of Cornwall, famous for its saffron buns.

Cosmetics: The early Celts were very concerned with their appearance. Chieftains bathed regularly and anointed themselves with oil and sweet-scented herbs. Women wore eye shadow, lip coloring, and rouge made from elderberries and other natural dyes. Lavender, roses, and other flowers provided perfumes for the skin and also scented the breath. For washing hair, a compound of herbs and spices in vinegar was added to an infusion of birch twigs in soft water and then was scented with rose petals. Flowers mixed with beeswax and lanolin from sheep's wool made pomades for the hair.

In a story from the fifteenth-century Irish *Book of Lismore,* an herbal bath is used for magical purposes. Two noblewomen beg Caoilte, Fionn McCumhaill's steward, for help in restoring their husbands' affections. Caoilte "brought the full of his right hand of potent faery herbs with him, such as he knew were used by the chief women of the Fenians, and he gave them to the women and they made a bath thereof, and bathed therein, and this brought back the love of their husbands on them."[7]

Skin lotions: Simple facial and body lotions were made by steeping herbs and flowers in warm milk, whey, or buttermilk. Meadowsweet, elderflowers, and thyme were among the most popular. The mixture was frequently sweetened with honey and thickened with oatmeal or bran.

Elderflower Lotion

This old folk recipe cools, cleanses, and softens the skin.

Method
1. Heat a handful of elder blossoms (stripped from the stalks) in 1½ cups of buttermilk until warm. Do not boil.
2. Keep on a low heat for about 30 minutes, covered, until the flowers soften.
3. Remove from heat, and allow to steep for three hours.
4. Reheat and add 1 ounce white honey, stirring well.
5. Cool and pour into a bottle or screw-top jar.

Broiled Salmon with Honey and Herbs

Every Saint John's Eve, the salmon fishermen of Port Ballintrae in County Antrim hold a famous community salmon dinner, which is considered the big event of the year. On the menu is fish soup, freshly caught salmon, new potatoes, and Bushmills whiskey. Salmon has been a prized food in Ireland from earliest times, whether roasted on a spit, boiled in a cauldron, or broiled on a gridiron. In the old tale, "The Wooing of Finnabair," King Ailill and Queen Medb of Connacht broil a salmon for the young chief, Fráech, with honey "well-made by their daughter, the Princess Finnabair." The king and queen would have basted the fish with a mixture of honey and salt, as in the following recipe, in which the salmon is served with a sauce of fresh summer herbs:

Ingredients
4 salmon steaks
¼ cup honey
1 teaspoon salt
For the herb sauce
4 tablespoons fresh dill
4 tablespoons fresh chives
4 tablespoons fresh parsley
4 tablespoons butter
Juice of 1 lemon

Method

1. Finely chop the herbs and add to lemon juice and melted butter in a small saucepan. Set aside.
2. Heat the honey with the salt until dissolved.
3. Brush the salmon steaks liberally with honey-salt mixture on both sides.
4. Grill steaks under broiler or on barbecue grill, turning once so that both sides brown. (Test for doneness with a fork: the flesh in the middle of the salmon must be opaque.)
5. When the salmon is almost done, bring the herb and butter mixture slowly to a boil, stirring.
6. Serve the salmon with sauce on the side.

Sláinte an bhradáin! (*slawn*-chuh uh *vrod*-awn)
The health of the salmon!
AN IRISH TOAST

FAERIES

*Where the water whispers mid
the shadowy rowan-trees
I have heard the Hidden People like
the hum of swarming bees:
And when the moon has risen and the brown
burn glisters grey
I have seen the Green Host marching
in laughing disarray.*
FIONA MACLEOD

On calm summer evenings in Ireland the faeries go hunting. The air is full of the faint sound of horns, the baying of hounds, the galloping of horses, and the cracking of whips. Their flight sounds like the humming of a swarm of bees.

Not so long ago, the fact of the faery race was taken for granted in the Celtic countries, as spirits are in most nonindustrial societies throughout the world. In Ireland they were known as the *aes sídhe*, literally, "the people who live in a mound." Once, it is said, they were the Tuatha Dé Danann, the race of gods who lived in Ireland and were defeated by the invading Milesians, the ancestors of the Irish people. Amergin, poet and judge of the newcomers, divided Ireland in two. While the Milesians would reign above ground, he allowed the Tuatha Dé Danann to live in the "hollow hills," the prehistoric burial mounds that dot Ireland's countryside today. As they prepared to depart, Manannán mac Lir gave them the gift of the *féth fiada* (*feyth fee*-uh-thuh), a magic mist or veil that made them invisible to human eyes. This is why they can be seen only at those special times and places when the veil between the worlds is thin.

A twelfth-century Irish poem describes the *aes sídhe* as a fiercely beautiful race of warriors:

THE HOSTS OF FAERY

White shields they carry in their hands,
With emblems of pale silver;
With glittering blue swords,
With mighty stout horns.

In well-devised battle array,
Ahead of their fair chieftain
They march amid blue spears,
Pale-visaged, curly-headed bands . . .

No wonder though their strength be great:
Sons of queens and kings are one and all;
On their heads are
Beautiful golden-yellow manes.

With smooth comely bodies,
With bright blue-starred eyes,
With pure crystal teeth,
With thin red lips . . . [8]

Faeries, however, are not all of the Dé Danann race, and they come in many forms. Those who have seen them might describe them as anything from a tall, graceful people to a passel of ugly hobgoblins, with many shapes and sizes in between. There are solitary faeries, like the household brownie who looks like a stocky little man with a gray beard, and the delicate watershee that haunts the marshes. Then there are those that W. B. Yeats called "trooping faeries" who band together and spend their time dancing, singing, and feasting in the faery mounds. There are also fearsome spirits such as the Púca (*poo*-kuh), a black goat with wicked horns, and the Ban-Sidh (*ban*-shee), whose piercing wail prophesies death. None of them, it needs to be said, bears any resemblance to the little boys and girls with butterfly wings so beloved of Victorian illustrators.

Other Celtic countries are as populous with faeries as Ireland. In Wales they are known as the Tylwyth Teg or Fair Family, who play in the meadows, leaving faery rings where they have danced. Cornwall has its Piskies, who have red hair, pointed ears, and turned-up noses. On the Isle of Man lives the Fenodyree, a hairy spirit so strong he can harvest a field of wheat in one night. Now that he is no longer seen, there is a saying: "There has not been a merry world since Fenodyree lost his ground!"

HOW TO ADDRESS A FAERY

Faery, or *fairy*, comes from the Latin word for the Fates: *fata*. This generic word conceals the vast number of names the Celts had for the many and varied inhabitants of the Otherworld. Here are a few of the more common ones:

Language		Pronunciation	Meaning
Irish Gaelic	*daoine sídhe* or *aes sídhe*	*dee*-nya shee or ees shee	people of the mound
	sídhe (modern Irish: *sí*)	shee	short for *aes sídhe*
	sídheog (modern Irish: *síóg*)	*shee*-oge	a single faery
Scottish Gaelic	*daoine sìth*	*duh*-nyuh shee	people of the mound
	sìthiche	*shee*-i-huh	a single faery
Welsh	*tylwyth teg*	*tuh*-loo-ith teg	Fair Family
Manx	*ferrish*	*feh*-rish	a single faery
Cornish	*Pobel Vyghan*	pobble *vee*-an	Little People

However, most country people would never dream of referring to faeries by anything other than a polite euphemism for fear of attracting the wrong kind of attention. Instead, they called them the Good People, the Gentry, the People of Peace, or, simply, Themselves.

So the answer to the question "How do you address a faery?" is: "With great respect."

THE GIRL WHO DANCED WITH THE *SÍDHE*

Not far from Tuam in the west of Ireland stands the great hill of Knockmaa, the home of Finvarra, King of the Connacht faeries. Below the hill is a stone castle that you can still see today. Now it is all in ruins and covered with ivy, but long ago there once lived in it a young servant girl called Kathleen who could see things no one else could see and hear things no one else could hear. The faeries loved her, and by night they would carry her away to the faery fort on the top of the hill. Most of all she was loved by Finvarra himself, who wanted nothing more than to make her his queen.

One Midsummer Eve, Kathleen put on a white gown and wove into her hair the flowers of the foxglove, the *lus na mban sídhe*, the herb of the faery woman. She left behind the lights and the laughter of the ball that was taking place in the castle hall and slipped out into the cool air. She had her own celebrations to attend.

On the faery fort, a host of strange figures began to take shape by the light of the rising moon. There were pixies and nixies and dwarves in gray coaties; hobbits and hobgoblins as big as my thumb. There were little men dressed in bright green suits with sky blue jackets and three-cornered hats, all tripping in with their ladies, decked in lace and silver bells. There was the leprechaun and the cluricaun, the faery shoemakers, sitting on a tree stump, stitching and singing as they sewed:

> *Big boots for hunting,*
> *Sandals in the hall,*
> *White for a wedding-feast,*
> *Red for a ball.*

Their needles went flying in and out like silver fish, as scarlet leather was sewn together and silver buckles shone bright.

In a circle sat the brownies, who visit poor cottages to entertain old folks with their merry pranks. They fill the air with the fragrance of flowers and sweet melody, and they grind corn and cut wood for a bowl of cream left on the doorstep at night. In spring they shake the tree buds open, help the corn to ripen, and make all green things to grow.

And a host of sprites no bigger than harvest mice, decked in green jacket, red cap, and white owl's feather, came swooping down like starlings, landing in the meadowsweet and startling a group of young faeries, who ran and sheltered behind dock leaves and ragwort stalks. Then in came Jackie-My-Lantern, Kit o' the Candlestick, and a hundred will-o'-the-wisps, bearing little lamps that seemed to bob and float like moons to light the dancing green.

On a small mound sat the musicians, faery fiddlers sawing away like grasshoppers, playing hornpipes and strathspeys, slip-jigs and reels. There were pipers that called down the songs of the wind on the mountain and the faery harper who could weave from his harp melodies like running water. But the faery music also brought, crawling and creeping from underneath rocks and out of damp caves, the stranger and not-so-beautiful inhabitants of Faerie. If you had looked closely in the shadows that night, you might have seen gringes and gallybeggars, Dick-a-Tuesdays, Jack-in-the-Wads, and even Jenny Greenteeth herself. Grogans and gruagachs, spriggans and spunkies, boggles and bogies and bugaboos that make strange noises in the night, howl pitifully, then laugh, cause great flame and sudden lights, fling stones and rattle chains, open doors and shut them, hurl down platters, stools, and pails, sometimes appearing in the likeness of hares, crows, or large black dogs . . . Sili Ffrit and Sili-Go-Dwt and Lob-Lie-by-the-Fire . . .

And up from the shores came the sea people, gentle merrows like beautiful girls with flowing hair and dark eyes but with fishes' tails and little webs between their fingers; kelpies riding the waves like water horses; and selkies, who are seals in the sea but who on land take off their skins and become human women. But loveliest of all were the Lordly Ones, tall shining faeries with gold bands about their brows, who moved like light on water, aquamarine and silver. All the faery host came to dance on the hill, and dance they did, as light as summer leaves, "footless and wild like birds of paradise."

Kathleen stood shyly watching them. Then out of the spinning dancers stepped Finvarra, the Lordly One, coming toward her, a gold light around his head. He whirled her into the dance, and when she looked at his face she suddenly knew she would never have to leave again. . . .

. . . and there she must be dancing still, for in the morning they found her lying dead on the hill, a smile upon her face and foxgloves in her hair. They buried her in the churchyard and raised the cross above her. But there are some who still see lights on Knockmaa every Saint John's Eve and hear the faint music of fiddle and pipes. They usually make the sign of the cross and walk as fast as they can away from Castlehackett and down the road to Tuam.

FAERY DWELLINGS

In Tír-n'an-Og,
In Tír-n'an-Og,
The blackbird lilts, the robin chirps,
the linnet wearies never,
They pipe to dancing feet of Sídhe
and thus shall pipe for ever.
ETHNA CARBERY

In the Celtic landscape are many thresholds to the secret country of the faeries. For rather than being located in an abstract region beyond the sky, the Otherworld intersects our world everywhere. It can be found beneath the earth, under ancient barrow mounds where the bones of the ancestors lie, in caves, and in mountains. Or it can be seen on summer evenings as you stand on the shore looking westward at the cloud-islands on the horizon. You might discover its gates at a lone tree or standing stone or by spending the night at a holy well. An unwitting step into a faery ring or onto an innocent-looking clod of earth known in Ireland as the "stray sod" might whisk you away to a land of extraordinary and unearthly beauty—not to mention danger for the unprepared.

This land has many lyrical names that hint of its delights: Tír na nÓg (*cheer* nuh *nawg*), Land of Youth; Mag Mell (*moy myall*), Plain of Honey; the Summerlands. It is an earthly paradise where summer perpetually reigns, and fruit and flowers grow together on the trees. Feasting, hunting, music, love, and games go on forever, and death does not exist.

Those who have wandered, stumbled, or been lured into the Otherworld—and been lucky enough to come out again—tell similar travelers' tales of a country that lives up to another of its Irish names: Tír-Na-Sorcha (*cheer* nuh *sor*-uh-khuh), Land of Light. The faery light may radiate out from beautiful Otherworld dwellings made of shining metals and precious jewels. Sometimes it streams out from one enormous gemstone set in the roof of an underground cavern. In the seventeenth century, Robert Kirk, a Scottish minister who believed in faeries, described their dwellings

as "having continual Lamps and Fires, often seen without fuel to sustain them."

Others have deliberately embarked on journeys into the Otherworld to learn the hidden wisdom of the faery realms. Scottish witch Isobel Goudie was led into the Downie Hills where she beheld a "fair big room as bright as day," while seventeenth-century occultist John Heydon journeyed into an earth mound in Somerset, where he held counsel with the faery queen in a glass castle. And as might be expected, inner-world voyagers from other cultures encounter a similar inner landscape. In Siberian shamanism, for instance, the shaman's soul flight takes him over "a celestial landscape, bathed in light,"[9] while Australian medicine men journey through subterranean caverns filled with the light of crystals glittering from the walls.

Today the doors of the faery hills remain sealed against us, for we keep the eyes of our mythic consciousness shut tight, refusing to allow cracks to appear in the walls of our present, desacralized worldview. Few of us dare to open what W. B. Yeats called the "flaming door" and explore the power that crackles on the thresholds of our reality structures. But to do so might send a revitalizing current through the wasteland of our culture, as Irish mystic and poet George Russell once dreamed:

When the quiet with a ring of pearl shall wed
   the earth,
And the scarlet berries burn dark by the stars
   in the pool;
Oh, it's lost and deep I'll be amid the Danaan
   mirth,
While the heart of the earth is full.[10]

EXPERIENCING FAERIES TODAY

Many sensitive people have encountered faeries in our own world. In the early twentieth century an American scholar who believed in faeries, W. Y. Evans-Wentz, recorded many firsthand experiences among ordinary people in Ireland and the British Isles. He also interviewed Irish poet George Russell (A. E.), who described them in vivid terms:

> There was at first a dazzle of light, and then I saw that this came from the heart of a tall figure with a body apparently shaped out of half-transparent or opalescent air, and throughout the body ran a radiant, electrical fire, to which the heart seemed the centre. Around the head of this being and through its waving luminous hair, which was blown all about the body like living strands of gold, there appeared flaming wing-like auras. From the being itself light seemed to stream outwards in every direction; and the effect left on me after the vision was one of extraordinary lightness, joyousness, or ecstasy.[11]

Others, while not seeing faeries directly, feel their presence through sound. Ella Young, poet and friend of W. B. Yeats and George Russell, describes hearing the *ceol sídhe* (*kyawl shee*), faery music, when she was staying on Achill Island:

> This faery music has in it the sound of every instrument used in a great orchestra, and the sound of many, many instruments that no orchestra possesses. It has singing voices in it, sweeter than human: and always it has a little running crest of melody like foam on a sea-wave or moon-gilding on the edge of a cloud. All these sounds, and sounds more indefinable are going on at the same time. . . .[12]

Although faeries are rarely seen with the outer eye, it is possible to sense their presence in places that are infrequently visited by humans. At "threshold" places that have a numinous quality—on hills and mountains, in certain woods, and beside streams—you

THE WONDROUS LAND

In the Irish saga "The Wooing of Étaín," the Faery King, Midir (*meer*), calls to his beloved, Étaín (*ey-deen*), to leave Earth and come with him to Tír na nÓg:

> *Fair Lady, will you come with me*
> *to a wondrous land where there is music?*
> *Hair is like the blooming primrose there;*
> *smooth bodies are the color of snow.*
>
> *There, there is neither mine nor yours;*
> *bright are teeth, dark are brows.*
> *A delight to the eye the number of our hosts,*
> *the color of foxglove every cheek . . .*
>
> *Warm, sweet streams throughout the land,*
> *your choice of mead and wine.*
> *A distinguished people, without blemish,*
> *conceived without sin or crime . . .*
>
> *Woman, if you come to my bright people,*
> *you will have a crown of gold for your head;*
> *Honey, wine, fresh milk to drink*
> *you will have with me there, Fair Lady.*

may catch a glimpse of them out of the corner of your eye if you are in a meditative frame of mind. When you turn to look more directly, however, what you saw may turn out to be a strange-shaped rock or tree stump. But you can't be sure it didn't just change . . .

It is not necessary to go far afield to develop a relationship with the faery kingdom. Hobs, brownies, or cluricauns are domestic spirits who attach themselves to a household. Invisible by day, the hob comes out at night when everyone is asleep to do his work, such as washing supper dishes or darning a pile of socks. For many rural families in the British Isles and Ireland, the hob was the "luck of the farm" and could be depended upon to reap, mow, and thresh the grain as well as herd the sheep. He also looked after the hearth-fire and gave good advice when needed. In return, he expected some cheese or milk left out for him at night.

It can be very rewarding to develop a relationship with the faeries that live in your garden, patio, or even window box. Faeries are already present wherever there are plants, so you are simply opening up to an awareness of their presence. Plan to spend at least a few minutes with your plants on a regular basis. Instead of moving into action with weeder or watering can right away, say hello to them. Be observant—not only to their physical presence, but also to their energy and "personality." As you tend them, get to know their needs and preferences, and treat them with the care you would give to a favorite animal. Just acknowledging their sentience will make the faeries come forth, which you will recognize when your plants look more awake and alive.

If you grow vegetables you can also ask the faeries to help the plants grow better and to provide protection from pests. Tune in to any advice they may give you about how you can improve their growth. Before you cut flowers or harvest vegetables, tell the faeries of your intention and do so with respect for the plants. When you take from the garden, be sure to leave an offering in return. (For traditional offerings, see page 229.)

LOB-LIE-BY-THE-FIRE

Keep me a crust
Or starve I must;
Hoard me a bone
Or I am gone;
A handful of coals
Leave red for me;
Or the smoldering log
Of a wild-wood tree;
Even a kettle
To sing on the hob
Will comfort the heart
Of poor old Lob:
Then with his hairy
Hands he'll bless
Prosperous master,
And kind mistress.

WALTER DE LA MARE[13]

Faery Healers
Despite the way the faery world has been banished to the hinterland of modern

consciousness, the healing powers of the Otherworld have always been available to those who are called to become healers themselves. These chosen ones were called "faery doctors" in Ireland, "wise wives" in Scotland, "wise men" in Wales, and "cunning men" in Cornwall. There were more women among them than men, and many had learned the healing secrets of the Otherworld by being "taken" by the faeries themselves. In west Ireland there was a belief that Finvarra and his band stole the prettiest girls from the Midsummer Eve dances and took them to be their wives in the faery palaces. When they had lost their youth and beauty, the women were sent back to their homes with the gift of healing as compensation. Other faery healers were "taken" to the Otherworld through sickness. While they lay unconscious they experienced themselves in the spirit world. When they returned to health they had supernatural skills, and their lives were totally changed. Their accounts often match the description of what today we call the near-death experience.

Because faery doctors had lived in the spirit world, and certain diseases were believed to be caused by spirits, people struck by unaccountable illnesses trusted their ability to understand hidden causes and also to find the cure. They never used surgery or other invasive treatment methods: Charms, incantations, herbs, and stones were the chief tools of their trade. They knew where to find special plants and the correct way to gather and administer them. Some also brought back the ability to see into the future. Forbidden to reveal their knowledge or the whereabouts of the herbs while they lived, these healers could only pass on their secrets as they lay dying, and then only to the eldest of the family.

Faery doctors, like the famous Biddy Early in County Clare, never charged for their services, as this would diminish the effectiveness of the treatment. But it was traditional to leave silver in exchange for herbal remedies, and donations of food and drink were gladly received. Biddy particular enjoyed some whiskey or poteen along with gifts of bread and cheese. She had grown up in the nineteenth century on a farm where she saw and played with faeries as a child. When she was older they taught her how to use wild herbs for healing and magic. At first Biddy only used her skills to help her family and livestock on their farm, but soon neighbors and friends were queuing up for her services. Before long her reputation as a wise woman and healer spread throughout the west of Ireland, and Biddy found herself in a lifelong battle with the local priest, whom she usually managed to outwit.

HEALING BLESSING

Deep peace I breathe into you,
O weariness, here:
O ache, here!
Deep peace, a soft white dove to you;
Deep peace, a quiet rain to you;
Deep peace, an ebbing wave to you!
Deep peace, red wind of the east from you;
Deep peace, grey wind of the west to you;
Deep peace, dark wind of the north from you;
Deep peace, blue wind of the south to you!
Deep peace, pure red of the flame to you;
Deep peace, pure white of the moon to you;
Deep peace, pure green of the grass to you;
Deep peace, pure brown of the earth to you;
Deep peace, pure grey of the dew to you,
Deep peace, pure blue of the sky to you!
Deep peace of the running wave to you,
Deep peace of the flowing air to you,
Deep peace of the quiet earth to you,
Deep peace of the sleeping stones to you!
Deep peace of the Yellow Shepherd to you,
Deep peace of the Wandering Shepherdess to you,
Deep peace of the Flock of Stars to you,
Deep peace from the Son of Peace to you,
Deep peace from the heart of Mary to you,
From Bridget of the Mantle
Deep peace, deep peace!

FIONA MACLEOD

SWAN

A CELTIC BESTIARY

I am the white swan,
Queen above them.
CARMINA GADELICA

Swans are faery women in the shape of birds, and as a mark of their noble lineage they often appear in Celtic tales linked in pairs by gold or silver chains. In the Irish story "The Dream of Angus," a beautiful woman playing the sweet-stringed instrument known as the *tiompán* (*tim*-pawn) appeared to the Dé Danann prince, Angus, while he slept. Angus fell so much in love with her he became sick with longing. His father, the Dagda, and mother Boand (*bo*-awnd), of the River Boyne, searched throughout Ireland for the girl and at last found her by a lake with "three fifties" of other girls. All the girls were linked two and two by a silver chain, but Angus's dream girl stood out from them all, for she was taller than the others and wore a silver necklace and chain of burnished gold.

He learned that her name was Cáer Ibormeth (*kyre ih*-vor-veyth), Yew Berry, and that she spent every other year in the shape of a swan. When Angus returned to the lake next Samhain-tide, he saw "three fifties of white birds with silver chains, and golden hair about their heads." He called to her to come to him, but she would agree only if he promised to allow her to remain in her swan shape. Then Angus turned himself into a swan, and they flew away together to his dwelling of the Brugh na Bóinne (*broo* nuh *baw*-nyuh), now called Newgrange, in County Meath, "and there they sang until the people inside fell asleep for three days and three nights."

QUEEN OF THE APPLE ISLANDS

In Wales the knowledge of herbal medicine was supposed to have been taught by a faery woman who lived beneath a lake. The legend tells how a young shepherd fell in love with the beautiful faery of Llyn y Fan Fach (*hlin* uh *vahn vahkh*), in the Black Mountains. To his delight, she consented to marry him. He took her back to his home in the village of Myddfai (*muth*-vie), where they were wed, but she warned him that if he ever struck her three times, she would go back to her underwater kingdom. They lived happily together, and she bore three sons, but over the years he thoughtlessly struck her three times, and she returned forever to her old home beneath the lake. But when her sons were grown she taught them all the wisdom of faery healing through the use of herbs, and they grew up to become the celebrated healers known throughout medieval Wales as the Physicians of Myddfai. Descendants of this renowned family were still practicing medicine in the eighteenth century, and there is at least one herbalist in Dyfed today who claims descent from the famous family.

Two of the blows the shepherd gave her were the result of his ignorance of faery wisdom. The first occurred at a village wedding, when she astonished the congregation by bursting into tears. Embarrassed and annoyed, her husband gave her a reproving tap on the shoulder. Afterward she explained that she could see into the future and she had seen trouble ahead for the newlyweds. The second time he gave her an angry shake because she burst out laughing at a funeral, knowing that the dead one had left the world of suffering for a realm of bliss.

Without a belief in the spirit world, the understanding of life and death remains limited. The shepherd was given an opportunity to learn the secrets of the Otherworld from his own soul—the part of us that is usually hidden in the waters of the subconscious—for the soul is connected to the invisible world that lies beyond time and the body. He was angry at his wife for breaking societal conventions, he rejected her wisdom, and he made it impossible for her to stay on land, in the world of everyday consciousness. But, fortunately, she was able to communicate her knowledge to her children, and the story ending is a reminder that true healing may be derived from plants that grow on Earth, but knowledge of their uses and application must come from the world of spirit. This is a truth known throughout the world in indigenous cultures, although one we are only recently rediscovering, thanks primarily to the work of modern pioneers in alternative medicine, such as Eliot Cowan, an herbalist who heals with the aid of plant spirits.[14]

The faery healer may also be found as the Queen of an Otherworld island, as in "The Silver Branch" (see April) or within a faery hill. All these places are, of course, regions of the Underworld. In British tradition she is the Queen of Avalon, familiar to us from Arthurian legend. *Avalon* is derived from the Welsh *afal*, "apple," and its queen is Morgen, or Morgan le Fay—Morgan of the Faeries. In the Arthurian cycle she is all too often portrayed as a scheming sorceress whose mischief and magic continually upset the Round Table. But the original Morgen was a wise woman and healer. In the twelfth-century *Life of Merlin*, the Welsh bard and prophet, Taliesin, describes her island country. It is clearly the British counterpart of the Irish Otherworld islands:

> The Island of Apples gets its name
> "The Fortunate Island" from the fact
> that it produces all manner of plants
> spontaneously. It needs no farmers to
> plough the fields. There is no cultivation
> of the land at all beyond that which is
> Nature's work. It produces crops in
> abundance and grapes without help; and
> apple trees spring up from the short
> grass in its woods. All plants, not merely
> grass alone, grow spontaneously; and
> men live a hundred years or more.

That is the place where nine sisters exercise a kindly rule over those who come to them from our land. The one who is first among them has greater skill in healing, as her beauty surpasses that of her sisters. Her name is Morgen, and she has learned the uses of all plants in curing the ills of the body. She knows, too, the art of changing her shape, of flying through the air, like Daedalus, on strange wings. At will, she is now at Brest, now at Chartres, now at Pavia; and at will she glides down from the sky on to your shores. . . .

It was there we took Arthur after the battle of Camlan, where he had been wounded. . . . Morgen received us with due honor. She put the king in her chamber on a golden bed, uncovered his wound with her noble hand and looked long at it. At length she said he could be cured if only he stayed with her a long while and accepted her treatment. We therefore happily committed the king to her care and spread our sails to favorable winds on our return journey.[15]

Morgen herself is a mysterious figure whose name may derive from *Mórrígan* (Irish: Great Queen), from *Modron* (Latin: Matrona), the Welsh mother goddess, or *Muirgein* (Irish: Sea-born). Morgen is of the "sea," the realm of the Celtic Underworld, and brings us the mysteries of the deep feminine—intuition, seership, and magic. Like the Irish queen of Emhain, in "The Silver Branch," she presides over a group of women. There are nine, the sacred Celtic number, and they are probably the same nine maidens who guard a magic cauldron, which they heat with their breath, in the mysterious Welsh poem "The Spoils of Annwn." In early Celtic times there may actually have been Wise Women living in islands off the western coast of the British Isles. Pomponius Mela, writing in the first century C.E., tells of nine virgin priestesses who lived on the island of Sena, which may have been the Île de Seins, Brittany, or one of the Isles of Scilly. They never left the island but acted as consultants to those who sailed out to them. Like Morgen, these women had magical powers: They could predict the future, shape-shift into animal forms, fly through the air, control the weather, and cure all diseases. At the time Pomponius was writing, this was already local legend, so we will never know if this was really so. Whatever the truth, the powers of the Otherworld queen are very real indeed and can be experienced today if we are willing to set sail for her island of the inner country.

APPLE

☉HE SACRED ☉ROVE

Precious apple-tree of spreading and low-
sweeping bough . . .
SYLVA GADELICA

The apple tree is among the most mysterious
and magical trees of the Celtic forest. Like the
hazel, it is often to be found at the center of
the Otherworld as a Tree of Life, as in "The
Silver Branch" (see April). Its magical fruit
gives out a heavenly fragrance, and eternal life
and bliss in the Summerlands come to whomever eats it. In the medieval Irish tale "Connla

the Fair," a beautiful faery woman arrives in a
crystal canoe, and Prince Connla falls deeply
in love with her. She throws him a golden
apple, and the moment he tastes it he can
never forget her. They set sail together for her
beautiful island country, where the trees bear
fruit and blossoms at the same time. There
they live in ecstasy together, taking turns
eating the apple, which never gets any smaller
and keeps them forever young.

Sometimes the Otherworld apple tree
gives out an enchanting music that dispels
"all want or woe or weariness of soul." For
the apple tree is a symbol of the earthly paradise in which it grows, and like Yeats's
Wandering Aengus, in his famous poem, a
part of the human mind will always be
searching for

. . . the silver apples of the moon,
The golden apples of the sun.

☉HE INNER
⊂AULDRON
HEALING

There are times on our journey through the
spiral of the year that we come up against
obstacles that make it hard for us to proceed.
The well of inspiration dries up, the leaves of

the tree shrivel, we feel depressed, isolated, and blocked. The spiral labyrinth becomes more like a maze. Instead of walking confidently on one path that leads us ever onward toward the center of our lives, we take wrong turns, meet dead ends, and are continually retracing our steps. Such times are common enough on any spiritual path, and part of the journey itself is healing the unintegrated parts of ourselves that keep tripping us up. To this end, it can be very useful to take a journey into the Otherworld to seek healing from Morgan of Avalon.

For this meditation you may want to prepare a comfortable place with cushions so you can lie down before your altar, as it will take you into a very deep state of relaxation, essential for healing. Before you begin, place an offering of fragrant flowers or herbs on the altar in the south, the direction that corresponds to summer. A vase of flowers or a scattering of petals and herbs will both work equally well. A flowery incense can also be burned. The addition of musical accompaniment greatly enhances its effects. A number of people in my workshops have reported healing benefits from this meditation after doing it for the first time and without knowing what to expect. Continued practice is even more beneficial. It's a good idea to write down what you experience afterward, as putting it on paper serves to anchor inner work in the physical world and prevent subtle insights and perceptions from fading away like dreams upon awakening.

Meditation: Sailing to Avalon

Close your eyes, take a few deep breaths, and begin to relax. . . . Let the breath carry you away to another place, another time, before the beginning of time. . . .

You are standing at the edge of a shore looking over toward an island. It is nightfall, and above you a full moon is rising. All is so still in the dim purple air, and the sounds of the evening seem magnified . . . a night owl softly hooting from a neighboring wood . . . the liquid sound of the water lapping at your feet . . . Moths flutter white in the purple twilight, and as you look over the water toward the island you see it is half-hidden by a mist, and the moon is shining through this mist, creating a filmy veil of white around it . . . translucent, opalescent light that seems to come from another world. . . . And now out of the swirling mist comes something moving toward you. . . . It is a small boat, and it is gliding swiftly but smoothly to the shore, and yet there is no one aboard. It seems steered by some magic will of its own.

You gaze in fascination as the boat approaches the very place where you stand at the shoreline edge, and you know, as it comes to rest, bobbing gently on the water, that it has come for you. You step lightly into the boat and sit in the center of the wooden bench, feeling it rock a little, and then it steadies, turns, and glides away from the shore, carrying you smoothly into the misty regions of the island.

At first the night breeze lifts your hair, but as you enter the mist a cold dew surrounds you and you can no longer see. You must trust that the little boat knows where it is taking you, trust the passage into the unknown. . . . And now the mist begins to lift a little and then rolls back fully like a curtain, to unveil the shore of the island under the full moon. A woman is standing there waiting for the boat to bring you to land. . . . She is tall and straight, dressed in dark blue robes, and the little boat takes you to where she waits.

As you approach the woman, she is silent and does not move. Her face is half-veiled, but you can see kind, wise eyes beneath the veil, and she extends her hand in welcome. Then without a word she motions you to follow her. She leads you through orchards of apple trees that bear ripe fruit and blossoms at the same time, all silvered by the moon. As you reach the center of the island you see a low stone building, the temple at the heart of the island.

She leads you through a small doorway hung with a curtain made of tiny crystal beads. . . . Inside, a dim amber light reveals bunches of herbs and flowers hung up to dry on wooden beams. The lady ushers you to a long low pallet made of straw and heather, and you lie down upon it. Beside it is a small copper brazier in which is burning a gold and blue flame. . . . Although she does not appear to speak, you sense she is asking you to let her know where in your body, mind, or spirit you need most to heal. And you ponder this for a few moments . . . and let her know.

She picks up a large shallow wicker basket and takes from it certain things: sprigs of herbs, roots, glittering stones . . . maybe some other things . . . and she lays them on your body where they most need to go, maybe where you have told her there is a problem, maybe other places besides. . . . Notice where she places them. . . . The scent of the herbs . . . the warm glow of the flame . . . are very soothing after the cold boat ride, and you feel yourself drowsily drifting into a half-sleep state, while the lady takes a stringed instrument and begins to play . . . every now and then stopping to throw a handful of powdered herbs onto the fire, which sparkle for a few moments and fill the air with a sweet heavy fragrance.... And the herbs lull you into a dreamy state, and you half-wonder if you hear the lady singing ... and time no longer exists ... and you drift away feeling very sweet and peaceful....

And after what may have been a short time or a long time or no time at all, you surface into wakefulness, spiraling up slowly as if through water. The eyes of the lady are smiling down at you, and she bids you rise. The fire is low, and a little breeze is now entering in through the low door, making the curtain stir. She leads you outside, and you are aware of feeling lighter, better than before, as if there has been a shift within the matrix of your being.... A healing has taken place.... The first rays of the sun are gilding the apple trees, turning the apples to pure gold.... She takes you back to the edge of the shore, where the little boat is still waiting for you. You thank the lady with all your heart and bid her a fond farewell ... then you get into the boat, and when you have found your balance on the seat, it begins to glide away.

As it turns away from the island you look back and wave, but she is no longer there, and then the mist is all about you and you can see no more until you emerge on the other side.... And now you are gliding along the golden path of the morning sun on the water, and after a while you find yourself deposited at the edge of the mainland once again. You step out, and the little boat glides away once more. You take several deep breaths, and with each breath you take, become more aware of your body. Now open your eyes, wide awake.

NINE DESIRES

The desire of the fairy women, dew;
The desire of the fairy host, wind;
The desire of the raven, blood;
The desire of the snipe, the wilderness;
The desire of the sea-mew, the lawns of the sea;
The desire of the poet, the soft low music of the Tribe of the Green Mantles;
The desire of man, the love of woman;
The desire of women, the little clan;
The desire of the soul, wisdom.

FIONA MACLEOD

HOUSE OF LIGHT

Come, heart, where hill is heaped upon hill:
For there the mystic brotherhood
Of sun and moon and hollow and wood
And river and stream work out their will.

W. B. Yeats

The Celts had two homes: the house inside and the universe outside. In winter the family orbited the hearth-fire; in summer the sun was their sacred center. From May to November their world was bounded by invisible columns that held up the roof of the heavens. God was the divine thatcher who built the house of the world. This at least, was the *felt* truth in Ireland, where people still speak of the *cranna na spéire,* the columns of the sky, and *frathacha na firminte,* the rafters of the firmament.[1] Now that it is July, the height of summer, we follow the Celts out of doors to learn from them the wisdom of this "house of light."

Early Ireland was in many ways a welcoming place. Tribal communities lived in clearings within broad-leaved deciduous forests. By the sixth century C.E. many of the trees had been cleared, leaving green plains, valleys, and hillsides for fields of grain and pastureland. Songbirds filled the woods with music, while kites, falcons, and golden eagles soared over the plains searching for prey. Wolves, wild boar, and herds of deer lived in the thickest parts of the forest. Rivers and lakes teemed with fish. Ireland's waterways were much broader than today and were surrounded by miles of reed beds—habitat for flocks of wild geese, swans, and other waterfowl. Tales of Fionn McCumhaill and the Fianna portray them living on the land as they roamed through Ireland, hunting and fighting battles from May to November. Through these stories we catch a glimpse of what it must have been like to enjoy the seemingly inexhaustible riches of the earth in summer:

> The place where they gathered was on the hill that was called Fionntulach, the White Hill, in Munster. They often stopped on that hill for a while. . . . And they had every sort of thing for food: beautiful blackberries, haws of the hawthorn, nuts of the hazels of Cenntire, tender twigs of the bramble bush, sprigs of wholesome gentian, watercress at the beginning of summer. And there would be brought to their cooking-pots birds out of the oak-woods, and squirrels from Berramain, and speckled eggs from the cliffs, and salmon out of Luimnech, and eels out of the Sionnan, and the woodcocks of Fidhrinne, and otters from the hidden places of the Doile, and fish from the coasts of Buie and Beare, and dulse from the bays of Cleire.[2]

It is no wonder the Venerable Bede, writing in the eighth century, described Ireland as a land flowing with milk and honey.

To the early Celts the universe was alive and ensouled, peopled by spirits and deities who were the deep invisible dwellers of the land. Ireland itself was seen as a great goddess, one of whose names, Eriu, gives us the country we know today as Éire or Erin. Her body was the land itself: in County Kerry, two hills like great breasts are named the Paps of Anu, another of her names. Cavernous earth chambers, like Newgrange in the Boyne River Valley, were regarded as entrances to her womb, where the spirits of the ancestors dwelled. Rivers were the streams of milk flowing from her breast.

In the Christian era the cosmos was still regarded as animate and sacred, but now it was seen as the creation of God, a masterpiece reflecting his divine image in every rock, leaf, and wave of the sea. When Saint Patrick set out to convert the daughters of the High King of Tara, he was asked who the new God was and where he dwelled. Patrick replied,

Our God is the God of all men,
God of heaven and earth,
God of the sea and the streams,
God of the sun, moon, and all the stars,
God of high mountains and deep glens,
God above heaven, in heaven, and under heaven.
He has a dwelling—heaven, earth, and sea,
And all they contain.

TRANSLATED BY MARA FREEMAN

The early church in Ireland adapted itself to the ancient tribal social system and consisted of small monasteries that were also farms with livestock and fields for crops. Churches were simple buildings made of wood, and mass was frequently held out in the open air. Church buildings were often deliberately situated in pagan groves where the druids once worshiped, and the new leaders cherished and fiercely protected the sacred trees. They lived in companionship with the animals and birds of the forest and showed compassion for their sufferings. Saint Columcille lovingly cared for an exhausted crane that had been blown onto Iona's shore in a storm until it was able to fly again. In County Wicklow, Kevin of Glendalough once lay fasting on the gray flagstone that was his bed when a blackbird hopped upon his outstretched palm and built her nest there. The saint didn't move a muscle until she had laid her eggs and hatched them.

Some monks were attracted to the hermit's life and lived on remote islands, mountaintops, or forests in wattle huts or even caves or trees. For them the walls that circumscribe our modern lives, cutting us off from intimacy with the outside world, were fragile or nonexistent. To live like this was to see oneself in perspective, small in a huge and teeming world, and a whole body of exquisite nature poetry arose out of their experience.

Here's how a tenth-century hermit describes his woodland oratory:

I have a shieling in the wood,
None knows it save my God:
An ash-tree on the hither side, a hazel-bush
  beyond,
A huge oak-tree encompasses it.

Two heath-clad doorposts for support,
And a lintel of honeysuckle:
The forest around its narrowness sheds
Its mast upon fat swine.[3]

The clarity and detail of his descriptions are typical of what has been called "hermit poetry," springing from a lived experience. Unlike the later medieval poetry of European courts, where nature has become a pale allegory of abstract qualities, these verses carry the fresh quality of everyday life. The sheer variety of natural phenomena in each poem provides for us, living as we do at a time when human carelessness has decimated so many species, a window onto a world that teems with biodiversity.

Glen of the sleek brown round-faced otters
that are pleasant and active in fishing;
many are the white-winged stately swans,
and salmon breeding along the rocky brink.[4]

Hermit poetry evokes an existence where all the senses are involved. We who have banished ourselves from the rich banquet of the natural world, preferring the empty calories of virtual realities and consumer items, can sense how it must have felt to our ancestors to be satisfied by the natural abundance of things:

Ale with herbs, a dish of strawberries
Of good taste and color,
Haws, berries of the juniper,
Sloes, nuts.

When brilliant summer-time spreads its colored
    mantle,
Sweet-tasting fragrance!
Pignuts, wild marjoram, green leeks,
Verdant pureness.

Swarms of bees and chafers, the little musicians of
    the world,
A gentle chorus:
Wild geese and ducks, shortly before summer's end,
The music of the dark torrent.[5]

The vividness of the imagery recalls Blake's famous phrase: "If the doors of perception were cleansed, everything would appear to man as it is—infinite." In every poem, the poet's relationship with the natural world is specific and intimate. In the following poem the poet addresses individual animals, plants, and trees, revealing an authentic relationship with each:

Little antlered one, little belling one, melodious
    little bleater, sweet I think the lowing that you
    make in the glen . . .

Blackthorn, little thorny one, black little sloe-bush;
watercress, little green-topped one, on the brink
of the blackbird's well . . .
Apple-tree, little apple-tree, violently everyone
shakes you; rowan, little berried one, lovely is
your bloom . . . [6]

The personal life of the poet is hardly mentioned in these poems. Only occasionally do we get a touching glimpse of a few domestic details, and then only in the poems about winter when the poet is confined inside: "Cosy is our pot on its hook," begins one verse of a poem known as "Winter Cold," but this line is only put in to contrast with the plight of wild animals:

The wolves of Cuan Wood get
Neither rest nor sleep in their lair,
The little wren cannot find
Shelter in her nest on the slope of Lon. [7]

The scarcity of details of the individual life highlight its relative insignificance compared to the huge drama being enacted outside. The poet makes himself transparent so that he can relate to nature from a deeper level. The German poet Novalis called this place "the seat of the soul," which he located as "where the inner world and the outer world meet,

and where they overlap, it is in every point of the overlap." [8]

And in becoming transparent, these long-dead poets have enabled us to participate in that relationship just a little, to taste air fresh from the morning of the world.

THE IVY CREST

In Tuaim Inbhir here I find
No great house such as mortals build,
A hermitage that fits my mind
With sun and moon and starlight filled.

'Twas Gobbán [the divine smith] shaped it
cunningly
—This is a tale that lacks not proof—
And my heart's darling in the sky,
Christ, was the thatcher of its roof.
Over my house rain never falls,
There comes no terror of the spear;
It is a garden without walls
And everlasting light shines here.
              NINTH-CENTURY IRISH [9]

WATERCRESS SOUP

... a meal of green-topped long-
lasting watercress,
a drink of cold water from a pure stream ...
IRISH, TWELFTH CENTURY

From earliest times Irish people have gathered an abundance of wild greens and roots for food in the summer months. The Irish monk Saint Kevin lived for seven years on nothing but nettles and sorrel—an unvaried diet, but traditionally good for the blood, as nineteenth-century Irish mothers knew when they fed boiled nettles to recalcitrant children for an internal "spring cleaning" each year. Legend has it that a diet of watercress enabled Saint Brendan to live to the ripe old age of 180. The saint would have approved of the following soup, which is as delicious as its rich green color suggests.

Ingredients
3 tablespoons butter
8 ounces potatoes
8 ounces leeks, white parts only
2 cups vegetable or chicken stock
1 cup whole milk
2 bunches watercress
salt and freshly ground pepper

Method
1. Slice the leeks, and sauté in butter in a heavy pot on medium heat.
2. Peel and chop potatoes and add to leeks. Add salt and pepper to taste, and give everything a good stir.
3. Pour in the stock, bring to a boil, cover, and cook until the vegetables are soft (about 20 minutes).
4. Remove the coarser stems from the watercress and chop the rest, leaving a few sprigs for garnish. Add to the pot and cook uncovered for 4 to 5 minutes. Don't overcook or the watercress will lose its bright green color.
5. Puree in a blender, return to pot, add milk, and reheat slowly. Adjust seasonings, decorate with reserved sprigs of watercress, and serve.

Serves 4

Note: Unless you have proof of the purity of the stream, you should be very careful about gathering wild watercress these days because of pollution. To be safe, buy watercress from your local store.

WISDOM OF THE ELEMENTS

O God of the elements,
O God of the mysteries,
O God of the stars . . .
Carmina Gadelica

In the Celtic world all aspects of creation were powerful, living forces to be respected and regarded with awe. These living forces are often referred to as the "elements," and according to different accounts they include sun, moon, stars, earth, sea, dew, wind, clouds, and stones. In early Ireland the most serious oaths were sworn *"dar brí na gréine is na gealaí"*—by the strength of the sun and the moon. A story tells how the High King Laegaire (*ly*-gha-ryuh) was defeated in battle by the people of Leinster. In return for his freedom he swore by sun and moon, water and air, day and night, sea and land, never to demand tribute from them while he lived. He was released but broke his promise and died shortly thereafter "of the sun and of the wind and of the other pledges."

The druids were skilled at harnessing the elements to work magic. They conjured up winds, storms, and impenetrable fogs to confound their enemies in battle. In the Christian era the elements were invoked along with the power of God, as in this eighth-century prayer for protection on a journey:

I draw to myself today
strength of heaven,
glory of sun,
brightness of moon,
radiance of fire,
swiftness of lightning,
speed of wind,
depth of sea,
stability of earth,
firmness of rock . . .

I draw to myself today
The guiding power of God:
God's might to uplift me,
God's wisdom to lead me,
God's eye to look before me,
God's ear to listen for me. . . .

Over a thousand years later the people who eked out a precarious existence on the windswept North Atlantic islands continued to regard the universe with the same reverence as their Celtic predecessors. Because they lived amid the turbulent weather patterns and extremes of seasonal light and darkness, close cooperation with the Divine and the forces of nature was essential for survival.

They, too, prayed for the aid of the elemental forces, as in this Scottish charm for treating a chest ailment, collected by Alexander Carmichael from a healer on Mull:

Power of moon have I over thee,
Power of sun have I over thee,
Power of rain have I over thee,
Power of dew have I over thee,
Power of sea have I over thee,
Power of land have I over thee,
Power of stars have I over thee. . . .[10]

In the wild isolated hills, glens, and shores of the Scottish Highlands and islands, the lives of the people moved in rhythm to the wheeling dance of sun, moon, stars, and sea. The sun was called *sùil Dhé mhóir,* "the eye of the great God," and was greeted with song and prayer morning and evening "as if it were a great person come back to their land." Mór MacNeill, a sprightly old woman who lived on the island of Barra, told Carmichael:

In the time of my father and of my mother there was no man in Barra who would not take off his bonnet to the white sun of power, nor a woman in Barra who would not bend her body to the white moon of the seasons. No, my

dear, not a man nor woman in Barra. And old persons will be doing this still, and I will be doing it myself sometimes. Children mock at me, but if they do, what of that? Is it not much meeter for me to bend my body to the sun and to the moon and to the stars, that the great God of life made for my good, than to the son or daughter of earth like myself?

The high status afforded the sun stretches far back into the Celtic past, when the sun was seen as a god driving through the heavens in a fiery chariot. Until quite recently in Ireland the sun was described as going to lie down in the evening, or "going into its chair," while the long evening rays were said to be the "legs of the sun."[11]

Where the sun was regarded as a mighty presence, the moon was like a dear friend who guided travelers through the dark night. The seafaring people of the islands could navigate the treacherous reefs and rocks without the sun by day, but by night moonlight could make the difference between life and death. And so they invoked its light with heartfelt prayers and called it *lochran mór an àigh,* "the great lamp of grace."

The ancient Celtic calendar was calculated by the phases of the moon, and in seventeenth-century Scotland a month was still reckoned as one full moon cycle. Everyday country life was attuned to its phases. The waxing moon, which encouraged growth and increase, was a good time to sow seed for crops that grew above the ground. It was also propitious for slaughtering livestock and beginning a journey or any new venture. Under a waning moon the life force was withdrawn, and it was good only for tasks that needed dryness, such as plowing, reaping, and cutting peat, or for planting root crops. After the dark of the month the new moon was welcomed back with songs of joy, and many customs attended its return. On the Isle of Skye people gathered at the holy wells when the moon was new to make a sunwise circle three times and cast an offering into the waters. Alexander Carmichael describes how in some districts people climbed the nearest knoll to greet the return of the "jewel of the night."

> They began their scrutiny in the west, turning slowly sunwise upon the right heel, till the object of their search was seen. Then they called out: *"Fhaic! Fhaic! Fhaic!"* (See! See! See!) . . . Herdboys and herdgirls were wont to whisper softly in the ear of the cows: "There is the new moon, thou beloved one among cows!"

The three most beautiful things in the world:
a full-rigged ship, a woman with child,
and a full moon.
SCOTTISH TRIAD

Greeting the Sun and Moon

Cultivating an awareness of the cycles of sun and moon is a simple way for us to reconnect with the rhythms of the natural world. If we make a point of greeting the rising sun each morning, we actively participate in the beauty and wonder of a sacramental universe. There enters in a feeling of awe and gratitude that we are part of a greater mystery, as visionaries like William Blake have always told us:

> When the Sun rises, do you not see a round disk of fire somewhat like a guinea? O no, no—I see an innumerable company of the heavenly host crying, "Holy! Holy! Holy is the Lord God Almighty!" I question not my corporeal or vegetative eye any more than I would question a window concerning a sight. I look through it and not with it.[12]

In the glare of artificial lighting in our cities, streets, and homes, we have lost the sensitive attunement to the shifting tides of day and night that characterized all Earth's inhabitants until a little over a hundred years ago. If we start noticing the phases of the moon again, we expand our awareness of how this mysterious and beautiful body affects our sleep patterns, our hormonal cycles, and even our moods. We become more conscious of the way we are all an intricate part of a cosmic dance to the music of the spheres. And we do not dance alone.

The Stars

The Celts had many evocative names for the stars, hinting of legends long since lost. In Scotland Orion was the Great Falconer, standing on the edge of a swift-flowing river, his dirk slung from his belt. In Wales King Arthur ruled the skies: the Lyre was Arthur's Harp, Orion Arthur's Yard, and the Great Bear was Arthur's Plowman. In Ireland the Milky Way is still called the Way of the White Cow.

One legend of the stars was preserved by a Gaelic-speaking storyteller whose family had emigrated from Scotland to Cape Breton, Canada. A beautiful woman named Deirdire (*jair*-jee-ryuh) was greatly in love with Naois (*nuh*-ish), one of three brothers known as the Children of Uisneach (*ush*-nyakh). But King Conchobor, who wanted Deirdire for himself, pursued the lovers and killed Naois and his two brothers. Deirdire's heart broke, and she threw herself into Naois's grave, but the king buried them in separate mounds so they would not be joined, even in death. But out of each grave grew a tree, and the two trees joined together, and their branches intertwined. The king ordered that the trees be cut down, but they grew once more. This happened many times, until at last the king decided to bury them on different sides of the loch. But the spirits of the lovers turned into stars and met each other in the skies: Deirdire, Naois, and his two brothers became the Track of the Children of Uisneach, or, as we know it, the Milky Way.[13]

A poem by medieval Welsh poet Dafydd ap Gwylim describes the constellations that lit his way on a night journey to be with his lover. He pours on more images than there are stars in the sky:

> God . . . lit for me the rushlights of the Twelve Signs, a thick shower to banish dire affliction. Proud and sudden the stars came out for me, the cherries of the night . . . like hailstones of the brilliant sun, the mirrors, the halfpennies of great God, lovely as red-gold under the hoarfrost, the saddle-jewels of the hosts of heaven. The

sunshine has hammered shield-rivets in the sky; skillfully they were driven in one by one, a throng in the wide pale sky; the swift wind cannot dislodge these sky-pegs from their peg-holes. Wide is their orbit, the wind does not wash them, they are embers of the mighty heavens; a set of pieces shining made for dicing and backgammon, on the vast game-board of the sky; head-dress pins of the great firmament, our thoughts are all on them. . . . Praise to the pure light, like a bright path, the clover-flowers on Heaven's face, that came to my aid, though I was so late, like gilded frost, marigolds of the air. The wax candles of a hundred altars . . . the well-formed rosary-beads of blessed God scattered from off their string, they showed me carefully the valley and the hill, the reward for all my folly, and the road to Anglesey. . . .[14]

Wind comes from the spring star in the East,
Fire comes from the summer star in the South,
Water comes from the autumn star in the West,
Wisdom, silence, and death come from the winter
star in the North.

FIONA MACLEOD

The Sea

The Celtic sea is full of spirits. Off the Irish coast were three magical waves: the Wave of Clíona (*klee*-nuh) near Cork; the Wave of Tuaithe (*tooi*-huh) at Derry; and the Wave of Rudraidhe (*roo*-ree) at Down. The roaring of the Three Waves on stormy days warned that Ireland was in deadly danger or prophesied the approaching death of a king. In the western sea of Scotland dwell the Blue Men of the Minch, who haunt the narrow channel between Lewis and the Shiant Islands, and also the Muireartach (*mur*-yar-takh), or Hag of the Sea, who stirs up tempests on the northwest coast. The Celts honored these gods of the sea as much as the spirits of the land. Each Samhain on the Isle of Lewis, fishermen used to gather on the beach to pay tribute to a sea god called Shoney. One of them waded into the water carrying a pitcher brimming with ale, which he poured into the waves as a libation, crying, "Shoney, I give you this cup of ale, hoping that you'll be so kind as to send us plenty of seaweed for enriching our ground the ensuing year."[15]

INVOCATIONS TO THE SUN AND MOON
(Bow three times before saying)

TO THE SUN
Greeting to you, sun of the seasons,
As you travel the skies on high,
Strong your steps on the wing of the
*   heights,*
Glorious mother of the stars.

You sink down into the perilous
*   ocean*
Free from fear and harm;
You rise up on the gentle wave
like a young queen in flower.[16]

TO THE NEW MOON
Greeting to you, new moon, guiding
*   jewel of grace,*
I bend my knee to you, I offer you my
*   love.*

I bend my knee to you, I raise my
*   hands to you,*
I lift my eye to you, new moon of the
*   seasons.*

Greeting to you, new moon, maiden
*   of my love,*
Greeting to you, new moon, maiden
*   of my joy.*

You journey on your course, you steer
*   the flowing tides,*
You light your shining face for us,
*   new moon of the seasons.*

Queen of guidance, queen of good
*   fortune,*
Queen of my love, new moon of the
*   seasons!*[17]

QUEEN OF THE NIGHT
Greeting to you, jewel of the night!
Beauty of the skies, jewel of the night!
Mother of the stars, jewel of the night!
Foster-child of the sun, jewel of the
*   night!*
Majesty of the stars, jewel of the
*   night!*[18]

RUNE OF THE FOUR WINDS

By the four white winds of the world,
Whose father the golden Sun is,
Whose mother the wheeling Moon is,
The North and the South and the East and the
*   West:*
By the four good winds of the world . . .
Be all well
On mountain and moorland and lea,
On loch-face and lochan and river,
On shore and shallow and sea!
                    FIONA MACLEOD

GODS OF THE CELTS: MANANNÁN

The Irish god of the sea is Manannán mac Lir—Manannán, Son of the Sea—ruler of the Land Under Wave. He is particularly associated with the islands between Ireland and Britain that the Irish believed to be Otherworld realms: Mona (now Anglesey), the Isle of Arran off Scotland, and the Isle of Man. Known as "the rider of the maned sea," he traveled over the water in his chariot named Ocean Sweeper with the waves for his horses. One horse, Enbarr (Waterfoam), was his particular favorite. He often wore a great shining cloak that could change color like the sea itself. To him the sea was a fertile country of orchards and flowers, and the fish were his flocks of sheep and cattle.

When the Tuatha Dé Danann were driven underground by the invading Sons of Míl, Manannán left his island kingdom to be the gods' adviser. He appointed a *sidh* mound as a palace for each of the nobles and gave them three gifts: the *féth fiada*, or cloak of invisibility; the Feast of Goibniu, which warded off old age and death, and some magical pigs that would come alive again after being killed and eaten.

The people of the Isle of Man looked upon him as their god. They climbed a mountain to pay tribute to him with bundles of green rushes on Midsummer Eve, and they regarded him as their great protector who surrounded the island with a magical mist—the *féth fiada*—to hide it from the ships of Viking raiders. Manannán could turn himself into the shape of three legs and roll like a wheel, a triskelion symbol that is still used for the Isle of Man today. Until quite recently, Manx fishermen said a prayer to him before putting out to sea:

Manannan Beg Mac y Leirr—
Little Manannan Son of the Sea,
Who blessed our Island,
Bless us and our boat, going out well.
Coming in better, with living and dead in
*   our boat.*

SEAL

A CELTIC BESTIARY

With their large liquid eyes and humanlike cry, seals were often regarded as human beings under enchantment. The *selkie*, or seal people, of northern Scotland only needed their sealskins to help them pass through the water from one region of air to another. They lived in underwater palaces or on lonely off-shore islands and were thus creatures of both realms: land and water, human and faery. They embodied both the wisdom and the loneliness of those who live in two worlds, as an old Gaelic saying affirms:

Is ann aig na roin tha brath.
Only the seals know.

Some of the seal people were very helpful to humans, bringing them gifts of fish or saving them from drowning. But when seals were hunted mercilessly for their skins, they raised storms and sank ships in revenge. In the West Highlands, where they were known as the Roane, from the Gaelic for seal: *ròn* (*rawn*), they could often be heard singing the *dàn nan ròn*, the song of the seals, a piteous, mournful air that stirred the soul to tears. In their human shape, the selkie were more beautiful than ordinary mortals, and it was easy to fall in love with them. There are many tales of marriages between humans and seals in Scottish and Irish tradition. Some families are supposed to be descended from the seal people, and their children were born with webs of skin between their fingers and toes. Members of the Clan MacCodrum of South Uist have been known for centuries as the Children of the Seals. This is their story . . .

THE SELKIE

Long ago on an island at the northern edge of the world, there lived a fisherman called Neil MacCodrum. He lived all alone in a stone croft where the moorland meets the shore, with nothing but the guillemots for company and the stirring of the sand among the shingle for song.

But in the long winter evenings he would sit by the peat fire and watch the blue smoke curling up to the roof, and his eyes looked far and far away as if he were looking into another country. And sometimes, when the wind rustled the bent-grass on the *machair* (mah-kher, the sandy pasture by the sea), he seemed to hear a soft voice sighing his name.

One spring evening the men of the *clachan* (*klakh*-un, the village) were bringing their boats full of herring into shore. They swung homeward with glad hearts, and their wives lit the rushlights so that the wide world dwindled to a warm quiet room.

Neil MacCodrum was the last to drag his boat up the shingle and hoist the creel of fish upon his back. He stood awhile watching the seabirds fly low toward the headland, their wings dark against the evening sky, then turned to trudge up the shingle to the croft on the machair.

It was as he turned that he saw something move in the shadows of the rocks. A glimmer of white and then—he heard it between birds' cries—high laughter like silver. He set down the creel, and with careful steps he neared the rocks, hardly daring to breathe, and hid behind the largest one. And then he saw them—seven girls with long flowing hair, naked and white as the swans on the lake, dancing in a ring where the shoreline met the sea.

And now his eye caught something else—a shapeless pile of speckled brown skins lying heaped like seaweed on a boulder nearby. Now

MacCodrum knew that they were *selkie,* who are seals in the sea, but who, when they come to land take off their skins and appear as human women.

Crouching low, Neil MacCodrum crept toward the pile of skins and slowly slid the top one down. But just as he rolled it up and put it under his coat, one of the selkie gave a sharp cry. The dance stopped, the bright circle broke, and the girls ran to the boulder, slipped into their skins, and slithered into the rising tide, shiny brown seals gliding away into the dark night sea.

All but one.

She stood before him white as a pearl, as still as frost in starlight. She stared at him with great dark eyes that held the depths of the sea, then slowly she held out her hand and said in a voice that trembled with silver:

"Ochone, ochone! Please give me back my skin."

He took a step toward her.

"Come with me," he said, "I will give you new clothes to wear."

The wedding of Neil MacCodrum and the selkie woman was set for the time of the waxing moon and the flowing tide. All the folk of the clachan came, six whole sheep were roasted, and the whiskey ran like water. Toasts overflowed from every cup for the new bride and groom, who sat at the head of the table: MacCodrum, beaming and awkward, unused to pleasure, tapped his spoon to the music of fiddle and pipe, but the woman sat quietly beside him at the bride-seat and seemed to be listening to another music that had in it the sound of the sea.

After a while she bore him two children, a boy and a girl, who had the sandy hair of their father but the great dark eyes of their mother, and there were little webs between their fingers and toes. Each day, when MacCodrum was out in his boat, she and her children would wander along the shore to gather limpets or fill their creels with carrageen (an edible seaweed) from the rocks at low tide. She seemed settled enough in the croft on the shore, and in Maytime when the air was scented with thyme and roseroot and the children ran toward her, their arms full of wild yellow irises, she was almost happy.

But when the west wind brought rain and strong squalls of wind that whistled through the cracks in the croft walls, she grew restless and moved about the house as if swaying to unseen tides, and when she sat at the spinning wheel she would hum a strange song as the fine thread streamed through her fingers. MacCodrum hated these times and would sit in the dark peat corner glowering at her over his pipe but unable to say a word.

Thirteen summers had passed since the selkie woman came to live with MacCodrum, and the children were almost grown. As she knelt on the warm earth one afternoon, digging up silverweed roots to roast for supper, the voice of her daughter, Morag, rang clear and excited through the salt-pure air, and soon the girl was beside her holding something in her hands.

"O mother! Is this not the strangest thing I have found in the old barley-kist, softer than the mist to my touch?"

Her mother rose slowly to her feet and in silence ran her hand along the speckled brown skin. It was smooth like silk. She held it to her breast, put her other arm around her daughter, and walked back with her to the croft in silence, heedless of the girl's puzzled stares. Once inside, she called her son, Donald, to her, and spoke gently to her children: "I will soon be leaving you, *mo chridhe* (muh *khree:* my heart), and you will not see me again in the shape I am in now. I go not because I do not love you but because I must become myself again."

That night, as the moon sailed white as a pearl over the western sea, the selkie woman rose, leaving the warm bed and slumbering husband.

She walked alone to the shore and took off her clothes, one by one, and let them fall to the sand. Then she stepped lightly over the rocks and unrolled the speckled brown bundle she carried, holding it up before her. For one moment maybe she hesitated, her head turning back to the dark, sleeping croft on the machair; the next, she wrapped the shining skin about her and dropped into the singing water of the sea. For a while a sleek brown head could be seen in the dip and crest of the moon-dappled waves, pointing ever toward the far horizon, and then, swiftly leaping and diving toward her, came six other seals. They formed a circle around her, and then all were lost to sight in the soft indigo of the night.

In the croft on the machair Neil MacCodrum stirred and felt for his wife, but his hand encountered a cold and empty hollow. The only sound was the rustle of bent grass in the wind, but it did not sigh his name. He knew better than to look for her, and he also knew she would never come to him again. But when the moon was young and the tide flowing, his children would not sleep at night but ran down to the sands on silent webbed feet. There, by the rocks on the shoreline, they waited until she came—a speckled brown seal with great dark eyes. Laughing and calling her name, they splashed into the foaming water and swam with her until the break of day.

PILGRIMAGE

A good season is summer for long journeys. . . .
IRISH, ELEVENTH CENTURY

One way to fully experience the sacredness of the universe is to become a pilgrim. A pilgrimage is a prayer in the shape of a journey to a place where spirit resides. Since the dawn of time people have sought out places of divine revelation in the landscape: on holy mountains, by curative springs, at oracular caverns, and at the shrines of saints. The last days of July are traditional times for major pilgrimages to Celtic sacred sites, especially in Ireland. The long days and warm weather of

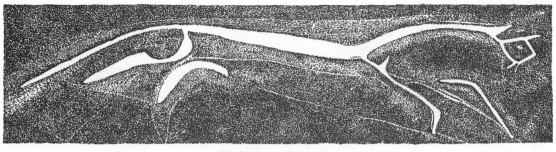

The Uffington White Horse

late July made traveling easier—the roads were less muddy and people on foot could bed down at night under the summer stars. More significantly, late July heralds the start of the quarter-day festival of Lughnasadh, when the early Celts traveled to special places to give thanks to the gods for the ripening crops. (We will be exploring the meaning and traditions associated with Lughnasadh more fully in August.)

In the sea-bound lands of northwest Europe, pilgrimage has been a deep-rooted part of the collective psyche for thousands of years. Although written records begin only with the journeys of monks in the Middle Ages, the landscape has another, older tale to tell. One of the most ancient roads in Europe is the Ridgeway, which runs eighty-five miles across the chalk downland of southern England. From at least five thousand years ago it led pilgrims westward from the Thames Valley to the great megalithic temple complex of Avebury, West Kennet, and Silbury Hill. Throughout the years pilgrims have passed by and wondered at the sacred markers of different ages that can still be seen today: burial tumps, the stone chamber of Wayland's Smithy, and the mysterious White Horse carved into the chalk, galloping forever over the downs.

The landscape of Ireland is full of places where the presence of an indwelling spirit can be felt. Most places of pilgrimage today are dedicated to Catholic saints, but the notion of pilgrimage in Ireland seems continually to emerge out of an older stratum of tradition than Christianity. The imposing quartzite peak of Croagh Patrick in County Mayo on Ireland's west coast is thought to have been a sacred mountain long before it was named for the patron saint who scaled it in 441 C.E. The second most popular pilgrimage place in Ireland is on Station Island in Lough Derg in County Donegal. Until the eighth century pilgrims entered a cave in the middle of the island, where, after much fasting and prayer, some had experiences of entering an inner kingdom as colorful as the pagan Otherworld. Local legend links the island cavern with the last bastion of druidry in Ireland.

Among the medieval tales of pilgrim monks is a story about Saint Scothíne (*sko*-hee-nyuh) of Leinster. He was a man of "great piety and of wondrous power," for he could travel from Ireland to Rome one day and return the next by walking on top of the sea. One day as he was striding across the waves, he met Saint Findbarr of Cork, who was rowing a boat.

"How is it that you are walking on the sea?" asked Findbarr.

"This is no sea, but a plain covered with clover," replied Scothíne, and he plucked a clover blossom and tossed it to the saint, saying, "But how is it that your boat floats on a plain?"

In answer to which, Findbarr dipped his hand into the water, drew out a salmon, and threw it to Scothíne.

This little tale echoes the Irish *imrama* sagas like "The Silver Branch," where Bran meets Manannán mac Lir riding his two-wheeled chariot over the sea, which is really the flowery plain of his country, the Land Under Wave. While Saint Scothíne appears to have the attributes of Manannán himself, Findbarr's swift response shows him to be a man of power, too. The salmon he effortlessly pulls out of the sea suggests he has the skills of the *fili*, who can land the Salmon of Wisdom up from the depths of the Otherworld's waters.

Findbarr, who was also known as Barrfhind, White Tops (like waves), once rode a white horse over the water from Wales to Ireland, when the wind was not favorable for sailing. The Irish Sea must have been full of saintly traffic at this time, because as the horse went plunging over the towering waves "as though on a level field," Findbarr came upon none other than the famous voyaging saint, Brendan the Navigator, riding on the back of a whale. They exchanged greetings, and Brendan promised to visit Findbarr's mentor, Saint David, when he got to Wales. Like the adventurers of Celtic legend, Saint Brendan sailed with a crew of monks in search of a mysterious island where the stones were jewels and the trees full of fragrant blossoms and apples. Known as the "Land of Promise of the Saints," the biblical overtones only thinly disguise its older name: Tír na nÓg, the Land of Youth. Many believe that Brendan's Land of Promise was in fact the east coast of North America.

INTO THE MYSTIC

Be thou a smooth way before me,
Be thou a guiding star above me,
Be thou a keen eye behind me,
This day, this night, forever.
SCOTTISH JOURNEY PRAYER

What blessed island do we hope to reach when we set out on pilgrimage? Will it be a place where we will find healing, clarity, inspiration, or perhaps a whole new perspective on life?

And will we be able to recognize it when the shoreline comes into view? An ordinary journey as tourist or traveler leaves one unchanged, but pilgrimage is a journey of the soul as well as the body and changes one forever. We leave familiar surroundings behind, not only to discover a special place but also to discover the part of ourselves that seems to have wandered away from our everyday lives. Stripped of our usual context, we travel to find out who we are in relation to sea, sky, and stone. As pilgrims, we move through an inner as well as an outer landscape, seeking the "blue remembered hills" of our soul's home.

The journey in search of the soul is symbolized by the labyrinth, a familiar image to the medieval pilgrim. In a number of French cathedrals, Chartres being the best known, it was carved on the floor so that people could walk the circuits on their knees as an alternative to traveling to holy places. A huge granite boulder carved with a labyrinth was found along the pilgrimage road to Saint Kevin's monastery in Glendalough, County Wicklow.[19] Similar stones have been found in Britain.

To walk a labyrinth, we step onto a circular path at its outer edge and are led inexorably around its many circuits until we reach the mystery at the center. There are many twists and turns, and at times it looks as if we are about to reach our goal, only to find ourselves winding toward the outside again. But, unlike a maze where we may come up against dead ends, a labyrinth has only one path, and we can trust it to lead us to our goal in its own time.

Pilgrimage to sacred sites, whether to a distant land or to a hill you can see from your window at home, takes us "from the outside to the inside." It also involves an element of trust that the journey will be worthwhile and not put us in harm's way. The word *pilgrim* derives from the Latin *peregrinus,* one who travels "through the land." In the Middle Ages, wandering monks called *perigrini* left their homelands and cast themselves on the mercy of the waves in tiny coracles to do the work of God in unknown lands. They surely must have been fired by the tremendous exhilaration that comes with leaving the safety of the known world for adventures in strange lands. When we voluntarily loosen the reins with which we control our everyday lives, we are thrust into the present, where at once we become more vibrant, more alive. With each breath we sip the cup of life and surrender to the intoxication of the universe as it unfolds each moment.

Planning a Pilgrimage

Six pointers for making a sacred journey:

Pack lightly. The essence of pilgrimage is to find out who we are outside the cocoon of our familiar milieu, so don't try to bring it along with you!

Take comfortable clothing and shoes. You will get to know the land only by walking on it, and many sacred places tend to be off the beaten track.

Be prepared to get dirt in your sandals. We are a society addicted to a lifestyle that promises to make us feel clean, safe, and protected from the environment rather than free and open to explore it.

Less is more. If you try to pack in too many places to visit, you will spend precious time on the road, especially in countries where poor or narrow roads make distances deceptive. We

can end up replicating our frenetic lives back home and return suffering spiritual indigestion rather than feeling nourished. Choose two or three special places, and prepare to spend time there for a few days, getting to know them—and the local people—in different lights, weather, and moods.

Let go of expectations. Pilgrimage is a gradual process of unfolding and discovery rather than a goal in itself. Spiritual experiences have a disconcerting tendency to happen at the least expected times and places, and they require us to stay open to a higher agenda than our own.

Embrace your shadow. Delays and inconveniences on the road or in less-than-perfect lodgings can make us annoyed and irritated. At these times we tend to see these things as roadblocks to the spiritual experience we hoped to have, whereas they are all part of it. If we observe ourselves compassionately under stress, we can learn a lot about how we operate outside our comfort zone.

"Wherever you go, there you are," or as Saint Brigit once told some pilgrims:

'Tis labor great and profit small
To go to Rome;
Thou wilt not find the king at all
Unless thou find him first at home.

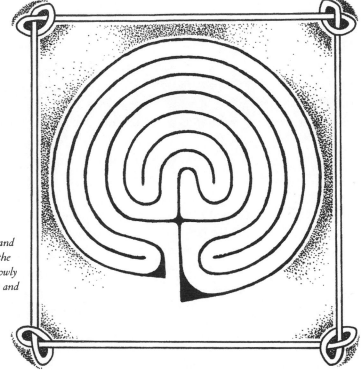

A Finger Labyrinth
for Meditation

Sit quietly, center yourself, and place your index finger at the entrance to the labyrinth. Slowly trace the path into the center and out again.

TROY STONES AND FINGER LABYRINTHS

On the north coast of Cornwall two labyrinths are carved on a rock wall next to a ruined water mill, possibly marking the path to the shrine of Saint Nechtan, a sixth-century monk. In a farm nearby there recently lived a famous wise woman, Kate "The Gull" Turner, who had a small piece of slate carved with the same pattern. It was a magical tool handed down from woman to woman through many generations. They were known as Troy stones (Troy Town was a common name for a labyrinth in England), and wise women used them by tracing their fingers along the labyrinth while humming a particular tune until they shifted into an altered state of consciousness and could enter the Otherworld.[20] With the recent renewal of interest in the labyrinth as a spiritual tool, "finger labyrinths" are once again being made, usually out of wood. A new generation of users finds them helpful as a moving meditation and a way to relax and calm the mind.

HOLY GROUND
FOUR ISLAND PILGRIMAGES

Islands, lying apart from the world and necessitating an often-perilous sea journey, have always been popular spiritual destinations in the British Isles and Ireland. Here are four famous ones, with some of the words they have inspired in pilgrims ancient and modern.

SCOTLAND: IONA

Delightful it is on the breast of an isle,
on the crest of a rock, to gaze upon
the faceted face of the sea; to view the swell
of the waves on a glittering ocean,
ceaselessly chanting plainsong to their Father.
SAINT COLUMCILLE

The great saint Columcille (*kol*-um *keel*-yuh) was probably thinking of Dun I, the highest point of Iona, when he wrote those words. He had sailed to the tiny island off the west coast of Scotland in 653 C.E. to found a monastic community for the conversion of the Picts. But legend says Iona has always been a center of spirituality from druid times and beyond. A sense of timelessness born of windswept white beaches, green marble rock, the scent of wild clover, and the constant breathing of the sea will continue to draw the pilgrims of the future to these ancient shores. Columcille once prophesied,

In Iona of my heart, Iona of my love,
Instead of monks' voices shall be the lowing of cows;
But ere the world shall come to an end,
Iona shall be as it was.[21]

WALES: BARDSEY ISLAND

There is an island there is no going
to but in a small boat the way
the saints went . . .

At the tip of the Lleyn Peninsula in North Wales, the ferry leaves for Bardsey Island, home to the bones of twenty thousand saints, according to legend, and to almost as many seabirds, according to naturalists. Bardsey was the site of the first monastic community in Britain, founded by Cadfan, a Breton saint, and pilgrimages to this island were considered almost as important as those to Rome in the Middle Ages. Another legendary inhabitant of this remote, bird-haunted island is Merlin, who lies in an enchanted sleep within a glass castle, surrounded by the Thirteen Treasures of Britain.

Was the pilgrimage
I made to come to my own
self, to learn that in times
like these and for one like me
God will never be plain and
out there, but dark rather and
inexplicable, as though he was here?
R. S. Thomas, *Frequencies*[22]

IRELAND: THE SKELLIGS

Twas thus I lived, skin to skin with the earth,
Elbowed by the hills, drenched by the billows,
Watching the wild geese making black wedges
By Skelligs far west and Annascaul of the willows.
Sigerson Clifford

Eight miles off the west Kerry coast, three islands rise like floating pyramids out of the Atlantic Ocean. These are the Skelligs (from *sceilig*, rock), and the largest is named after the archangel Michael, who guides the departed soul to its eternal home. On moonlit nights local fishermen have seen the souls of the dead hovering over the islands. Step ashore, and a steep rock stairway leads you upward, past dizzying ledges where gannets nest to a cluster of beehive-shaped stone huts, once home to a small colony of spartan monks. Further up, those with a head for heights can climb through a narrow hole in the rock called the "eye of the needle" and gain heaven that way.

A place for the pilgrim
A sanctuary of time
Fourteen steps to nowhere
Out of solid stone
Clannad, *Skellig*

Glastonbury Tor

ENGLAND: GLASTONBURY

Light born, see the pilgrim wend
To Glastonbury and journey's end,
For where light shines it must unveil
The presence of the Holy Grail
MARA FREEMAN

Glastonbury is no longer an island, since the Romans reclaimed it from the sea, yet the enigmatic shape of Glastonbury Tor with its ruined tower stands like a beacon from the Otherworld, rising out of Somerset Levels.

Pilgrims can walk the seven-tiered labyrinth leading to the summit of the Tor, once the seat of Gwynn ap Nudd, king of the Welsh faeries; wander through the ruined medieval abbey; or spend time in the peaceful gardens of the Chalice Well, where legend says the Holy Grail was hidden. Around the hill the apple orchards remind us that we are indeed on Avalon, the faery Isle of Apples.

It is to this Avalon of the heart the pilgrims still go. Some in bands, knowing what they seek. Some alone, with the staff of vision in their hands, awaiting what may come to meet them on this holy ground.
None go away as they came.
DION FORTUNE, *Avalon of the Heart*[23]

JOURNEY BLESSING
May the road rise with you,
And the wind be always at your back,
May the sun shine warm upon your face,
And the rain fall soft upon your fields,
And, till we meet again, may God hold you
In the hollow of his/her hand.
TRADITIONAL IRISH

BLACKTHORN

ᛏHE SACRED ᛕROVE

Then off to reap the corn, and leave
where I was born,
I cut a stout blackthorn to banish ghost
and goblin . . .
"The Rocky Road to Dublin,"
Irish ballad

Pilgrims have traditionally set out on their travels with a stout blackthorn walking stick. It has a particularly hard wood that polishes up to a pleasing shine, but that may not be the only reason for its choice. The blackthorn is a small tree full of sharp thorns, which protect nesting birds. Blackthorn hedges were used in early Ireland as a defense in times of tribal warfare, and the druids of Anglesey were reputed to have kept the Romans out of their stronghold with a dense blackthorn thicket. Fashioned into a stick, a branch was said to have the power of warding off evil spirits and was also used as a magical staff by witches. Hence it was an ideal companion for rambles into the unknown.

Like its cousin the whitethorn, it is a faery tree, guarded by a thin, wiry old man with pointed ears and long teeth, arms, and fingers—a personification of the sharp thorn itself. This is the *lunantishee,* one of a faery tribe that guards the tree and will not allow a stick to be cut either on the eleventh of May or November (the old Beltaine and Samhain). To do so on those days is bound to bring misfortune. The thorns also protect white flowers in the spring, which ripen into black sour fruit called sloes, an ancestor of our orchard plums. They make a fine red dye or a tangy jelly but are most famous when used to make sloe gin, a delicious deep pink liqueur.

SLOE GIN

Pick about 1 pound of sloes, and pierce their skins with a thorn or a skewer to liberate the juices. Add an equal amount of sugar, and half-fill your bottles with gin. Seal the tops and let stand at least three months, shaking occasionally to dissolve the sugar. Strain the clear liquid and enjoy.

THE INNER
CAULDRON
SACRIFICE

So will I build my altar in the fields,
And the blue sky my fretted dome shall be,
And the sweet fragrance that the wild flower yields
Shall be the incense I will yield to thee.
S. T. COLERIDGE

In June we looked at ways in which the plants and the spirits of the earth bestow healing upon the human world. Sacrifice is the act of giving back to the earth in return, and it is healing for us, too, for it brings us closer to a genuine participation in the reciprocal flow of the universe. Modern society has come to view the world as an inanimate supplier of human needs whose resources we have the right to continually plunder. Forests, wetlands, mountains, minerals, rivers, animals and birds—all the living, intricate, marvelous forms of the universe are reduced to economic units to feed the insatiable appetite of human desire. The Celtic awareness of the need to walk in balance with the Earth can teach us ways to honor, respect, and show gratitude to the universe that sustains us.

Pre-Christian Celtic religious practices derive from ancient Indo-European cosmology whereby the universe was created from the body of a god. This deity was a willing sacrifice, and at his death the different parts of his body became the elements of the universe: his skull became the sky, his blood the rivers, his bones the mountains, his breath the wind, his hair the plants, and so on. The god's sacrifice became a model for later sacrifices, which were considered necessary for the renewal of the world. The death of a divine being led to the creation of the world, so a living sacrifice was required to ensure the universe would be continually restored and not just die out through entropy. The offering of a creature from the microcosm would guarantee the continuation of the macrocosm. In early times human beings might be sacrificed; in later times an animal, usually an ox or a sheep, was ritually slain, and offerings were made of herbs, plants, and other fruit of the earth.

This month, rather than work at the altar in our home, we are going to look at some ways in which we can make our sacrifices on the altars on the land. Remember: a sacred site does not have to be famous or located in a distant country. It can also be a quiet, secret place you have found in the woods or, if you live in the city, a favorite old tree in a local park that has a special atmosphere.

Three Ways to Honor the Earth
  1. Offerings and Libations
  Traditional offerings to the spirits of the land are grain, ale, or milk. At a number of old Celtic sacred sites are stones that form natural altars. In Ireland they are called *balláns* (*bahl*-awns), meaning "little bowls," while in Scotland some are called "dobby stanes" or "gruagach stones," the gruagach being a *genius loci*, or spirit of the place. Libations of milk fresh from the cow, custard made with eggs, or ale were poured into the hollow. In other places people sprinkled grain in the form of bread, cake, or porridge straight onto the earth. When I am traveling in Ireland I always carry a spare chunk of soda bread; in Scotland a packet of oatcakes. These are easily portable and a local food source from crops used as offerings in the past. In the rainy season in California I like to hike out to a beautiful old oak under which wild chanterelles grow. Before I fill my basket I leave an offering to the tree whose plentiful fallen leaves enable the mushrooms to grow—usually a granola bar or apple from my backpack! Sprigs of heather and posies of flowers are also good offerings, but bring your own bunch or a garland rather than picking the wild ones. Leave only offerings that are biodegradable or will be appreciated by wild birds and animals.

When you approach a sacred site:
  Circle around it three times in a sunwise direction.
  Silently ask permission of the invisible guardians before you enter. If it feels like you have permission to proceed, enter quietly and find a place to sit or stand.
  Close your eyes, and take some deep breaths to calm body and mind.
  Open your eyes. Greet the *genii loci*, and make your offering. Speak words that come from your heart, or use a simple rhyme (spirits enjoy childlike rhythm and song!) like the following:

> *Powers of the living Earth,*
> *Hear me as I greet*
> *Sky and stars above me,*
> *Earth below my feet*

Old Ones, Ancestors,
Water, stone and tree,
Shining Ones, Faery Folk,
Lords of the Sídhe:
Please accept this offering, given in love.
  May your kingdoms be preserved and
  protected forever.

Spend as long as you like in communion with the place. Listen, smell, touch, and drink in its special atmosphere. If you are lucky you will receive a response, either as an inner voice or image or in the movements of wind, clouds, leaves, birds, or animals. The more often you can frequent a place, the easier it is to develop a relationship with its indwelling guardians.

2. Cleaning Up

Many sacred sites, once known only to locals or devout pilgrims, all too often attract the wrong kind of visitors today. It is disheartening to enter a lovely glen and find it full of litter and beer cans. This is where the best sacrifice we can offer is to clean the place up. Carry a trash bag in your backpack, and know that you are doing sacred work.

A more recent form of desecration, sad to say, is often the result of people who visit sacred sites to perform ceremonies. Standing stones that have stood undisturbed for thousands of years end up covered with candle wax or, worse still, blackened and cracked because someone has lit a fire on them. At other places the ground is disturbed because of people burying crystals all around. In case it needs to be said, *none* of these bears any remote relation to traditional Celtic practices. Apart from causing damage to priceless cultural treasures, they disturb and alter the subtle energies of the place, anger the guardian spirits, and even drive them away so that the site becomes energetically dead. In the end the best thing to bring to a sacred site is your calm, peaceful awareness and respect for the land and its invisible guardians. The best thing to take away is the knowledge that you have done your best to leave it in a pristine condition.

3. Healing the Earth

A special kind of pilgrimage is the journey taken to a place where the Earth has been wounded or is in danger of being defiled due to human ignorance or greed. This is a sacred journey in service to the Earth, which aligns us with the Celtic ethos of honoring the web of life. For example, in recent years thousands of people in the western United States have walked through the Nevada desert to protest nuclear weapons testing or have spent months at the Headwaters Forest in northern California to protect old-growth redwood trees from commercial logging. A theologian, one of sixty thousand people who traveled to Seattle to protest the destructive economic policies of the World Trade Organization, has called this modern pilgrimage "an actively mobilized process of bearing witness to woundedness and to the mysterious possibilities of the sacred."[24]

On this kind of pilgrimage all Earth becomes our altar, and our sacrifice produces ripples that expand throughout the living cosmos and down in time to future generations. Like the early Celts, we perform a sacred act in the hopes that we, too, might restore the universe.

BLESSING OF THE ELEMENTS

Grace of the love of the skies be thine,
Grace of the love of the stars be thine,
Grace of the love of the moon be thine,
Grace of the love of the sun be thine,
Grace of the love
and the crown of heaven be thine.
CARMINA GADELICA

THE FESTIVAL OF LUGHNASADH

Month of August . . . blithesome the bee,
Full the hive; better the work of the sickle
Than the bow.

WELSH, FIFTEENTH CENTURY

The third great festival of the Celtic year takes place on August 1, known in Ireland as Lughnasadh, "the assembly of Lugh," one of the chief gods of the Tuatha Dé Danann. It marks the midpoint of the summer half of the year between May and November and is the first of the three autumn months. In early Ireland it marked the beginning of the harvest season, which continued till the last sheep and cattle were brought down from the highland pastures in time for Samhain. Farmers reaped the first ears of wheat, oats, and barley and, in later centuries, dug up the first new potatoes. Lambs were weaned so that their mothers would mate and conceive new offspring to be born the following year in time for Imbolc. Soft fruits swelled and ripened—gooseberries in the

FESTIVAL NAMES

Language	Name	Pronunciation
Irish Gaelic	Lughnasadh	*loo*-nuh-suh
Scottish Gaelic	Lùnasdal	*loon*-uhsd-uhl
Manx	Luanys	*loo*-uh-nis
Welsh	Gwl Awst (the August Feast)	gooil oust
Cornish	Goel Est	gole est
Breton	Gouel an Eost	gweyl un yost

garden, bilberries on the moors. The gods had kept their covenant with the people, and it was time to celebrate earth's bounty.

Lughnasadh falls directly opposite Imbolc on the Celtic Wheel of the Year. Imbolc marked the halfway point of the dark, *gam*, or feminine, half of the year and was very much a women's festival, associated with childbirth and the dairy and presided over by Brigit. Celebrations clustered around the home and family. Lughnasadh stands at the center of the light half of the year and was more of a men's festival. Festivities took place at large outdoor conventions and fairs and included traditionally masculine activities such as commerce, horse racing, and settling legal matters. Even as late as the nineteenth century when the great assemblies of old were reduced to picnics, patterns, and country fairs, the festival was known as "Men's Sunday" in many parts of Ireland.[1]

In the Christian era the festival on August 1 became Lammas, the name derived from *hlaf-mæsse* (loaf-mass), the Old English name for the feast, when a loaf made from the first ripe grain was taken to church to be consecrated upon the altar.

Summer's over: Today is Lughna Day,
the night stretches.
CAPE CLEAR SAYING

LUGH THE MANY SKILLED

The god who initiated the August feast in early Ireland reveals himself less clearly than Brigit, who in her guise as saint remained a living presence in people's lives long after the advent of Christianity. We have to go further back in time to discover Lugh, but Julius Caesar gave us a clue as to his identity and function when he wrote that the god worshiped most by the Gauls was Mercury, whom they declared to be "the inventor of all arts," the guardian of roads and travelers, and a patron of moneymaking and commerce. The Gauls called this god Lugus, and his name was given to many European cities, such as Leiden, Liegnitz, and Lyon (Lugdunum), where a great festival was held on August 1 in Roman times.

In Ireland Lugus became Lugh, a renowned hero of the Tuatha Dé Danann. Some scholars believe his name derives from the Old Irish word *lug*, "light, brightness." He was known as Lugh Lámhfhada (*loo law-vo-duh*), Lugh of the Long Arm, which could refer to the rays of the sun. Others consider it more likely that his name derives from a Celtic word, *lugio*, meaning an oath, because Lugh was the patron of social contracts. His "long arm" may simply describe the way his weapons had a long range, since he was famed for his skill with sling and spear.

Among the Tuatha Dé Danann, Lugh was known as Samildánach (*saw-vil-dawn-ukh*), Many Skilled, meaning he was master of many arts. This referred not only to crafts but also to magic and warfare. An eleventh-century tale, "Cath Maige Tuired," the (Second) Battle of Moytirra, tells how this Celtic superhero first came to the Tuatha Dé Danann in the days when they ruled Ireland.

Lugh Comes to Tara

Núadu, King of the Tuatha Dé Danann, was giving a great feast at Tara, but despite the lavish food and entertainment it was clear that his people were ill at ease. Their enemies, the host of the Fomorians, were mustering their forces to attack Ireland, and they were a huge and formidable host. The doorkeeper was on watch outside when he saw an unknown band of men riding toward the gates. At their head was a strong, handsome young warrior wearing a royal crown. As they drew up to the door, one of his men announced him as Lugh of the Fierce Combats.

"Now, what do you want?" asked the doorkeeper. "Unless you have something to offer us, I'm not about to let you in."

"Just ask me," said Lugh. "I'm a builder."

The doorkeeper began to turn away. "We

don't need you. We have a builder already, Luchta mac Lúachada."

"Ask me again, doorkeeper!" said Lugh. "I'm a blacksmith."

The doorkeeper shook his head. "We have a blacksmith already, Colum Cúaléinech of the three new techniques."

Lugh said, "Go on—ask again. I'm a champion fighter."

The doorkeeper yawned. "We don't need you. We have a champion already, Ogma mac Ethlend."

"Ask me again, doorkeeper. I am a harper."

"We don't need you. We have a harper already, Abcán mac Bicelmois; the men of the three gods chose him in the *sídhe*-mounds."

"Then I'll have you know I am also a warrior."

"We don't need you. We have a warrior already, Bresal Etarlam mac Echdach Báethláim."

"Well, how about this? I'm a poet and a historian."

"We don't need you. We already have a poet and historian, Én mac Ethamain."

Lugh said, "Try this, then: I'm a magician."

"We don't need you. We have more druids and people of power than we know what to do with."

Lugh said, "Well, here's another one, then: I'm a physician."

"We don't need you. Dían Cécht's our physician."

"Could you do with a cupbearer?"

"We have plenty of cupbearers: Delt and Drúcht and Daithe, Tae and Talom and Trog, Glé and Glan and Glésse."

Lugh said, "I'm sure you need a bronzesmith."

"We do not need *Lugh*," said the doorkeeper, pointedly. "We have a bronzesmith already, Crédne Cerd."

Lugh put his face up very close to the doorkeeper's and whispered, "Ask the king whether he has one man who can do everything. If he does, then I'll leave Tara."

The doorkeeper went into the royal hall and told everything to the king.

"A warrior has arrived whose name is Samildánach—the One of Many Skills. He practices every one of the arts and is master of them all!"

Núadu listened thoughtfully, then ordered his best players to challenge Lugh to a game of *fidchell* (*fith*-yell), a game like chess. Lugh won every game—not surprising, since he invented it—and at last Núadu declared, "Let him to be brought into court, for the likes of him has never before come to Tara!"

The doorkeeper let him through, and Lugh was led up to the seat of the sage because he was a master of every skill. But Ogma the Champion thought to test his boasts. Muscles bulging, he heaved up a flagstone that was so heavy it took fourscore yoke of oxen to move it and hurled it through the wall. Lugh calmly went outside and tossed it back in again so that it landed in its place, then flicked the piece of the wall after it to fill up the gap.

The assembled warriors were greatly entertained by Lugh's feats.

"Play us some music now, if you're a harper!" they shouted. So Lugh took up a harp and began to play. He played the Music of Sleep, which set them nodding for a whole day; he played the Music of Sorrow so that they cried like babies into their mead; he played the Music of Joy so that they wiped their tears on their sleeves and began carousing.

Núadu began to think that maybe here was the warrior that could save them from the dreaded Fomorians. He held a council with his druid advisors and gave Lugh his place on the royal throne of Tara for thirteen days and nights.

Lugh went on to lead the Tuatha Dé Danann to victory against the Fomorians. At first his men tried to keep him out of the actual battle because he was too valuable to lose, but he managed to give his guardians the slip and appeared on the front lines, urging on his side. Balor, one of the most monstrous and feared of the Fomorians, heard Lugh as he darted about on one leg and with one eye closed (a magical posture), shouting encouragement and chanting spells designed to weaken the enemy. Balor had a unique and terrible weapon: a poisonous eye, which he would turn on his enemies and strike them dead. An eyelid with a polished ring-pull covered it when it was not in use, and it took four men to raise it.

"Lift up my eyelid, lad, so I may see the babbler who wants a word with me!" sneered Balor. But just as his eye began to open, Lugh fitted a stone to his sling and hurled it at Balor's eye. It went straight through Balor's head and out the other side, causing the Fomorians themselves to look upon the deadly eye. Now the tide of battle turned in favor of the Tuatha Dé Danann, who soon put the Fomorians to rout across the sea.

One of the Fomorians whom they were about to kill, Bres mac Elathan, bargained for his release with Lugh by giving away the secrets of plowing, sowing, and reaping. This may point to the symbolic meaning of the battle between the Tuatha Dé Danann and the Fomorians as a war waged between human beings and the forces of nature that held the power to yield or withdraw the fruit of the earth. Such mythic battles are well known in other early cultures, notably the gods and Titans of ancient Greece, and the Devas and Asuras of India. The Battle of Moytirra is none other than a Celtic version of the primal conflict between the forces of light and dark, good and evil, civilization and chaos, culture and nature. Lugh himself can be regarded as a culture hero who wrested the secrets of cultivation from the wild for the good of the tribe. As the "many-skilled" one, he is the personification of the greatest achievements of early Celtic society.

THE GATHERING OF THE TRIBES

Corn, milk, peace, happy ease,
Full nets, ocean's plenty,
Graybearded men, chieftains in amity . . .
IRISH, ELEVENTH CENTURY

The great Lughnasadh assemblies of early Ireland celebrated both the firstfruits of the land and the "ripened" talents of human society. Like the Greek Olympics, they featured races, games, and athletics and were also festivals of the arts and forums for political and legal debate. The most famous Lughnasadh assembly was held at Teltown, the burial place of Lugh's foster mother, Tailtiu (*tal-chuh*), the last queen of the Fir Bolg, the race that ruled Ireland before the Tuatha Dé Danann. Her name derives from Old Celtic *Talantiu*, "The Great One of the Earth." Tailtiu cleared a great forest to form what is today the county of Meath, in which lies some of Ireland's richest farmland. But she collapsed from exhaustion, and as she lay dying she asked Lugh to hold funeral games every August in her honor. As long as they were held, she prophesied that there would be "corn and milk in every house, peace and fair weather" for the feast.[2] In fact, Lughnasadh has an older name, Brón Trogain, which refers to the fertile earth.

In Celtic tradition a plentiful harvest could not be won without the cooperation of the earth goddess, of whom Tailtiu is a local manifestation. Before a new king could be inaugurated, he had to undergo a ritual marriage with the goddess of the land in her role as Sovereignty, for only she could confer upon him the authority to rule. We first came across this theme in March, in the story of the "The Voices of the Wells." When the well maidens were raped by an evil king, the land became blighted and barren. This theme recurs in the Grail Cycle, where a wounded king lies close to death in a Wasteland that can only be restored when the Grail (as a chalice, a symbol of the goddess) is recognized. Lugh and Tailtiu may once have been related as king and consort, but if so the original myth has been lost.[3] In a medieval tale, "Baile in Scáil," Lugh appears as the husband of the Sovereignty goddess as she initiates a future king.

In early Ireland a good harvest depended upon the king being a just and worthy ruler, for he was a representative of the people. Under such a monarch, the weather was mild, sheep and cattle multiplied, granaries overflowed, and orchards hung heavy with fruit. If he was either physically defective or morally reprehensible, the land would not be fertile and the people would fail to thrive. He represented the creative, masculine principle of the universe as symbolized by the "stone phallus," the Lia Fáil at Tara, which was reputed to cry out when touched by a man destined to become king.

Teltown was only fifteen miles from Tara, the seat of the High King, who presided over the festival. Chieftains from outlying areas came bearing special Lughnasadh tributes to him: seafood, watercress, wild bilberries, venison, fish from the River Boyne, and water from the sacred well of the goddess Tlachtga (*tlokht*-ghuh). Bread was not included, probably because it is made from a cultivated crop, whereas wild foods are the natural fruit of the earth. When the king ate a ritual meal from the offerings, he was eating the food of the goddess, and this guaranteed a plentiful harvest season.

A number of other Lughnasadh festivals took place in other areas of Ireland, all at places connected with mysterious Otherworld women. A famous assembly took place at Carman, an unidentified place in eastern Ireland named after another goddess figure whose original lore has been lost. That she, too, represented the earth's bounty is clear in that this festival was held to ensure corn and milk, choice fruits and plenty of fish, heroic men, tender women, and good cheer in every household. Without the festivities, there would be decay, early grayness, and immature kings. For the festival of Lughnasadh represents the culmination of a successful partnership between the king and the goddess of the land, between the people and the earth.

Three abundances in Ireland: an abundance
of ears of corn, an abundance of flowers, and
an abundance of fruit.

IRISH TRIAD

These early assemblies may have lasted up
to three weeks. As well as providing an arena
for resolving important social issues and sanc-
tioning laws, they were an opportunity for a
lavish display of all the arts under Lugh's
patronage—athletics, craftsmanship, ball
games, and horse racing, the last two of which
he was supposed to have invented. The original Lugus-Mercury was patron of commerce,
so it followed that there would also be a
market, where different tribes, isolated for
most of the year, could trade goods. The Celts,
who always loved colorful costumes and finery,
no doubt came dressed in their best. Artists
and entertainers displayed their talents, and
there were storytelling recitations and music
contests, with prizes of gold or jewels awarded
to the best performers by a chieftain, queen,
or other person of high rank. In other parts of
the fair riders on horseback delighted audiences with feats of skill and acrobatics, while
crowds gathered around showmen, jugglers,
and clowns sporting grotesque masks and
painted faces or watched conjurers perform
fantastical magic tricks. The entertainment
was accompanied by all the cacophony of the
modern fairground, according to an eleventh-
century poem about the Fair of Carman:

Trumpets, harps, hollow-throated horns,
pipers, timpanists, unwearied,
poets and gentle musicians . . .

. . . fiddlers, gleemen,
bone-players and bag-pipers,
a rude crowd, noisy, profane,
roaring and shouting.[4]

But the high-spirited revelry never got out
of hand, for strict rules prohibited any kind of
brawling or fighting. Part of the Fair of
Carman was set aside for traders who had
come from all over Ireland to sell produce
and farm animals, together with a

great market of the Greek foreigners
where there is gold and fine raiment . . .[5]

The festival was also an occasion for hand-
fasting, or trial marriages. At Teltown, young
men and women lined up on either side of a
wooden gate in a high wall in which a hole was

carved, large enough for a hand. One by one, girl and boy would grasp a hand in the hole, without being able to see who was on the other side. They were now married and could live together for a year and day to see if it worked out. If not, the couple returned to next year's gathering and officially separated by standing back-to-back and walking away from each other. This was known as a "Teltown marriage."

As night fell the skies provided a dazzling show of a different kind as meteor showers danced in the dark. They are still known in Ireland as "The Games of Lugh."

HORSE

A CELTIC BESTIARY

Whether on ancient battlefield or modern racecourse, the horse has captured the hearts and minds of the Celts for centuries. Revered for their speed, elegance, and sexual vigor, they were a symbol of prestige among the highest-ranking members of Celtic society. Both gods and goddesses are associated with the horse and mare. The Irish god Eochaid (*o*-khith) from *ech*, "horse," was a rider of the heavens whose horses were Wind and Sun; Manannán had a horse that could ride over the sea as well as land; the Welsh Rhiannon (hree-*ahn*-non) was deeply connected to the white mare, as was Epona of Gaul, who is shown sitting sidesaddle upon a small horse, accompanied by a bird, a dog, and a foal.

The early Celts outfitted their horses in the finest bronze trappings, often inlaid with coral and enamel, so that they looked magnificent whether drawing the two-wheeled chariots used in times of war or galloping over the plains in races for the entertainment of kings. Their delight in richly caparisoned horses is clearly apparent in myths and sagas, such as the Welsh "Culwch and Olwen," where King Arthur's young cousin goes to court: "The boy went off on a four-year-old steed with a gleaming grey head, sturdy-legged, hollow-hoofed, a tubular gold bridle around his head, and a precious gold saddle upon his back. . . . A purple four-cornered mantle about him, with a reddish-gold apple mounted at each corner, each apple worth a hundred cows."[6]

Faery queens and princes ride on white horses into our world, sometimes to take a human lover, as did the Queen of Elfland with Thomas the Rhymer. The beautiful Otherworld princess Niamh (*nee-uv*) came riding out of the sea on a white horse and invited Fionn McCumhaill's son, Oisín, to come with her to Tír na nÓg. Not one to waste time, Oisín leaped up behind her, and the lovers galloped away until they reached the western shore. As soon as the horse's gold-shod hoofs touched the water, he neighed three times and "plunged forward at once, moving over the face of the sea with the speed of a cloud-shadow on a March day."[7]

LAMMAS FAIRS

The Lughnasadh festivals of early Ireland were the grandest events of the summer, until the dynasty of the High Kings came to an end with the Norman Conquest in the twelfth century. But all over Ireland, right up to the middle of the twentieth century, country people have celebrated the beginning of harvest at revels, wakes, and fairs—and some still continue today as lively as ever.

"Lammas," or "Gooseberry," Fairs were usually held on the Sunday nearest to August 1 so that a whole day could be set aside from work. Booths and stalls sprang up, like mushrooms overnight at well-known holy wells and other places of summer pilgrimage, until the Victorians banned the fairs for being too rowdy. They were colorful, noisy gatherings where people came from miles around to sell farm animals, local produce, or horses. Tinkers and trick-of-the-loop men hawked their wares at booths and sideshows. Stalls were piled high with silks and homespuns, pots and pans, while gooseberries, currants, and cherries lay heaped like jewels. Vendors did a roaring trade in such delicacies as pigs' trotters, gingerbread, and sticky yellow toffee, beloved by children, while others provided "strong beer and maddening whiskey for wranglers and busybodies." Fortune-tellers and entertainers of all kinds plied their trades in makeshift stalls, and "open-doored booths were filled with lovers."[8] Musicians and dancers competed for prizes under a decorated pole called a *craeb*, while in other areas the air resounded with the whacks and blood-curdling yells of faction fighters engaged in the ancient art of stick fighting. An Irish folktale calls this season the "little lunacy week in August."

Gatherings also took place at rivers and lakes, where young men rode horses and cattle into the water, a ritual designed to keep the animals healthy. Those standing on the shore cast spancels, halters, and lumps of butter into the water as offerings, praying for protection on their animals. The most daring of the young bucks competed with one another in swimming races on horseback, sometimes even in the sea—a dangerous sport that proved fatal on more than one occasion.[9]

But most Lughnasadh gatherings took place on high hills and mountaintops, where the sky seems to go on forever and the landscape of Ireland is laid out in splendor: all her rivers, peaks and woods, rolling hills and curving coastline. For our ancestors, who knew the lore behind every one of these

THE FAERY SHOEMAKER

As on the other quarter days, the faeries ventured out into the human world at Lughnasadh, although they were not quite as evident as on the three spirit nights of the year. One celebration in County Cavan was held on a hill near a cave where once a fiddler had wandered in to play a few tunes. He was never seen again, but Lughnasadh revelers in later years often heard the sounds of fiddle music and faery dancing within the cave. One August the festival was in full swing on top of the rock above the cave when people heard the "sweetest, strangest music imaginable" down below. Out of the cave appeared a tiny fiddler in old-fashioned clothes. The party danced to his music till the sun went down and he disappeared.[10]

One particular kind of faery associated with Lughnasadh is the leprechaun, the faery shoemaker. Some believe his name derives from _Lugh-chorpán,_ "little Lugh-body." The Gaulish Lugh was the patron of shoemakers, an association that has found its way into Welsh myth, where Llew Llaw Gyffes (_hluh_-ee hlow _guh_-fess), Lugh's Welsh counterpart, is a shoemaker.

features, it must have been like turning the pages of the book of the land to reveal the pageant of the gods: *That plain is where Fionn pursued his runaway wife. That glen is where she and her lover hid! Those peaks are the rocks the Old Woman dropped as she flew down to the sea! That lake was formed from one who wept for Princess Gile. . . .*

For many, this joyful day was known as "Bilberry," "Heatherberry," or "Fraughan" Sunday, for as they climbed the heathery slopes of the hill they gathered the little blue fruit called *fraughans (fraw-huns)*—from *fraoch,* heather. The boys liked to show off to their sweethearts by weaving little wicker or rush baskets for their berry collecting. Others made berry bracelets and slipped them onto a slim wrist to make romantic feelings known. On top of the hill, they sang and danced barefoot to the music of melodeons, fiddles, and flutes; played leapfrog and rounders; wrestled, raced, and competed in other contests of skill; gossiped with old friends; and listened to stories from the elders. It was all "all high spirits, open air and joy."[11] Often the chosen hill was topped with an ancient stone, reputed to have magical properties, on which people sat for healing and good luck. In some places, a young woman—or an effigy of one—crowned with the last of the summer's flowers, sat in state upon a stone chair, with garlands strewn at her feet. Dancers whirled around her, touching her garlands or pulling off a ribbon for good luck. In this way, perhaps, the earth goddess was still remembered with honor.

BLUEBERRY JAM

> *On Summer Sunday's afternoon*
> *The old rock was a sight:*
> *The boys and girls would congregate*
> *With wild unfeigned delight*
> *And pass the hours till milking time*
> *When home they would return*
> *With baskets filled with fraocháns*
> *From the Rock of Carrickbyrne.*

The full baskets were taken home to the kitchen, where the girls made sweet fraughan cakes topped with purple fraughan cream, to give to their beaux at the Fraughan Bonfire Dance. If any berries managed to last till the next day, they might be made into pies, jam, or even bilberry wine, which had a reputation for kindling romance and hastening on the wedding! Because these hilltop gatherings often required a long walk followed by a strenuous climb, the berry pickers always set aside some of their harvest for weaker members of the community who had stayed behind.

The following recipe makes seven to eight half-pint jars of jam, which should be plenty for you to share with others. It comes from Scotland, where the fruit is called blaeberries (blueberries) and is made with rhubarb for a sharper taste and better texture. North American blueberries work just as well.

Ingredients

8 cups blueberries, bilberries,
    or huckleberries
4 cups rhubarb, chopped into 1-inch pieces
1 teaspoon lemon rind, grated
2 tablespoons lemon juice
1 cup water
4 cups granulated sugar

Method

1. In a large heavy saucepan, combine blueberries, rhubarb, lemon rind and juice, and water.
2. Bring to a boil, stirring frequently; reduce heat and simmer, very gently, for 10 minutes.
3. Add sugar; increase heat to high and boil vigorously, stirring often.
4. After about 20 minutes, test jam for setting by putting a small amount on a cold plate and pushing it gently with your thumb. If it wrinkles, it's ready.
5. Remove from the heat, skim off foam, and stir for 3–5 minutes to suspend fruit evenly throughout the jam.
6. Fill sterilized jars and seal.

CELEBRATE COMMUNITY

In an age where many of us feel all too disconnected from one another, the high days of August are an ideal time to come together with friends and neighbors to foster a sense of community. Lugh, as the Celtic Mercury, presides over communication, travel, and gatherings where there is a creative interchange of ideas.

At this time of year some areas put on Renaissance fairs or Highland games, which often capture something of the atmosphere of the old Lughnasadh gatherings. If there are none near you, visit your nearest county fair. Stroll among the show animals and prize vegetables, sample the baked goods, and admire the traditional crafts. Pay your respects to the farmers through whose labor and skill we have food on our tables. They connect us to the earth-centered ways of our ancestors.

Start a family or neighborhood tradition by organizing your own Lughnasadh event, like a potluck picnic in the park, by a river, at the beach, or on a nearby hill. Alternatively, you can hold it in your own backyard, where you can pay more attention to decorating the table with flowers, ears of grain, fruit, and other seasonal produce.

- If you have a large group, organize team games such as volleyball, tug-of-war, swimming races, or whatever is appropriate to the space. Bring ears of wheat and barley to make harvest knots and corn dollies. Encourage people to bring musical instruments, songs, and stories to share.
- Ask people to bring food and drink made from the new harvest of fruits, vegetables, and grains, such as fruit drinks and salads, homemade bread, cakes, and scones. When the tribes came together for the national assembly at Teltown, they brought regional goods to share. If you live in an ethnically diverse community, you might have people bring the food of their ancestors. Have everyone share stories, personal or cultural, about their dish before you eat.
- Before you get down to the feast, give thanks for the blessings of the firstfruits with a grace, such as this modern Irish one:

ALTÚ

*I láthair mo mhuintire
siar go dtí tús na beatha,
i bhfianaise na ndéithe
agus na n-aindéithe,
in ómós do fhéile
ollmhór na cruinne,
gabhaim buíochas
roimh mo chuid*

GRACE

*In the presence of my
    people
back to the beginning of
    life,
In the witness of the gods
and the ungods,
In homage to the
    immense
generosity of the universe,
I give thanks
before my portion.*
DENNIS KING

MAKING A HARVEST KNOT

At harvesttime it was traditional for men and women to give each other woven harvest knots as tokens of affection. The women often wore them in their hair, while the men pinned them to their buttonholes. These are quite simple to make and fun to do at a group gathering, especially for those less inclined to more boisterous Lughnasadh activities.

Gather together
4 wheat straws with heads
string for tying straws together
Many types of braids can be used to create a
    traditional love knot. This knot uses four

straws to create a tubular plait, which is quick and easy to weave.

Method

1. Soak the straws in hot water until they are flexible. Make sure to remove the leaves from the straws by cutting just above the first node and peeling off the leaves. Only use the head and first joint of the straw for the weave.

2. Tie together the straws just below the heads, and bend them to lie in a 90-degree angle from the heads. Envision the face of a clock: straw A points to one o'clock, straw B points to four o'clock, straw C points to eight o'clock, straw D points to eleven o'clock. Don't position the straws at right angles to each other. This weave fills in the gaps created when a straw is moved, by using the next straw clockwise to the one just used. This creates a rounded tubular plait that can be used as woven or can be stretched to increase the length and change the look.

3. Always move in a clockwise direction, picking up the straw next to the gap just filled and placing it in the open space.

4. Complete six to eight inches of braid, tie it into a loose pretzel knot, then use thread to tie the end of the braid to the base of the heads. Give the knot to one you love.

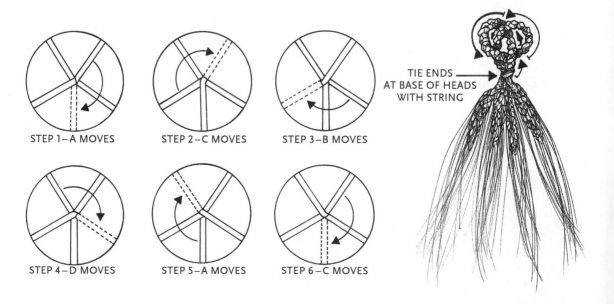

STEP 1–A MOVES   STEP 2–C MOVES   STEP 3–B MOVES

STEP 4–D MOVES   STEP 5–A MOVES   STEP 6–C MOVES

TIE ENDS AT BASE OF HEADS WITH STRING

HOLY GROUND
CROAGH PATRICK
(COUNTY MAYO, IRELAND)

Many Lughnasadh pilgrimages and gatherings are held on hilltops and mountains, for high places have always been associated with Lugh (as they are with the Roman Mercury). The tallest of these is Croagh Patrick (Cruach Phádraig, "Patrick's Cone") in County Mayo, which is visited by thousands of pilgrims every year on the last weekend of July. This impressive quartzite peak rises like a serene blue pyramid 2,510 feet above the western sea, earning its name as Ireland's holiest mountain. According to Christian legends, Saint Patrick fasted upon the summit forty days and forty nights in 441 C.E. and drove out snakes and other demonic forces from the site. One of the "demons" was a woman, perhaps once a local goddess of the waters, whom he banished to the bottom of a nearby lake, while the other was Crom Dubh (*krom duv*), the old pagan god of the harvest.

Although Christianity has obliterated older traditions, local stories and customs offer a few glimpses into the mountain's pagan past. One legend tells that inside the mountain was a palace where lived a group of faery women who loved to dance. Barren women used to spend the night of August 1 at a certain magical spot in hopes that they would conceive. Archaeologists have recently discovered scores of prehistoric remains scattered about the mountain, which suggest that Croagh Patrick has been an important ritual landscape for over five thousand years.

GODS OF THE CELTS:
CROM DUBH

Around Croagh Patrick, and in other parts of Ireland, the Lughnasadh holiday was known as Domhnach Chrom Dubh, "Crom Dubh's Sunday." Little is known about the mysterious Crom Dubh, whose name means the "Dark, Bent One," yet he seems to have been the dominant god of the harvest in Ireland before the coming of Christianity. Until quite recently he was remembered in Munster as "the little black man who first brought wheat into Ireland." He was "bent" because he carried it upon his back, rather like Kokopelli, the humpbacked spirit of southwestern Native American tribes, whose hump was actually a bag of seeds that he brought as a gift to the people. A story from Sligo describes how Crom Dubh taught the people to sow and reap, advised them about weather conditions, and gave the laborers the first food at the feast day dinner. He was also the guardian of a sacred bull, the most highly valued of Celtic animals. In the nineteenth century people used to climb Slieve Callan in County Clare on August 1 to pay honor to Crom Dubh, even though they did not remember who he was. On top was a weathered dolmen on which they strewed wildflowers in memory of the forgotten little god of the harvest.

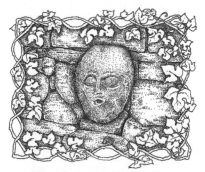

The stone head of Crom Dubh at Clochane, County Kerry

OAK

THE SACRED GROVE

Choose the Oak of the Sun . . .
RHYME OF THE SACRED WOODS, SCOTLAND

Famed for its endurance and longevity, oak has always been synonymous with strength and stability. Known in early Ireland as the "Tara of the wood," it has natural associations with Lugh, who was a protector of kings. Lugh's counterpart in Welsh mythology is the hero Llew Llaw Gyffes, "the Fair One of the Steady Hand," whose adventures are recounted in the fourth branch of the *Mabinogi*. In this story

Lleu turns into an eagle and perches atop a magical oak tree, where he suffers "nine-score hardships." Lleu's fate reminds us of the way Odin hung on the World Tree, Yggdrasil, for nine days, and indeed, Lugh is often compared to the great god of Norse mythology.[12]

Like a good king, oak supports those in need of protection. A west country folktale tells of an oak that helps a girl escape a cruel king by sending a bough crashing onto his head. The king's men come to fell the tree but meet with a sorry fate:

Oh they rode in the wood, where the oaken tree stood
To cut down the tree, the oaken tree
Then the tree gave a groan and summoned his own,
For the trees closed about and they never got out
Of the wood, the wonderful wood.[13]

In another tale from the same region, "The Vixen and the Oakmen," oak-tree spirits hide an exhausted vixen who is being pursued by hunters, for "they guard all forest beasts." When the pursuers are gone, the oakmen invite the vixen to "Wipe your sore paws in our oak tree rain pool," which makes her pads heal and her torn fur grow again.[14]

If you feel in need of strength and restoration, stand with your whole body against an oak and soak in the calm steadying energy of this monarch of the woods.

A number of folktale fragments from the British Isles and Ireland describe a harvesting contest between a human hero and a formidable magical being: an evil spirit or the devil himself. The human hero, representing culture, usually outwits his opponent, who originally represented the untamed forces of nature. Often he does this through the use of iron, which is traditionally abhorred by Otherworld beings, some say because they are the folk memory of the pre—Iron Age inhabitants, who were displaced by the Celts with their superior iron tools and weapons. In what are probably the oldest versions, nature is represented by a *Cailleach*, or hag: the death aspect of the Earth Goddess, who can cause the crops to fail. Her other face is the young, life-bringing goddess of springtime. In the following story I have taken themes from Irish, Scottish, and Cornish lore to create a new quilt out of the patchwork pieces.

DONAGH MÓR AND
THE HAG OF THE FIELDS

Along time ago an old woman and her daughter set up house in the Glen of Dogs in County Galway. They told no one where they came from, and no one asked any questions. The old woman was very wealthy, and she bought a big house with plenty of fields, which she sowed with oats and barley. But whenever a lad came to work for her, she warned him that he would not be paid unless he could keep up with her, and she would give him nothing to eat except bread, gruel, and stirabout (porridge). Now the old woman was an Ancient One of the Earth, who had once created the very mountains themselves by flying over Ireland with an apronful of rocks that she dropped wherever she fancied. Strong as the storm she was, and swift as the wind. Not a lad remained with her for more than two weeks. They all went home and died.

One summer news of the terrible Hag of the Fields came to the ears of Donagh Mór (*don*-uh more), Big Donald, a giant of a lad who lived with his old mother some miles across the hills. Now Donagh was as sturdy as a stallion and swift footed as a deer. He was a champion stick fighter at every fair in the land, and he seldom went anywhere without his ash pole. When Donagh heard how many lads had died he said they must be a poor lot if they could not keep up with an old woman.

"I will go myself, tomorrow," said he, "and unless I beat her, I'll drown myself."

"O, love of my heart!" cried his mother, "that's a terrible woman, that is! Never a lad went into her service but is in his grave now."

"You'll see, Mother, I'll get the better of her before a month from this day. I often heard that wit was better than strength, and I have both wit and strength a-plenty."

Next morning Donagh walked over the hills to the hag's house and bade her a hearty "Good morning!" On the table was a dish of stirabout, and she made him sit down and eat, "for you cannot do hard work on an empty stomach." Donagh sat down, and the hag went out to fetch her sickle for the day's work. He had eaten only two spoonfuls when the hag's daughter came in. She had a face on her like a misshapen turnip, but Donagh stood up with a beaming smile and swept his hat off his head.

"How lucky I am to be working in a place with a girl as lovely as yourself!" he cried.

"Hush!" said she. "My mother may be listening."

"If the whole parish were listening, I would praise a pretty girl," said Donagh.

Before long the hag returned. "Be stirring," she said. "We have the whole top barley field to reap today."

All that day Donagh Mór reaped as fast as he could, but always she was ahead of him. He called out, "Hag of the Fields! Wait for me! Wait for me!"

But she called back, "Donagh Mór! Keep up with me! Keep up with me!"

He worked until the sun set and clouds covered the moon, and he called out, "The clouds are over the moon and I cannot see. Wait for me! Wait for me!"

But she answered, "I have no light either. Keep up with me! Keep up with me!"

Then he called, "I am wearied with this morning's journey. Wait for me! Wait for me!"

And she answered, "This morning I climbed the hill of seven peaks. Keep up with me! Keep up with me!"

The night wore on till it was nearly midnight, and he cried after her, "My sickle wants sharpening. Wait for me! Wait for me!"

She replied, "My sickle would not cut garlic. Keep up with me! Keep up with me!"

And at that she reached the end of her last furrow, and as Donagh Mór staggered up behind her, pouring with sweat, she whirled around and held her blade against his neck.

"You will not last long, my big strong lad!" she sneered, as he gave a weak cry and fell to his knees.

That night Donagh crawled off to sleep in the barn, but he had lain down only a few minutes when he saw the light of a flickering candle in the darkness, and the next moment the hideous face of the hag's daughter came into view. When she asked him how he had fared that day he told her with a groan that he would not remain another moment, except that he was in love with the daughter herself.

"Please stay, then, and let me help you!" said the hag's daughter. "You must know that my mother's sickle is made of stone and magic spells are set into the blade. But iron it cannot abide. I will rise early in the morning and plant iron stakes all among the dock leaves in the barley field, and you will have no more trouble from her."

Donagh Mór thanked her with profusions of love and even kissed her twisted lips. And that night she came to him in his dreams, only she was a beautiful maiden with hair of flax and he was walking with her in the fields of springtime among green springing corn.

The next morning Donagh and the hag went out to the second barley field. The hag began on the first strip where the girl had driven the iron stakes into the ground. She swung her sickle, it hit the stake, and the edge was taken from her blade.

"A hard dock weed, that!" said she.

"It is," said Donagh Mór.

She hit another, and another. Soon the edge was very dull indeed, and the magic no longer worked. She began to fall behind.

"I must sharpen my sickle, Donagh Mór. Wait for me! Wait for me!"

"You would not wait for me yesterday. Keep up with me! Keep up with me!" said Donagh.

The hag stopped to sharpen her blade, but before long she hit another stake and it was blunt again.

She called out, "Donagh Mór, my sickle is blunt, and only a new edge will cut the barley. Wait for me! Wait for me!"

"No, Hag," said he. "Only a good man can cut the barley. Keep up with me! Keep up with me!"

The Hag of the Fields was so furious that she threw down her sickle and ran up behind Donagh Mór, intending to throttle him with her bare hands. But Donagh turned around just in time to see her. He held up his sickle, and she ran herself through on the curved, shining blade. As Donagh watched, her long flying hair turned into yellow barley, her glaring eyes turned into stones, her body melted into the loam of the field, and where her blood flowed out, scarlet poppies sprang up all around.

Donagh Mór found himself standing with the last sheaf of barley in his arms, alone in a newly harvested field. Whistling, he tucked his sickle into his belt and strode over the fields toward his home. As he went, he spared a glance for the hag's daughter, who stood watching him from the farmhouse doorway.

"I'll come back in the spring," he said to himself.

FIRST FRUITS

In Ireland Lughnasadh was often called Colcannon Sunday, after a dish made from the first of the new potatoes. The head of the household, playing what was probably the role of the king in tribal days, lifted the first spadeful of potatoes ceremoniously and sprinkled them with holy water. Back at home the woman of the house put on a special white apron kept for the occasion, boiled a huge pot of potatoes over the fire, and mashed them with a wooden mallet. Often they were seasoned with onions, garlic, or cabbage. The cooked vegetables were then turned out onto a platter, and a well was hollowed out in the middle for plenty of butter and hot milk. The family sat round and ate, while the cook ate hers from the pot itself— a special privilege. In more well-to-do households the meal would be accompanied by meat: a flitch of bacon, newly slaughtered sheep, or roast chicken, followed by seasonal fruits such as gooseberries and blackcurrants. It was thought to be unlucky not to eat potatoes on this day, so people often made sure to share theirs with less fortunate neighbors.

In Scotland Lughnasadh customs flowed into the celebration of the Feast of Saint Mary, which took place on August 15, a few days after the old Lammas Day reckoning. Carmichael described how in the early morning the crofters would go into their fields to pick the first fruits of the crops, usually bere, a kind of barley. They laid them on a sunny rock to dry, husked them by hand, winnowed them in a riddle, ground them in a quern, and kneaded them on a sheepskin. The resultant little cake, or bannock, was called *Moilean Moire,* the "fatling" of Mary. It was toasted before a fire made from wood of the sacred rowan, and the father of the house ceremoniously broke it into pieces, which he gave to his wife and children in turn. Then the whole family sang the "Iolach Mhoire Mhather," the Paean of Mary Mother, who promised to protect them from all harm.

On the feast day of Mary the fragrant,
Mother of the Shepherd of the flocks,
I cut me a handful of new corn,
I dried it gently in the sun,
I rubbed it sharply from the husk,
With my own palms.

I ground it in a quern on Friday,
I baked it on a fan of sheepskin,
I toasted it to a fire of rowan,
And I shared it round my people.

I went sunways round my dwelling
In the name of Mary Mother,
Who promised to preserve me,
Who did preserve me,
And who will preserve me,
In peace, in flocks,
In righteousness of heart . . .

As they sang they circled the fire. Then,

The man puts the embers of the fagot-fire, with bits of old iron, into a pot, which he carries sunwise round the outside of his house, sometimes round the steadings and his fields, and his flocks gathered in for the purpose. He is followed without as within by his household, all singing the praise of Mary Mother the while. The scene is striking and picturesque, the family being arrayed in their brightest and singing their best.[15]

THE INNER CAULDRON
FRUITION

Now that most of us in the Western world take plentiful, year-round food for granted, it is hard for us to imagine the relief and gratitude our Celtic ancestors must have felt when harvesttime began. For poorer people, it wasn't always possible to stretch out the stores till next year's harvest, and this was especially true in the dark days of Ireland's oppression in the eighteenth and nineteenth centuries. Before the first potatoes were mature there was "Hungry July" or "July of the Cabbage," when the *Cailleach Rua*, the Red-haired Hag of Hunger, stalked the fields or squatted by the empty cooking pot. An old woman in County Mayo gave voice to the meaning of Lughnasadh during this era when she proclaimed in ringing tones: "The harvest is in and the hunger is over!"[16]

Even if you don't produce what you eat, this is a good time to connect with those who do by visiting farmers' markets or spending a day in the countryside picking your own fruit for jams and pies. As you watch the black and red jewels of berries, musky peaches, and nectarines spill out onto your kitchen table, let your eyes feast on their colors and shapes.

Smell, touch, and taste the fullness of summer
and the blessings of life bestowed upon us by
the earth at this time of the year. Think of
the human labor and skill that midwifed them
into being in your kitchen at this very
moment.

In the modern world August is also vaca-
tion time when work is set aside for lazing on
the porch or the nearest sunny beach. We,
too, can rest from our labors, celebrate
summer, and enjoy the fruits of our daily toil.
This can give us a good opportunity to take
stock of what the seasons so far have yielded:
to reflect upon our hopes and dreams that
were sown in the dawn of the year, came to
life in the springtime, and are now maybe
ready to bear fruit. On the spiritual level we
can ask ourselves what wisdom we have gar-
nered so far this year: What will be the harvest of our souls?

Meditation: The Hill of Vision

Sit before your altar. In the center, place a
chalice, cup, or bowl to symbolize the fruitful
womb of the earth goddess. This could also
be represented by a basket, especially one in
a cornucopia shape, filled with fruit or
vegetables. If you have grown or picked them

yourself, this will be even more meaningful.

Close your eyes and take a few deep
breaths. See yourself walking slowly up a
steep hill in the height of summer. . . . Feel
the warm sun on your shoulders, listen to the
song of a lark far above you in the clear blue
sky. . . . Fat bees with yellow pollen clinging to
their legs buzz sleepily among the mauve and
white heather bells. . . . Every now and then
you stoop to collect tiny blue-black berries
that grow among them. . . . Some you pop into
your mouth and enjoy the sweet burst of
juice, others you pocket for later. . . . Now you
have reached the top of the hill, and the
whole vista of the landscape opens up before
you. In the shimmering August heat, you can
see tiny fields and villages below and, beyond
them, woods, hills, and, far off in a blue haze,
mountains and the sea. . . . This is the landscape of your life, and today you have an
opportunity to take stock of it from above, to
get the bigger picture . . . to pause and see
how your soul is proceeding toward its harvest
for this year.

Look over toward the east. Here are some
newly cleared fields of grain beginning to
sprout. Let images emerge of new hopes,
dreams, and ideas that have come into your
life this year. Are they developing the way you
want them to? . . . Look at your life and see

where you have aimed, and if you are still on target.... What do you still have to get done?

Now turn and look toward the south. Here are some fields thick with golden corn coming into full ripeness. What is coming into fruition in your life now that you have been working on diligently all this year? ... What have you accomplished in the way of creative projects, training courses, business plans, relationships, family matters, community work, or whatever you have been focusing on? ... How are these projects bearing fruit in your life? Are you reaping the rewards you hoped for? ... Are you satisfied with these firstfruits? ... What do you feel most good about having harvested this year?

Turn and look toward the west. Here is a field where the grain is unhealthy, covered with black spots of mold and strangled by weeds.... Look at any results that you have not been happy about this year. Ask yourself in what way you may have knowingly or unknowingly contributed to them through the choices you made.... If so, what can you change so that you won't make the same mistakes at next year's planting?

Now turn toward the north. Here is a field ready to be plowed under. What things are drawing to a close in your life? What do you feel ready to let go of or know instinctively,

even if you don't want them to go, that they must? ... A situation or relationship whose time is past, that must be sacrificed to give way to new life.... You may feel somewhat sad to know that this lovely golden field will soon be shorn, but you know that the sacrifice of the grain is made so that new life may be born, new nourishment that will feed and sustain you through the winter months to come....

And now you turn to the center of the hill, and, standing before you on either side of a rough-hewn slab like a stone altar, are the Lord and Lady of the harvest. He is small, dark, and muscular with black, curling hair. He wears a light-colored tunic of rough woven cloth, and his arms are bare. In one bronzed hand he bears a shining, curved sickle. In the other is a sheaf of freshly cut wheat. She is a strong and lovely woman with flaxen hair streaming over broad shoulders. She wears a white linen gown, sprigged with blue cornflowers and brilliant red poppies, and she carries a shallow, woven basket in both her hands. She steps forward and holds the basket out to you and silently offers you the gift within.... This gift is the harvest reaped by your soul ... the reward of all your efforts and labors of this cycle. Take it and look at it closely; if it is a gift you do not understand, you can ask them to clarify its meaning ... (long pause)

Then you give the Lord and Lady thanks and, reaching into your pocket, take out the berries you have saved and place them on the stone altar as an offering. . . . And now, bearing your gift, you walk slowly down the hill again . . . back into your everyday life.

May the harvest of your dreams be winnowed by the stars!

THE HILLS OF THE HEART

In the hollows of quiet places we may meet,
the quiet places where is neither moon nor sun,
but only the light of amber and pale gold
that comes from the Hills of the Heart.

There, listen at times,
there you will call,
and I hear.

There will I whisper,
and that whisper will come to you,
as dew is gathered into the grass,
at the rising of the moon.

FIONA MACLEOD

CREATIVE FIRE

The Awen I sing,
From the deep I bring it . . .
TALIESIN

September is a month of changes. Up on the moorlands the bracken is turning to deep bronze, and scarlet rowanberries blaze against a surreally blue sky. Blackberries and hazelnuts swell into ripeness in the hedgerows. The slanting evening light tells us that autumn has come, and the night hours are once more equal to the day. Leaves redden, and fields of golden grain turn into stubble under the scythe, for this is the month when the full harvest gets under way in most of the Celtic countries. Alexander Carmichael describes the first day of reaping in the Hebrides:

The day the people began to reap the corn was a day of commotion and ceremonial in the townland. The whole family repaired to the field dressed in their best attire to hail the God of the harvest. Laying his bonnet on the ground, the father of the family took up his sickle, and facing the sun, he cut a handful of corn. Putting the handful of corn three times sunwise round his head, the man raised the *Iolach Buana,* the reaping salutation. The whole family took up the strain and praised the God of the harvest, who gave them corn and bread, food and flocks, wool and clothing, health and strength, and peace and plenty.

Throughout the British Isles and Ireland great ceremony attended the cutting of the last sheaf, the last refuge of the harvest spirit. The sheaf was often braided into the shape of a woman and sometimes dressed in a gown. In the Highlands it was called A'Mhaighdean (uh *vy*-jun), the Maiden, or the Cailleach, the Hag, and, according to district, was lucky or unlucky, just as the Celtic goddess traditionally has two faces—of life and of death. At the end of the harvest everyone came together for a big party called the Maiden

Feast, where the decorated sheaf sat in state and was offered the toast: "Here's to the one that helped us with the harvest!" Afterward, it might be hung in the farmhouse for good luck throughout the winter or plowed back into the earth the following year. Sometimes it was kept to make Bride's "bed" at Imbolc, for the harvest goddess was another aspect of Bride herself.

In the Hebrides September 29 was Saint Michael's Day, a festival that shared many of the features of Lughnasadh. Michael was an immensely popular Celtic saint who took over the role of Lugh in the Christian era. In Carmichael's time he was actually invoked as "the god Michael" and, like Lugh himself, was associated with horses, a shining spear, and high places. A number of old churches situated on top of hills or rocky mounts are dedicated to this saint: Saint Michael's Mount in Cornwall, Skellig Michael in Kerry, Aird Michael in Uist, and Mont Saint Michel in Brittany, to name a few. Lugh's routing of the Fomorians was transferred to Saint Michael's victory over the evil dragon. On his feast day an unblemished male lamb was sacrificed, and women made a special cake, the *struan Micheil,* "Michael's bannock," from all the types of grain grown on the farm, kneading it with butter, eggs, and sheep's milk. The bannock was marked with a cross and cooked on a stone over a fire of sacred oak, rowan, and bramble wood. All day long there were processions, songs to "Michael the Victorious," athletics, and horse racing, climaxing in a boisterous *céilidh* (*kyey*-lee) with music, dancing, and the exchange of gifts.

The pagan origins of the festival showed clearly through some of the dances. One of these, known as Cailleach an Dùdain, the Hag of the Mill Dust, was particularly significant, for the dancers, a man and a woman, dramatized the seasonal cycle to come. The man held the Slachdan Druidheachd, the druid wand, first over his head and then over hers, at which she dropped down as if dead. He then mourned for her, dancing about her body to the changing music. Then he raised her left hand, touched it with the wand, and the hand came alive and began to move up and down. The man became overjoyed and danced about her. Next he would bring her other arm and her legs to life. The he knelt over her, breathed into her mouth, and touched her heart with the wand. She leaped up, fully alive, and both danced joyously. So were played out the mysteries of the harvest: the death of the fertile Mother of Life in the barren months that were to come and the promise of her resurrection in springtime.

A good season for staying is autumn,
there is work then for everyone before the very
* short days.*
Dappled fawns from amongst the hinds,
the red clumps of the bracken shelter them;
stags run from the knolls at the belling of the deer
* herd.*
Sweet acorns in the wide woods,
stubble around the wheatfields over the expanse of
* brown earth.*
There are thornbushes and prickly brambles
by the midst of the ruined court;
the hard ground is covered with heavy fruit.
Hazelnuts of good crop fall from the huge old
* trees on dykes.*

IRISH, ELEVENTH CENTURY

BARLEY BREAD SHEAVES

All among the barley,
who would not be blithe,
When the ripe and bearded barley
is smiling on the scythe?

In Wales barley bread was "the prime bread in days of old, eaten with all meals."[1] In this recipe, adapted from the traditional Welsh *bara barlys*, the barley flour is mixed with wheat to make the lighter loaf we are more used to today, and it is shaped into a sheaf of grain to grace the harvest table.

Ingredients

2 packages active dry yeast

1 cup warm water (110–115 degrees)

2 cups milk

½ cup light brown sugar or 4 tablespoons honey

1 tablespoon salt

¼ cup butter (you can substitute vegetable oil)

3 cups barley flour

5 cups finely ground whole wheat flour (for a lighter-textured bread use 3 cups whole wheat flour plus 2 cups all-purpose flour)

3 tablespoons melted butter

olive oil for greasing bowl and baking sheet

Method

1. Sprinkle yeast over the warm water in a large bowl. Stir to dissolve yeast.
2. In a small saucepan over medium heat warm the milk until bubbles form around the edges. Remove from heat. Add sugar, salt, and ¼ cup butter, and stir until butter melts. Cool mixture to lukewarm.
3. Stir milk mixture into yeast mixture with a wooden spoon. Add 2 cups barley flour and 2 cups whole wheat flour to yeast mixture, stirring with a wooden spoon until smooth. Gradually add the remaining flour, incorporating the last of it with your hands until the dough is stiff enough to leave the sides of the bowl.
4. Place dough on a lightly floured surface and knead for 10 minutes. Dough should be smooth and elastic.
5. Place dough in a lightly greased large bowl, turn dough, greased side up. Cover with a towel and let rise in a warm place, till doubled, about 1 hour.
6. Punch dough down and divide in half. Each half will make one barley sheaf. Divide half of dough into 3 medium-sized balls and 1 small ball. Form the three medium-sized balls into10-inch-long loaf strips. Place the loaf strips side by side, bending the two outer strips outward at the top. Take the remaining ball and divide in half. Roll into two long strips. Join the strips by folding them in half around one another. Twist the strips into a braid. Place the braid around the center of the loaves to bind the sheaves together. Tuck the ends of the braid under the sides of the loaf. Cut diagonal indentations, using a sharp knife, into the top of each loaf strip to simulate the heads of wheat.

7. Repeat with the other half of the dough.
8. Place on greased baking sheets, cover, and let rise in a warm place, free from drafts, till doubled, about an hour.
9. Bake in a 350-degree oven for 40 to 50 minutes or till crust is a deep golden brown and loaves sound hollow when tapped.
10. Turn onto wire racks to cool, and brush with remaining melted butter. Sprinkle with sesame seeds if desired.

Makes 2 loaves

At each stage—mixing the ingredients, kneading the dough, leaving it to rise, and baking the loaf—you might wish to imbue the bread with a blessing, as the women once did in Scotland as they made Michael's Bannock:

Peace and plenty to all in our family, Mystery of Michael, protection of the Sacred Three.
Carmina Gadelica (slightly adapted)

A CAPFUL OF BARLEY

The farmer's wife rose early one morning to bake bread for the men in the fields. There was only a small quantity of new barley meal, and she was hard-pressed to bake enough loaves to go around. As she began to mix the dough, a little woman in green came in and politely asked for the loan of a capful of meal. The farmer's wife thought it best not to refuse and gave her the last of her measure. A little later the woman in green returned with an equal amount of meal, which the farmer's wife stored in the wooden barley chest. But it must have been very special meal indeed, for however much she used, the chest was always full. That September she baked enough loaves to serve her own family and the reapers throughout the harvest and had enough left for barley bread all winter long.

ROWAN

⚓HE SACRED ⚓ROVE

A handful of red rowanberries
To safeguard her . . .
HIGHLAND CHARM

The scarlet berries of the rowan, or mountain ash, brighten the September hillsides like the last of summer's fire. Valued throughout the Celtic countries for its powerful magic, the rowan is called in an early Irish poem the "wizard's tree." The druids spread interwoven rowan boughs, or wattles, over the hides of sacrificed bulls, on which they lay to journey to the spirit world, a practice that gave rise to the Irish expression "to go on the wattles of knowledge," meaning to do your utmost to find something out.

In Irish mythology the Tuatha Dé Danann were said to have brought rowan from Tír Tairngire (*cheer tar*-ing-ih-ruh), the Land of Promise. Its berries possessed the "exhilaration of wine and the satisfaction of old mead" and also were able to restore youth to the aged. Their reputation as a food of the gods may have sprung from a strong and delicious drink that was brewed from them. The seventeenth-century herbalist John Evelyn seems to confirm this when he writes, "Ale and beer brewed with these berries, being ripe, is an incomparable drink, familiar in Wales, where this tree is reputed so sacred, that there is not a churchyard without one of them planted in it. . . ."[2]

Country people protected themselves from ill luck with rowan wood, which they used to make every sort of domestic and farming tool from distaff to churn dash, plow pin to water mill. They made little crosses of rowan wood and placed them over stable doors or under milk pans or tied them to the cow's tail with red thread. For in the days when witches were believed responsible for all misfortunes, from ill health to farming troubles, it was well known that:

Rowan tree and red thread
Keep the witches from their speed.

Although the recipe for the fabled rowan ale has been lost, rowan jelly is popular in Scotland as a piquant accompaniment to rich meat and game.

ROWAN JELLY
Ingredients
4 cups rowanberries (preferably from European mountain ash, *Sorbus aucuparia,* which produces sweeter berries than the North American native *Sorbus americana*)
2 or 3 apples, peeled and quartered
1 cup sugar for each cup juice

Method
Cover the washed berries and apples with water. Simmer about 40 minutes or until water is red and berries are very soft. Strain off the juice, but do not press the fruit or the jelly will become clouded. Measure the juice and return it to the pan. Add equivalent amount of sugar. Boil rapidly for half an hour or until some of it sets quickly on a plate when cold. Pour into sterilized jars and seal.

COOKING THE SALMON OF WISDOM

The transformation of grain into bread is the ultimate triumph of Lugh, the culture god. As Lugh is also the inventor of all arts and skills, the achievement of Celtic art and music is another kind of harvest we will look at in this chapter. What turns corn into bread and raw materials into works of art is the same element: fire. What cooks the fruit of the earth is the fire that is kindled; what cooks the fruit of the human soul is the "fire in the head," the passion of the creative mind.

In early Irish culture wisdom was expressed in the form of poetry and magical knowledge. This was the province of the *fili* (*fih*-luh), or poet-seer, a master of wisdom to whom the secrets of the Otherworld had been revealed. *Fili* comes from the root "to see," for to the Celts vision and poetry—the rapture of illumination and the inspired voicing of it—were inseparable, the in-breath and out-breath of the ecstatic experience. Unlike our conception of a poet today, the Celtic image of poet was more akin to the shaman, "a mediator between the supernatural powers and the human race,"[3] whose gifts came from the Otherworld. Poets were trained in mantic techniques that taught them how to leave the body and ascend to the sky or descend to the Underworld to communicate with spirits and the dead. To the *filidh*, the fire of inspiration and creativity was called *imbas forosnai*, the "knowledge that enlightens." This process is illustrated in the well-known story of Fionn McCumhaill's initiation as a *fili*.

When he was young, Fionn went by the name of Demne (*jev*-nuh), and his teacher was an old master poet called Finnéces (*fin-yey*-guss), Finn the Poet. For seven long years the old man had been waiting and watching by Féc's Pool, hoping to catch sight of the Salmon of Wisdom that lived in its shadowy depths. An old prophecy had foretold that one day he would eat the salmon and be filled with the knowledge of all things.

Shortly after Fionn arrived, Finnéces spotted the salmon and caught it in his net. The young Fionn helped him make the fire and prepare the spit on which the giant fish would be roasted. Trembling with joy, Finnéces withdrew to prepare himself spiritually for the sacred feast that was to be the fruition of his hopes and dreams. Before he left, he ordered Fionn to watch over the

roasting fish and warned him not to taste a single bit but to bring it to him when it was fully cooked. Finn nodded obediently and spent the day feeding the fire with twigs and branches, carefully turning the spit to make sure the salmon cooked well on all sides. When it last it was done, Fionn brought the splendid fish to his teacher with pride, but as he approached, the old man went very still and looked into Finn's eyes.

"Did you eat any of the salmon, lad?" he asked gravely.

"I did not!" said Fionn in surprise. "But as I turned the fish on the spit, I burned my thumb and put it in my mouth."

The old man gave a long sigh. "What is your name, lad?"

"Demne," the boy replied.

The poet shook his head slowly. "Fionn is your name," he said, "and it is for you the fish was given. I can teach you no more." He gave the salmon back to Fionn, and after Fionn ate it he was filled with the light of inspiration. He looked about him as if seeing the world for the first time, and the poetry poured forth from him in a spontaneous paean of praise for Earth's beauty.

In this story, transformation occurs by the two kinds of fire: the physical fire that cooks the salmon, and the Otherworld fire that "cooks" the poet. In fact, Fionn actually *becomes* a salmon himself and is often referred to as the "Golden Salmon of Knowledge"—golden, perhaps, because he is filled with the radiant vision of the spirit world, which is the home of all the arts.

Fionn's experience may sound more like a mystical than a poetic initiation to modern readers, for whom poetry belongs more to the realm of literature than religion. But to the early Irish, a poet was "a mediator between the supernatural powers and the human race,"[4] whose gifts came from the Otherworld, borne in fire and water.

The poet's initiation has much to teach us about the creative process in our everyday lives. Creativity begins when we gaze into the waters of the soul and get in touch with what we feel. If we look deeper into the river, we may also discover the deepest springs of our intuitive powers. Feelings and intuition speak to us through the power of our imagination— the images reflected in the water. Creativity also comes as the lightning flash, the bolt of illumination. What we call a "lightbulb going on inside our heads" was, to the early Celts, the "fire in the head" that the *fili* Amergin sang about (see May), the *imbas forosnai* (im-bus *for*-oss-nee). It speaks to us in ideas,

insights, flashes of inspiration, knowing. Although we all tend to favor one way over the other, true creativity has to include a balance of "fire" *and* "water," thought *and* feeling, mind *and* soul.

Just as Fionn underwent his initiation on the banks of the river, a liminal place, we often make major leaps of growth and understanding at those times in our lives when we are on the threshold between one stage and another: leaving school, at midlife, when our children leave home, or when a job or a marriage has begun or ended. At such times we tend to be more on the edge of the unknown, open to whatever may leap up out of the currents of change. This is often the time when a teacher or guide appears in dreams or meditations to help us align with our higher purpose in life. Sometimes this guide is a part of ourselves, our higher self, as Finnéces may have been of Fionn. Although Fionn is called by his childhood name of Demne in this story, the boy was already known as Fionn to his peers, so on one level the story is about the older, wiser spiritual self (Fionn the Poet) initiating his younger, personality self (Fionn-Demne). The prophecy was right—the salmon was meant for a Fionn, but the younger, not the older one.

This guide teaches us how to prepare and cook the salmon of wisdom that our many life experiences, both painful and joyful, have enabled us to bring up out of the waters of the soul. At first we may not be aware of the tremendous gift the salmon has to offer us; we may not even believe it can be for *us*. Finn was just a student and a *gilla*, a servant lad who was doing his job. Illumination can sometimes come by accident, "like a thief in the night," to the humble and innocent.

The first thing Fionn did when he ate the salmon was to utter a paean of praise to the beauty all around him, as if the taking in of the magical fish had opened his eyes to the wonder of the world. When we are fully open to the creative spirit we become fully present to ourselves and the wonder of all of creation in the moment. We know what it is like to feel fully alive.

THE BIRTH OF TALIESIN

Fionn McCumhaill's Welsh counterpart was called Gwion (gwee-on). Both these names derive from a root word meaning "white" or "shining," suggesting the illumination of poetic inspiration. Like Fionn, Gwion underwent a transformation from which he emerged as the great Welsh bard, Taliesin (tahl-yess-in), a real poet who lived in sixth-century Wales.

Long ago, in the time of King Arthur, there was a wisewoman called Ceridwen (*kair*-id-wen), who was mistress of the three arts of magic, enchantment, and divination. She lived by the shores of Bala Lake in North Wales with her husband, Tegid Foel, and their two children, a girl and a boy. The girl was called Creirwy (*kry*-rooy), Dear One, and she was as fair as the moon upon water. But her son, Morfran (*mor*-vrahn), Black Crow, was so ugly he was nicknamed Afagddu (ah-*vahg*-thee), Utter Darkness. Yet Ceridwen loved her misshapen son and longed to bring brightness into his life, so she spent days and nights poring over the oldest and most secret tomes until she had mastered the secret art of brewing a cauldron of Inspiration and Knowledge. Just three drops of this precious liquid would bestow understanding of all the arts, together with the gift of seership, upon her hapless son. Ceridwen learned under which moon to gather the herbs and under which stars to steep them, and she began to boil them in her great iron cauldron for a year and a day.

To tend the fire she hired a blind man called Morda, and to watch over the brew she brought in a little peasant boy called Gwion. All that year Gwion stirred and stirred the simmering cauldron with a great wooden spoon, while Morda fed the fire with twigs and dead leaves. But one day, toward the end of the year, as Ceridwen was out culling herbs and chanting spells, three drops sprang out of the cauldron and landed on Gwion's hand—and without thinking, the lad sucked the burn and swallowed the three drops of Inspiration. And in that moment he was filled with a great light that burst open the horizons of his young mind. Everything that had ever happened and was going to happen in the world rolled out before his inner eye like a highway.

But with his outer eye, he saw Ceridwen running toward him—her art had told her what had happened—and her face was twisted with rage. Gwion dropped the wooden spoon and ran, but she came close behind and he heard her footsteps like thunder upon the path. The boy ran and ran, and in his thoughts he was Hare leaping to safety—and he turned into a hare and leaped away. But she turned into greyhound, and though Hare was swift, Greyhound was swifter, and soon the little animal could feel her breath on his neck. He bounded to the edge of the lake and leaped into the water, and in his thoughts he became a fish, and as Salmon he swam away through the dark reedy waters of the lake.

But Ceridwen leapt into the water and became an otter, and though Salmon was swift, Otter was swifter, and her paws flexed for the kill. But the fish leaped out of the water, and in his thoughts he became a bird. He was Crow, beating at the air with his wings, and away he flew. But she leaped out of the water, and she turned into a hawk. And Crow was swift, but Hawk was swifter, and she swooped down and dug her talons into the neck of the smaller bird. But at the last minute, he turned into a grain of wheat and dropped down between the cruel talons onto the threshing floor of a nearby mill. And there he hid with thousands of other grains of wheat.

But Ceridwen turned into a black hen, and she fluttered down to the threshing floor and scratched and pecked until she had found him—and she swallowed him up whole. But the grain of wheat began to grow inside her. It grew, and it grew, and when nine months were over, she lay on her back and gave birth to a baby boy. As soon as the child was born she took a dagger—for well she knew who he was—and went to slit his throat. But she made the mistake of looking into the child's face. He was so beautiful, he was her own son, and she couldn't bring herself to kill him. She threw the dagger down with a clatter, and instead she made a coracle out of leather, wrapped the baby up in layers of animal skins, and placed him gently in the little boat. Then she tucked it under her arm and strode over mountain and moorland until she came to the ocean. There she cast the coracle upon the salt-cold waters. The boat was sent spinning and tossing by the waves and currents and winds of the sea for hundreds of years, but in all that time the child wrapped in skins did not age by a single day.

Now, many years later, a Welsh prince called Elphin lived at the mouth of the river Conway. He was a wastrel and a gambler and heavily in debt. But on the Eve of Beltaine, he heard that the salmon were running, so he said to himself, "Now if I stretch some nets across the river banks, I can catch some salmon and make some money."

So he stretched his nets across the estuary, and all night long he waited there under the bright stars, and in the morning he waded into the water to see what he had caught. There he found not a single fish, but caught in the nets was a little coracle, all encrusted with limpets and barnacles.

And inside the coracle something lay wrapped in animal skins.

Elphin folded back the skins one by one, and when the last one slipped off, there lay a baby boy, and around his head shone a bright light. Elphin could not believe his eyes. All he could say was, "Look at that shining brow!" which in Welsh is *Taliesin*. And when the child heard his name calling him back into the world of time, he opened his eyes, and said, "Taliesin am I!" And he grew up to be the greatest poet and prophet that Wales had ever known.

THE BREATH OF AWEN

The basic meaning of *Awen* is "blowing, breath, wind," for *inspiration*, literally, means to breathe (inspire) in. Although it refers primarily to poetic inspiration, where the words flow out on the breath, it is essential to the smooth and skillful execution of all forms of art, as masters know. For example, in Japanese calligraphy the brushstrokes are dependent on the correct flow of breath as pen is applied to paper.

Do this meditation before embarking on any particular form of artistic expression, whether playing an instrument, dancing, writing, or weaving:

Sit in front of your altar or other comfortable place, and imagine that you are sitting over a pool that is as deep as the ocean. As you take a long, slow, deep breath in, breathe the energy of that pool up into your body like a river . . . and allow that river to float into your lower body up through your feet, your legs, and your pelvis like a silver stream of light. . . . Now bring it up through your solar plexus to your heart, and let it circulate there before breathing it out and down . . . down . . . down your lower body and out through your legs again. . . .

Do this a number of times until you feel it's happening automatically in the background of your awareness. . . . And now imagine that above you is a bright golden sun that is sending down beams of light through your body. Feel the golden light stream through your head, down through your neck and shoulders, and into your heart, where it mingles and circulates with the other stream from below. . . . Now every time you breathe in, breathe *in* the energy of the realm of Sea, the silver light of the Underworld . . . and breathe *out* the energy of Sky, the golden light of the Upperworld . . . and keep up the breathing until you feel a sensation of warmth, tingling, or fullness in the heart area. . . . Let some of this flow down through your shoulders, arms, and hands. . . .

Continue for at least ten minutes, then, still staying in this feeling, open your eyes and express yourself through playing music, painting, dancing, writing, and so forth. You can relax the breathing now, but still remember to breathe freely and deeply and let the inspiration flow from your heart into your work. If you feel blocked, totally let go of the idea that you are "producing" something, and play spontaneously like a child. Don't worry about the outcome. Just babble, scribble, or jiggle with abandon—and have fun! This will free you up to bring more joy into your creative expression.

HOLY GROUND
BALA LAKE
(GWYNEDD, WALES)

Bala Lake is the largest natural lake in Wales at four and a half miles long by a half mile wide. In Welsh its name is Llyn Tegid (*hlin tey*-gid), after Tegid Foel (Bald Tegid), Ceridwen's husband, who is said to have been a giant. The smooth waters of the lake make it a favorite recreation area for boating and fishing today, but in the past the lake was steeped in danger and mystery. Strange lights are often seen above the lake on old Christmas Eve, January 4, while a dragon is said to haunt its deep waters. Occasionally it swims to the surface, as it did one spring morning in 1995, to the astonishment of local fishermen.

Once, according to legend, there was no water at all but a green and fertile land ruled by a tyrannical king who mercilessly oppressed his people. One night the king held a splendid feast to celebrate the birth of his son's first child. A poor harper from the neighboring hills was fetched to play music at the event. The old man marveled at the lavish banquet, the mounds of food, the rivers of wine, and the magnificent dress and manners of the noble lords and ladies. But around midnight, during an interval in the dancing while he sat alone in a corner, a voice suddenly whispered in his ear, "Vengeance! Vengeance!" He turned and saw a tiny bird, hovering and beckoning him to follow. The harper hesitantly followed him out of the castle, and the bird led him higher and higher up a nearby hill. Whenever the old man wavered, the cry would come again: "Vengeance! Vengeance!" At last he stopped, worn out by the climb, only to find that the bird had disappeared. Feeling rather foolish, the harper tried to make his way back to the castle, but soon he found himself lost in the darkness. When dawn broke he could look down below to where the castle had been, but now there was nothing but a calm, deep lake, with his own harp floating on its waters. For years boatmen claimed to see the tops of ruined towers below the lake on quiet moonlit nights at harvesttime.

ART OF THE GODS, ART OF ANGELS

To contemplate the flowing curves of Iron Age Celtic art, the pouring out of circles and spirals in vigorous, organic swirls, is to perceive the universe as a river of swirling energy out of which forms continually rise and fall. Often we seem to be looking at a world *in potentia* that is trembling on the brink of form, witnessing the gods in the very act of creation. What at first appears to be an abstract geometrical pattern may reveal itself as the curved neck of a swan, and then a beaked face comes plainly into view. Or we

Bronze meat hook from Ballymoney, County Antrim, Ireland

discover a human face peering out of foliage like a woodland spirit.

Was this the way the world looked to the people who lived in the vast oak forests of northern Europe, used to the ambiguity of light and shadow, the continual shifting of leaves, branches, and clouds? Theirs was an untamed natural environment, vastly removed from the formal architecture of the civilized world. In fact, the Romans dismissed Celtic art as barbaric, since it did not measure up to the classical benchmark in which the proper subject of art was the natural or idealized human form.

The Celtic artists preferred to depict the forms found in nature, weaving vines and tendrils, blossoms and plants, into dynamic, free-flowing designs. The creatures with whom they shared their world also appear in their art, such as bulls, deer, birds, horses, boar, cattle, sheep, and dogs, along with fantastic, mythical beasts: sphinxes, griffins, dragons, lions, and dolphins. There is often a shape-shifting quality about these designs reminiscent of the Celtic myths where human beings turn into animals and vice versa. A bronze bit of a horse from first-century Ireland looks like a human face when viewed one way and a design of crested ducks when held upside down. These fluid, ambiguous forms remind us of the way the material plane and the realm of spirit continually intersect in the Celtic worldview. Is Bran sailing on an ocean or over a flowery plain? The riddling Celtic mind answers, "Both!"

In Celtic society there was no distinction between "fine" arts and crafts, as there is today. The best art is found in the design and decoration of functional objects, from cups and bowls, combs and mirrors, to horse and chariot trappings and implements of war. Sometimes the most engaging pieces are found on the most utilitarian objects, such as the row of tiny waterbirds that perch along the handle of a meat fork or the comically long horse's face on a harness mount.

The anonymous makers of these works of art were wood carvers, sculptors, glass workers, potters, leatherworkers and stonemasons, but most of all they were metalsmiths, who worked in iron, bronze, silver, gold, and enamel. In many early societies smithcraft was a sacred function because of the smith's power over fire and mysterious ores. An adept of the arts of transformation, a smith could also heal and foretell the future. Brigit was a patron of smithcraft as well as of healing and prophecy. Metals were gifts of the gods because they came from the Underworld. They seemed imperishable, and above all, they were filled with light. Faery palaces were made of them:

I have a house in the land to the north,
one half of it of red gold, the lower half
of silver. Its porch is of white bronze
and its threshold of copper, and of the
wings of white yellow birds is its
thatch. . . . Its candlesticks are golden,
with a candle of great purity, with a gem
of precious stone in the very middle of
the house.[5]

An early Irish prayer of protection invokes
the power of precious metals:

I invoke my Silver Champion who has not died,
  who will not die.
May a time be granted to me of the quality of
  white bronze![6]

Metalworkers had a direct line to the
Otherworld for inspiration: an early Irish tale
describes how the great Ulster warrior,
Cúchulainn, demanded from the craftsman
MacEndge a silver shield engraved with an
original design. (Designs on shields often contained talismanic symbols to protect the
bearer.) The artisan protested he had already
used up all his ideas, but Cúchulainn threatened to kill him unless he came up with
something new. MacEndge went off to his
workshop in a state of profound gloom, but a

being from the Otherworld flew down through
the smoke hole in the roof to help him out.
Using a pair of wooden compasses, the god
traced a design in the ashes, and MacEndge
made a wonderful shield for Cúchulainn that
was given the name of Dubán.

For the gods were artists, too. The Tuatha
Dé Danann had a trio of gods called *na trí
dee dána,* the Three Gods of Craftsmanship.
These were Goibniu the smith, Luchta the
carpenter, and Credne the worker in bronze.
In the Second Battle of Moytirra, Lugh com-
missioned these three to make magical
weapons for the gods' fight against the Fomorians. Earthly metalworkers made magical
weapons, too, decorated with totem animals
designed to instill fear into the foe. Warriors
wore helmets crested with pointed horns,
birds of prey, and other ferocious beasts; Scottish tribes charged into battle to the blare of
the bronze trumpet known as a carnyx. A
long, curving pipe that ended in a stylized
wild boar's head with glaring eyes and gaping
movable jaw, this must have looked as terrifying as it sounded on the battlefield. As Professor John Carey writes, in his essay on Celtic
art and poetry, "The Waters of Vision,"

The makers of the beautiful, intricate,
mysterious things which have come

down to us thought of the gods as being like themselves, but also of themselves as being like the gods. . . . The goldsmith, the enameller, the illuminator, must have seen their work as being in some way the same as that of the masters of the fabric of perception. Their power to create, to transform, to delineate was as absolute, and as miraculous.[7]

On a less dramatic scale, Celtic craftsmen also made jewelry: beads of glass and amber, bone combs and pins, and bronze and iron rings inlaid with intricate mosaic patterns. For the royal families there were golden torcs, circles of twisted gold worn around the necks of those of high rank as a symbol of authority. Royal men wore heavy bronze armlets; women displayed bracelets of the most delicate filigree made from fine threads of gold; and for all there were finger rings and thumb rings of copper, enamel, or tin. Craftsmen inlaid their work with colored glass and gemstones wherever possible, using coral, hematite, garnets, and quartz crystal, amber from the North Sea, and jet from Yorkshire.

Medieval Celtic tales are often full of long descriptions of gorgeously bedecked heroes and heroines or catalogs of their exquisite treasures. Here is a description of Étaín, the loveliest faery woman in the world, when first seen by her future husband, King Eochaid:

By the brink of the spring sat Étaín, in her hand a comb of silver adorned with gold. Next to her, for washing, was a basin of silver on which four birds had been chased, and there were little gems of carbuncles on its rim. A bright purple mantle was clasped over her breast with a golden brooch. A tunic she wore, with a long hood that might cover her head attached to it; it was stiff and glossy with green silk beneath red embroidery of gold, and was clasped over her breasts with marvelously wrought clasps of silver and gold; so that men saw the bright gold and the green silk flashing against the sun. On her head were two tresses of hair, and each tress had been plaited into four strands; at the end of each strand was a little ball of gold. . . . (Irish poem, ninth century)

The coming of Christianity brought new momentum, new techniques, and new subject matter for Celtic art. From the sixth to the twelfth centuries, the monasteries of Britain and Ireland produced some of the greatest treasures of Christian heritage, from the illuminated Gospels to the magnificent High Crosses. The astonishing interweaving patterns, whether on vellum or stone, reflect a world filled with the endless delight of movement, a perfect, precarious balance between the orderly and the unbounded.

These heirs to the legacy of Iron Age Celtic art were monks themselves. In Saint Brigit's time there was a famous school of metalsmiths near her church, presided over by Saint Conleth, the first bishop of Kildare, and an accomplished artist himself. In the sixth century Saint Dega was chief artist to Saint Ciaran of Clonmacnoise. Besides being a smith, he was a scribe, a bronzeworker, and a leather-crafter, and he made 150 bells, 150 croziers, and leather cases for 60 Gospel books.

The new interlacing designs that entered Celtic art at this period speak to us of the forest clearings where the monks lived and worked in their workshops

Spirals from the Book of Durrow *carpet page*

and *scriptoria*. Here and there an animal or bird appears out of the tangle of knotwork, as if from the shadows of trees. Human forms intertwine with animal, both joined by twisting and turning filaments that connect the whole tapestry. Sometimes a form that starts out as human may end up as beast or bird. This rhythmical interpenetration of forms can be seen as a reflection of the interconnectedness between human beings and the natural world found in the Celtic wisdom tradition, whether pagan or Christian.

For some of the most detailed illuminated letters, like the famous "chi-ro" page in the *Book of Kells*, they used brushes no thicker than a hair's width, and, as so much of the design is barely discernible with the naked eye, the artist may have used a quartz crystal as a magnifying glass. The letters bloom and expand to dominate the whole page, the product of endless hours of pure and intense creativity that confronts us with a "fanatical, almost frightening, command of complex form and microscopic detail."[8] And yet within the dazzling glory of the first two letters of Christ's name, there is room for a cartoon of two cats who sit watching mice share a communion wafer, and an otter with a fish in its mouth.

Some pages in these holy books are given over totally to ornamentation, with no lettering at all. These are the richly decorated "carpet pages," such as the one in the seventh-century *Book of Durrow*, painted in saturated hues of red, yellow, green, and deep brown. The flowing pattern of triple spirals demonstrates the way the cosmos comes into being and returns unto itself in the perpetual ebb and flow of creation. It may have been designed as a tool for the monks to meditate upon to prepare themselves for the teachings that follow.

Just as myths of the Iron Age Celts tell of their work as inspired by the gods, so the Christian monks were given divine guidance by angels. A scribe of Kildare in Saint Brigit's time was about to begin a book. The night before, an angel came to him in a dream and showed him an unusual design. The angel asked the scribe, "Do you think you can make this drawing on the first page of the book you are about to begin?"[9]

The poor scribe felt he could not attempt anything so marvelous, but the angel encouraged him to ask Saint Brigit to pray for him

to gain the necessary skills. This the saint did—like her predecessor, Brigit, the Goddess of Inspiration—and the scribe was able to create the wonderful book according to the designs the angel showed him night after night in his sleep. No wonder Gerald of Wales, a visitor to Ireland in the twelfth century, declared that the manuscript art was the work "not of men, but of angels."

GODS OF THE CELTS: GOIBNIU

The weapons of Goibniu (*gwiv*-nyuh), the smith of the gods, carried an unbeatable guarantee:

> Even if the men of Ireland continue the battle for seven years, for every spear that separates from its shaft or sword that will break in battle, I will provide a new weapon in its place. No spearpoint which my hand forges will make a missing cast. No skin which it pierces will taste life afterwards.[10]

His boast was made good at the Second Battle of Moytirra, where the spear he made for Lugh pierced Balor's eye and sealed the victory for the Tuatha Dé Danann.

Goibniu also possessed other characteristics of the divine smith. Like Hephaestus, the Greek smith god who supplied the Olympian gods with drink, he was the provider and host of the Otherworld "Feast of Goibniu," where the Tuatha Dé Danann drank an intoxicating ale that kept them immortal. Smithcraft was also associated with healing, and although we have no stories portraying Goibniu in this role, an old Irish charm for the removal of a thorn invokes his protection.

In later Irish and Scottish folklore he is known as the Gobán Saor (*gob*-awn *sweer*), Gobán the Wright, who was a master mason and carpenter as well as a smith, and the builder of the round stone towers of Ireland's medieval monasteries. He was a fellow of ready wit and cleverness. Once, he had almost completed a tower when the monks tried to lower his wages. When he protested, they waited until he was on top of the tower, then they removed all the scaffolding and ladders, refusing to put them back until he had agreed to their terms. At this, Gobán began throwing down the stones one by one to make himself some steps for the downward journey, whereupon the monks hurriedly agreed to pay him his due.

CAT

A CELTIC BESTIARY

One has only to look at the cats that have managed to insinuate themselves among the interlacing designs of Celtic art to know that the Celts were fond of felines. Cats may stare out unblinkingly from a High Cross at an Irish monastery, totally disinterested in the serious biblical dramas being enacted all around them, or curve impossibly around the corner of an illuminated page to stalk a bird. In early Ireland each household had its cats to keep both home and granary free of mice, but they were also beloved pets, especially among women, while children were given kittens to play with. These favored ones might sleep indoors in a basket or even on their mistress's pillow.

Old Irish names tell us what these cats looked like: Glas Nenta (*gloss nyen*-tuh) was Nettle Gray, while Bréone (*brey*-oh-nuh), Little Flame, was no doubt a marmalade cat.

The most famous Celtic cat of early Ireland was a white one called Pangur Bán (*pang*-ur *bawn*), who kept the monk who owned him company while he toiled over his books and so was immortalized in verse:

I and Pangur Bán my cat,
'Tis a like task we are at:
Hunting mice is his delight,
Hunting words I sit all night.

Better far than praise of men
'Tis to sit with book and pen;
Pangur bears me no ill-will,
He too plies his simple skill.

Oftentimes a mouse will stray
In the hero Pangur's way;
Oftentimes my keen thought set
Takes a meaning in its net.

'Gainst the wall he sets his eye
Full and fierce and sharp and sly;
'Gainst the wall of knowledge I
All my little wisdom try.

When a mouse darts from its den
O how glad is Pangur then!
O what gladness do I prove
When I solve the doubts I love!

So in peace our tasks we ply,
Pangur Bán, my cat, and I;
In our arts we find our bliss,
I have mine and he has his.

Practice every day has made
Pangur perfect in his trade;
I get wisdom day and night
Turning darkness into light.

TRANSLATED BY ROBIN FLOWER[11]

DRAWING A CELTIC KNOT

Celtic design can be a meditative practice, akin to walking a labyrinth. Drawing the figures can bring about perceptual shifts that take us to the heart of the sacred geometry underlying many of the patterns, leading us to an experiential awareness of truths that lie beyond words.

You will need:
Graph paper or plain white paper
Pencil
Eraser
Felt-tip pen

Method
1. With a pencil, copy the alternating dot pattern on your graph paper, or use a copy machine to copy the grid to plain paper, then trace the pattern with a pencil.

2. Using a pencil, connect the large dots in a crisscross pattern as shown in the diagram. These lines determine your knot pattern.

3. Create the strands of the knot pattern by drawing parallel lines on either side of the crisscross pattern. These lines create the spaces surrounding the small dots and the

intersections of the knot strands. Keep the thickness of the strands consistent, as the knot is created as one continuous strand, without beginning or ending.

4. The next step is to join the ends of the crisscross strands with curves. Use the large dots on the outside of the rectangle as reference points for the outside of the curves. Keep the thickness of your strand consistent by creating the inside curve around the small dot.

5. The next step is to "weave" your knot with an over-under pattern. It may help you to trace the arrows on the diagram with your finger or a pen to "feel" the direction of the weave. You will end at the starting point.

6. Beginning in the upper left corner, use your eraser to erase one set of diagonal lines at each intersection. Continue to alternate the removal of diagonals as you continue weaving the strand. You might silently repeat to yourself, "Over, now under; over, now under," to create a rhythm as you weave.

7. To complete the knot, trace over the remaining lines with a felt-tip pen. The knot can be left plain or shaded in a variety of ways to create depth.

CELTIC MUSIC: SOUNDS OF THE OTHERWORLD

Thig crioch air an saoghal,
ach mairidh gaol is ceòl.

The world will pass away,
but love and music last forever.
SCOTTISH PROVERB

When the Tuatha Dé Danann won the Second Battle of Moytirra, Lugh, the Dagda, and Ogma chased after the fleeing Fomorians because they had stolen the Dagda's harp, Úaithne. Bursting into the enemy's banqueting hall where the retreating hosts had fled, they saw the harp hanging on the wall. Now no music could be played on this harp unless the Dagda himself summoned the melodies by chanting this spell:

Come, Daur Dá Bláo (Oak of Two Meadows),
Come, Cóir Cethairchuir (Four-Angled True One),
Come, summer, come, winter,
Mouths of harps and bags and pipes!

The Dagda sang the spell, and the harp sprang from the wall, killing nine men that were in its path. Like a bird, it flew to the

Dagda's arms, and he began to play. He played the Music of Sorrow for them so the women wept. He played the Music of Joy until the women and youths held their sides with laughing. He played the Music of Sleep, and all the fierce warriors who had risen to kill the three intruders dropped their weapons and fell fast asleep. When they awoke, the three gods and harp were long gone.

This short piece, which falls at the end of the Second Battle of Moytirra, tells us a lot about the nature of Celtic music. It was a magical art belonging to the gods themselves and woven about with spells. The father of the gods, the Dagda himself, owned a harp, for this instrument held pride of place in early Celtic music. It was given a name, like a ship. The Dagda demonstrated the three feats of the harper, as indeed Lugh had done when he first came to Tara: the *suantraí* (*soon*-tree), sleep music, the *geantraí* (*gyan*-tree), laughter music, and the *goltraí* (*gol*-tree), weeping music. Another story tells how these three strains came about: Boand, the goddess who gave her name to the River Boyne, was in labor with her three sons. The harp began crying and mourning with her in the intensity of her contractions. Then it played music to rejoice and welcome her first two sons into

the world. Finally, it played a soothing music as the last one was born, sending mother and babies into a restful sleep.

Many Irish tales describe women of the Otherworld as purveyors of magical music that can soothe and heal. When the voyager Tadg (*tathg*), son of Cian, visits an island of divine women, he meets the goddess Cliodhna, who gives him three magical birds:

> . . . a blue one, with crimson head; a crimson with head of green; a pied one having on his head a colour of gold, and they perched upon the apple-tree that stood before them. They eat an apple apiece, and warble melody sweet and harmonized, such that the sick would sleep to it.
>
> "Those birds," Cliodhna said, "will go with you; they will give you guidance, will make you symphony and minstrelsy and, until again ye reach Ireland, neither by land nor by sea shall sadness or grief afflict you."[12]

The same magical music permeates the apple branch that is the passport to the Otherworld in the stories of Cormac mac Art and Bran mac Febal. These tales give us a glimpse into the Celtic regard for music as a gift of

THE FAERY MUSIC OF INISICÍLEÁIN
(IN-YISH-I KEEL-YAWN)

In the old days, when this island was inhabited, a man sat alone one night in his house, soothing his loneliness with a fiddle. He was playing, no doubt, the favorite music of the countryside, jigs and reels and hornpipes, the hurrying tunes that would put light heels on the feet of the dead. But, as he played, he heard another music without, going over the roof in the air. It passed away to the cliffs and returned again, and so backwards and forwards, again and again, a wandering air wailing in repeated phrases, till at last it had become familiar in his mind, and he took up the fallen bow, and drawing it across the strings followed note by note the lamenting voices as they passed above him. Ever since, that tune, *port na bpúcaí*, the "fairy music," has remained with his family, skilled musicians all, and if you hear it played by a fiddler of that race, you will know the secret of Inisicíleáin. . . . That fairy music, played upon an island fiddle, is a lament for a whole world of imaginations banished irrevocably now, but still faintly visible in the afterglow of a sunken sun.[13]

the spirit world that can both guide those who walk between the worlds and also heal "all want and woe or weariness of soul."

In later times music was seen as a gift from the faeries. In Ireland those who hear the faery harp become possessed with the spirit of the *ceol-sídhe*, the faery music that haunts them for the rest of their lives. Countless folktales and local legends of the Celtic countries tell of people who have become musicians after an encounter with the faeries. Often this happens when a traveler is passing a faery hill, usually after sunset, and hears music from within. The famous seventeenth-century blind harper, Turlough O'Carolan, whose music has been recorded by many modern Celtic musicians, supposedly slept out on a faery fort one night and heard the faery music in his dreams. When he awoke he remembered every note and played them all from memory.

This powerful gift was not to be taken lightly, and often special conditions surrounded faery music. A piper in eighteenth-century Ireland who was walking through the hills one evening heard a faery piper play a beautiful tune, called "Móraleana." He was told that he could play it only three times in his life before an audience; any more and a doom would fall upon him. He kept strictly to this injunction until he found himself in the finals of a piping competition, and to make sure he would win he played the faery tune. The beauty of the melody carried the day, and he was declared the winner. But the moment he was crowned with the winner's garland he grew pale and fell dead upon the stage. His punishment stems from his misuse of a spiritual bequest that he used to further his worldly ambition. Like the shaman's ability to heal, the gift of music cannot be taken for granted.

Perhaps the most poignant tale of supernatural music comes from the Isle of Skye in Scotland and tells "How Music First Came to the Western Isles." A boy once found a wooden harp floating in the sea. He fished it out and held it up to the wind, which made it sing with a plangent melody. Day after day,

the boy sat fingering the strings, trying to make the magical music again, but only discordant sounds would come. In desperation, the boy's mother consulted a *dubh-sgoilear*, a black magician, to beg him to either give her son the gift of music or take the desire from him.

"Give me your soul," said the magician, "and I will put the skill of music into your boy; or give me your body and I will quench his longing for it."

The mother chose to give her son the gift of music. He was radiant with joy as the sweet sounds flowed from his fingers, but when he found out what she had done, he became distraught with horror and remorse. From that moment on, he played music so sad that the birds of the air and the fish of the sea all stopped to listen to him, and that is the reason for the sorrowful strains of the music of the Western Isles.[14]

Delighted with Harps

Just as the Celts viewed the Otherworld as closely intersecting their own, so music, whose origins are in that world, was a constant presence in everyday life. From the chieftain's hall to the lowly cottage, music has flowed through the lives of the people at celebrations, religious meetings, fairs, and wakes. It has lent rhythm to the unending daily chores of subsistence living and provided the continuo to innumerable personal joys and sorrows. Like the mythical three strains of harp music, it has cheered, moved, and consoled countless generations and continues to do so today.

Although the origins of Celtic musical instruments are obscured by time, we know that the earliest musicians played stringed instruments and pipes. In early Ireland pride of place belonged, of course, to the harp (*cruit* or *cláirseach*), although the *tiompán*, a plucked or bowed lyre, was also popular, and a prototype of the modern fiddle is mentioned as one of the instruments heard at the Fair of Carman. Carvings on early Irish and Scottish stone crosses show both a four-sided harp with rounded top and bottom, and the classic triangular shape. They were originally carved from a solid block of bog willow and strung with bronze wire. In medieval times harps were valuable and treasured possessions wrought by expert craftsmen and often exquisitely decorated with carvings and set with precious stones. A number of harps have survived from the medieval period, the most famous being the fourteenth-century "Brian Boru" harp, which is on display in Trinity College, Dublin, and also graces Irish coins. In

the tenth-century *Laws of Wales*, a pair of triads declare that the three most indispensable things for a gentleman are his harp (*telyn*), his cloak, and his chessboard, while at home he should have a virtuous wife, a cushion for his chair, and his harp in tune.[15]

In Ireland and Scotland harpers themselves were skilled specialists who held positions of honor in political and cultural life. Every noble household employed a harper to compose and play eulogies to the family and its ancestors. The harpers of both countries enjoyed high prestige, and their expertise made a deep impression on Gerald of Wales when he wrote of the Irish in 1185:

> They seem to me to be incomparably more skilled in [musical instruments] than any other people I have seen. . . . They glide so subtly from one mode to another, and the grace notes so freely sport with such abandon and bewitching charm around the steady tone of the heavier sound, that the perfection of their art seems to lie in their concealing it, as if "it were better for being hidden. An art revealed brings shame."[16]

With the demise of Gaelic culture in the seventeenth century, the great families could no longer afford to maintain their harpers, and most were forced to become itinerant musicians, wandering the roads telling tales and singing songs to whomever would listen in return for a meal and bed for the night. Yet, as late as 1691, the Reverend Robert Kirk was able to write in his *Secret Commonwealth* that Highlanders were "much addicted to and delighted with harps." Fortunately, an authentic revival of interest in the harp in recent years means we can continue to indulge that addiction today.

> Three accomplishments well regarded in
> Ireland: a clever verse, music on the harp,
> the art of shaving faces.
> IRISH TRIAD

Piping Wild

Wind instruments are the oldest instruments in the Celtic realms to have survived, because some were constructed of metal. Four superbly crafted bronze trumpets were discovered in a lake near the great stronghold of Navan Fort, once the Ulster royal seat of Emhain Macha in Northern Ireland. Archaeologists believe they were cast into the lake as a deliberate votive act. But these ceremonial pieces were only one kind of wind instrument; in the Middle Ages, there were also horns for the hunt and battleground and reeds, stalks, and hollowed wood for playing dance tunes and airs. Like the harp, pipes are faery instruments. In Scottish ballads faery lovers sound the horns of Elfland to lure young maidens away from this world.

Bagpipes did not become popular in Ireland till the fifteenth century, when pipers played them to lead battle marches and funeral processions and also to provide music at assemblies and sporting events. Originally, pipers blew through a mouthpiece to inflate the bag, but in the seventeenth century the *uillean* (*ill*-en), "elbow," pipes emerged, where players use their arm to pump a simple bellows, giving a more muted, haunting sound to Irish pipe music. The more well known Scottish bagpipe, or *piob mhór* (peeb vor), "great pipe," came into its own in the Highlands and islands of Scotland. Originally, it may have been used in warfare, where its terrifying skirl could be heard even above the roar and din of battle, for a good piper can make himself heard at least two miles away. In the seventeenth century a more complex musical form developed, known as the *piobaireachd* (*pee-broch-k*) and sometimes called *an ceol mór,* "the great music," giving rise to many

TO A HARP

Harp of Cnoc Í Chosgair, you who
    bring sleep
to eyes long sleepless;
sweet subtle, plangent, glad, cooling
    grave.

Excellent instrument with smooth
    gentle curve,
trilling under red fingers,
musician that has charmed us,
red, lion-like of full melody.

You who lure the bird from the flock,
you who refresh the mind,
brown spotted one of sweet words,
ardent, wondrous, passionate.

You who heal every wounded warrior,
joy and allurement to women,
familiar guide over the dark-blue
    water,
mystic sweet sounding music.

You who silence every instrument of
    music,
yourself a pleasing plaintive instrument,
dweller among the Race of Conn,
instrument yellow-brown and firm.

The one darling of sages,
restless, smooth, sweet of tune,
crimson star above the faery hills,
breast-jewel of High Kings.

Sweet tender flowers, brown harp of
    Diarmaid,
shape not unloved by hosts,
voice of the cuckoos in May!

I have not heard music ever such as
    your frame makes
since the time of the faery people,
fair brown many-coloured bough,
gentle, powerful, glorious.

Sound of the calm wave on the beach,
pure shadowing tree of pure music,
carousals are drunk in your company,
voice of the swan over shining streams.

Cry of the faery women from the Fairy
    Hill of Ler,
no melody can match you,
every house is sweet-stringed through
    your guidance,
you the pinnacle of harp music . . .
    GOFRAIDH FIONN Ó DÁLAIGH,
    FOURTEENTH CENTURY[17]

beautiful laments, marches, salutes, and splendid pieces for clan gatherings and special occasions.

A family from Skye, the MacCrimmons, were said to have developed the *piobaireachd,* and legend has it that they learned the art from a faery woman who gave the first of their line a silver chanter. One version, interesting because it gives us a glimpse into the role of the piper within the clan system, tells how Iain Òg MacCrimmon was sitting on a faery hill in the west of Skye, feeling disconsolate because he was not considered a good enough piper to attend a competition promoted by the chieftain, MacLeod, at Dunvegan Castle. A faery woman approached him, saying,

Your handsome looks and sweet music
Have brought you a faery sweetheart.
I bequeath you this silver chanter:
At the touch of your fingers,
It will always bring forth the sweetest music.

She gave him the silver chanter for his pipes and taught him the art of the *piobaireachd.* Iain Òg hurried off to Dunvegan Castle and won the contest over pipers from all over the Highlands, for all could tell that his music had the gift of faery fingers

on the chanter. He became the hereditary piper to the Macleods, and from that day on the MacCrimmons of Skye produced many generations of renowned pipers and composers. He founded a famous school for pipers at Borreraig, his home in the west of Skye, where people came from all over Scotland and Ireland to study for a full seven years.

But MacCrimmon had been warned by his faery sweetheart that should he or any of his descendants treat the silver chanter disrespectfully, the gift for music would be removed from his family forever. One stormy day, one of his descendants was returning to Skye from the nearby island of Raasay with the chief of the Macleods. As he played in the pipers' seat at the prow of the chieftain's galley, the swell of the waves caused his fingers to slip. Finally, he laid down the pipes with a derogatory remark, blaming the silver chanter for his mistakes. At that moment the chanter, of its own accord, rose from the galley and slipped over the gunwale and into the sea, where it has since remained. From that time on the MacCrimmons' hereditary gift dried up, their school of piping fell into decay, and the family's fortunes declined. A lone cairn marks the spot where the school of piping stood, and it is said that the sound of ghostly

piping can still be heard in the sea cliffs and caverns of Borreraig.

After the failure of the Jacobite Rebellion in 1746, the playing of the pipes was forbidden in Scotland, but large numbers of Highlanders were recruited into the British army, where they employed the pipes for regimental marching music to the beat of drums, giving birth to the modern pipe band. More recently the bagpipes have been given a new lease of life in the Celtic music revival of the last thirty years. Their wild, indomitable skirl can be heard in modern recordings and performances, weaving in and out of an array of other instruments, ancient and modern. In fact, they are becoming so popular it has been said that more pipers are playing today than at any other time in the history of the pipes.

"There's meat and music here," as the fox said, when running away with the bagpipe.
SCOTTISH SAYING

The Singing Word

> *A sharing of gold is but brief,*
> *but a sharing of song lasts long.*
SCOTTISH PROVERB

Among all the other instruments that contribute to the unique sound of Celtic music—fiddles, *bodhráns*, whistles, to name a few—none is so enduring in its appeal as the human voice. In the chieftains' halls, the voices belonged to the bards, who sang or chanted praise-poems to their masters and declaimed the great stories to music at feasts and assemblies. Although the bardic colleges were dissolved in the seventeenth century, these ancient songs could still be heard only a hundred years ago in Ireland and Scotland. In 1873 the Irish scholar Eugene O'Curry recalls one of his father's friends singing the old lays of Fionn and the Fianna, which date from the twelfth century:

He had a rich and powerful voice, and often, on a calm summer day, he used to go with a party into a boat on the Lower Shannon . . . where the river is eight miles wide, and having rowed to the middle of the river, they used to lie on their oars there to uncork their whiskey jar and make themselves happy, on which occasions Anthony O'Brien was always prepared to sing his choicest pieces, among which were no greater favorites than Oisín's poems. So powerful was the singer's voice that it often reached the shores at either side of the boat in Clare and Kerry, and often called the laboring men and women from the neighbouring fields at both sides down to the water's edge to enjoy the strains of such music (and such performance of it) as I fear is not often in these days to be heard even on the favoured banks of the soft flowing queen of Irish rivers.[18]

In the cabins, out in the fields, or on the waves, the voices were of the ordinary people of Ireland, who recorded their own histories in songs of loves and betrayals, dreams and awakenings, banishments and reunions. The soft sounds of a lullaby welcomed the newborn child into the world, while the anguished wail of the *caoine* (*kwee*-nyuh), or keening, marked her passage out of it. In Scotland in particular, singing provided a much-needed counterpoint to such daily tasks as churning milk, grinding grain, herding cattle, and spinning wool. Boswell, writing of his tour through the Hebrides in the 1785, experienced this flow of song firsthand: "As we came to shore, the music of the rowers was succeeded by that of the reapers."[19]

Many of the richest work songs arose out of cloth production, especially the process known as "waulking," the shrinking of the cloth. All the women in the community sat around a long trestle, pounding the cloth with their hands and feet, singing rhythmically as they worked. These waulking songs preserve some of the most ancient remnants of Gaelic culture—ballads, faery songs, clan lore, songs of love and heroism. The women also spontaneously improvised verses and created their own songs as they worked, often witty and caustic ones about local people and events.

Alongside the communal songs that helped weave the fabric of everyday life were songs written from individual experience, wrung from the soul by passionate and often intolerable feelings. And yet these anonymous singers touch such a universal chord that even today we can be moved by long-forgotten tales of events far outside the context of our modern lives: "Ny Kiree Fo Niaghtey" (The Sheep Under the Snow), from the Isle of Man, tells of a farmer who lost his entire flock in an unexpected snowstorm, while "Bádaí na Scadán" (The Herring Boats) was composed spontaneously by a distraught man searching the beach for his sons' bodies after a fishing boat disaster. And, of course, the perennial songs of exile:

*O my country, I think of thee, fragrant, fresh Uist
    of the handsome youths,
Where nobles might be seen, where Clan Ranald
    had his heritage.*

*Land of bent grass, land of barley, land where
    everything is plentiful,
where young men sing songs and drink ale.*

*They come to us, deceitful and cunning, in order
to entice us from our homes;
They praise Manitoba to us, a cold country
    without coal or peat . . .*

*If I had as much as two suits of clothes, a pair of
shoes and my fare in my pocket,
I would sail for Uist.*[20]

Music and song were for everybody, not just for professional performers. People sang "as they breathed: unselfconsciously and spontaneously."[21] A nineteenth-century woman who lived in the Highlands discovered: "In every cottage there is a musician." In Ireland Sailí Gallagher, a traditional singer from Donegal, told her interviewer:

I always sing when I'm working—I never stop singing! I never stop—and somebody'll see us the other day, and I was makin' tea and I was singin' away, and they said, "Well, *you're* happy, anyway." But I never stop singing—I always keep on![22]

The merciful word, the singing word,
and the good word.
May the power of these three holy things be
on all men and women for evermore!

IRISH TRIAD[23]

Discovering Celtic Music Today

The rich legacy of Celtic music and song is available to us today, performed by those dedicated to singing the song onward into the new millennium, despite the near demise of Celtic culture and the ubiquitous presence of television. As well as performing instrumental pieces and songs in English, a number of today's Celtic artists sing in Gaelic, Welsh, Breton, and Cornish.

In Celtic communities practically everyone played some kind of instrument or sang, because music was a shared experience rather than a passive form of entertainment. In the evenings, especially in winter, people gathered at a specified house for songs, stories, and *craic,* good fun. Donegal singer Neilí Ní Dhomhnaill remembered: "Anybody that could sing—when he would come . . . maybe there would be a couple of people—and they would ask him to sing a song. And maybe someone would tell a story—everyone would have to do something."[24]

We can counteract the passivity of modern entertainment, keep Celtic culture alive and well, and also have enormous fun by getting involved in singing, dancing, or playing music from the Celtic countries. Many communities now provide resources for beginners, and you will find some numbers in the back of this book to get you started.

THE INNER CAULDRON
TRANSFORMATION

All art involves transformation, and to create art, we ourselves must be transformed. Even if we do not think of ourselves as artists in the usual sense of the word, conscious living is a creative act in which every day is our canvas to paint, our metal to forge, our song to craft. "The Birth of Taliesin" teaches us about transformation. On one level Gwion (the "shining" one) represents the sun, which is "swallowed up" by the lengthening night as winter approaches. He emerges from the sea just as the "shining brow" of the sun arises at Beltaine, the first day of summer. On the inner level, Gwion represents our essence, which is often portrayed as a shining light. As the Earth orbits the sun, so does our personality self turn toward the light at the center of our being.

Gwion's death and rebirth as a poet-seer is reminiscent of the initiation rites within the mystery schools of late antiquity, where the candidate descended into the realm of the Great Goddess who was both receiver of the souls of the dead and giver of new life. Her two children, who represent the darkness and light of the world, suggest that Ceridwen is a Welsh aspect of the Great Goddess. Her cauldron, her womb, and the ocean are all vessels of regeneration out of which the peasant boy emerges as Taliesin, bard and seer. The fisherman who discovers him does indeed land a fish: Little Gwion has been reborn as the all-knowing creature of the Otherworld—the Salmon of Wisdom.

Often our own lives become transformed by unexpected events, as Gwion's was when he ingested the magical drops by accident. That is when Ceridwen, keeper of the cauldron of changes, begins to hunt us down, forcing us to be fluid, to adapt, to shape-shift into new roles that challenge our ideas of who we are. A marriage ends, we lose our job—whatever hook we have hung our identity on is suddenly snatched away—and, like Gwion, we are plunged into the womb of the Goddess to be remade.

A woman who works with victims of domestic violence says of this process in her life:

For Ceridwen I have tried many forms—not all necessarily ones that I thought I wanted, not always necessarily ones she was going to allow me to stay in. She has turned her face away at times others might have thought I was most vulnerable—like the babe upon the ocean—but in the end the outcome has always been that I am so much more, with so much more left to become— even though I am not quite yet the Taliesin I might be!

Meditation: Ceridwen's Cauldron
Sit before your altar with the chalice or bowl in the center. Think about something in your life you would like transformed. This could be a feeling, a situation, a relationship, a habit, or anything that you know needs to be regenerated. Write this down on a piece of paper, and keep it by you as you prepare to take a journey to meet Ceridwen, Mother of Changes.

You are standing among the reeds of a green water-meadow near Bala Lake. An orange sun is beginning to set in the west, and silhouettes of herons and other waterbirds fly across its face as they seek their evening nests among the rushes. On the other side of the lake crouches the dark bulk of a circular house, with a tall conical roof out of which a thread of smoke is curling. Walking sunwise around the lake, you make your way to the house, and as you approach you see someone by the door. It is a thickset, black-browed boy of about fourteen. On his shoulder a raven squats, and you know it is Ceridwen's son, Morfran. He silently lifts the skins that cover the doorway, and you enter.

At first you are aware only of the flickering light and shadows on the walls. The shifting light reveals bunches of plants hanging down from the thatched roof, and now and again you catch glimpses of shelves on which lean precarious stacks of books, flasks of colored glass, and strangely shaped objects, some of which you recognize and others to which you cannot put a name. There is one large shadow of a stooping figure, and, moving your gaze to the center of the room, you see it belongs to a tall, middle-aged woman who stirs a steaming cauldron. She wears a long, crimson robe, and her hair is braided in two thick plaits, one black and one white. By her side stands her daughter, a slender girl of about sixteen, with yellow hair that curls over her shoulders. Ceridwen straightens up and looks at you with a direct, unswerving gaze. She asks, "What do you wish to have transformed?" and beckons you toward the cauldron. You step toward her with the paper on which you have written your desire, and she motions you to cast it into the steaming brew.

(*At this point, take your piece of paper and place it in the bowl or chalice in the center of your altar. Now close your eyes again.*)

As it disappears, the liquid in the cauldron begins to boil and seethe with a fizzing sound. As you watch, bubbles form and break on the surface and sparkling drops fountain up into the air. When at last they subside, the liquid becomes very still again, and Ceridwen smiles and motions you toward the cauldron. The surface is mirror-clear, and in it you can see images of the transformed situation. . . . Notice what is different about it . . . how you act . . . how others around you act . . . what you say . . . what you think and feel. . . . Be aware of holding a different attitude, of res-onating at a different vibration . . . of stepping into a whole new way of being. . . . (*long pause*) Then the girl comes forward holding in her two hands a chalice on which many crea-tures and birds are finely chased in silver.

Ceridwen dips a ladle into the cauldron and pours some of the potion into the chalice, and her daughter offers it to you, saying, "This is the elixir of Awen. May you be transformed." You drink the liquid and immediately feel refreshed and filled with a sense of hope for the future and a strong commitment to positive change.

And now it is time for you to leave, so you thank the two women and walk around to the door, which Morfran is once more holding open. As you pass through, you become more and more aware that you are sitting here, in *this* place, in *this* time, and you come all the way back to the present, opening your eyes and feeling refreshed and alert.

THE MUSIC OF WHAT HAPPENS

Once, as the Fianna-Finn rested on a chase, a debate arose among them as to what was the finest music in the world.

"Tell us that," said Fionn, turning to Oisin.

"The cuckoo calling from the tree that is highest in the hedge," cried his merry son.

"A good sound," said Fionn. "And you, Oscar," he asked, "what is to your mind the finest of music?"

"The top of music is the ring of a spear on a shield," cried the stout lad.

"It is a good sound," said Fionn.

And the other champions told their delight: the belling of a stag across water, the baying of a tuneful pack heard in the distance, the song of a lark, the laughter of a gleeful girl, or the whisper of a moved one.

"They are good sounds all," said Fionn.

"Tell us, chief," one ventured, "what do you think?"

"The music of what happens," said great Fionn, "that is the finest music in the world."

JAMES STEPHENS

THE FESTIVAL OF SAMHAIN

I have tidings for you;
The stag bells,
Winter snows,
Summer has gone.

At the end of October the doorway to the dark half of the Celtic year swings open. The dying sun is swallowed up by the lengthening nights; the green fields of summer have become brown and sere. In groves of oak and beech, leaves drop to earth, and animals prepare for winter sleep. It is Samhain, the season of frost and firelight.

Samhain comes from two words meaning "summer's end." In the seventh century it was Christianized as All Saints' Day, also known as Hallowmas or Hollantide, which commemorated the souls of the holy dead. The night before, which was the most important time for the festival, we know as *Halloween*. Throughout the centuries, pagan and Christian beliefs have intertwined in a gallimaufry of customs and celebrations from October 31 through the middle of November, all designed to usher in the mysteries of the dark half of the year.

In the country year Samhain marked the time when herders led the cattle and sheep down from their summer hillside pastures to the shelter of stable and byre. The hay that would feed them during the winter was heaped into sturdy thatched ricks and tied down securely against the storms to come. Animals destined for the table were slaughtered, and in pre-Christian times they would first have been devoted to the gods with much ceremony. Everyone worked their hardest to gather in the last of the harvest—barley, oats, wheat, turnips, and apples—for come November, the faeries would blast every growing plant with their breath, blighting any nuts and berries remaining on the hedgerows. Peat or wood for winter fires lay in stacked rows by the hearth. It was a joyous time of family reunion, when all members of the household worked together baking, salting meat, and making preserves for the winter feasts to come. The endless horizons of summer gave way to a warm, dim room; the symphony of summer sounds was replaced by a counterpoint of voices, young and old, human and animal.

FESTIVAL NAMES

Language	Name	Pronunciation
English	Halloween, Hallowmas	
Irish Gaelic	Samhain	*sow*-ihn
	Oíche Shamna (Samhain Eve)	*ee*-huh *how*-nuh
Scottish Gaelic	Samhuinn Oidhche Shamhna	*sah*-vin uh-*ee*-hyuh
	(Samhuinn Eve)	*how*-nuh
Manx	Sauin Oie Houney	*sow*-in oh-ee *how*-nee
	(Sauin Eve)	
Welsh	Nos Calan Gaeaf	noss *cal*-ahn *gie*-ahv
	(First Day of Winter)	
Cornish	Nos Kalann-Gwav	noss *cal*-ahn gwahv
Breton	Noz Kala-Goañv	noz *cal*-a-*gwah*

THE FEAST OF TARA

Just as the Celtic day began at night, Samhain may have actually marked the Celtic New Year, for our ancestors knew that from dark silence come whisperings of new beginnings and the stirring of the seed underground. Certainly, in early Ireland Samhain was the most important of all the four great calendar festivals. A great feast, the *feis temrach*, was held at Tara every third year, attended by much drinking and feasting. Its main purpose seems to have been the renewal of kingship and the kingdom itself, with the four provincial kings and their people arranged foursquare around the High King, who sat in state at the center.[1] This was of utmost importance for outside the walls of Tara the forces of chaos reigned as the *sídhe* mounds opened wide and all kinds of Otherworld beings streamed out, at the height of their powers on this in-between time that was the third and greatest spirit night of the year. According to one tale, Tara was almost overcome by an evil spirit every Samhain, until the arrival of Fionn McCumhaill.

The Enchantment of Tara

When Fionn came to manhood, he went to Tara at Samhaintide to the gathering of the High King and found he had walked into a national crisis. Every Samhain for the last nine years, a Dark Lord of the *Sídhe* called Aillén mac Midna (*al*-yeyn muck *meeth*-nuh) from the northern stronghold of the Tuatha Dé Danann had burned Tara to the ground, and each year there was not one champion among the Irish who could stop him.

"However much we bar the doors, he simply walks through playing the sweetest music you ever heard on the *tiompán,* and as soon as we hear those magical notes, not one of us can stay awake—not even wounded men and women in labor," lamented the king. "When we're all asleep, he breathes fire from his mouth and burns the whole place down. If any man could save us, I would give him the reward of his choice."

Fionn decided to have a try, for he wanted to win back the leadership of the Fianna, the warrior band that his father had lost through treachery. A man called Fiacha, the son of one of his father's old friends, gave him a magic spear, which would help him stay awake.

That night all of Tara was barricaded against the fiend, and everyone huddled together in fear or paced feverishly about in an attempt to stay awake. But Fionn sat in a corner of the hall, the spear butt against the floor between his legs, the point against his forehead. It was not long before the sweet strains of faery music wafted into the hall, and no matter what they were doing, one by one the whole court fell fast asleep. But whenever Fionn started to nod off, the spear point jabbed his forehead and he jerked upright again. The third time this happened, he was just in time to see a tall, ethereal figure drift like a shadow into the hall, playing a silver-stringed instrument. Fionn watched, mesmerized, as the *Sídhe* Lord parted his lips, almost as if he was going to sing, but instead, out from a cavernous mouth poured a great roaring flame that streamed toward the roof. Fionn struggled to his feet and hurled his purple-fringed mantle at the jet of flame. The fire missed its mark and plummeted into the earth, taking the mantle with it. At that, the shadowy lord spun on his heels and fled like a gray mist back to his home in the northern mountains. But Fionn caught up with him just as he was entering his *sídhe* mound, aimed his magic spear, and pierced him right through the back. When Fionn returned to Tara, the king was so pleased that he restored to him his rightful inheritance as leader of the Fianna.

THE FIRES OF SAMHAIN

Meat, beer, nut mast, chitterlings,
They are the dues of Samhain;
A merry bonfire on the hill,
Buttermilk, fresh-buttered bread.
EARLY IRISH CALENDAR POEM[2]

At the Feast of Tara the druids commemorated the start of the new cycle with a sacred fire on the hilltop at Tlachtga, twelve miles to the northwest. Lighting fires at this time has continued right up to the present in Ireland and the British Isles, although different reasons are usually given for doing so. In the 1860s the Halloween bonfires were still so popular in Scotland that one traveler reported seeing thirty fires lighting up the hillsides all on one night, each surrounded by rings of dancing figures, a practice that continued until the First World War. Young people and servants lit brands from the fire and ran around the fields and hedges of house and farm, while community leaders surrounded parish boundaries with a magic circle of light. Afterward, ashes from the fires were sprinkled over the fields to protect them during the winter months—and of course, they also

improved the soil. The bonfire provided an island of light within the oncoming tide of winter darkness, keeping away cold, discomfort, and evil spirits long before electricity illumined our nights. In Wales the sinking of the last flame was a signal for all the children present to run as fast as they could for home, screaming, "The black sow without a tail take the hindmost!"

In many bonfire ceremonies an effigy is burned—an echo, perhaps of the ancient sacrifices that the early Celts offered up to the gods at the Samhain fires. In Queen Victoria's time a huge bonfire was kindled in front of her Scottish home, Balmoral Castle, to "burn the witch," a hideous old crone called the Shandy Dann, who was sent to her doom with the skirl of the bagpipes. In Britain Bonfire Night falls on November 5 and commemorates Guy Fawkes's attempt to blow up the Houses of Parliament in the seventeenth century. Since then, many a "guy" has been consigned to the flames, though in some parts of the country, such as Lewes, Sussex, other despised figures—of the pope, Margaret Thatcher, and the local bank manager, among others—have been joyfully cremated. Bonfires continue to light up the skies every year and probably always will, as there will probably always be a human need to make fires against the winter's dark.

THE WILD HUNT

As the gates of Winter open wide, the great cavalcade of spirits known as the Wild Hunt sweeps through the skies. They ride to gather the lost and wandering souls of the dead and lead them home. At their helm rides an illustrious huntsman, who in Wales is Gwynn ap Nudd, King of the Faeries; in England he is Herne the Hunter; and in many places he is King Arthur himself:

> *Arthour knyght he rade on nycht*
> *With gylten spur and candil lyght.*

In the northern dusk people trembled to hear the unearthly cries of wild geese overhead. They believed it must be the yelping of the huntsman's spirit hounds, who like all Otherworld animals, have white bodies and red ears. In Scotland the ghostly hunters have hawks on their wrists and ride westward on the wind toward Tír na h-òige, the Land of Youth, and Tír fo thuinn, the Land Under Wave.

THE DARK GODDESS

Samhain was the time of the ritual wedding feast, or *banais rígh*, between the king and the sovereignty goddess who represented the land and gave him the right to rule. Many tales describe this goddess as having two aspects: old and young, foul and fair, the hag and the maiden, and we have come upon her in one or other of these guises throughout this book. She arrived as the lovely Queen of Elfland to Thomas the Rhymer but changed into her hag aspect when he kissed her. As Ceridwen, she appeared as the goddess who both took Gwion's life away and yet gave birth to him as a poet. These stories tell us something about her role as an initiator into the mysteries of poetry. She also often appears in her hag aspect first to initiate a would-be king.

In the Irish tale "The Adventures of the Sons of Eochaid Mugmedón," five brothers go out hunting in the woods to prove their manhood. They lose their way and set up camp among the trees to light a fire to cook the game they have killed. One of the brothers is sent in search of drinking water but finds a monstrous black hag guarding a well. She will give him water only in exchange for a kiss. He turns away, repelled, as does each of the brothers who follows him in turn, except for Niall, who gives her a wholehearted embrace. When he looks at her again, she has turned into the most beautiful woman in the world, with lips "as the crimson lichen of Leinster's crags . . . her locks . . . like Bregon's buttercups."[3]

"What art thou?" said the boy. "King of Tara, I am Sovereignty," she replies, "and your seed shall be over every clan."

By appearing in her most repulsive aspect, Sovereignty is able to test for a true king, one who is not fooled by appearances, who knows the value of the treasure that is concealed in unlikely places. He is willing to put aside self-gratification and submit to unappealing demands out of compassion. Above all, by kissing or mating with the Dark One, he understands the mysteries of life and death as two sides of the same coin and so will be able to draw upon the wisdom of the Otherworld during his reign and be in right relationship with the gods.

The Cailleach

In Scotland Samhain ushers in the reign of the Cailleach Bheur, whom we first met in February as the hag queen who rules over the winter season until the return of Bride in early spring. Her name literally means the "Veiled One," an epithet often applied to those who belong to hidden worlds but that later came to mean simply "Old Wife." *Bheur* means "sharp" or "shrill," because she personified the cutting winds and harshness of the northern winter, which came to be known as "Cailleach weather." She was also said to be the daughter of *grianan*, the "little sun," which in the old Scottish calendar shines from Samhain to Bride, followed by the "big sun" of the summer months. She is the weather spirit responsible for the gales that lash the northeast, and local fishermen gave her the ironic epithet of "Gentle Annie."

She was terrible to behold:

her face was blue-black, of the lustre of coal,
And her bone tufted tooth was like rusted bone.

In her head was one deep pool-like eye
Swifter than a star in winter
Upon her head gnarled brushwood
like the clawed old wood of the aspen root.[4]

The Cailleach Bheur lived in a cave below Ben Nevis, the "mountain of snows," in the Scottish Highlands. Dressed all in gray, a dun-colored plaid wrapped tightly about her shoulders, she leaped from mountain to mountain across the arms of the sea. When an unusually heavy storm threatened, people told one another, "The Cailleach is going to tramp her blankets tonight," for at the end of summer she washed her cloak in Corrievreckan, the whirlpool off the west coast, and when she spread it out to dry the hills appeared white with snow. She wielded a magic rod or hammer with which she struck the grass into blades of ice. In early spring she could not bear the growing light and would fly into a temper, throwing down her wand beneath a holly tree, before whirling away in rage: "and that is why no grass grows under holly trees."[5]

At winter's end some said she turned into a gray boulder until the warm days were over.

But others declared that she became Brigit, the beautiful young goddess of spring. They said she fled westward to the legendary Green Isle where springs the Well of Youth and, in the first rays of the sun on Brigit's Day, drank the water that bubbles up from a crevice of a rock and was transformed into the fair maid whose white wand turns the bare earth green again.

But the Cailleach had other aspects, too, showing her to be one of the old, wild goddesses of the land. She was an Earth Shaper, an old Mountain Mother, who gave birth to rocks and islands. She built all the hills in Ross-shire, and Ben Wyvis was formed of rocks carried in her creel. Once her creel upset, and the rocks fell out and formed Little Wyvis, the smaller peak nearby. When her creel tilted sideways, rocks called "the spillings from the creel of the big old woman" turned into the Hebridean Isles. In Ireland she flew over the land with a heap of stones in her apron, dropping them on the way to form mountains, such as the Sliabh na Caillighe (*shlee*-uv nuh *kal*-ee) in County Meath, which you can still climb today in order to sit on the great stone known as the Hag's Chair and make a wish.

On the threshold to the dark half of the year, the Cailleach has much to teach us

LETTING GO: A BANISHING SPELL

Ask yourself the following, and write a list for each:

1. What old habits, patterns, and ways of being no longer serve you and your relationships?
2. What things from the past adversely affect your family or your community's well-being and would best be forgiven and forgotten?
3. What does our planet need less of to make it more healthy?

Choose *one* item from each list that you genuinely wish to release.

Now take a piece of yarn, string, or cord, and make three knots in it, one for each issue. As you make each knot, visualize each situation clearly, and imagine every aspect of it being firmly bound into the knot. Bury the knotted cord where sun, wind, and rain cannot touch it, and let it rot away.

about darkness. Beltaine, the other great gateway of the Celtic year, initiated us through light, bringing sunshine and communion. Samhain is the yin (Celtic: *gam*) to Beltaine's yang (Celtic: *sam*), the *via negativa* rather than the *via positiva*. At Beltaine we learn through relationship; at Samhain we learn through separating and allowing to die that which is no longer useful or relevant in our lives. Having harvested the kernels of our soul's growth this year, we now begin clearing our inner fields of leftover stalks and stubble. By doing so, we align ourselves with the cosmic cycle of death and rebirth.

SHEELA-NA-GIG

The stone figure known as Sheela-na-gig may represent the only image of a goddess to be found in Ireland today. (Others exist in Britain, too.) She is carved as a naked figure, who squats with her legs apart, holding open her vulva. Is she the Earth Mother giving birth, or is she the Sovereignty goddess challenging the would-be king to mate with her? Although the carvings are usually found on medieval churches, most commentators agree that they are stylistically much older. Some may have originally come from riverbeds or graveyards or stood sentinel at sacred springs. Although some writers have dismissed these carvings as images of lust meant as a warning by the church, ordinary people have visited them for centuries to rub or scrape rock dust from the vulva for good luck, fertility, and protection. And they continue to do so in the twenty-first century, so strong is the pull of this ancient goddess on the human psyche.

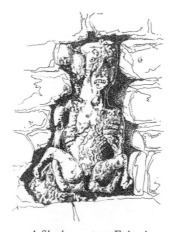

A Sheela-na-gig at Fethard,
County Tipperary, Ireland

I have had my day with kings,
drinking mead and wine;
today I drink whey and water
among shriveled old hags . . .

The flood-wave,
and the swift ebb;
what the flood brings you
the ebb carries from your hand . . .[6]

GODS OF THE CELTS:
MÓRRÍGAN

The Mórrígan (*mor*-ree-un), whose name
means "Phantom Queen," was a battle fury.
Along with Badb (*both*-uv), Crow, and Macha
(*mokh*-uh), she formed a terrifying triplicity
known as the Mórrígna, who unleashed their
powers of enchantment to bring mists, clouds
of darkness, and showers of fire and blood
over their enemies. Their howls of menace
froze the blood and caused soldiers to flee the
battlefield. Any aspect of this triple goddess
might appear among opposing armies as carrion crows or ravens, hopping about on the
spears and shields of the army who were to be
victorious. Or warriors might catch a glimpse
of an old lean hag hovering above the fray.
Another of her aspects was as the Washer at
the Ford, an old woman seen washing the
linen of a soldier about to die in battle.

HOLY GROUND
THE HAG OF BEARA
(KERRY, IRELAND)

On the Beara Peninsula in the far southwest
of Ireland, a strange outcrop of metamorphic
rock shaped like a woman's face gazes out to
sea. It is the Cailleach Bhéarra (*vyey*-ruh), the
Hag of Beara, whom local tradition calls the
Shaper of the Land. Once an immortal ancestral goddess, she was changed by the pen of a
medieval scribe into an old nun grieving over
her lost youth and beauty. The poem might
be the lament of the goddess herself for the
end of the pagan era:

Beholding her at this liminal place, a warrior knew that he would soon be crossing the river that separates life and death.

Yet she was also regarded as a strong protector of her people and shows aspects of being a goddess of the land and fertility. One Samhain, before the Second Battle of Moytirra, the Dagda came upon her as she was washing herself in a river in Sligo, with one foot on either bank, her hair hanging down in "nine loosened tresses." The two had sexual intercourse, reminding us of the Samhain ritual marriage between the leader of the tribe and the goddess of the land to ensure prosperity for the coming year. The Mórrígan warned the Dagda of the approaching Fomorian host, counseled him on how to win the battle, and promised him she would strike fear into the heart of the enemy king. When the Tuatha Dé Danann won, she announced the victory by proclaiming:

Peace up to heaven,
Heaven down to earth.
Earth beneath heaven,
Strength in each,
A cup very full,
Full of honey;
Mead in abundance,
Summer in winter . . .
Peace up to heaven . . . [7]

RAVEN

A CELTIC BESTIARY

"What is blacker than the raven? Only death," goes an old saying, and certainly no other bird has such a reputation for the dark side of life than this bird and its cousins in the crow family. Its sharp beak, harsh cry, and fondness for carrion, whether on battlefield or roadside, create an altogether sinister image. Along with the Mórrígan, the banshee may appear as a hooded crow to warn of impending death, while in Scotland the Cailleach sometimes assumes raven shape.

And yet "raven-knowledge" is a proverbial term for wisdom, and the raven is also associated with Lugh and other Celtic divinities as an intelligent bird that offers good counsel and prophecy. A stone relief from Burgundy shows a pair of ravens perched one on each shoulder of a god, apparently croaking words of advice into his ears. These may be the two magic birds that warned Lugh of the approach of the Fomorians in the Second Battle of Moytirra, or perhaps the two white ravens of the faery god Midir. After King Arthur's death, his soul took the shape of a raven and is often to be seen hovering over his favorite haunts. For this reason it is unlucky to kill a raven in many parts of Wales and Cornwall.

In the *Mabinogi,* the great king Brân the Blessed was named for a raven (*Brân* means "raven" in Welsh). Before his heroic death in battle, he asked his followers to cut off his head and bury it on the White Hill in London, facing France. As long as it remained, Britain would be safe from invaders. When the Tower of London was built on the site, a flock of ravens appeared in order to protect the kingdom, and there they remain to this day, strutting about Tower Green, their wings clipped so they will not fly away.

ELDER

ᏫHE SACRED ᏮROVE

The elder is a small but bountiful tree, covered in summer with fragrant white blossoms and in autumn juicy purple berries, which country people have used for centuries in jams, jellies, medicinal syrups, and wine. It is associated with the goddess in her hag aspect, and in many parts of the British Isles the tree spirit was addressed as the "Old Lady." Bathing one's eyes in the green juice of the wood confers the ability to see invisible beings, while if you stand under an elder tree at Samhain in Scotland, you can see the faery host riding by. A protective amulet can be traditionally made by plucking an elder twig just before the October full moon. The wood between the nodes must be cut into nine pieces and bound in a piece of linen. It is hung around the neck so that the pieces of wood touch the heart. They must hang there until the thread breaks, at which point the amulet has to be buried where it will not be found.

MISCHIEF NIGHT

On Samhain Eve Manannán mac Lir lifted his cloak of concealment from the Shining Ones, and anyone out near faery forts at dusk might hear their sounds of revelry or catch a glimpse of dancing feet. Most late wayfarers took steps to protect themselves from a closer encounter by carrying a black-handled knife or sticking a needle in coat collar or sleeve, as the faeries shrink in fear from iron—because, some say, they were the pre–Iron Age dwellers in these isles. However, more adventurous souls knew that at this time you could enter a *sídhe* mound by walking nine times around it, at which point a door would appear in the hill.

It was Samhain-tide—the Night of the Laughter of the Gods—tonight. Their palaces flamed tonight upon the heights and windy ridges of the world; and across the far-stretching plains—wide open. Tonight a mortal could enter there: could drink, ungrudged—from vats of mead and hydromel—the golden-beaded heady drink of immortals.

Ella Young

Samhain was known as "Mischief Night" in some areas, as young people gleefully gave full rein to their shadow side. Fantastical figures with blackened faces trooped through country lanes bearing turnip lanterns carved into deaths' heads, while grotesque masks and costumes transformed village regulars into cross-dressers and cavorting hobbyhorses. Ordinary folk had become archetypal figures acting out the forces of darkness and the Underworld.

In the eighteenth and nineteenth centuries—and no doubt long before that—they careened through the village, whitewashing windows, smearing doorknobs with treacle, or filling locks with glue. If their fathers did not admonish them, it was probably because they themselves were out concocting even more diabolical amusements. An old favorite in Ireland was to quietly unharness the horse and take apart the cart of a neighbor who had arrived home the worse for drink and, while he slept, reassemble horse and cart again *inside* his living room, looking forward to his bemused discovery in the morning. It was also a time of delicious daring, when the foolhardy might be egged on to fetch a dead man's bone from a churchyard or gather fernseed at midnight in a solitary wood.

Halloween pranks wedded to the custom of going door to door begging for goodies gave rise to the modern custom of trick or treat, although originally children filled their pockets with apples and nuts, not candy. In County Cork a band of young men blowing horns and making a general hullabaloo marched through the countryside led by a man wearing white sheets and a horse's head. He represented the White Mare (Láir Bhán), an aspect of the goddess. On hearing the horns approaching her house, a housewife would rush to the door with offerings of cakes or coins, while the leader sang the traditional verses.

The goddess also put in an appearance in South Wales, where men and boys went around the houses wearing women's clothes and singing a song about the White Lady. They were known as *gwarchod,* or hags, and wore sheepskins, ragged clothes, and masks. Each house they visited gave them harvest fare, and when they returned home to the "big house" or farm, they were rewarded with a traditional supper called "the mash of nine sorts," a stew made from a variety of vegetables including turnips, peas, parsnips, potatoes, carrots, and leeks mashed up with pepper, salt, and milk. The sacred number nine made this a very special feast indeed.

Underlying the mischief and merrymaking was a more serious ritual. The masked figures represented the spirits of the dead. To refuse them food was to invite their vengeance on the household—hence the trick if there were no treats.

TURNIP LANTERNS

The original Halloween lantern was a turnip, mangelwurzel, or swede (rutabaga), for pumpkins do not grow readily in the short summers of the Celtic lands. These paler root vegetables are actually shaped more like a skull and give off an eerie yellow glow when a candle is lit inside. They remind us of the early Celts' veneration of the head, which they considered the seat of the soul.

Materials

1 large turnip. Try to find one with the proper skull shape—slightly tapered toward the chin. Find a big one!

One sharp knife and teaspoon

Newspaper

Container for the turnip shavings

Candle

Sturdy wire, about 12 inches

Method

1. Cut the top off the turnip—not too far down.
2. Using the knife, carve out a hole in the top of the turnip. Once there is enough room, use the teaspoon to hollow out the turnip so that the turnip becomes translucent—that is, when you hold it up to the light you can see it glow.

3. Using a sharp knife, carve a Celtic face into the turnip shell. Remember, this is not a pumpkin, so no gap-toothed smile! Select a good Celtic face like this one:

4. Flatten out the inside of the base, making a slight depression to hold the candle.
5. Light candle and drip wax into depression in the center. Stick candle upright in the wax.
6. Pierce a hole in each side of the top of the turnip. Insert the wire for a handle.
7. Use the resulting grated turnip for soup!

Reproduced by permission of Conrad Bladey

JANET AND TAMLIN

It was always roses—the scent that blew like a faery wind through the narrow windows of the castle tower. Or with no scent at all, just the yellowing papery petals pressed to my breast where soon a child will suck. Without the roses, I would already have been lost, delivered up to be wed to some doddering old friend of my father's, like one of the pieces in the endless games of chess I used to play. With the roses' help, I can remember. I *must* remember ... and then I can defeat the whole host of them: my father, the Faery Queen, and all ... and be with the only one that ever could unlock my sullen heart—Tamlin. So, as I wait here at the ancient well on this bitter cold Halloween night, let me remember how it all began. ...

> *O I forbid you, maidens all,*
> *That wear gold on your hair,*
> *To come or go by Carterhaugh*
> *For young Tamlin is there.*

If my father had taken the trouble to get to know his only daughter, he would have realized that his warning was like honey to the bear. With my poor weak mother gone, I defied every rule he made; every "don't" I did. I was fifteen and bent on enjoying my freedom as much as I could before I was forced to wed some foul-breathed lord and breed his brats. For word had come that a Faery Knight was haunting the well at Carterhaugh. His name was Tamlin, and any girl who passed that way had to pay him a fee: a gold ring or a green mantle—or else her maidenhead. Well, I was too young even to know what that meant! But a faery well sounded a lot more interesting than the dreary sewing circle I had to attend every day ... especially in summer, when the whole greenwood was alive with birdsong and the fragrance of wild roses.

I slipped out next morning and rode over Ettrick Water into Carterhaugh Woods. There was the old moss-covered well, overhung with a tangle of briar rose. I was disappointed to see it deserted. Clearly, the rumors were untrue. I slid down from my horse to pick a spray to take back as proof of my adventure. The scent of the flowers was heady and sweet, and they seemed to draw me toward them. It was then that the trees seemed to huddle closer round the well and the morning became very slow and quiet. The air sparkled with shards of light as I pulled a double rose. In that moment I heard his voice for the first time, rippling through the silent pool of morning:

> *"Why pullest thou the rose, Janet,*
> *And why breaks thou the wand?*
> *And why comes thou to Carterhaugh*
> *Withouten my command?"*

I spun round to face him, clutching the roses to my breast. He was not tall, but very slim, with fair hair that hung in elf-locks around his shoulders. I could not take my gaze away from his gray eyes, which had both a light and a sorrow in them. But I was used to standing my ground:

> *"Carterhaugh, it is my own,*
> *My daddy gave it me,*
> *I'll come and go by Carterhaugh,*
> *And ask no leave of thee."*

"Then," said the Faery Knight, "you must pay my fee."

When he took a step toward me, I held my breath but felt no fear. And when he led me deep into the greenwood, I was not loath to follow. And when he laid me down on a bed of moss my heart leaped into his, and, body and soul, we became as the double rose.

I was never so free and never so bound.

When they discovered I was pregnant by a Faery Knight, they locked me in the tower room until a husband could be found desperate enough for a dowry to accept the Earl of March's soiled goods. It was several months before I managed to escape and ride back to Carterhaugh. The woods were no longer green. The last brown leaves were whipped from their branches by the late October wind. The roses at the well had lost their petals and were now red hips, as ripe and firm as my womb. As soon as I plucked one Tamlin appeared as before, and the next moment I was in his arms. We wept together tears of love and parting. At last I cried, "Tell me, my love, for our baby's sake, if ever you were a mortal man!"

Tamlin gave a sigh and answered, "In the beginning I was known as the second son of the Earl of Murray. I left that life the winter's day I went hunting in these woods.

"There blew a drowsy, drowsy wind,
And sleep upon me fell,
The Queen of Faeries she took me
In yon green hill to dwell.

"But worst of all, Janet," he ended, with quiet hopelessness, "every seven years, the queen must pay a tithe to hell, and I fear the next time it will be me. And the hour is almost come, for tonight is Halloween when the Faery Host rides and the devil takes his due. Yet, Janet, at this time when the two worlds meet, you may yet win me back, if your courage is strong."

I pledged my faith in a silent kiss. He continued, "Go to Miles Cross in the deep of night. Fill a cup with holy water and sprinkle it around you in the *caim*, the magic circle of protection. At midnight the faeries will come riding by in companies, and I shall be among them:

"Oh, first let by the black, black steed
And then let by the brown,
But haste ye to the milk white steed
And pull the rider down.

"For I'll be on the milk white steed
With a gold star in my crown,
Because I was an earthly knight
They gave me that renown.

"Run swiftly to my horse, take the bridle, and I will slip down. They will turn me into all manner of terrible shapes, but if you love me, Janet, you must hold me tight, however much it hurts. If you endure, they will be forced to change me back into a naked man. Then cast your mantle over me, and I shall be yours."

Which is why I am here tonight to fight for my love under the frosty stars of a Samhain Night. And now there is no longer time for reflection. Like a wind they are upon me, the *sluagh*, the host: first a gale of black horses with wild laughing riders, and now a gust of brown horses with flame-faced warriors. They cannot see me, protected by the *caim* as I am, but I am ready to spring the moment I see him. . . .

. . . And here he is at last, riding the white horse at the head of the third company, the gold star in his crown. A crouch and a leap—and my fingers close around his bridle. I am almost swung off the ground as the horse rears—a white wave breaking against an invisible rock. The rider falls—he is in my arms! He is—

He is an adder.

The poison tongue flicks out. He writhes in my hands. . . .

Remember the rose, Janet!

A thousand bells are ringing in my ears. I am confused by flickering lights and cold, grinning faces. . . .

Remember the rose, Janet! Remember!

I remember. I see with my heart what my eyes cannot see. I hold him fast. I feel his dear man's body pressed to mine. . . .

But now he has become a huge and ferocious bear! Red eyes gleam with murderous fire. I am being smothered by the stench of foul breath. . . .

Remember the rose, Janet! Remember me!

I close my eyes and feel against my lips the warm kiss of a human mouth.

But I make the mistake of opening my eyes. He is no longer a bear but a small hard bar of iron. A bar that glows white-hot. My head is full of the clangor of bells. I can no longer feel his body, only a pain that sears my flesh and sends me falling, falling backward into a dark abyss. Only I refuse even now to let him go . . . even if I fall into the arms of death. . . .

. . . Not death, but the sweet sharp shock of water rises to meet me. I gasp, open my eyes—and he is there with me, body and soul—my own true love, Tamlin! Gasping, we stagger together, up to our knees in well water, then I throw my green mantle about his naked body and make him mine forever.

> *Then up and spoke the Queen of Faeries,*
> *And an angry woman was she,*
> *"She's taken away the bonniest knight*
> *In all my company!"*

But her voice is fading, and she and all her host are turning pale and transparent, like stars before the sun. They spur their horses and rush past us in the dawn wind. There is a sound of great gates closing.

The Dream has ended. And only just begun.

DIVINATION AT SAMHAIN

> *For on Hallowmas Eve*
> *the Nighthag shall ride,*
> *And all her nine-fold sweeping on by her side,*
> *Whether the wind sing lowly or loud,*
> *Sailing through moonshine or swathed in a cloud.*

> *He that dare sit in St. Swithin's Chair*
> *When the Nighthag wings the troubled air,*
> *Questions three, when he speaks the spell,*
> *He may ask, and she must tell.*
> SIR WALTER SCOTT

Sir Walter Scott's poem highlights another aspect of the Cailleach's power at Halloween: to grant oracles. Samhain was a significant time for divination, perhaps even more so than May or Midsummer's Eve, because this was the chief of the three spirit nights.

Divination customs and games frequently featured apples and nuts from the recent harvest, and candles played an important part in adding atmosphere to the mysteries. In Scotland a child born at Samhain was said to be gifted with *an dà shealladh* (un *dah hyel*-lugh), "the two sights," more commonly known as "second sight," or clairvoyance.

Apple Magic

At Samhain the apple harvest is in, and old hearthside games, such as apple bobbing, called apple dookin' in Scotland, are reminders, perhaps, of the journey across water to obtain the magic apple from Emhain Ablach (*a*-win *owl*-ukh), the Otherworld Island of Apples.

DOOKIN' FOR APPLES Place a large tub, preferably wooden, on the floor, and half fill it with water. Tumble in plenty of apples, and have one person stir them around vigorously with a long wooden spoon or rod of hazel, ash, or any other sacred tree.

All players take their turn kneeling on the floor, trying to capture the apples with their teeth as they go bobbing around. Each gets three tries before the next person has a go. Best to wear old clothes for this one, and have a roaring fire nearby so you can dry off while eating your prize!

If you do manage to capture an apple, you might want to keep it for a divination ritual, such as this one:

THE APPLE AND THE MIRROR Before the stroke of midnight, sit in front of a mirror in a room lit only by one candle or the moon. Go into the silence, and ask a question. Cut the apple into nine pieces. With your back to the mirror, eat eight of the pieces, then throw the ninth over your left shoulder. Turn your head to look over the same shoulder, and you will see an image or symbol in the mirror that will tell you your answer.

(When you look in the mirror, let your focus go "soft," and allow the patterns made by the moon or candlelight and shadows to suggest forms, symbols, and other dreamlike images that speak to your intuition.)

Dreaming Stones
Go to a stream that marks a boundary, and, with closed eyes, take from the water three stones between middle finger and thumb, saying these words as each is gathered:

I will lift the stone
As Mary lifted it for her Son,
For substance, virtue, and strength;
May this stone be in my hand
Till I reach my journey's end.

(Scots Gaelic)
Togaidh mise chlach,
Mar a thog Moire da Mac,
Air bhrìgh, air bhuaidh, 's air neart;
Gun robh a chlachsa am dhòrn,
Gus an ruig mi mo cheann uidhe.[8]

Carry them home carefully and place them under your pillow. That night, ask for a dream that will give you guidance or a solution to a problem, and the stones may bring it for you.

COLCANNON

A popular Halloween custom in Ireland was to blindfold young girls and send them off in pairs to the cabbage patch. With much shrieking of laughter, each would grope about for the cabbage of her choice and pull it from the ground, root and all. The characteristics of the root—long, short, crooked, hairy, and so on—would tell her what kind of future husband she would have. The cabbage would then be whisked off to the kitchen for further prophetic usage in the traditional dish known as colcannon (from *cal ceann fhionn*, "white-headed cabbage"). A wedding ring was concealed in the big skillet of mashed potatoes and cabbage, and, armed with spoons, the girls feverishly competed with one another to get the ring in their mouthful, a sure sign that she would be next to marry.

Colcannon was traditionally served with a well of melted butter in the middle and was a favorite in all country Irish households, as the old poem attests:

Did you ever eat colcannon,
When 'twas made with yellow cream,
And the kale and praties blended
Like a picture in a dream?
Did you ever scoop a hole on top
To hold the melting lake
Of the clover-flavored butter
That your mother used to make?
Ah, God be with the happy days
When troubles we had not,
And our mothers made colcannon
In the little skillet pot.

Ingredients

2 pounds organic potatoes, scrubbed and
   sliced, skins left on
1 leek chopped small, white and pale green
   parts only
6 green onions, white and green parts sliced
¾ cup half-and-half or thin cream
8 tablespoons butter
3 large garlic cloves, chopped
Salt to taste
Lots of freshly ground black pepper

Method

1. Boil the potatoes in salted water until soft.
   Drain and set aside.
2. Boil the cabbage in a small amount of salted
   water until nearly tender but still retaining
   some crispness. Drain and add a little butter
   and black pepper. Chop and set aside.
3. While cabbage cooks, sauté the leek and
   garlic until limp in 2 tablespoons butter.
   Add the cream and heat, but do not boil.
4. Mash the potatoes by hand with the seasonings and 2 tablespoons butter until very
   smooth. Pour in the leek mixture and
   whisk some more.
5. Add the cabbage. Potato and cabbage
   should be roughly equal. If the colcannon
   has cooled down by now, you may want to
   reheat it to piping hot in oven or under
   broiler.
6. With the back of a spoon, make a hollow
   in the middle of the colcannon and add the
   butter, or melt the butter on top of individual servings.
   Serves 6–8 as a side dish, 3–4 as main dish

THE INNER CAULDRON
RECLAIMING

Samhain teaches us about our Shadow: all the
fears, blind spots, negativity, and unresolved
issues about ourselves and life in general that
must be recognized, accepted, and reclaimed
before we can become whole. Much of the
power of Celtic spirituality lies in this willing-

ness to embrace our dark side. Rather than insisting we turn ever toward the light, as certain New Age spiritual paths would have us do, the Celtic Dark Goddess takes us *down* to bring us face-to-face with our own hidden darkness, for, as Jung once said, "One does not become enlightened by imaginary figures of light, but by making the darkness conscious."

The Cailleach, the Mórrígan, and all Hag aspects of the goddess play the role of the Dweller on the Threshold, the figure who guards the entrance to the inner planes. She is the Queen of Air and Darkness, who embodies our Shadow in a fearsome manner, yet she is not evil in herself; she is merely reflecting back to us our own weaknesses, illusions, and fears. If we cannot face our own negativity, we are not ready to proceed further on the spiritual path. But if we can meet the Shadow with equanimity, its formidable appearance dissolves, and we are initiated into deeper truths and realities.

The story of Tamlin, on one level (for it has many levels and this is just one), teaches us about facing our Shadow on the way to achieving the unity of self required for spiritual work. The heroine, Janet, dares to defy her family and rescue her lover from his Underworld bondage to the Faery Queen, an aspect of the Dark Goddess. Love gives her the courage to hold onto him even though he

shape-shifts into some terrifying forms. Because she "holds him tight, however much it hurts," the Faery Queen is vanquished. Tamlin can be seen as Janet's hitherto unintegrated "masculine" side (or *animus*), who emerges from the "well" of her subconscious when she does a bold, courageous act. In the original ballad version of the story, they marry—her feminine and masculine sides unite—and Janet's child, her true Self, is born.

The following inner journey will take you to meet the Cailleach to help you reclaim hidden parts of yourself.

Meditation: The Hag's Chair
Now we have arrived at the gate of Samhain at winter's threshold. Place a stone in the center of your altar to symbolize the Cailleach's mountain and to remind you of her strength and enduring wisdom. According to ancient cosmology, our bones are formed from the stones of the earth, and indeed, it is our bones that last longer than any part of our earthly substance. Important Celtic centers were marked by a stone: the Lia Fáil, or Stone of Destiny, stands at Tara, the royal center of Ireland, as mentioned in January, while the Stone of Divisions stands on the hill at Uisnech in

County Meath, marking the sacred center (navel, or *omphalos*). of the five provinces. Like the Tree of Life, a standing stone is an *axis mundi* that connects us with both the worlds below and above. Choose a stone that appeals to you, one that you have found at the beach or river: smooth and round, worn by water, or striated with many colors.

If you wish, play a drumming tape or have someone beat a drum. Earthy sounds invoke the power of the Cailleach. An album of ancient-sounding music, such as *The Kilmartin Sessions*, which features Bronze Age musical instruments, is also effective during this inner journey.[9]

It is midnight. You are standing at the foot of a mountain in the North Country. A glimmer of starlight reveals huge boulders strewn over a rocky landscape of cliffs and moraines. It is very cold as you stand there breathing in the icy air, and you can see the vapor of your breath as you exhale. The silence is profound, but every now and then it is broken by the sound of the wind as it blows down from the peaks.

As your eyes grow accustomed to the dim light, you discern a narrow white trail switchbacking through the rocks ahead, and you know this is your path. You begin the steep ascent up the forbidding slopes, following the faint white ribbon in front of you, passing an occasional cairn of stones marking the way and showing that others have gone before you. . . . And after a long time, or a short time, or no time at all, you are aware that the path has led you to a huge pile of stones in the shape of a chair, carved with many spirals and concentric circles.

It is the Hag's Chair, and she is sitting there, looking down at you from an eye in the middle of her forehead: a huge Old Woman, with a face of midnight blue in which her one eye shines like a star. Frost white hair falls down like snowdrifts about her body. Two iron claws emerge from her midnight blue robes; one holds a great iron hammer. On one shoulder perches an owl with unblinking topaz eyes; at her feet lies a long, gray wolf, asleep.

As you approach her, she slowly stands, and it is like a mountain rising. She motions you to follow her, and she leads you over starlit rocky ground to a high cliff top. There she tells you to lie down on your stomach and peer over the edge. You find yourself gazing into a deep, dark boiling whirlpool, out of which an image arises . . . the image of your Shadow self—a part of you that you usually keep hidden. Your Shadow self may personify your anger, fear, jealousy, pride, or any part of you that you find hard to accept. Look closely at this figure. Observe what feelings arise within yourself as you do so. Now tell your Shadow honestly how you feel about it. . . . And now give your Shadow a voice and let it respond. . . . Ask your Shadow what it really wants from you. . . . Again, listen to its response. . . . Why does it want that? . . . What has it to offer you if you meet its needs? . . . Dialogue back and forth in this manner until the two of you have reached an agreement. Once you have reached an agreement, look at your Shadow again and notice if it has changed in any way. . . . Thank your Shadow for this meeting, and see its image slowly dissolve away again back into the whirlpool.

And now the boiling waters become still, and you are gazing into a calm silvery surface on which no ripple stirs. You find you can reach out and touch it—and it is not water at all, but a hard reflecting surface, and an ancient croaking voice is saying, with an undertone of dry amusement, "Welcome to the mirror of your mind!"

You stand up and take a step back—and see that now you are no longer looking at a mirror but into the one deep, pool-like eye of the Cailleach as she sits before you on her stone chair. And as you continue to look into that eye, it is like gazing into the vast reaches of the midnight sky itself, illumined by countless shining stars. . . . You are filled with a sense of calm, peace, and well-being that seems to last a very long time. Gradually you become aware that you are indeed gazing into the starry sky, and the Old Woman is no longer there. Her stone chair is empty, the owl and the wolf are gone, and you stand alone on a wintry mountainside, with the wind blowing about you. As you walk back down the narrow white trail, you gradually become aware that you are lying in *this* room, in *this* time and place, and when you reach the foot of the mountain, your eyes open and you return fully, feeling wide awake, calm, and relaxed.

Note: This can be a very profound meditation that should be done several times. You may want to write down what you experience as soon as possible so that you can review it later.

THE FAERY RIDE

Forget the hearth,
Forget the roof,
Set the wheel aside:
Leave your weaving,
Warp and woof,
Steal out to us this Samhain-Tide.

Steal out to us, our tossing hair
Sets sun and moon and stars aflare.
The racing winds are hounds beside
The cloud-maned horses that we ride.
Come ride with us, have heart to dare
The plunging steed; the steeps of air;
The swirling, high, tumultuous flight,
The aery hooves—this Samhain Night![10]

ELLA YOUNG

THE LAMP OF MEMORY

Thou fill'st the winged chalice of the soul
With thy lamp, O Memory . . .
DANTE GABRIEL ROSETTI

The dark days of November lead us deeper into the mysteries of
Samhain, with All Saints' Day on November 1 and All Souls' Day
on November 2, two Christian festivals that overlaid the earlier pagan
festivals of the dead. In modern America we tend to regard death as
something of an aberration, but our Celtic ancestors viewed life as a
never-ending spiral of birth, death, and rebirth. They believed that after
death the soul journeyed to the Summerlands beyond the western sea,
where the grass was always green and fruit and flowers grew together.
Feasting, hunting, music, love, and joyous sporting contests went on forever; and if any were wounded or killed one day, they sprang back to life
the next. In the Iron Age men and women of noble rank were buried

with everything they were likely to need in the afterlife: drinking horns, cauldrons, jewelry, weapons, and even chariots. Because of their beliefs, they were fearless in the face of death, which they considered to be "but the center of a long life."[1] In fact, it was not uncommon for a man to lend money and agree on repayment in his next lifetime.

THE DEAD AT CLONMACNOIS

In a quiet, watered land, a land of roses,
Stands Saint Kieran's City fair;
And the warriors of Erin in their famous generations
Slumber there.

There beneath the dewy hillside sleep the noblest
of the clan of Conn,
Each below his stone with name in branching Ogham,
And the sacred knot thereon.

There they laid to rest the seven Kings of Tara,
There the sons of Caibrè sleep—
Battle banners of the Gael, that in Kieran's plain of crosses
Now their final posting keep.

And in Clonmacnois they laid the men of Teffia,
And right many a lord of Breagh;
Deep the sod above the Clan Creidè and Clan Conaill,
Kind in hall and fierce in fray.

Many and many a son of Conn the Hundred-Fighter
In the red earth lies at rest;
Many a blue eye of Clan Colman the turf covers,
Many a swan-white breast.

ENOCH O'GILLAN, TRANSLATED BY T. W. ROLLESTON

THE SEVEN DAUGHTERS

November ushers in the rising of the Pleiades, a cluster of seven small bright stars in the constellation of Taurus. In Ireland they are known as *an Tréidín*, the Little Herd, and in Scotland *grioglachan*, from *griogag*, meaning "bead" or "crystal." In the Gaelic-speaking community of Cape Breton, Canada, they were known as the Seven Daughters of the Sea. These were seven maidens who came ashore and fell in love with the seven sons of a great chieftain. Their love was not returned, and one by one they died. Their spirits rose into the sky, where they can be seen on northern winter evenings, clustering together in their sorrow.

GODS OF THE CELTS: DONN

Some miles off the southwest coast of Ireland stands a small rocky island against which the sea surges with tremendous force. This is Tech Duinn, the House of Donn, an ancestor deity of the Gaels. The souls of the dead assembled here before embarking on their last journey to Tír na nÓg across the western ocean, to follow the path of the setting sun. Donn's name means "Dark One," and he is a shadowy figure who was relegated to mortal status as a brother of the bard Amergin. He drowned off the coast of Kerry and was buried at Tech Duinn, as a ninth-century poem relates:

> A stone cairn was raised across the broad sea for
> his people,
> A long-standing ancient house, which is named
> the House of Donn after him.
> And this was his mighty testament for his hun-
> dredfold offspring:
> "You shall all come to me, to my house, after
> your death."

Nowadays the island is simply known as Bull Rock. A lighthouse rises from it, and seabirds—fulmars, kittiwakes, storm petrels, and puffins—nest on its cliffs. Far below, the sea rushes through rock archways like entrances to a dolmen tomb.

VOYAGE OF THE DEAD

In Brittany, one of the last druid outposts, the fishermen of the northern coast were supposed to ferry the souls of the dead to their new homes on an Otherworld island across the English Channel, here called "Brittia," according to the sixth-century Roman writer Procopius:

Carvings on the pillar stone from Trecastle, Wales, may depict the transmigration of souls after death.

> At a late hour of the night they are conscious of a knocking at their doors and hear an indistinct voice. . . . They see skiffs in readiness, with no man at all in them, not their own skiffs, however, but of a different kind, in which they embark and lay hold of the oars. And they are aware that the boats are burdened with a large number of passengers and are wet by the waves to the edge of the planks and the oarlocks, having not so much as one finger's breadth above the water; they themselves, however, see no one, but after rowing a single hour, they put in at Brittia. And yet, when they make the voyage in their own skiffs, not using sails but rowing, they with difficulty make this passage in a night and a day. Then when they have reached the island and have been relieved of their burden, they depart with all speed, their boats now becoming suddenly light and rising above the waves, for they sink no further in the water than the keel itself.
>
> And they, for their part, neither see any man either sitting in the boat with them or departing from the boat, but they say that they hear a kind of voice from the island which seems to make announcement to those who take the souls in charge, as each name is called of the passengers who have come over with them. . . .[2]

YEW

THE SACRED GROVE

Of all the trees in the greenwood,
Oak, Elder, Elm, and Thorn,
The yew alone burns lamps of peace
For them that lie forlorn.

In early times the darkly glorious yew tree was probably the only evergreen tree in Britain. Both druids, with their belief in reincarnation, and later Christians, with their teaching of the resurrection, regarded it as a natural emblem of everlasting life. An old Irish verse calls yew the "patriarch of long-lasting woods," for this tree was revered as one of the most ancient beings on Earth: "Three lifetimes of the yew for the world from its beginning to its end" was a medieval saying. Recent research has shown that some yews in British churchyards may be as many as four thousand years old. These churches were probably built over pagan sacred sites, and indeed, the druids used yew wood to make magic wands and staves on which they carved the ogham runes. Yew's reputation for long life derives from the unique way in which it grows. The branches reach down to the ground, take root, and form new stems, which then rise up around the old central growth as separate but connected trunks. After a time they cannot be distinguished from the original tree, so the yew has always been a symbol of death and rebirth, the new that springs out of the old. To come upon one of these venerable trees today is a humbling experience. They are not tall, but their branches sometimes spread out in a canopy so wide it is like stepping into a mysterious, Otherworldly cavern.

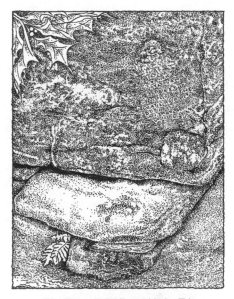

The Wizard's Well at Alderley Edge

HOLY GROUND
ALDERLEY EDGE
(CHESHIRE, ENGLAND)

Many legends tell how the great kings and heroes of old did not die but lie asleep in certain caves and hills. When the country is in its hour of greatest need, they will awaken and ride out to save her from her enemies.

One such place is Alderley Edge, a sheer sandstone cliff rising above the flat plain of Cheshire. Riddled with caves and ancient copper mines dating from the late Bronze Age, it was most likely an important economic and religious center for the Celtic tribe known as the Cornovii.

The Legend of Alderley Edge tells how one autumn a farmer rode over the hill on his way to Macclesfield market to sell his white horse. Halfway across, an old man suddenly appeared, "tall and strangely clad in a deep, flowing garment." He offered the farmer a sum of money for the fine beast, but he was refused. The old man prophesied that no one would buy his horse that day, and his words came true. When the disappointed farmer returned that evening, the old man was waiting. He ordered him to follow, "by the Seven Firs, the Golden Stone, by Stormy Point, and Saddle Bole."

They arrived at a rocky cliff face, where the wizard touched a rock with his wand, and a massive pair of iron gates appeared, which flew open with a sound like thunder. He led the terrified farmer and his horse through a maze of passages where hundreds of men in shining armor and their milk white steeds all lay sound asleep. But the horse of one warrior was missing.

"Your horse is needed to make the number complete," said the wizard. "Remember my words: There will come a day when these men and these horses will awaken from their enchanted sleep and ride out to save their country in a great battle. Leave your horse with me, and take this for your price."

He pointed to a cavern heaped high with treasure, and with trembling hands the farmer stuffed his pockets with gold and jewels. The wizard bade him be gone, and the iron gates clanged shut behind him and were never seen again.

Today one can walk through the woods to ancient healing springs, such as the one called Merlin's Well, where the carved face of the wizard gazes down inscrutably from the outcrop above.

THE SILENT COMPANY

On November 2, the eve of All Souls' Day in Ireland, families lit a candle in the window to guide the souls of the dead back to their old homes. As the veil between the worlds thinned, a *sluagh*, or host, of spirits walked the land and encountered the same hospitality the Celts have always shown the living. Doors and windows were left unfastened, and any passage through the house that they once used was kept open. The table was laid with the best white cloth, and special food was left out for them to enjoy.

In Wales they were known as the "silent company," and the food was called *bwyd*

cennad y meinv ("the food for the embassy of the dead"). In Brittany it was *boued gouel an Anaon* ("the food for the feast of the dead") and usually consisted of warm pancakes, curd cheese, and mugs of cider. When the family retired for the night, they sometimes heard the scraping of stools and clatter of plates and forks, as the spirits enjoyed their meal. Neither did they forget the homeless spirits, sadly roaming about the countryside with nowhere to go. Food and drink were set out on doorstep and windowsill so that they, too, might have a share.

Until quite recently in the Irish Gaeltacht, families kept a *seomra thiar*, or "room to the West"—sometimes just an alcove or nook— where they placed objects that reminded them of departed ones. At sunset the family solemnly turned toward the setting sun and spent time in loving remembrance of them. A candle was lit for each soul, then the whole family sat down to a communal feast in their honor.

Making a Shrine for the Dead
1. Choose part of a western wall for the shrine. This could be an alcove, shelf, windowsill, or small table. Cover it with a black or purple cloth.
2. Now arrange upon it mementos of relatives and friends who have passed over to the Summerlands this year or in the recent

past—photographs, small personal possessions or pieces of jewelry, and perhaps some branches, leaves, or flowers.

3. You may also feel moved to remember individuals or groups of people throughout the world whose deaths this year have touched you deeply. Photos from newspapers, symbolic objects, poems, and so on can also be added to the shrine.

4. Stand a candle by each one, and place a large candle in the center, symbolic of the one light that unites us all.

5. At dusk, light the candles, beginning with the central one, and sit or stand facing the shrine, contemplating each one in turn.

WAKES

The wake for the dead was once a great social occasion in Ireland and Scotland, when the family, relatives, and neighbors gathered at the house of the deceased before the burial. The dead person's praises were sung and the death mourned loudly, often by women who were professional "keeners." Their wailing and lamentations served the function of leading the community in a cathartic experience. But this was also a time for storytelling, singing, dancing, and games, washed down with copious drafts of whiskey and *poitín*. During the festivities the corpse was often treated as if he or she were alive, sometimes being taken out to dance or dealt a hand of cards! Complex ritual dramas were enacted through the night, clearly remnants of pagan rituals designed to propitiate the spirits of the ancestors and the Otherworld, but because of their sexual content they were suppressed by the priests in the seventeenth century, and none remain today. One was called "Building the Ship," where a group of men and women positioned themselves in the shape of a ship, perhaps to ritually encourage the dead one's voyage across the sea to the Blessed Isles.

Allow any emotions that may arise simply to be present, and express them naturally, as the Celts freely gave vent to their feelings at death.

6. If you are doing this in a group, you may wish to share stories, songs, poems, or words of inspiration. Each member of the circle can give a short tribute to one or more of those remembered here.

7. On All Souls' Eve, those who may be trapped in the limbo between heaven and earth, known as purgatory in Christian tradition, can be released. You may want to offer the following prayer, adapted from Scottish sources, to anyone who has recently died or whose death was particularly difficult:

> *You are going home to your home of winter,*
> *To your home of autumn, of spring,*
>   *and of summer;*
> *You are going home to the Land of the*
>   *Living,*
> *To the restful haven of the waveless sea.*
> *Peace of the Seven Lights be upon you, beloved,*
> *Peace of the Seven Joys be upon you, beloved,*
> *Peace of the Seven Loves be upon you, beloved,*
> *On the breast of the Mother of Blessings,*
> *In the arms of the Father of Peace.*

8. Prepare a special feast for yourself, family, or group for after the ritual at the shrine. Eat and drink with gusto! This is the time to wholeheartedly celebrate the great round of life and death. Finally, make sure you set aside a special dish for the departed ones before you go to bed.

BOAR

A CELTIC BESTIARY
BOAR

The fierceness and untamed power of the wild boar naturally led to its association with war and death among the early Celts. Warriors went to battle urged on by the terrifying squeal of the carnyx, the boar-headed trumpet, while some dressed in boar skins or wore menacing boar crests upon their helmets.

The boar was one of their favorite animals to hunt, for its strength and valiant defense when cornered appealed to Celtic notions of warriorhood. Celtic mythology is rich in tales of heroic boar hunts. Fionn hunted Formael, a huge boar that was "enough to cause mortal terror, for he was blue-black, with rough bristles . . . gray, horrible, without ears, without a tail, without testicles and his teeth standing out long and horrid outside his big head . . . and it raised the mane on its back so high that a plump apple would have stuck on each one of its rough bristles."

The early Celts prized boar meat above all food, and the centerpiece of the Feast of Tara was the freshly slaughtered *banb samna,* the young pig of Samhain. Pig bones and even whole joints of pork have been found in the graves of chieftains, no doubt in anticipation of a banquet in the afterlife. Guests at the *bruidne,* or Otherworld feasting halls, could eat all the pork they wanted from the cauldron, since pigs that were killed and eaten one day sprang up alive the next in the Celtic warriors' paradise.

CELTIC STORYTELLING

*A tune is more lasting than
the voices of birds,
A word is more lasting than the riches
of the world.*
Douglas Hyde

In the dim light of the long wooden hall, rushlights and flames from the central fire reveal figures lounging on pallets of dried grasses and animal pelts. On a raised couch at the head of the hall reclines the chieftain himself. They eat from low carved tables covered with food. Daggers glint as they slice hunks of boiled pork brought to them by women and young folk from the cauldron that hangs over the fire. A handsome woman circles the tables, filling drinking horns from a flagon of mead. The loud, boasting speech of the warriors and the chatter of the women are stilled as a man steps into the center carrying a small wooden harp. Although he is dark and slight compared to the fair muscular fighting men around him, his presence commands attention, partly, perhaps because of the bright-feathered cloak that swings from his shoulders, gleaming in the firelight. The harp spills sweet notes into the silence of the shadowy hall, and a clear voice rings out. . . .

A Storehouse of Tradition

The truths of the tribe are locked up in its stories. And in the Celtic countries the old tales are not buried beneath the earth with the bones of the ancestors; neither do they lie in fragments in museum cases. They endure, even when the people who first told them are dust in the landscape. "Myths and the characters whose stories they are live in the quiet of mountains and valleys, forests and meadows, rocks and springs, until someone comes along and thinks to tell them. They have other hiding places, too, inside the language we use every day, in the names of places where they happened, or the names of trees or days on the calendar."[3]

In early Ireland all that the tribe held of value was entrusted to the memory of the druids. Guardians of an oral-based culture, they were living libraries of its history, genealogies, mythology, and law. When the druid order was destroyed, others took up the flame of tradition. First of these were the *filidh,* poet-seers whose intensive education spanned at least twelve years, during which time they learned hundreds of stories in categories such as Destructions, Cattle Raids, Courtships, Battles, Deaths, Feasts, Adventures in the Otherworld, Elopements, and Visions.

As keepers of ancestral wisdom, the *filidh* were held in high acclaim. They wore a cloak of purple decorated with feathers, and a golden branch was carried above them to a special seat in the chieftain's hall. Together with the lesser order of the bards, the *filidh* kept their culture alive through the Middle Ages and Renaissance eras in Ireland, Wales, and Scotland, where, remarkably, the bardic schools were still active as late as the eighteenth century. After this, much of the precious tapestry of story came unraveled, but much also survived, carefully passed on into the modern age by generations of village storytellers known as *shanachies.*

Many of these unlettered men and women were sorcerers of the spoken word who could recite a different tale for every winter night. In the nineteenth century a visiting professor described the great Kerry shanachie, Seán Ó Conaill, a seventy-year-old farmer-fisherman who had never been to school, as

> one of the best-read men in the unwritten literature of the people whom I have ever known, his mind a storehouse of tradition of all kinds, pithy anecdotes, and intricate hero-tales, proverbs and rhymes and riddles. . . . He was a conscious literary artist. He took a

deep pleasure in the telling of his tales. His language was clear and vigorous, and had in it the stuff of literature.[4]

As Seán spun a tale, using all his well-honed skills of gesture and narrative, the audience would respond "with a hearty laugh at the discomfiture of the villain, or at some humorous incident and applaud with appropriate remarks the valor of the hero fighting against impossible odds seven-headed giants or monsters from the sea, or the serried ranks of the armies of the King of the Eastern World."

When he finished speaking he would lean forward and take a burning ember from the fire, press it down with a horny thumb on the tobacco of his pipe, lean back in his straw-bottomed chair, and enjoy the vigorous applause of listeners who were no doubt familiar with the tale from previous winters. After a while, conversation would turn in a desultory way to local news and gossip, until a visitor would request another story from "the man of the house," and the assembly would once again be transported to the magical islands of story.

THE SHANACHIE

Shanachie is an Anglicization of the Irish *seanchaí* and Scots Gaelic *seanachaidh*. The root word is *sean*, meaning "old," reflecting the shanachie's original function as a reciter of ancient lore, a custodian of tradition.

Scenes like this took place in cottages, crofts, barns, and alehouses throughout the Celtic lands, starting on November 1 and lasting until May brought the summer back. Orkney poet Edwin Muir remembers, "The Winter gathered us into one room as it gathered the cattle into the stable and the byre; the sky came closer; the lamps were lit at three or four in the afternoon, and then the great evening lay before us like a world: an evening filled with talk, stories, games, music and lamplight."[5]

In the Hebrides each community had a *céilidh* house, where everyone would gather on winter nights. There might be some singing and playing, but mainly the evening was spent in the telling of stories and personal anecdotes, the asking of riddles and quoting of sayings. The *céilidh* house symbolized the living heart of the community. The last one on the Isle of Lewis was burned down by the owner's request as he sailed past his homestead on the emigrant ship that would take him from Scotland forever.

Many of the tales in the shanachie's repertoire were so long they would burn a dip candle down in the telling and last until dawn whitened the sky. A far cry from a modern evening of television fare punctuated by sound bite news and commercial breaks! Where we now move restlessly from the screen world to the refrigerator and back, once the shanachie began, "There was, in old times, and in old times it was, a king of Ireland. . . ." or perhaps, "There was a fisherman once in Kinsale who had seven children . . ." you knew you were setting sail on a long voyage for "perilous seas in faery lands forlorn." Some, like the famed Scottish wonder tale, "The Leeching of Kian's Leg," were told over twenty-four consecutive nights.

KEEPING STORYTELLING ALIVE TODAY

> *They shall be remembered for ever,*
> *They shall be alive for ever,*
> *They shall be speaking for ever,*
> *The people shall hear them for ever.*
> W. B. YEATS

Although Celtic storytelling was almost swept to oblivion in the twentieth century, there has recently been a spirited revival of this ancient art, both in the Old world and the New. An up-and-coming generation of storytellers is breathing new life into the flame of story, regarding the few aging masters of the tradition with the same reverence once accorded the bards of old. Storytelling festivals are popping up all over Ireland, Great Britain, and the United States, and students are sharing the stage with septuagenarians.

In Scotland, people flock to hear Duncan Williamson, a member of a traveling family, who has a repertoire of over three thousand tales, riddles, jokes, and songs. In America, Norman Kennedy, an Aberdeen native now living in Vermont, who spent hundreds of hours listening to the old storytellers before they died, travels around the United States telling tales and teaching songs. And in many parts of the countryside there will be one or two people quietly recognized as the local shanachie, although unknown outside their area. Like the hero in a wonder tale, the storyteller appears to die then leaps up alive once more, to the delight of the audience.

In the United States, teachers, ministers, psychologists, and others involved in the helping professions are recognizing the power of the story to teach, impart wisdom, and heal. We are beginning to realize that to lose our stories is to lose our basic connection with one another, with our ancestors, and with our children. Sharing stories makes us laugh—and cry— together, strengthening the bonds of family and community even while we are entertained, something that will never be fostered by the passive and solitary act of watching television.

It's time to switch off the television and computer and form our own living circles again. Here we can recapture and retell our own stories, listen to the stories of others, and allow this most basic form of human communication to reconnect us.

You do not have to have the training of a shanachie to tell stories. Here are some suggestions to help you rekindle this living tradition within your family or community.

1. Storytelling is a nighttime activity. Gather around a fire, inside or out. If you have no fire, a candle in the center works just as well. Turn off the electric lights, and just sit for a while enjoying the light, the shadows, the silence. Feel the daytime world ebb away and the dreamtime flow in to take its place.

2. If you have been working with the meditations in this book, you should now be familiar with entering inner space. This is the land where all stories are born. Your own treasury of stories is already here. We might call it the "House of Memory."

3. Choose one person to guide the members of the group to their own "House of Memory." The leader says,

   "Let's begin by looking into the flame. This flame is just like the ones our ancestors looked into for thousands of years.... (pause) Now close your eyes and continue to see the flame.... (pause) Using it as a guide, let yourself go back in your imagination to a time when something happened with *fire*.... Now go back and daydream about that time.... See it like a movie in your mind ... and let the movie play from beginning to end.... (long pause) Now store the movie in your memory, and come back to the room."

4. When everyone has opened their eyes, the leader says, "Now each of us will share our memory. It doesn't have to be very long, and you don't have to worry about the words. Just start running the movie in your mind again, and describe what you see as the story unfolds."

5. This simple exercise offers a direct experience of how stories arise from inner images, with the words coming naturally later. Now the stage is set for some rich

and rewarding excursions into the Land of Story, with many treasures to share as you move on to further topics.[6]

Telling Celtic Tales

If you want to learn to tell stories in the Celtic tradition, the very best thing you can do is listen to traditional tellers. The resource section at the end of the book will show you where to begin. Here are some specifically Celtic techniques:

1. Entering the Otherworld

In the bardic colleges, students lay down in a darkened hut with a stone on top of their chests to enter fully into the inner world of the imagination. (I can personally attest that sensory deprivation concentrates the mind and memory wonderfully, although I draw a line at the stone!) Make sure your environment is as free from distraction and sensory stimulation as possible.

2. The Keys to Memory

While some traditional storytellers may use the method of seeing the story play out in images in the mind's eye, others learn some or all the words by heart (especially in the case of dialogue, lists of items, and standard descriptive passages known as "runs"). In this situation mnemonics come in handy. The early bards used triads to aid memory, such as this one:

Three Elders of the World:
The Owl of Cwm Cowlwyd,
the Eagle of Gwernabwy,
and the Blackbird of Celli Gadarn.[7]

You can adapt this method to your story to remind you of lists, sequences of events, and the like.

3. Playing with Words

Repeating certain words and phrases is what distinguishes the oral from the written tale. Skillful use of verbal techniques, such as repetition and alliteration, lifts a story out of plodding prose and makes it dance with the rhythm of a reel. It will also help you remember the story more easily. A fun and simple-to-learn story that features rhythm and repetition is the Irish folktale "The Man Who Had No Story."[8]

4. Story Openers and Closers

Traditional tags at the beginning and end of a tale are like spells that ritually mark the boundary between ordinary time and the "once upon a time" of story. For example:

Once long ago, and a long time it was. If I were there then, I should not be there now. If I were there now and at that time, I should have a new story or an old story, or I should have no story at all. . . .

THE MAGICAL POWER OF STORIES

In early Ireland the spoken word was considered so powerful that a story could bring good fortune to the listeners. For this, the storyteller expected to be paid well. This is how one tale ends:

> There are thirty chief virtues in this story; a few of them will suffice as examples. The married couple to whom this story is told on their wedding night will not separate without offspring; they will want for neither food nor clothing. A new house in which this is the first tale told, no dead will be brought out from it, it will lack neither food nor clothing, fire will not burn it. A king to which this tale is told prior to battle or conflict will be victorious. This tale should be told at offering drinks, feeding princes, or taking over inherited land. The reward for reciting this tale is a white-speckled, red-eared cow, a shirt of new linen, a cloak of fleecy wool with brooch, from kings and queens, from married couples, from stewards, from princes, to the one who can recite it and tell it to them."[9]

The everyday mind is arrested and confused, the world of cause and effect is suspended, and we enter those marvelous realms where dreams unfold:

Once it was where it was not beyond seven times seven countries and the Sea of Operencia behind an old stove in a

crack in the wall in the skirt of an old hag and there in the seven times seventh fold . . . a white flea; and in the middle of it the beautiful city of a king.

Story endings tend to be more conventional to bring us back to earth and ease the transition to normal conversation:

They feasted and they drank, and if the wine hadn't run out, I'd still be there with them instead of here talking to you.

And sometimes there are ingenuous disclaimers:

If my story is not true, may the soles of my shoes turn to buttermilk!

For to learn the craft of the Celtic storyteller is in some ways to assume the mantle of druid and psychopomp, one who takes us through the gates of the Otherworld to see many marvels then leads us safely home again. It may take you to the dwelling places of the *sídhe* and the realms of the ancestors.

If you are accepted, you will emerge singing the song of the bardic initiate:

Under the Earth I go.
On the oak leaf I stand.
I ride on the filly
That was never foaled,
And I carry the dead in my hand.

THE CHILDREN OF LIR

This tale formed part of the Irish bards' repertoire and was known as one of the "Three Sorrows of Storytelling." The flight of the enchanted swans can be understood on many levels: at this time of year it may remind us of our search for connection with the past and the longing of the exiled soul for home.

Out of the world's thread, fates' fingers spinning. Some lives are shot with gold, others with shadow. This is a tale of enchantment and exile, of four lives woven together by white swan's feather, storm and ice, and the sound of a little bell.

Long ago, when the high gods and goddesses known as the Tuatha Dé Danann lived in Ireland, there was a great king whose name was Lir (*lihr*). And this Lir had four lovely children—Fionnuala (*fin-oo*-luh), Conn, Fiachra (*feekh*-ruh), and Aodh (*ee*). Fionnuala was the eldest, and she was as fair as the young rowan tree; her brothers Fiachra and Conn were as swift as running water, and Aodh was a little bright-eyed baby boy. Everyone in Lir's court on the Hill of the White Field loved them— except their stepmother, Aoifa (*ee*-fuh), who was jealous of their father's love for them. And her hatred pursued them as the wolf pursues the fawn.

One day Aoifa took them in her chariot to the lake of Derravaragh to bathe in the waters. But as they played on the shore's edge, laughing and splashing, catching rainbows of mist and light between their fingers, she struck them with a rod of enchantment and turned them into four white swans.

"You will swim on this lake for three hundred years," she said, "then three hundred years on the narrow sea of Moyle, and three hundred years upon the Western Sea. This only will I grant you: that you shall still have human voices and there will be no music in the world sweeter than yours. And so shall you stay until a druid with a shaven crown comes over the seas, and you hear the sound of a little bell."

The swans spread their wings and rose up, circling the lake, and as they flew they sang their sorrow in the voices of human children. When the king found out what had happened, he turned Aoifa into a demon of the air and banished her from his court forever. He rode like the wind to the lake and called his children to him. "Come to me, Fionnuala; come, Conn; come, Aodh; come, Fiachra!" And there they came, flying to him over the lake: four white swans, and they huddled sadly around him as he knelt by the water's edge.

King Lir said through his tears, "I cannot give you back your shapes till the spell is ended, but come with me now to the house that is mine and yours, dear white children of my heart."

But the swan that was Fiachra said, "We cannot cross your threshold, Father, for we have the hearts of wild swans. We must fly into the dusk and feel the wave moving beneath us. Only our voices are of the children you knew, and the songs you taught us—that is all. Gold crowns are red in the firelight, but redder and fairer far is the dawn on the water."

The king reached out his hand to touch them, but the swans rose into the air, and their voices were lost in the sound of beating wings.

Three hundred years they flew over Lake Derravaragh and swam upon its waters. Many came to listen to their singing, for their songs brought joy to those in sorrow and lulled the sick to sleep. But when three hundred years were over, the swans rose suddenly and flew away to the straits of Moyle that flow between Ireland and Scotland. A cold, stormy sea it was and lonely. The swans had no one to listen to their songs and little heart for singing on the wild and chanting sea. Then one winter a great storm rushed upon them and scattered them far into the dark and pitiless night.

In the pale light of morning, Fionnuala fetched up on the Carraig-na-Rón (*kar*-ig nuh rohn), the Rock of Seals. Her feathers were broken and bedraggled with salt seawater, and she lamented long for her brothers, fearing never to see them again. But at last she saw Conn limping toward her, his feathers soaked, his head hanging, and now Fiachra, tired and faint, unable to speak a word for the cold. Her heart gave them a great welcome, and she sheltered Conn under her right wing and Fiachra under her left.

"Now," said Fionnuala, "if only Aodh would come to us, we would be happy indeed."

And as the first evening star rose in the sky, they caught sight of the little swan that was Aodh paddling valiantly over the waves toward them. Fionnuala held him close under the feathers of her breast. As they huddled together, the water froze their feet and wing tips to the rock, so that when they flew up skin and feathers remained behind.

In the morning they turned westward toward the wild Atlantic Ocean, and there they flew among the bird-haunted islands till three hundred more years had passed. Then, at last, the Children of Lir were free to return once more to the Hill of the White Field. Homeward they soared on wings of joy, eager to see the face of their father once more. But when they arrived, they found all desolate and empty, with nothing but roofless green raths and forests of nettles: no house, no fire, no hearthstone. Gone were the packs of dogs and drinking horns, silent the songs in lighted halls. And that was the greatest sorrow of all—that there lived no one who knew them in the house where they were born. They rested the night in that desolate place, singing very softly the sweet music of the *sídhe.*

At dawn they flew back to the western sea, for now they had no other home, and they lighted down on the island of Glora, off the coast of Connacht. There they made their nest among the reeds of the Lake of Birds.

Now, it was about this time that blessèd Patrick came into Ireland to spread the faith of Christ. One of his followers, Saint Caemhoch (*kwee-vokh*), built a little church by the lakeshore on the Isle of Glora. In a break of day, the saint arose from his heather bed, wrapping his rough brown robe around him to keep out the chill, and rang the bell for matins. On the other side of the island the swans started up and stretched their necks in fear.

"What is that dreadful thin sound we hear?" asked the brothers.

Fionnuala said, "That is the sound of the bell of Caemhoch, and soon our enchantment will be passing away."

They began to sing gladly, and the sweet strains of faery music floated across the lake and in through the reed walls of the cell. St. Caemhoch rose in wonder and walked down to the shore's edge and saw them, lit by the morning sun: four white swans singing with the voices of children! They came to rest at the saint's feet and told him their story, and he brought them to his little church. Every day they would hear mass with him, sitting on the altar. Their beauty gladdened his heart, and the hearts of the swans were at peace.

Then one day Fionnuala asked the saint to baptize them, but no sooner did the holy water touch the swans than their feathers fell away, and in their place stood three lean, withered old men and a thin, withered old woman. In a cracked whisper the woman that was Fionnuala said, "Bury us, cleric, in one grave. Lay Conn on my left, and Fiachra on my right, and on my breast place Aodh, my baby brother."

So they were buried, a cairn was raised above them, and their names written in ogham. And that was the fate of the Children of Lir.

But it is said that on windy days in the west of Ireland, by lakeshore or ocean strand, you can sometimes hear children's voices in the air, singing sweeter than you've ever heard, as they play with their father at home in the blessed Summerlands.

SOUL CAKES

A soul, a soul, a soul cake,
Please, good missus, a soul cake,
An apple, a pear, a plum or a cherry,
Any good thing to make us all merry.

In Wales and many parts of Britain, November 2 was the day to make soul cakes. These were spiced buns or cakes shaped like human figures. From the sixteenth century onward, poor people came around the houses begging for the cakes, which they would then give to the priest in payment for prayers for their dead relatives. In later times the original reason to go "a-souling" was forgotten, but the cakes continued to be made for children and other visitors that came by on All Souls' Day. The original Welsh recipe has been lost, but since gingerbread has always been a popular Welsh cake, here is a version based on an old gingerbread recipe.

Spirited Soul Cakes

Ingredients
½ teaspoon mace
½ teaspoon cloves
1 teaspoon baking powder
1 teaspoon baking soda
½ cup milk
1 ounce brandy (optional)
½ cup butter, softened
½ cup brown sugar
2 eggs
1 cup molasses
2½ cups flour
1½ teaspoons ginger
1 teaspoon nutmeg

Method
1. Cream together butter and brown sugar.
2. Add eggs and beat well. Add molasses.
3. Sift dry ingredients together in a medium bowl. Add dry ingredients alternately with milk to creamed mixture. Blend in brandy.
4. Pour batter (it will be thick) into two greased 13-inch-by-9-inch baking pans. Bake for 30 minutes in a 350-degree oven.
5. Cool cakes for approximately 15 minutes, then turn out onto a foil-lined flat surface.
6. Using a 1-inch-thick gingerbread man cookie cutter, cut figures from cakes. If cutter does not completely slice through, cut around edges with a sharp knife. Trim excess cake from around figures.

THE INNER CAULDRON
REMEMBERING

The songs of our ancestors are also
the songs of our children.
PHILIP CARR-GOMM

Irish folklorist Kevin Danaher remembers how, as a child, he asked an old storyteller from Limerick "if he wasn't afraid to go into the haunted house." The shanachie replied, "In dread, is it? What would I be in dread of, and the souls of my own dead as thick as bees around me?"[10]

Because the Celts of bygone days have always been aware of the invisible as well as the visible worlds, they did not share our modern notion of death as total separation. In the Celtic worldview time is an endless, connecting thread that enables the living to feel the wise and loving presence of the ancestors, who care as deeply about their descendants as a living family would. They weep with us when we are troubled and celebrate our good fortune. In early times people sought their advice by ritually fasting and sleeping on their graves in hopes of meeting with them in their dreams. As late as the sixteenth century, the chieftain Hugh O'Neil encamped his entire army on a burial mound before a great battle to gain the assistance of the "spirits of the mighty dead who dwell within."[11]

In America today we have lost the sense of connection with our ancestors that gave so much meaning to life in the past. Our sense of clanship, of being a branch of a great family tree whose roots are solidly anchored in tradition, is missing from our modern world. We live in a country to which people have come fleeing the bondage, not the security, of tradition. We pride ourselves on being the "New World," a nation of individuals, mavericks, and entrepreneurs. But in our haste to sever the ties that bind, we have also cut ourselves off from a sense of continuity with the truths of the tribe and its sacred connection with the land. It is no wonder so many of us feel so rootless and seek restlessly outside of ourselves for the way back home. We are seeking to *remember,* in the sense of identifying ourselves as members of a larger family of souls. Then we can become aware that we are part of a bigger story than our own fleeting appearance on Earth. Like the mushroom in the woods, we may appear to be a single entity, but we are invisibly connected by a network of mycelium as wide as the forest floor. The silent company of our ancestors stands behind us, lending their unspoken support to our future because *we* give meaning to *them* as well as the other way around. And likewise, we ourselves are the ancestors of generations who are to come. As Orkney poet George Mackay Brown once wrote, "We cannot live fully without the treasury our ancestors have left to us."

1. How does an awareness of your ancestors help you define who you are today?
2. Who in your family of origin has had the most spiritual impact on your life?
3. As an ancestor to future generations, what is the most important thing you would wish them to inherit from you?

Meditation: The Yew Tree Path

This inner journey will take you to meet one of your ancestors. The ancestor may be of your bloodline, from a past incarnation, or simply a spiritual ancestor. He or she will be someone who has influenced your spiritual life or shaped you in a positive way. Do not choose who will appear; let the choice be made for you.

FOOTSTEPS INTO THE PAST

A practical way to connect with your ancestral roots is to trace your family tree through genealogy. To get started:

Write down everything you know about your family, starting with yourself and working backward through your parents, grandparents, great-grandparents, and so on. Include dates and places of birth, marriage, and death as well as places of residence. Information such as occupation, military service, or church affiliation may also come in useful.

Talk or write to family members, especially the older ones. You may be surprised at how many memories may surface under gentle questioning and how old letters, diaries, photographs, and other useful documentation may come to light.

Many tools—books, software, Internet sites, and professional consultants—exist today to help you go further with your search. You'll find some of these in the resource section at the back of this book.

Close your eyes and take a few deep breaths. See before you a long avenue of ancient yew trees. Their branches have spread over the centuries so that they now entwine to form an arching tunnel, so densely interwoven it appears completely black, except that at the end you can see a small circle of pale yellow light. . . . As you take your first steps into the tunnel, become aware of stepping beyond present time into the deep ageless realm of the yew trees that stretches before the dawn of time. . . . Feel the power of the Underworld embodied in these dark tree-beings, as they brood upon the wisdom of the deep. . . .

And after what may be a short time, or a long time, or no time at all, the pale circle of light at the end of the tunnel is growing bigger and shedding a glow . . . and the interwoven branches are beginning to thin so that you begin to see patches of a violet-blue evening sky above you. . . .

And now at last you step out of the tunnel and see before you a figure tending a small fire of fragrant wood that crackles now and then, sending out sparks of green and gold. On the eastern horizon to your left, a group of seven stars is rising. You approach the fire tender. This is your ancestor. . . . He or she has been expecting you. Approach the fire and greet this person. . . . Notice what he or she looks like . . . clothes . . . hair . . . face . . . Is your ancestor old or young? Tall or short? Listen carefully while your ancestor tells you who she or he is and the role played in your spiritual development. . . . (long pause) Your ancestor has a gift of wisdom for you today. Sit by the fire with this person and receive the gift, which may come in the form of words or an object that is placed into your hands. . . . Thank your ancestor for this gift, and if you have any questions, ask now. . . . When it becomes clear the conversation is drawing to a close, take leave of your ancestor in the way that feels most appropriate, then walk back through the yew tree tunnel bearing your gift into the world of time . . . into your present life.

ORCHIL

I dreamed of Orchil,
the dim goddess who is under the brown Earth,
in a vast cavern, where she weaves at two looms.
With one hand she weaves life upward through the grass;
with the other she weaves death downward through the mould:
and the sound of the weaving is Eternity,
and the name of it in the green world is Time.
And, through all, Orchil weaves the weft of Eternal Beauty,
that passes not,
though her soul is Change.

Fiona MacLeod

WINTER SOLSTICE

I am a beam of the Sun . . .
AMERGIN

Winter Solstice is the time when light is born out of the womb of winter's darkness. Every year, on or around December 21, the sun appears to stand still, or rise and set in the same place for a few days. It is the time of the longest night, when Earth's very breath seems to falter in the face of the overpowering dark. Then, imperceptibly at first, the sun begins its long journey toward the south, and all of creation begins to exhale.

Rituals for welcoming back the sun date from the dawn of civilization, as communities came together to celebrate life with feasting, music, dance, drama, and, above all, light and fire. Whereas today we tend to think of Christmas as a single day or weekend event, most cultures suspended normal work routines and celebrated for at least twelve days.

In ancient Rome the Winter Solstice was welcomed with a joyous and unruly feast known as the Saturnalia. By the second century C.E. they also celebrated the Birthday of the Unconquered Sun on December 25, a custom that originated in Syria. Farther north, Scandinavians celebrated Yule, a name that could mean "wheel" or that possibly gives us the root word for "jolly."

The exact nature of early Celtic celebrations are not known because in the fourth century C.E. the Church of Rome overlaid the old festival of the birth of the Sun with the birth of the Son. The actual birthday of Christ had never been certain, so after much debate the ancient midwinter feast was chosen because people were used to celebrating the birth of a sun god or hero at this time of year. Even then, the Church fathers had to continually remind believers that they were supposed to be worshiping the birth of Christ, not the Sun.[1] For although this holiday now had a new name, many of the same customs were carried on as they had been for thousands of years and for the same reason: to banish the dark and welcome back the light.

CELTIC CHRISTMAS

In the eighth century the traditional twelve-day pagan festival was declared a sacred season by the Church, and it became the Twelve Days of Christmas, with peaks at December 25, January 1, and January 6. During this time the Church prohibited all work or public business, except for the labor of cooks, bakers, or any others who contributed to the delights of the holiday.

Twelve days of feasting, merrymaking, sporting contests, singing, dancing, and all sorts of joyous anarchy and "misrule" got under way on the magical threshold between the old year and the new. Some of the fun and games probably once belonged to Samhain, the original time for the Celtic New Year but were transferred to the Christian festival in later times.

Released from work, all sorts of little bands toured the community offering entertainment in exchange for food and drink. Singers known as waits sang traditional carols unaccompanied or with harps, fiddles, and pipes. Mummers and guisers came out in full force, dressed in colorful costumes, which might include animal skins, masks, and bells, and brightened the winter season by performing plays around the community. Often the central theme of these plays was the death and subsequent resurrection of one of the characters, echoing the drama of the old year as it prepared to give way to the new.

Scotland

In Scotland the revelry was particularly lively and joyous. Under the influence of Scandinavian settlements it retained the old pagan name of "Yule" in many parts, while the Twelve Days became known affectionately as the "daft days." But in the sixteenth century jollity was snuffed out with the candles. Feasting gave way to fasting when the newly established Reformed Scottish Kirk denounced Yule as an abominable popish practice. The puritanical leaders even went so far as to prosecute citizens for such sins as "playing, dancing and singing of filthy carols on Yule day at even."[2]

Only in the Catholic Highlands and Islands did the old ways continue, while in the rest of Scotland the psychological need for a midwinter feast was met by transferring the festivities to the New Year. By the 1800s the Kirk had relaxed its grip on Scotland and some of the old celebrations were restored, but ever since, the heart of Scotland's midwinter celebrations has been the New Year feast of Hogmanay.

Ireland

In Ireland the holidays lasted from *Nollag Mór*, Big Christmas, on December 25 to *Nollag Beag*, Little Christmas, on January 6. It was the most important festival of the year, a time to contemplate the special mystery of both human and divine love. People were more than usually devout and generous to others. It was commonly held that the gates of heaven were open at this time and that anybody who died during the Twelve Days went straight to paradise.

Preparations for the season began many weeks in advance, when country people flocked to the *Margadh Mór*, or Big Market, to "bring home the Christmas." They took butter, eggs, hens, geese, turkeys, and vegetables to sell and returned home laden with meat, tea, tobacco, whiskey, wine and beer, dried fruit, spice, sugar for the Christmas puddings, toys and sweets for the children, new clothes, and household gear.

Everybody gave gifts, a custom that had its roots in ancient law. Shopkeepers gave Christmas boxes of fruitcakes and drinks to their customers, sized according to the amount of business they did there during the year. Farming families gave bacon, hens, eggs, and potatoes to friends and relatives in towns, while they in return received town supplies

SON OF THE DAWN

In the Hebrides a band called the *gillean Nollaig*, or Christmas lads, traveled around the houses dressed in white gowns and disguised by tall white headpieces. They lifted up the youngest child in the house, and if there was none they made a "baby" out of a sheet or blanket and cradled it. This was the *Cristean*, or Little Christ. The infant was placed on a male lambskin and carried three times around the fire sunwise by the leader of the band while they sang and paid homage to the baby.

A HEBRIDEAN CAROL

Refrain:
Hey the Gift, ho the Gift,
Hey the Gift on the living.

Son of the dawn, Son of the clouds,
Son of the planet, Son of the star,
(refrain)

Son of the rain, Son of the dew,
Son of the welkin, Son of the sky,
(refrain)

Son of the flame, Son of the light,
Son of the sphere, Son of the globe,
(refrain)

Son of the elements, Son of the
heavens,
Son of the moon, Son of the sun,
(refrain)

Son of Mary of the God-mind,
And the Son of God first of all news,
(refrain)
CARMINA GADELICA

HOW TO SAY "MERRY CHRISTMAS!"

Language		Pronunciation
Irish Gaelic	*Nollaig shona!*	*no-*lihg *ho-*nuh
Scottish Gaelic	*Nollaig chridheil dhuibh*	*nol-*lig *chree-*al ghooiv
Welsh	*Nadolig llawen!*	na-*dol-*ig *hlou-*en
Manx	*Nollick ghennal!*	*nol-*lick *ghen-*uhl
Cornish	*Nadelik looan!*	na-*del-*ik *low-*en
Breton	*Nedeleg laouen!*	ne-*dey-*lek *lou-*en

and coins for their children. Prosperous farmers gave generously to their workers and poorer neighbors: fresh-killed meat for their Christmas dinner and sometimes a Christmas log to burn.

But the greatest gift was to have the whole family beneath one roof again. Sons and daughters who worked in distant towns left work early on Christmas Eve to be back in their old homes before nightfall. Those who lived across the sea made sure they were there in spirit. Many a poor family eagerly awaited the "American letter," not least because of the substantial sum of money almost certain to be wrapped up in it. And in return the woman of the house made sure she sent greetings cards containing all the year's news to "the people away," providing possibly their only link to home.[3]

Giving from the Inside Out

In Celtic clan-based societies, gift giving arose simply and naturally out of a love of family and concern for the old woman in the glen who couldn't afford a good dinner. Reduce holiday season stress by giving from a place of peace. This means that instead of looking "out there" and getting dazzled by the overwhelming array of consumer items on offer, sit down quietly in your sacred space, tune into one person at a time, and allow your intuition to tell you what he or she really needs from you. This may just as likely turn out to be a nonphysical as a physical item. Don't forget to include in your thoughts needy people in your community and also wild birds and animals. Giving from the "inside out" will deepen and enrich this season for both giver and receiver.

THE YULE LOG

Heap on more wood—the wind is chill;
But let it whistle as it will,
We'll keep our Christmas merry still.
Sir Walter Scott

Like an "unconquered sun" in the heart of the home, the blazing Yule log was the crowning glory of the Scottish midwinter feast. It was called the *Cailleach Nollaigh*, Christmas Old Wife, or *Yeel-Carline*, Old Woman of Yule, for it personified the Cailleach who had swallowed up the light during her winter reign. To burn her was to set the sun free.

Ideally it was big enough to burn throughout Christmas Day and the nights before and after. In Wales the Yule log was called *Y Bloccyn Gwylian*, the Festival Block, and in the border counties a little of it was burned each evening in the embers of other wood until Twelfth Night. In Ireland the Yule log was called the *bloc na Nollaig*, or Christmas Block.

The ceremonies began with a ritual cleaning of the entire house. This was no ordinary cleanup but a thorough purification ritual, where beds were stripped and mattresses turned, floors scrubbed and polished, and windows washed inside and out. The hearth was thoroughly dusted and a new coat of whitewash applied to the hob. Inglenooks were garlanded with evergreens, although those living by the sea might gather seaweed for decoration.

The male head of the household selected a thick branch or hefty stump of a tree, preferably oak, and hauled it home from the woods on Christmas Eve. He carved it into the shape of old woman—the Cailleach. As the embodiment of cold and death, she was thrown onto the fire on Christmas Eve, and the family had the satisfaction of seeing winter and darkness reduced to ashes before their eyes. This ritual had the added benefit of ensuring that death would bypass the house during the coming year.

In some areas it took a whole group of people to haul the Yule log home, sometimes with small children seated astride it. As merry hunters bringing home the sun, they became actors in a cosmic drama. It was good luck to come upon the little procession on its way home from the woods, and those that did raised their hats in respect as the log went by. When they staggered over the threshold with the log, tired but triumphant, the more artistic members of the family came forward to decorate it with long sprays of ivy and other greenery. Last, it was sprinkled with a libation of cider or ale before being consigned to its fate upon the hearth.

The Yule log was traditionally placed upon a piece of last year's wood, which was used for kindling the new one. Musicians played and drinks flowed as it blazed up, filling the room with warmth, light, and cheer. The whole household sat around it drinking whiskey, ale, or wine, eating cake, and telling jokes and stories. For a while dark and cold were defeated; poverty, hunger, and disease—all too often the unwelcome gifts of midwinter—were kept at bay outside the protective circle of the sun brought back to earth.

After the Yule log had burned down, it still had a job to do. In Wales the ashes were kept and mixed with seed corn for the spring sowing, for luck and fertility. And in most places a piece of it was carefully put away for the following year when the cycle would continue, a reminder that the sun could always be counted on to return and that the unbroken continuity of light and warmth was assured.

Around the Yule Fire

Burn a dry oak log and contemplate the miracle of fire—especially its power to activate and transform the hidden sunlight within the wood.

Spend a few moments meditating on the theme of "hidden potential." What buried talents, passions, and desires that lie deep within you would you like to see brought to life and light in the coming year?

Practice on old Scottish ritual: toss sprigs of rowan, or holly if none is available, into the fire as a symbolic way to burn away any bad feeling between family, friends or neighbors.

If you are with two or more people, sing the "Yule Round."

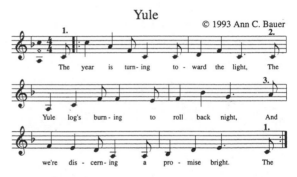

Yule

© 1993 Ann C. Bauer

The year is turn-ing to-ward the light, The Yule log's burn-ing to roll back night, And we're dis-cern-ing a pro-mise bright. The

YULE CANDLES

One of the simplest and loveliest of customs is the lighting of the Yule candles. In pre-Christian times these probably would have been blazing torches, as in old Scandinavia, but in later centuries they were white or colored candles, with red being the most popular, perhaps because "the red blood reigns in the winter's cold." The family might have one huge individual candle or a number of smaller candles, one for each member of the family and little colored ones for the children. Those who could afford it had a one-week candle, called in Ireland *coinneal mór na Nollaig*, the "Great Christmas Candle." The candles were lit with great ceremony on Christmas Eve, marking the transition from the ordinary daily world into the magical realm of Christmas. First, they were placed in holders made from a hollowed turnip decorated with colored paper and holly, then they were set in the window. In her autobiographical book, *An Irish Country Christmas*, Alice Taylor remembers how it was for her as a child on a Kerry farm in the 1940s:

> We gathered in a semicircle around the window, where the candle rested on the deep sill. The world outside was dark, and when my father cracked a match the flame was reflected in the windowpane. When he put it to the candle, at first the wick spluttered and blackened but then it slowly reddened and a yellow flame kindled and rose upward. Its reflection glowed in the window and another family looked in at us. . . . The lighted candle was the symbol that Christmas was finally here. The magic of Christmas was out in the moonlit haggard with the cattle and down the fields with the sheep, but most of all it was here in the holly-filled kitchen with the little battered crib under the tree and the tall candle lighting the window. The candle was the light of Christmas and the key that opened the door into the holy night.[4]

A special reason for lighting candles on Christmas Eve was to show Mary and Joseph, who found no room at the inn in Bethlehem, that here they could be sure of a welcome. In nineteenth-century West Limerick, a candle was lit in every window of the house and a table set for three "to have a proper welcome before the 'Travelers to Bethlehem.'"[5] A dish of water was also left out for the holy family to bless, which could afterward be used for healing.

In many places children were taken up to a high point after dark to see the whole landscape aglow, as every village and isolated farmhouse far and near prepared to receive the divine gift.

Lighting the Candle

Place a candle in your window this season. If you want to follow the traditional Irish custom, choose a red one. A more elaborate candle-lighting ceremony is given below. It can be equally effective alone or with a large family group.

1. Place a large red or golden candle in the center of the table or floor, representing the sun.
2. Sit in front of it, or, if doing this in a group, have everyone sit in a circle around it. Have some matches ready, and a taper for each person.
3. Turn all lights out. Experience the feeling of sitting in utter darkness—the silence, the stillness, the inwardness. If children are present, have them say out loud what it feels like (soft, scary, cold). Ask them to imagine what life would be like without the sun.
4. Now consider all the gifts the sun brings us. Again, if children are present, have them call out what comes to mind.
5. Contemplate how the seed of light is even now being born within the womb of darkness. (An adult can explain to children how the wheel of the year is now turning toward the light.) Light the central candle.

6. Now all in turn light their tapers from the sun candle and wish out loud for something they would like to have happen in the coming year.
7. When the room is filled with light and warmth, finish the celebration with seasonal song, circle dance, or food.
8. At the end of the gathering, individual candles can be snuffed out with the reminder that the flame continues to burn brightly within our hearts. If possible, let the central candle stay alight throughout the night (with obvious safety precautions!) to welcome back the sun.

May peace and plenty be the first to lift
the latch on your door
and happiness be guided to your home
by the candle of Christmas.

IRISH BLESSING

HOLLY

ᲧHE SACRED ᏩROVE

And the first tree in the greenwood,
it was the holly!
CORNISH CAROL

Bright holly with its glossy leaves and scarlet berries brings the hope of undying life to the dark days of winter. Because it signifies the green of growth together with the warmth of blood and fire, it has always been the most popular evergreen in northern Europe.

The Romans decorated their homes and temples with holly during the Saturnalia and sent one another sprigs of it with wishes for good health and prosperity. The druids considered holly sacred and used it in healing the sick. It repelled evil spirits and protected the house from lightning. Country people hung it up in house and stable, particularly at Christmas, for cattle were supposed to thrive if they looked at it on Christmas Day. With the coming of Christianity, holly continued to deck the halls, only now its prickly leaves and red berries were a reminder of the crown of thorns and the shedding of Christ's blood.

In the medieval romance of "Gawain and the Green Knight," the giant Green Knight enters Arthur's court at the New Year bearing a great bush of holly as his insignia. He and one of Arthur's knights, Sir Gawain, whose name means the "Hawk of May," engage in a beheading contest. Gawain, who, as his name suggests, symbolizes the waxing year, strikes off the head of the Green Knight, but the knight springs up alive again, reminding us of the ever-renewing cycle of life.

DECKING THE HALLS

Now with bright holly all your temples strow,
With laurel green and sacred mistletoe.
JOHN GAY

Throughout the Twelve Days people festooned their homes with evergreens. They served as a reminder of the indomitable green world and also provided the forest spirits with a retreat from winter storms. Holly often mingled with other plants: together with hazel, it kept mischievous faeries away. If holly was not available, rowan—that other red-berried tree of protection—was hung above the lintel in house, stable, and byre. In many places it was paired with ivy as a male and female pair. Holly was particularly lucky for men, whereas ivy was the women's plant.

O the Ivy O, she's the Queen of old,
And the Holly he is red.
Hang 'en high in the farm, and us won't come to
*   no harm*
Till the Chrissimas days be told.

Other evergreens, such as box, bay, and crimson-berried yew, were also popular, together with fragrant bunches of rosemary. Before electricity, branches from the Scots pine were used as torches, but in later years these, too, became part of the decorations.

Making a Solstice Wreath

A solstice wreath symbolizes the wheel of the year and the completion of another cycle of seasons.

Gather together materials and tools.

At a craft store buy:
    a 16-inch straw wreath form
    a spool of thin-gauge paddle wire

Around the house gather:
    natural jute or waxed sinew twine
    wire cutters
    pruning shears or scissors
    thin bamboo skewers (to attach fruits)
    small screw eyes (to attach cones, nuts,
        or oak galls)

Collect in the woods or garden, or purchase:

A large basket of bay laurel branchlets 6
inches to 9 inches long

8–10 branchlets of holly with berries

Vines of flexible ivy 12 to 15 inches long

10–12 sprigs of rosemary at least 6 inches
long

Other symbolic greenery could include
wintergreen, pine, or oak leaves.

Decorations could include small apples,
pinecones, tiny oranges, unshelled nuts, oak
galls, and ribbons.

As you bind the plants into place, meditate
about the year now past and what you want to
manifest in the coming year.

Method

1. Working at the edge of a table makes the
binding of the herbs and plants onto the
straw base easier. You will use lengths of
paddle wire about 10–12 inches long to
wrap around the wreath, twisting the ends
together to hold the bundles of herbs in
place. Cut 20 lengths of paddle wire
10–12 inches long. Cut 10 lengths of
paddle wire 5 inches long to wrap herb
bundles. To make a loop for hanging, cut a
20-inch length of twine. Fold it in half, loop
around the wreath, and knot to secure.

2. Start filling the inside of the wreath using
short, small-leafed sprigs of herbs. Using
the 5-inch length of wire, bundle together
two sprigs of rosemary and two sprigs of
bay, 6 inches long. You will need 8–10
bundles of herbs to complete the inside
of your wreath. Holding the bundle
against the inside of the wreath, wrap a
long piece of wire around the wreath
base, looping over the herb bundle stem
ends, binding them into place as you
twist the wire ends together. If necessary,
form the bundle to the circle and bind
the opposite end of the bundle in the
same way. Continue to attach all the
bunches around the inside of the wreath
base with the stems going in the same
direction, overlapping the bunches to
conceal stem ends.

3. Still going in the same direction, attach the
prickly lengths of holly to the front of the
wreath, tucked beside the rosemary or bay
ring. The overlapping sprigs of holly form
the stable base through which you weave
the long vines of ivy around and through,
blending the qualities of the greenery
together.

4. The long-leafed branchlets of bay bundled
together in groups of two or three are
inserted around the outside of the wreath.

Continue to bind the sprigs to the wreath using the long lengths of wire, overlapping the stem ends, covering the straw base. Weave the wire over and through the greenery, twisting ends of wire together. The intertwining of the wire and greenery adds form to the wreath, keeping its circular shape as well as securing the bundles to the form.

5. Hang the wreath. Balance the greenery by adding sprigs of rosemary or other greenery where necessary.
6. Decorate the wreath by adding apples, holly berries, and wintergreen berries. Pierce the apples with the thin bamboo skewers. Insert skewer securely into the straw base. Tie on berries, and stemmed fruits with wire. Attach a screw eye to oak galls and cones, insert wire through the screw eye, and tie in place.

Plant Symbolism

Rosemary is for remembrance. Rosemary and bay leaves purify and protect. As you bind these sprigs together, remember the highlights of the past year. Use the bay to cleanse away events or happenings that were unsettling. The sun is the ruling planet of both herbs, as it is the rebirth of the sun we celebrate at the Winter Solstice.

The twining together of the holly and the ivy represents the integration of the masculine and feminine parts of yourself. The holly is the fiery, protective masculine aspect. The ivy represents the intuitive, emotional feminine. The magical pairing of the two brings balance and luck for the coming year. Which is more prominent in your wreath? What does one offer the other?

Apples are symbols of immortality and love. Wintergreen is healing.

Walnuts are wishes. What would you like fulfilled in the coming year? Combine these with the fertility of the pinecone. What would you like to manifest in the coming year?

Hang the completed wreath over the door to welcome visitors. You can also mount it above a fireplace where the warmth will enhance the release of aromatic fragrances. It can also be laid flat with candles inside, as a centerpiece to the Yuletide feast. If you celebrate Winter Solstice with children, this is a good time to gather everyone around the wreath and teach them about the Sacred Circle and Wheel of Life.

At the end of the Twelve Days you can decide which Celtic custom to follow in disposing of your wreaths and other natural decorations. In some areas evergreens were ceremonially burned on Twelfth Night, but another old custom ruled that they should stay up until Imbolc, while others kept them until the following year to protect the house from lightning and other misfortunes.

MISTLETOE: THE DRUIDS' HERB

"The Druids . . . hold nothing more sacred than mistletoe and a tree on which it is growing," wrote the Roman author Pliny in the first century C.E. about the druids of Gaul. He went on to describe an elaborate ceremony held on the sixth day of the moon, when a white-robed priest climbed the tree and cut down this rare parasitic plant with a golden sickle. The proceedings began with an invocation to the moon as one who "healed all things," and since the druids regarded mistletoe as a universal healer, perhaps they believed its pearly white berries contained the essence of the moon. In Scotland one of the old Gaelic names for mistletoe was *druidh-lus,* "druid's herb," and it was highly prized as a powerful magical and healing plant, especially for heart conditions. Its modern Gaelic name is *uil'-ioc,* "all-heal."

Mistletoe was banned from church Christmas decorations because of its druidic associations, but in eighteenth-century Wales, where it grows in profusion, it found favor in country homes as the centerpiece of the kissing bough. This was a double hoop made of willow, ash, or hazel to form a sphere, which was then decorated with mistletoe, either alone or with other evergreens. More elaborate ones might also include fruit and nuts, oat ears, candles, dolls, and ribbons. A bunch of mistletoe was tied to the bottom and the whole edifice hung from a beam just inside the front door. Here it hung in shining splendor, slowly revolving in the candles' draft, long before the modern Christmas tree made its appearance in the mid–nineteenth century. After the season the kissing bough was left up for magical protection until the next year.

The custom of kissing beneath the bough originated in the Middle Ages, when it was called the Holy Bough. In the middle was placed a little model of the Christ Child or the Holy Family. As each visitor entered the house over the Christmas season, they were greeted with a "kiss of peace," a sign that any bad feeling that might have arisen during the year was now forgiven and forgotten.

Making a Kissing Bough

At a craft store buy:

2 small grapevine wreaths, one approximately 7 inches in diameter, one approximately 6 inches in diameter (the smaller wreath must fit inside the larger wreath)

Spool of paddle wire

2-inch wide gold wire-edged ribbon, about 4 yards

1 spool ⅜-inch gold-accented wire-edged ribbon

1 spool ⅛-inch gold-accented wire-edged ribbon

Around the house gather:

Wire cutters

Scissors

Glue gun and glue sticks

Gather from your garden or purchase:

6–8 sprigs of rosemary

A small limb of pine

2 miniature pinecones (cedar or hemlock)

One small orange

1 small apple

¼ pound mixed unshelled nuts (especially Brazil nuts, almonds, walnuts, filberts)

A sprig of mistletoe

Method

1. Interlock the small wreath inside the large wreath at a 90-degree angle. This basic structure creates a nesting place for the fruit and nuts.

2. Using the ⅜-inch ribbon, wrap the orange in an X pattern, leaving 2-inch ends on the ribbon.

3. Twist the ribbon ends together and wrap with an 8-inch length of paddle wire.

4. Secure the orange inside the wreath circles using the paddle wire.

5. Wrap the stem of the apple with an 8-inch length of wire, and tie to the inside of the wreath circles. Using hot glue, glue the unshelled nuts around the fruits. Tuck small sprigs of rosemary and pine in the spaces between the fruit and nuts, decorating and concealing the glue.

6. Tie a loop of ⅜-inch ribbon at the top of the bough for hanging.

7. Glue sprigs of rosemary and pine to the top of the wreaths.

8. Decorate the top of the wreaths with gathered bows of 2-inch and ⅜-inch ribbons. Tie in place with ⅛-inch ribbon with long end pieces.

9. Glue pinecones in the center of bows.

10. Wire a sprig of mistletoe to the bottom center of the wreaths. Conceal the ends of the mistletoe with gathered bows of 2-inch and ⅜-inch ribbon. Leaving all the ribbon ends long allows for additional decorative curling.

Hang your kissing bough in a doorway or entryway.

Symbolism of the Kissing Bough
Interlocking circles: eternity
Apple: love
Orange: love, luck
Rosemary: love, lust
Pine: fertility
Nuts: fertility, wishes, prosperity, love, luck
Mistletoe: love, hunting, fertility, protection
Gold: abundance
Pinecones: fertility, longevity, comfort

WREN

A CELTIC BESTIARY

Throughout old Ireland on St. Stephen's Day (December 26), bands of singers, musicians, and dancers, all dressed in straw costumes, paraded through the district carrying the body of a little wren on a holly bush or in a tiny wooden coffin. These were the wren-boys, and they stopped at each house singing:

The Wren, the Wren, the king of the birds,
St. Stephen's Day was caught in the furze,
Although he is little, his honor is great,
Put your hand in your pocket and give us a treat.

The "treat" of food, drink, or money was put toward a *ceili*, the Wren's Ball, at the end of the proceedings. The custom was also enacted in Wales and recently has been revived in some parts, although nobody uses a real bird nowadays.

From early times the wren has been closely associated with the druids, who foretold the future by listening to its call. But why was the wren called king of the birds? The story goes that all the male birds had a parliament to decide which of them should be king. There was a lot of squabbling because each thought he was the best: The thrush sang his sweetest song; the goldfinch displayed his glorious plumage; the swallow showed how he could dart and swoop. To settle the matter the eagle suggested they have a contest to see who could fly highest, knowing full well he was the strongest bird. They all agreed and soared into the sky, but soon the eagle had left them all behind. Hovering triumphantly over the treetops, he screamed, "Birds, behold your king!" But the little wren had hidden himself under one of his broad wing feathers. He hopped out and perched on the eagle's head, chirping, "Not so, not so. I'm above him. I'm above him." Down dropped the eagle, and down dropped the wren, breathless, but King of the Birds.

CHRISTMAS OF THE ANIMALS

In honor of the Christ child's birth in a stable, country people were especially kind to their animals at Christmastime. Remembering how the beasts kept the baby Jesus warm, farmers fed their cows, horses, and donkeys extra amounts of hay or bran mash, while the hens received a double measure of grain. On Christmas Eve in Cornwall the last sheaf of the harvest was taken down from its pride of place in the farmhouse kitchen and presented to the cattle. In Scotland bunches of oats were hung on rowan trees to feed wild birds.

In some areas families lit lanterns in byre and stable and hung evergreens all around. Children loved to decorate the animals themselves and festooned the horned beasts with garlands of holly.

But the most elaborate animal rituals took place in Wales. On Christmas Eve the master of the household prepared a bowl of hot ale, sweetened with sugar and flavored with spices, while the mistress took up a basket containing a cake. They decorated bowl and basket sumptuously with evergreens, holly, and ivy wreaths then bore them out to the stall of the finest ox, followed by the rest of the household in procession. Inside the stable, the men stood on one side and the women stood opposite them. Now the mistress ceremoniously impaled the cake on the ox's horns; the master stirred the ale, drank a mouthful, and passed the bowl around; and everyone sang a hearty Welsh toast.

If the ox behaved placidly during these extraordinary proceedings, it was a token of good luck for the coming year, but if it became restless and angry, it was a bad omen. The merry householders also kept their eyes on the cake: If it fell on the women's side, they would rule the household next year; otherwise, the men would triumph.

But the most wonderful occurrence took place at midnight on Christmas Eve, according to a long-standing belief throughout the British Isles and Ireland. This was the magic time that all the animals in the byre were thought to kneel in adoration of the newborn child. At the same moment, another miracle happened: the animals were given the gift of human speech.

As midnight struck inside the farmhouse, the children must have found it hard to contain themselves from running out into the frosty stable yard to hear the animals talking, but they were not allowed to do so for it would have spoiled the sacred moment. What the animals said to one another was left to the imagination.

Many other kinds of miracles occurred at Christmastide. In Cornwall it was believed the faeries met at the bottom of tin mines to perform a Christmas mass. In many areas bees were thought to leave their hives at three o'clock on Christmas morning, swarm around buzzing loudly, and return. In Brittany the great standing stones at Carnac walk down to the river to drink.

One famous miracle that can still be witnessed today is the flowering of the Holy Thorn at Glastonbury. When Joseph of Arimathea brought the Holy Grail to Glastonbury, he planted his staff in the ground, where it burst into a blossoming hawthorn tree. And although the hawthorn is only supposed to bloom in May, the Glastonbury Thorn shows white flowers every Christmas Day in honor of the divine birth. The following story brings together two Christmas miracles.

THE CHRISTMAS THORN

There was once a man from Ilminster who went to Glastonbury on a pilgrimage. Before he left, the villagers asked him to bring back a holy relic to bless the village. They were most disappointed when he returned bearing only a sprig of the common hawthorn. But the man planted the little shoot in the village square and prayed beside it morning and evening. It began to grow at an incredible rate, and by Christmas it had grown to a slender young tree. The villagers looked suspiciously at the pilgrim and crossed the street when he passed by. The pilgrim took no notice of their slights. He continued his prayers and predicted that the hawthorn tree would bloom on Christmas Day.

Christmas Day came and nothing happened. But just before midnight on January 4—Old Christmas Eve—the whole village was awakened by a great clatter in the street. People threw on their clothes and ran to the windows, and there below them was an extraordinary sight: all their sheep and cattle were streaming into the streets. Leading the herd was the great master bullock that belonged to the wealthiest farmer. The villagers tumbled out of doors and followed the animals to the village square, where the little thorn tree stood blossoming white in the moonlight. There they saw the pilgrim kneeling down in prayer.

Just then the church clock chimed the midnight hour. At that, the great bullock lowed aloud and knelt down on the frosty ground, and every beast knelt with him. One by one, the villagers slowly knelt down along with their animals.

And that is how Ilminster knows that it has a holy thorn.

A YULETIDE FEAST

There the huge sirloin reeked; hard by
Plum porridge stood and Christmas pie;
Nor failed old Scotland to produce,
At such high tide, her savory goose.
SIR WALTER SCOTT

Roast Goose

The traditional Celtic meat for a winter feast was wild boar, roasted on a spit over an open fire or boiled in a cauldron. When the boar was hunted out of existence a sheep or ox, roasted over the Yule log, became popular. But it was the humble goose that won pride of place on most Christmas tables in Ireland in later years. Here is a traditional recipe with herb stuffing:

Ingredients
1 goose, 7–9 pounds
1 cup chopped celery
1 medium onion, chopped
1 apple, diced
4 cups bread crumbs
3 tablespoons fresh sage leaves
2 tablespoons each fresh thyme and parsley
½ cup chicken stock
1 egg, lightly beaten
Salt and freshly ground black pepper
½ lemon and cider for basting

Method

1. Preheat oven to 400° F.
2. Wash and dry goose. Cut off any excess fat from around neck cavity. Prick skin all over and rub with lemon, salt, and pepper.
3. Combine celery, onion, and chicken stock, and simmer till soft. Mix with bread crumbs, herbs, and apple; season; and bind with egg. Add more stock if too dry.
4. Stuff goose loosely, and truss with skewers and string. Place on rack above roasting pan, high enough to avoid the fat that drains into the pan.
5. Roast 15 minutes, then reduce heat to 350° F and continue roasting 20 minutes per pound or until goose is very well browned and leg joints move easily.
6. During roasting, baste with cider.
7. Serve with giblet gravy, apple or rowan-berry sauce (see below), roast potatoes, and buttered cabbage.

Makes 6–8 servings

Rowanberry Sauce

2 shallots, finely chopped
1 lemon
1 orange
3 tablespoons rowan jelly (see September, or use red currant jelly instead)
⅔ cup port
2 teaspoons red wine vinegar
Pinch ground ginger

Method

Scald shallots in boiling water and drain. Slice the rind of the fruits into very fine shreds. Blanch in boiling water for 1 minute, then drain. Squeeze the juice from the fruit. Melt the rowan jelly in a small saucepan and add shallots, citrus rind, fruit juice, port, vinegar, and ground ginger. Bring to a boil, remove from heat, and serve warm or cold.

Plum Pudding

It was the Dagda, the chief god of the Tuatha Dé Danann, who cooked the original "plum porridge" in his magic cauldron: a mess of grain, meat, and fruit. Perhaps it was because the Dagda was associated with the sun that this dish became popular at the Winter Solstice. In later centuries it turned into plum pudding, a rich fruit dessert, but a vestige of sun worship remains associated with it: To this day it is traditional for everyone in the household to take a turn stirring it three times sunwise while making a wish. Plum pudding—or Christmas pudding, as it is more often called today—is found throughout the British Isles and Ireland.

Ingredients

1½ cups raisins

1 cup currants

¾ cup golden raisins

¾ cup pitted dates

¾ cup soft dried figs

1 8-ounce stick unsalted butter

½ cup dark brown sugar, firmly packed

1½ cups bread crumbs, from stale white loaf

¾ cup all-purpose flour, sifted

grated zest and juice of 1 lemon

grated zest of 1 orange

4 large eggs

¼ cup slivered almonds (optional)

1 teaspoon each cinnamon, nutmeg, allspice, ground ginger

¼ teaspoon salt

½ cup brandy

Method

1. In a large mixing bowl, beat the butter and sugar until thick and creamy, then slowly beat in the eggs, brandy, orange, and lemon zests. (This can be done by hand or with an electric mixer.)

2. Coarsely chop the figs, raisins, and dates, and add to the bowl with the currants, stirring well. Add the flour, spices, and salt, then fold in the bread crumbs.

3. Butter a 2-quart ceramic or Pyrex pudding basin, and spoon in the mixture. Cut a round piece of wax paper 2 inches larger than the top of the basin, and pleat it in the middle so it can expand as the pudding rises. Place it over the pudding bowl, put a sheet of aluminum foil, cut and pleated in the same way, over the top, and tie both firmly under the rim with string.

4. Set the basin in a large covered pot or Dutch oven, and fill with boiling water until it is halfway up the side of the basin. Boil gently for 4 hours, topping up with boiling water as necessary.

5. Remove basin and leave pudding to cool. Store in a cool, dark place to mature for up to two months.

6. Steam again for 2 hours before serving. Turn it out of the basin and decorate with a sprig of holly. Pour warm brandy over the top and set alight. Serve with brandy butter.

About 12 servings

Brandy Butter

3 ounces butter at room temperature

3 ounces fine sugar

3 tablespoons brandy

1 teaspoon lemon juice

Method
Beat the butter until white and creamy, then gradually add the sugar. Beat in the brandy a little at a time, and last, the lemon juice. Chill at least 2 hours before serving.

Mulled Wine

Yuletide feasts were washed down with a special treacle ale in Scotland, while beer was favored in Wales. Birch, elderberry, and dandelion wines were popular, too. But as early as the fifth century, imported wine flowed freely at the great feasts given by Irish chieftains, while a thirteenth-century poem describes a bard going from "one feast of purple wine to another."

Ingredients
1 magnum of good-quality red wine
$1\frac{1}{2}$ teaspoons freshly ground nutmeg
$\frac{1}{2}$ teaspoon ground ginger
$\frac{1}{2}$ teaspoon ground cinnamon
1 teaspoon allspice
1 teaspoon whole cloves
1 cinnamon stick
Honey or sugar to taste

Method
Simmer gently in a large saucepan for 1 hour, being careful not to boil. Strain through a cheesecloth and serve warm.

THE SUN CHILD

That one of the few Christmas stories out of the Scottish Highlands and islands features Bride (Brigit) as the central character has something of a mythic inevitability. The tale also weaves together Bride's life as a druid on the island of Iona with her later role as Christian saint.

A winter's sun was slowly going down over *Innis nam Druidneach* (*ee-nish nun droo-yakh*), the Isle of the Druids, sending long shadows across the heathery grass. Within a ring of standing stones on a small hill, a circle of white-robed figures waited in silence, their faces turned toward the southeast. As the sky dimmed to a soft purple, many gasped as the horizon began to brighten with an unearthly silver glow. A star rose, trailing a shimmering tail of light.

An elderly druid stepped forward, preparing to speak. But at that moment a girl of about fourteen stumbled into the center of the circle. She pointed to the star, made as if to speak, then fell into a dead faint at the old druid's feet.

"It is Dubhtach's daughter, Bride," said one, as they gathered around her. "Take her to the Pool of Healing, and perhaps she will revive."

A strong, black-bearded druid gently lifted the fallen girl and carried her to the small triangular pool below the stones. He cradled her in his lap, dipped a piece of moss into the well water, and gently bathed her brow. The icy water revived the girl. She sat up suddenly, stared straight ahead, and said abruptly, "The star. I must go."

"Bride of the Visions, tell us what you see," said the old druid.

Bride focused glowing eyes on the small, anxious crowd. "A new sun is rising in the east," she said simply, "and I must attend his birth."

She closed her eyes again, and this time the druids knew where to take her. On a litter of woven hazel branches, they bore her away to the *Sìthean Mór*, the Faery Hill in the center of the island. There they laid her in the small cave reserved for those who would make the spirit journey.

The hot stench of unwashed flesh and animal dung made her reel. First there had been the cool night air of Iona and the soft wave sounds that had been in her ears from birth. Then the glittering arms of the star reaching down through the skies to bear her eastward. But she had been unprepared for the heat, the clamor, and the press of bodies that hemmed her in on all sides. And now—a shove between the shoulder blades, and a harsh voice: "Wake up, girl, and fetch the water. And mind you don't spill any. It'll be our last for days, what with this accursed drought. And we've got guests in every room tonight."

Bride forced her way through the crowd of men, women, children, and animals that were jostling through the dusty courtyard of the inn. It took her a while to walk to the muddy hole that passed for a well and fill her pitcher. Although she walked back to the inn as fast as bare feet on baked ground could go, she found the gates already shut. Inside, the frenzy had quieted down to a soft murmur of voices as oil lamps were lit and bedding rolled out for the night. But as Bride was about to let herself in through the small door cut in one of the gates, a voice spoke to her out of the shadows.

In the dim light Bride could just make out the speaker: a small, balding man holding the reins of a donkey on which sat a young woman, heavily pregnant and swaying with fatigue. In a low, pleading voice, he begged Bride to find his wife some food, drink, and a place to rest for the night. Now, Bride knew that the inn was full and the innkeeper most unlikely to be sympathetic. Her heart went out to them, and without hesitation she gave them the pitcher of water.

When they had drunk their fill, she led them around the back of the inn to the stables. She left the old man making a bed out of hay for his wife and returned to the kitchen with the empty pitcher. The innkeeper loomed large in the doorway.

"What took you so long?"

"The well was so low, it took me forever to fill, sir," stammered Bride, wondering what would happen to her when the pitcher was found to be dry. He ordered her to fill bowls for his wealthier guests to wash in, and with trembling hands Bride tried to obey. To her astonishment, sparkling water poured from the pitcher, filling every bowl to the brim.

As soon as she could get away Bride took the pitcher, still full, with a heel of bread from the kitchen and slipped out of the back door. Over the stable shone the star with the glittering tail. Inside, Bride found she was just in time to help the young wife give birth to her child and receive him into the world. She sprinkled three drops of water on the child's brow and blessed him in the druid fashion. From the muddy well a pure spring of water bubbled up and flowed down the hillside in a never-ending stream.

And so from that time on, Bride was known as *Ban-chuideachaidh Moire*, the Midwife of Mary, and *Muime Chriosda*, the Foster-Mother of Christ, while Christ was called *Dalta Bride bith nam beannachd*, the Foster-son of Bride of the Blessings.

Far away on the Isle of the Druids, a procession of white-robed men and women circled the Hill of Stones three times and climbed through grass and heather to the top. At their head walked a young girl, a yew-berry garland around her brow. In the east the sun of the New Year leaped up over the horizon.

The Spiral Stone at the entrance to Newgrange

HOLY GROUND
NEWGRANGE
(COUNTY MEATH, IRELAND)

Behold the sidh before your eyes . . .
built by the strong Dagda,
it was a marvel, a court, a wonder hill.
THE BOOK OF BALLYMOTE

Aligned to the Winter Solstice is perhaps the most mysterious and awe-inspiring Neolithic monument in Ireland. This is the Brugh na Bóinne, Hostel of the Boyne, known in English as Newgrange, the largest earth chamber in Europe. Located only a few miles from Tara, it is believed to be over five thousand years old, and as well as a burial mound, it seems to have also been a place of religious ceremony.

Newgrange is featured in countless Irish stories. In some tales it was built by the Dagda. It was also the home of the goddess Boand, who gave her name to the nearby Boyne River. The lustful Dagda tricked Boand's husband, Elcmar, by sending him away on an errand then lying with his beautiful wife. Elcmar was to return by nightfall, but the Dagda caused the sun to stand still for nine months, at which point Boand gave birth to a child, Angus Óg.

The astonishing thing about this myth is that it is acted out in the landscape itself. Newgrange was once covered with chunks of white quartz, which have been partially restored. Seen from afar, it must have looked like a huge gleaming egg set in the middle of the green river meadows. A miracle of ancient engineering, the entrance was designed to align perfectly with the Winter Solstice sunrise. On the first morning of the year's turning toward the light, sunbeams shoot down the narrow passageway into the heart of the chamber. The earth-womb of the goddess is impregnated by the Dagda, a solar god. The result of this divine union is the birth of the new year: Angus, the Young Son/Sun. Newgrange is both a burial chamber and the womb of the Earth, which, when fertilized by the sun, gives birth to new life.

Thousands of years ago, in the freezing cold of an Irish winter, initiates might have sat, fasting and praying, in the impenetrable dark of its innermost chamber to await the coming of the light. And still today, to pass beyond the great spiral stone that guards its entrance and squeeze through the narrow passage that leads to the central womblike chamber is a profound experience. There is a sense of peace and tranquillity within this ancient temple of rock, a feeling of oneness with the Earth, in whose body we are cradled. Mysteriously beautiful carvings of swirling shapes and spirals cover the walls like a book that our minds cannot read but that the soul understands.

GODS OF THE CELTS: ANGUS

Angus Óg (Angus the Young) was the god of youth and love. *Angus* means "true vigor," suggesting his youthful energy. He is also known as Mac Óg, the Young Son, because of the way he was conceived and born. Boand said, "Young is the son who was begotten at the beginning of a day and born between that and the evening." The Dagda took him to be reared at the palace of the faery king

Midir, where he became a champion hurley player. When he was older he became something of a trickster god, who won the Brugh na Bóinne for his own residence by his cunning. Angus appears in many stories about love, either as a helper of eloping couples or because he is in love himself, for which he has been compared to Adonis or Eros. This beautiful young god wore a cloak of rainbow colors and played the harp, while above his head circled four birds that were said to be kisses of the bringer of love.

THE INNER CAULDRON
RENEWAL

We have arrived at last at the close of the year, a time of endings and new beginnings. At Winter Solstice the seed of light is tightly folded within the bud of darkness. From now on, as the days grow longer, the sun-seed slowly unfurls from this center, through the spring days of Imbolc and Beltaine, to its full flowering at Summer Solstice. At this point it will reach the outermost ring of the year's spiral and begin to contract slowly toward the center once again. Perhaps this is the meaning of the spiral art carved by the ancient ones on the walls at Newgrange, aligned as it is to this most important time of the year. (It is also believed that there may be a hidden passage on the other side of the mound, aligned to the Summer Solstice sunset.)

As we look toward the threshold of a new year, we become more aware of our journey as a spiral that circles around yet continually moves us onward to the next cycle of our soul's evolution. Amid all the busy Christmas preparations, it is important to take some time to tune into the deep, dark womb of the year's midnight, to feel and enjoy the quiet interval that comes when the curtain has gone down over the stage of this year's rich drama and the new play has not yet commenced. (In my experience, a failure to take this "down" time in winter is the real reason behind those cold and flu bugs that make us rest whether we want to or not.) In the following and last meditation, we enter the silence of the Earth itself to experience its mysteries and to prepare for our rebirth into the light of a new cycle.

Meditation: The Wonder Hill

Close your eyes, take a few deep breaths, and bring your attention into the still center of yourself. You are standing at the edge of a wood on a hill looking down at a twilight scene. Below you the trees have given way to a low-lying river valley, silvered by a waking moon that sails high in a clear sky. The moon's reflection makes a path of sparkling silver coins over the surface of the river as it smoothly slides through the valley, but your eye does not linger long on the beauty of this scene, for a greater wonder lies on the other side of the river: a huge earthen mound, or knoll, which appears to be covered with crystal, glistens in the pearly light like a terrestrial mirror of the moon herself. Circling the mound is a ring of small sharp standing stones like jagged teeth.

You set off down the hill in the direction of the mound, and now you have reached the banks of the river where young willow trees grow. . . . The water looks much wider than it appeared from above, and with disappointment, you see no way across it at all. . . . But as you stand there on the riverbank, reluctant to leave, you notice a white swirling mist that appears to rise from the water. . . . And now it has turned into the shape of a woman with long swirling hair and white robes, by whose side is a white cow, also made of mist but with a silver star shining on its forehead. The Lady of the River asks you why you have come. Think hard before you answer. What is the real reason that brings you here? What do you hope to gain by this journey? If your answer springs from a true desire for wisdom, she will approach you and bid you climb on the back of the white cow, who then turns and bears you easily across to the other side. . .

And now you are approaching the crystal hill, and you reach the ring of stones. But as you go to step between two of them, there is a sudden blaze of light, and each one shoots up into a tall flame like a torch, flickering to left and right, barring your way, sending great unearthly shadows over the gleaming walls of the mound. You step back hurriedly, and now a voice comes, hissing like the flames themselves, challenging your right to be here. And if your answer is sincere and courageous, the flames will die down and let you through. . . .

You arrive now at the narrow doorway to the mound. . . . Two stone pillars capped by a third frame a narrow black recess. In front of the doorway, blocking the way, lies a huge

recumbent gray stone, completely covered with spiral carvings. It seems to give off a kind of electricity, as if it is alive and could give you a shock if you walked around it. As you stand there, wondering what to do, you are all at once aware that the spiral patterns are beginning to move. Your gaze is drawn into them, and you lose perspective so that you seem to be watching the movement of the spiral galaxies themselves. Pieces of quartz sparkle within their gray bed, so that you are not sure whether you are looking down at stone or up at the stars themselves. A deep and resounding voice, which seems to come out of the stone itself, asks you why you wish to enter the chamber. Answer well, and you will be allowed to pass beyond. . . .

And as you move toward the dark opening in the earth, a robed figure steps out of the shadows with a greeting of welcome. This is your Guide come to escort you within, pleased that you have passed the three trials of water, fire, and stone. Holding a lantern to guide your feet on the uneven ground, your Guide leads you down a narrow chamber where you have to stoop beneath the low roof. The air is close, almost warm. Then, all at once, you find you have emerged into the inner chamber, where you can see the faint shadows of a circle of people sitting around the walls. . . . Your Guide ushers you to a place in the circle, then extinguishes the light. . . . The darkness envelops you like a velvet cloak. . . . From time to time there is a deep humming all around you of a chant droned in a strange tongue. . . . Sometimes it is accompanied by rhythm instruments: a thudding drum and the sound of shaken pebbles . . . or flute sounds like the wind in the reeds. . . . At times you enjoy the sounds or the silence. . . . Sometimes, you seem to see pictures floating past your eyes, as if you are dreaming . . . images of your life in the year gone by. . . . Observe them with detachment. . . . Let them go, let them go. . . .

And now something at last is happening. . . . The drum is sounding more urgently . . . the chant is rising . . . You begin to see the shapes of the people around you and realize that a faint gray light is entering the chamber. . . . The growing light reveals some people swaying to the rhythm. . . . Their faces show ecstatic trance, while others sit as still as statues in deep meditation. . . . Notice if there is anyone you recognize here. . . . The chanting and drumming are rising to a crescendo now . . . and at the highest point of

sound it stops abruptly. In the silence a golden ray of light, like a river of liquid amber, flows down the passageway into the chamber . . . the first light of the newborn Sun. . . . Slowly it glides over the stones, illuminating with its golden sheen mysterious symbols carved on the walls: spirals, sunbursts, concentric circles, and diamond shapes . . . as if pointing to words on a stone book that, if understood, would reveal the secrets of the universe. . . . And now the beam of the sun has reached you. . . . It touches your feet, your body, your face. . . . You soak in the light through every pore. . . . You become radiant with light in every cell of your body . . . rejuvenated . . . recharged . . . renewed. . . . (long pause) At last, the beam of light moves on, but its radiance remains deep within the core of your being . . .

. . . even after it has passed on, and you are filing out one by one, stooping through the narrow passageway . . . walking around the spiral stone . . . beyond the stone circle . . . and out into the light of day, the light of a new year. . . . And you come all the way back to the present, opening your eyes, feeling wide awake, refreshed, and renewed.

WITH THE EBB,
WITH THE FLOW

Mar a bha,	*As it was,*
Mar a tha,	*As it is,*
Mar a bhitheas	*As it shall be*
Gu brath. . .	*Evermore . . .*
Ri tràgadh,	*With the ebb,*
'S ri lionadh.	*With the flow.*

CARMINA GADELICA

SPIRITUAL RESOURCES
Solas Bhríde
14 Dara Park
Kildare
Ireland
Phone: + 353 4552 2890
E-mail: solasbhride@tinet.ic
    The community center of the Brigidine Sisters who relit Brigit's Flame in Kildare. You can purchase a candle lit from the central flame.

Two North American groups where members take turns tending Brigit's Flame:
Ord Brighideach (for men and women)
Web: www.ordbrighideach.org

Daughters of the Flame (women only)
c/o #14–2320 Woodland Drive
Vancouver, BC
V5N 3P2
Canada
Web: www.obsidianmagazine.com/Daughtersofthe-Flame/index.html

The Order of Bards, Ovates and Druids (OBOD)
P.O. Box 1333
Lewes
East Sussex BN7 1DX
England
Web: www.druidry.org
    Probably the largest and most established of the modern Druid groups in existence today, with over 7,000 members in twenty countries, and a distance learning program. Their aim is, first, to help individuals develop their full potential and, second, to cherish and protect the natural world.

CULTURE AND LANGUAGE
The following organizations promote Celtic culture and languages. Learning to speak the languages of the Celtic countries deepens and enriches one's appreciation of the culture immeasurably. As well as checking out the following resources, look for groups in your area who come together to sing in Gaelic or Welsh. Singing is one of the most pleasurable and easiest ways of learning a language that I know.

Comhaltas Ceoltóirí Éireann (A Gathering of Irish Musicians)
32 Belgrave Square
Monkstown
County Dublin
Ireland
Phone: + 353 1280 0295
Web: www.comhaltas.com/index.htm
    An international organization with many American regional branches open to anyone interested in traditional Irish culture. Comhaltas's branches usually sponsor activities such as dance lessons, music lessons, Irish language lessons, sessions, and *céili*.

An Comunn Gàidhealach America (The Gaelic
    Society of America)
110 Westwind Cove
Florence, AL 35634
Web: www.acgamerica.org
    Promotes Scottish Gaelic language, music, art,
and history, with many regional branches.

Celtic League, American Branch
c/o Margaret Sexton
P.O. Box 20153
Dag Hammarskjold Postal Center
New York, NY 10001-0002
Web: www.manxman.co.im/cleague/index.html
    An inter-Celtic organization that campaigns for
the social, political, and cultural rights of the Celtic
nations.

Gaelic College of Celtic Arts and Crafts
P.O. Box 9
Baddeck, NS B0E 1B0
Canada
Phone: (902) 295-3411
Web: www.gaeliccollege.edu
    Located in Cape Breton, Canada, it promotes
traditional crafts, music, dance, and language.

Centre for Manx Studies
Dr. Peter Davey, Director
6 Kingswood Grove
Douglas
Isle of Man, IM1 3LX
United Kingdom
Phone: + 44 1624 673 074
Web: www.liv.ac.uk/ManxStudies

International Committee for the Defense of the
    Breton Language (ICDBL)

U.S. Branch
169 Greenwood Avenue, B-4
Jenkintown, PA 19046-2629
Phone: Lois Kuter, (215) 886-6361
Web.www.breizh.net/icdbl/saozg/index.htm
    Offers a quarterly newsletter about Breton
culture called *Bro Nevez*.

Cymdeithas Madog (Welsh Studies Institute of
    North America)
Anne Smith, Secretary
Cymdeithas Madog
27131 NE Miller St.
Duvall, WA 98019
Web: www.madog.org/index.html
    A clearinghouse for information about Welsh lan-
guage resources.

Gaelic.net
    Provides information about the Gaelic language,
culture, and worldwide community.

Kowethas an Yeth Kernewek (Cornish Language
    Fellowship)
c/o Graham Sandercock
Trewynn, Lodge Hill
Liskeard, Kernow
Cornwall
United Kingdom
Phone: + 44 1579 345 152
Web: nexus6.robots.eeng.liv.ac.uk/~evansjon/
    kowethas.htm

Books, Audio, Video
Ó Siadhail, Mícheál. *Learning Irish*. New Haven: Yale
    University Press, 1988.
Rhys-Jones, T. J. *Teach Yourself Welsh*. Lincolnwood,
    IL: NTC Publishing Group, 1992.

Robertson, Boyd, and Iain Taylor. *Teach Yourself Gaelic.* Lincolnwood, IL: NTC Publishing Group, 1993.

Speaking Our Language, a Scottish television series, offers a complete guide to learning Gaelic for all ages through books, CD-ROMs, videos, and audio-tapes. Contact:

Sìol Cultural Enterprises
3841 Highway 316
P. O. Box 81
St. Andrews, NS
Canada, BOH 1X0
Phone/Fax: (902) 863-0416
Website: www.gaelicbooks.com

Learn the Language On-line
Irish language tuition: http://homepage.tinet.ie/~eofeasa
Interactive Irish lessons with audio: www.maths.tcd.ie/gaeilge/gaelic.htm
Begin Scottish Gaelic through cartoons supported by sound: www.smo.uhi.ac.uk/gaidhlig/ionnsachadh/bac
Yn Ghaelg (Manx Gaelic), Manx Language Resources: http://homepages.enterprise.net/kelly/smenu.html
Beginners' Breton on-line with sound: www.kervarker.org/english/Kenteliou.html

You can also join e-mail lists to practice a new language with other beginners. Choose from:
GAELIC-L (for Irish, Scots Gaelic, and Manx)
WELSH-L (for Welsh, Cornish, and Breton)
To join, send a message to: listserv@irlearn.ucd.ie containing the line: subscribe listname yourfirstname yoursurname. For example, Subscribe GAELIC-L Sarah Flynn

Learn in a Celtic Country
Some overseas colleges also offer short courses for learning the language and experiencing the culture—a rewarding way to spend time in a Celtic country. Here are a few located in exceptionally beautiful surroundings:

Sabhal Mór Ostaig
An Teanga
Sleite
Isle of Skye IV44 8RQ
Scotland
Phone: + 44 1471 844 373
Web: www.smo.uhi.ac.uk/beurla
Scotland's Gaelic college on the island of Skye runs short courses for learning the Gaelic language and studying Gaelic music and culture through the summer, at weekends, and other times scattered through the year. It also puts on a summer festival of Celtic-based concerts, *céilidhs,* dances, and workshops.

Oideas Gael
Gleann Cholm Cille
Contae Dhún na nGall
Éire
Phone: + 353 73 30248
Web: www.oideas-gael.com
E-mail: oidsgael@iol.ie
Language learning and cultural activity vacations and tours in Donegal, the Irish-speaking heartland of Ireland.

National Language Centre
Nant Gwrtheyrn
Llithfaen, Pwllheli
North Wales LL53 6PA
United Kingdom
Phone: + 44 1758 750 334
Web: www.nantgwr.com
    Situated in a former quarrying village by the sea
on the Lleyn Peninsula in North Wales, this institute
offers year-round Welsh learning at all levels.

GENEALOGY
Tracing your ancestors has been made much easier
with the advent of the Internet. Here are some on-
line resources:
    www.genuki.org.uk
    www.cyndislist.com
    www.rootsweb.com/~irish

You can also contact:
Irish Family History Society
P.O. Box 36
Naas
County Kildare
Ireland
Web: www.mayo-ireland.ie/geneal/ifhissoc.htm

North of Ireland Family History Society
    c/o Graduate School of Education
The Queen's University of Belfast
69 University Street
Belfast BT7 1HL
Northern Ireland
Web: www.nifhs.org

The Scottish Association of Family History Societies
Hon. Secretary Alan J. L. MacLeod
51/3 Mortonhall Road

Edinburgh EH9 2HN
Scotland
Web: www.safhs.org.uk

Association of Family History Societies of Wales
Geoff Riggs, Secretary
Peacehaven
Badgers Meadow
Pwllmeyric
Chepstow, Mon.
Wales NP16 6UE
United Kingdom
Web: www.rootsweb.com/~wlsafhs

The Isle of Man Family History Society
David Christian
3 Minorca Hill
Laxey
Isle of Man LM4 7DN
United Kingdom
Web: www.isle-of-man.com/interests/genealogy/fhs

Cornwall Family History Society
5 Victoria Square
Truro
Cornwall TR1 2RS
United Kingdom
Web: www.cornwallfhs.com

Books
Cory, Kathleen B. *Tracing Your Scottish Ancestry.*
    Edinburgh: Polygon, 1997.
Grenham, John. *Tracing Your Irish Ancestors:*
    The Complete Guide. Dublin: Gill and Macmillan,
    1993.
Herber, Mark D. *Ancestral Trails: The Complete*
    Guide to British Genealogy and Family History.
    Baltimore, MD: Genealogical Publications, 2000.

Rowlands, John, and Sheila Rowlands, eds. *Welsh Family History: A Guide to Research.* Aberystwyth: Association of Family History Societies of Wales, 1998.

MUSIC

The best way to hear traditional Celtic music is, of course, live, at a pub, *céilidh,* or *fest-noz* (Breton night-party). But many excellent recordings are available, too. Literally hundreds of Celtic bands, duos, and solo musicians have sprung up in the last thirty years, since the enthusiastic revival of traditional music, and new performers and recording artists are still arriving every year. Here are a just a few whose recordings have stood the test of time and are easily available in the U.S.

Ireland: The Chieftains, Bothy Band, Altan, Clannad, De Danann, Patrick Street, Lunasa, Christy Moore (singer), Dolores Keane (singer), Mary Black (singer), Andy Irvine (singer), Jimmy Crowley (singer), Martin Hayes (fiddle), Davey Spillane (uilleann pipes), Joe Burke (accordian), Matt Molloy (Irish flute).

Scotland: Battlefield Band, Silly Wizard, Old Blind Dogs, Runrig, Tannahill Weavers, Sileas, Capercaillie, Dougie McLean (singer), Jean Redpath (singer)

Wales: Carreg Lafar, Ar Log, Plethyn, Fernhill, Robin Huw Bowen & Crasdant

Brittany: Kornog, Skolvan, Barzaz, Alain Stivell (harp)

Isle of Man: Charles Guard (harp), Emma Christian (harp, singer)

Cornwall: Anao Atao

Spain: Miladoiro (from Galicia); Llan de Cubel (from Asturias)

Traditional Music Sung by Native Speakers
Portland America Distributing
496 Congress Street
Portland, ME 04101
Phone: (800) 797-3868
Web: www.portlandamerica.com
Carries otherwise hard-to-find Scottish and Cape Breton music and stories.

Cerdd Ystwyth Music
7, Upper Portland Street
Aberystwyth, Ceredigion
Wales SY23 2DT
United Kingdom
Phone: + 44 1970 623 382
Web: www.cerddystwyth.co.uk/index.htm
Has a large stock of Welsh recordings and can also put you in touch with upcoming Welsh festivals and *eisteddfods.*

Ossian USA
118 Beck Road
Loudon, NH 03307
Phone: (603) 783-4383
Web: www.ossianusa.com/about.html
Carries music from legendary singers and musicians from all parts of Ireland.

Cló Iar-Chonnachta (CIC)
Indreabhán
Conamara
Co. na Gaillimhe
Éire/Ireland
Phone: + 353 91 593 307
Web: www.cic.ie
Located in Galway, this distributor carries rare archival recordings of traditional music, including *sean-nós.*

Ceolas
844 Fremont St.
Menlo Park, CA 94025
Phone: (650) 326-0680
  The most comprehensive Web page on Celtic music: www.ceolas.org/ceolas.html
  Has information and links on all aspects of the tradition, including musical instruments, dance, and resources for those who would like to learn to play the music themselves.

STORYTELLING
Moore, Robin. *Creating a Family Storytelling Tradition*. Little Rock: August House, 1999. A step-by-step guide for beginning a storytelling tradition in your family.

Anthologies of Celtic Stories for Children and Adults
Glassie, Henry, ed. *Irish Folktales*. New York: Pantheon Books, 1985.
Jacobs, Joseph, comp. *Celtic Fairy Tales and More Celtic Fairy Tales*. London: F. Muller, 1972.
Matthews, John, ed. *Classic Celtic Fairy Tales*. London: Blandford, 1999.
Philip, Neil, ed. *The Penguin Book of Scottish Folktales*. New York: Penguin Books, 1995.
Stephens, James. *Traditional Irish Fairy Tales*. New York: Dover Publications, 1996.
Thomas, W. Jenkyn. *The Welsh Fairy Book*. Cardiff: University of Wales Press, 1995.
Williamson, Duncan. *Fireside Tales of the Traveller Children*. Edinburgh: Canongate, 1983. See his other books as well.
Young, Ella. *Celtic Wonder-Tales*. New York: Dover Publications, 1995.
A few rare recordings of the old, traditional storytellers are available from Cló Iar-Chonnachta, Portland America Distributing, and Ossian USA (see the Music section).

Some more recent tellers who have produced recordings:
Robin Williamson (the Bard!)
Pig's Whisker Music
P.O. Box 114
Chesterfield
Derbyshire S40 3YU
England
Phone: + 44 1246 567 712
Web: www.thebeesknees.com/bk-pw-in.html

Fiona Davidson (Scottish storyteller, singer, and harpist)
Web: www.the-bard.co.uk

Norman Kennedy (Scottish storyteller who learned from the old tellers)
P.O. Box 473
Plainfield VT 05667
Phone: (802) 426-3140

Eamon Kelly (Irish shanachie)
Recordings available from:
Rego Irish Records
P.O. Box 1515
Green Island, NY 12183-0515
Phone: (800) 854-3746
Web: www.regorecords.com/spokenarts.html

  And finally, if you are ever in Ireland in early September, take the ferry to Cape Clear Island for the International Storytelling Festival held there every year across the whole island—an unforgettable experience! Contact:

  Chuck Kruger
  Glen West

Cape Clear Island
County Cork
Ireland
Phone/fax: + 353 28 39157
Web: indigo.ie/~ckstory/index.htm

SACRED LAND
The Ancient Sacred Landscape Network (ASLAN)
Web: www.symbolstone.org/archaeology/aslan
Focus for a number of British organizations that aim to preserve and protect sacred sites and their setting, and the maintenance of access to them.

The Sacred Land Project
ICOREC
3 Wynnstay Grove
Manchester M14 6XG
United Kingdom
Phone + 44 161 248 5731
Web: www.els.salford.ac.uk/env-res/wwf/about.html
Aims to rehallow the environment of Britain.

Trees
The Global ReLeaf Project
American Forests
P.O Box 2000
Washington, DC 20013
Phone: (202) 955-4500
Web: www.americanforests.org/global_releaf/

Trees Foundation
P.O. Box 2202
Redway, CA 95542
Phone: (707) 923-4377
Web: www.treesfoundation.org

Trees for Life
The Park
Findhorn Bay
Forres IV36 3TZ
Scotland
Phone: + 44 1309 691 292
Web: www.treesforlife.org.uk

MISCELLANEOUS
Green Man Essences
Web: www.greenmantrees.demon.co.uk

Ogam Oils and Essences
Celtic Tree Oils Ltd.
Ogam Apothecary
Carlingford
County Louth
Ireland
Phone: + 353 42 73793
Web: http://homepage.tinet.ie/~celtictrees1/

Herb and Potpourri Suppliers
(U.S. West Coast)

San Francisco Herb Company
250 14th Street
San Francisco, CA 94103
Phone: (800) 227-4530
Web: sfherb.com/index.html

(U.S. East Coast)

Atlantic Spice Company
2 Shore Road
P.O. Box 205
North Truro, MA 02652
Phone: (800) 316-7965
Web: www.atlanticspice.com

Craft Suppliers
The Cedar Tree Crafts
205 Washington Street
Millsboro, DE 19966
Phone: (302) 934-9550
Web: www.thecedartreecrafts.com

Black Beards (Wheat Weaving suppliers)
512 Washington Drive
Turtle Lake, ND 58575-4300
Phone: (701) 448-9171
Web: www.geocities.com/wheatfarmer_1

A number of the illustrations in this book plus other sacred and magical art can be purchased as greetings cards and prints from:

BlueFeather Arts
The Studio of Linda Carol Risso
P.O. Box 375
Carmel Valley, CA 93924-0375
Phone: (831) 659-7470
Web: www.bluefeatherarts.com
Or send for a current catalog of original artwork.

CELTIC SPIRIT RESOURCES

WORKSHOPS AND RETREATS

For a schedule of Mara's upcoming presentations, go to www.chalicecenter.com, or subscribe to her free quarterly newsletter by e-mail:
news@celticspirit.org
Mara is also available for speaking engagements, workshops, weddings, rituals, and retreats.

THE WELL OF WISDOM:
CORRESPONDENCE COURSE

Those wishing to follow a spiritual path in the Celtic tradition are invited to join the Druid Clan of Dana, an Irish magical order in which Mara Freeman is an Archdruidess. Members can participate in a worldwide distance-learning program, "The Well of Wisdom," a sevenfold path of self-actualization through the Celtic Mysteries.

ANAMCARA: READINGS AND COUNSELING

Anamcara is an old Irish word meaning "soul friend," a companion on the spiritual path. Mara offers readings and soul guidance in the spirit of Anamcara, drawing upon her extensive experience as a transpersonal psychotherapist, intuitive, and astrologer. Consultations can be conducted by telephone.

CELTIC SPIRIT PILGRIMAGES

Join Mara on pilgrimage to some of the most beautiful sacred places in the Celtic realms. For details and registration, see below."

THE AVALON MYSTERY SCHOOL

For those wishing to go deeper into Celtic and related Western magical traditions: you are invited to enter into the Mysteries of Avalon through a correspondence course that also offers optional workshops with Mara Freeman in the U.S.A. or Britian. The path of the Mysteries leads to higher consciousness of the self as connected with all beings, visible and invisible, on the great Tree of Life, and ultimately with the Source of All. Training in the arts of sacred magic will teach you ways to mediate spiritual energies into the physical world for healing.

AUDIO SERIES (CDs)

CELTIC SPIRIT MEDITATIONS

All twelve meditations in this book guided by Mara Freeman to musical accompaniment.

CELTIC TALES OF ENCHANTMENT

A selection of magical stories from *Kindling the Celtic Spirit* set to the harp and other instruments.

CELTIC TALES OF BIRDS AND BEASTS

Five stories of animals and shape-shifters: wise and humorous tales of wonder set to Celtic music.

Contact Mara at:
P.O. Box 3839, Carmel, CA 93921, USA
E-mail: office@celticspirit.org
Phone: (800)-694-1957
Web site: www.celticspirit.org

NOTES

INTRODUCTION

1. A. E. [George Russell], *The Candle of Vision* (New York: University Books, 1965).

JANUARY

1. A. Rees and B. Rees, *Celtic Heritage* (London: Thames and Hudson, 1961).

2. Personal communication from Alexei Kondratiev.

3. Trefor M. Owen, *The Customs and Traditions of Wales* (Cardiff: University of Wales Press, 1991).

4. Translation by Mara Freeman, from Alexander Carmichael, *Carmina Gadelica*, vols. 1–6 (Edinburgh: Oliver and Boyd, 1940).

5. Henry Glassie, *All Silver and No Brass* (Bloomington and London: Indiana University Press, 1975).

6. Kevin Danaher, *Irish Country Households* (Cork: Mercier Press, 1985).

7. Michael Slavin, *The Book of Tara* (Dublin: Wolfhound Press,1996).

8. P. W. Joyce, *A Smaller Social History of Ancient Ireland* (Dublin: Longmans, Green, 1908).

9. Lady Augusta Gregory, *A Book of Saints and Wonders* (London: John Murray, 1907).

10. Kenneth MacLeod, *The Road to the Isles* (London: Adam & Charles Black, 1943).

11. Ronald Hutton, *The Stations of the Sun* (London: Oxford University Press, 1996).

12. F. Marian McNeill, *The Silver Bough*, vol. 3 (Glasgow: William MacLellan, 1959).

13. John G. Neihardt, *Black Elk Speaks* (New York: Washington Square Press, 1972).

FEBRUARY

1. Alexander Carmichael, *Carmina Gadelica,* vols. 1–6 (Edinburgh: Oliver and Boyd, 1940).

2. Whitley Stokes, ed., *Cormac's Glossary* (Dublin: Irish Archeological and Celtic Society, 1868).

3. Miranda Green, *Celtic Goddesses* (New York: George Braziller, 1995).

4. John T. Koch and John Carey, *The Celtic Heroic Age* (Massachusetts: Celtic Studies Publications, 1995).

5. Kevin Danaher, *The Year in Ireland* (Cork, Ireland: Mercier Press, 1972).

6. Séamas Ó Catháin, *The Festival of Brigit* (Dublin: DBA Publications, 1995).

MARCH

1. Trefor M. Owen, *The Customs and Traditions of Wales* (Cardiff: University of Wales Press, 1991).

2. Alexander Carmichael, *Carmina Gadelica* (Edinburgh: Oliver and Boyd, 1940).

3. Walter L. Brenneman and Mary G. Brenneman, *Crossing the Circle at the Holy Wells of Ireland* (Charlottesville and London: University Press of Virginia, 1995).

4. Lady Augusta Gregory, *A Book of Saints and Wonders* (London: John Murray, 1907).

5. Charles Hope, *Holy Wells of England* (Detroit: Singing Tree Press, 1968).

6. Paul Devereux, *Re-Visioning the Earth* (New York: Fireside, 1996).

7. Hope, *Holy Wells.*

8. Arthur C. L. Brown, *The Origin of the Grail Legend* (New York: Russell & Russell, 1966).

9. T. S. Eliot, *The Wasteland and Other Poems* (London: Faber and Faber, 1971).

10. F. Marian McNeill, *The Silver Bough,* vol. 1 (Glasgow: William MacLellan, 1959).

11. McNeill, *Silver Bough.*

12. Carmichael, *Carmina Gadelica.*

13. Miranda Green, *Celtic Goddesses* (New York: George Braziller, 1995).

14. Mary Beith, *Healing Threads* (Edinburgh: Polygon, 1995).

15. R. S. Loomis, *Wales and the Arthurian Legend* (Cardiff: University of Wales Press, 1956).

APRIL

1. Alexander Carmichael, *Carmina Gadelica* (Edinburgh: Oliver and Boyd, 1940).

2. R. I. Best, "On the Settling of the Manor of Tara," *Eriu* 4 (1910).

3. Edward Gwynn, *The Metrical Dindshenchas,* vol. 3 (Dublin: Hodges, Figgis, 1924).

4. A. T. Lucas, "The Sacred Trees of Ireland," *Journal of the Cork Historical and Archaeological Society* 68 (1963).

5. Nora Chadwick, "Geilt," *Scottish Gaelic Studies* 5, part 2 (1942).

6. Geoffrey Grigson, *The Englishman's Flora* (London: Phoenix House, 1960).

7. Personal communication with Dusty Miller.

8. Interview with Ella Young on KPFA Radio, Berkeley, CA, 1957.

9. Jeffrey Gantz, *Early Irish Myths and Sagas* (London: Penguin, 1981).

10. Robert Van de Weyer, *Celtic Parables* (London: SPCK, 1997).

11. Mircea Eliade, *Shamanism* (New Jersey: Princeton University Press, 1964).

MAY

1. Miranda Green, *Dictionary of Celtic Myth and Legend* (London: Thames & Hudson, 1992).

2. Kevin Danaher, *The Year in Ireland* (Cork: Mercier Press, 1972).

3. Alexander Carmichael, *Carmina Gadelica* (Edinburgh: Oliver and Boyd, 1940).

4. Carmichael, *Carmina Gadelica.*

5. Danaher, *The Year in Ireland.*

6. Mircea Eliade, *Studies in Comparative Religion* (London: Sheed and Ward, 1971).

7. Trefor M. Owen, *Welsh Folk Customs* (Llandysul: Gomer Press, 1994).

8. Translated from Katharine Briggs, *The Vanishing People* (New York: Pantheon, 1978).

9. A. Rees and B. Rees, *Celtic Heritage* (London: Thames and Hudson, 1961).

10. Translation by Patrick K. Ford, *The Celtic Poets: Songs and Tales from Early Ireland and Wales* (Belmont, MA: Ford & Bailie, 1999).

11. Seán O' Faoláin, *The Silver Branch* (New York: Viking Press, 1938).

12. James Carney, *Medieval Irish Lyrics* (Berkeley and Los Angeles: University of California Press, 1967).

13. W. B. Yeats, *Selected Poems and Two Plays of William Butler Yeats* (New York: Collier Books, 1962).

14. Norman A. Jeffares, ed., *Irish Love Poems* (Dublin: O' Brien Press, 1997).

15. Edward O. Wilson, *Biophilia* (Cambridge: Harvard University Press, 1986).

16. Anne Ross, *Pagan Celtic Britain* (London: Routledge and Kegan Paul, 1967).

JUNE

1. Dáithi Ó hÓgáin, *Myth, Legend, and Romance* (New York: Prentice-Hall, 1991).

2. Gerald and Margaret Ponting, *The Standing Stones of Callanish* (Stornaway: Essprint, 1977).

3. Alexander Carmichael, *Carmina Gadelica* (Edinburgh: Oliver and Boyd, 1940).

4. Marie Trevelyan, *Folk-lore and Folk-stories of Wales* (London: Elliott Stock, 1909).

5. Kenneth Jackson, *A Celtic Miscellany* (London: Routledge & Kegan Paul, 1951).

6. Robert Graves, *The White Goddess* (London: Faber and Faber, 1948).

7. W. G. Wood-Martin, *Traces of the Elder Faiths of Ireland* (London: Longmans, Green, 1902).

8. Kuno Meyer, *Selections from Ancient Irish Poetry* (London: Constable, 1928).

9. Mircea Eliade, *Shamanism* (New Jersey: Princeton University Press, 1964).

10. A. E. (George W. Russell), *Collected Poems* (London: Macmillan, 1928).

11. W. Y. Evans-Wentz, *The Fairy-Faith in Celtic Countries* (Bucks: Colin Smythe, 1977).

12. Ella Young, *Flowering Dusk* (New York: Longmans, Green, 1945).

13. Walter de la Mare, *The Complete Poems* (New York: Alfred A. Knopf, 1970).

14. Eliot Cowan, *Plant Spirit Medicine* (Mill Spring, NC: Swan Raven, 1995).

15. Basil Clarke, *Life of Merlin* (Cardiff: University of Wales Press, 1979).

JULY

1. Dáithi Ó hÓgáin, *Irish Superstitions* (Dublin: Gill and Macmillan, 1995).

2. Lady Augusta Gregory, *Gods and Fighting Men* (Gerrards Cross: Colin Smythe, 1970).

3. Kuno Meyer, *Selections from Ancient Irish Poetry* (London: Constable, 1959).

4. Kenneth Jackson, *A Celtic Miscellany* (London: Routledge and Kegan Paul, 1951).

5. Meyer, *Ancient Irish Poetry*.

6. Jackson, *Celtic Miscellany*.

7. Meyer, *Ancient Irish Poetry*.

8. Robert Bly, ed., *News of the Universe* (San Francisco: Sierra Books, 1980).

9. Robin Flower, *The Irish Tradition* (London: Oxford University Press, 1947).

10. Alexander Carmichael, *Carmina Gadelica* (Edinburgh: Oliver and Boyd, 1940).

11. Ó hÓgáin, *Irish Superstitions*.

12. William Blake, *The Complete Poetry and Prose of William Blake*, ed. David V. Erdman (Berkeley and Los Angeles: University of California Press, 1982).

13. From the telling of Joe Neil MacNeill, of Sydney, Cape Breton, in *Cape Breton's Magazine* 19 (June 1978): 31.

14. Jackson, *Celtic Miscellany*.

15. Carmichael, *Carmina Gadelica*.

16. Translated by Mara Freeman from Carmichael, *Carmina Gadelica*.

17. Carmichael, *Carmina Gadelica*.

18. Carmichael, *Carmina Gadelica*.

19. Peter Harbison, *Pilgrimage in Ireland* (New York: Syracuse University Press, 1992).

20. Nigel Pennick, *Celtic Sacred Landscapes* (London: Thames and Hudson, 1996).

21. F. Marian McNeill, *Iona: A History of the Island* (Glasgow: Blackie and Son, 1920).

22. S. Thomas, *Frequencies* (London: Macmillan, 1978).

23. Dion Fortune, *Avalon of the Heart* (London: F. Muller, 1934).

24. Ken Butigan, "We Traveled to Seattle," *Earthlight, the Magazine of Spiritual Ecology* no. 36 (Winter 2000).

AUGUST

1. Máire MacNeill, *The Festival of Lughnasa* (Dublin: University College, 1982).

2. Edward Gwynn, *The Metrical Dindshenchas,* vol. 3 (Dublin: Hodges, Figgis, 1924).

3. MacNeill, *Festival of Lughnasa.*

4. Gwynn, *Metrical Dindshenchas.*

5. Gwynn, *Metrical Dindshenchas.*

6. Patrick K. Ford, *The Mabinogi and Other Welsh Tales* (Berkeley and Los Angeles: University of California Press, 1977).

7. P. W. Joyce, *Old Celtic Romances* (London: David Nutt, 1879).

8. Kevin Danaher, *The Year in Ireland* (Cork: Mercier Press, 1972).

9. MacNeill, *Festival of Lughnasa.*

10. MacNeill, *Festival of Lughnasa.*

11. MacNeill, *Festival of Lughnasa.*

12. A. Rees and B. Rees, *Celtic Heritage* (London: Thames and Hudson, 1961).

13. Ruth L. Tongue, *Forgotten Folk-Tales of the English Counties* (London: Routledge & Kegan Paul, 1970).

14. Tongue, *Forgotten Folk-Tales.*

15. Alexander Carmichael, *Carmina Gadelica* (Edinburgh: Oliver and Boyd, 1940).

16. MacNeill, *Festival of Lughnasa.*

SEPTEMBER

1. Bobby Freeman, *Traditional Food from Wales* (New York: Hippocrene Books, 1997).

2. John Evelyn, *Silva, or, A Discourse of Forest-Trees* (London: J. Dodsley, 1776).

3. Dáithi Ó hÓgáin, "The Visionary Voice," *Irish University Review* 9 (1979): 44–61.

4. Ó hÓgáin, "Visionary Voice."

5. Kenneth Jackson, *A Celtic Miscellany* (London: Routledge and Kegan Paul, 1951).

6. Kuno Meyer, *Miscellanea Hibernica,* vol. 2 (Urbana: University of Illinois Press, 1916).

7. John Carey, "The Waters of Vision and the Gods of Skill," *Alexandria* 1 (1991).

8. Carey, *Waters.*

9. Giraldus Cambrensis, *The History and Topography of Ireland,* trans. John O'Meara (Portlaoise: Dolmen Press, 1951).

10. Elizabeth A. Gray, *Cath Maige Tuired* (Kildare: Irish Texts Society, 1982).

11. Robin Flower, *The Irish Tradition* (London: Oxford University Press, 1947).

12. Standish O Grady, *Silva Gadelica* (London and Edinburgh: Williams and Norgate, 1892).

13. Robin Flower, *The Western Island* (New York: Oxford University Press, 1945).

14. Keith Sanger and Alison Kinnaird, *Tree of Strings* (Temple, Midlothian: Kinmor Music, 1992).

15. Roslyn Rensch, *Harps and Harpists* (Bloomington: Indiana University Press, 1989).

16. Giraldus Cambrensis, *History and Topography of Ireland.*

17. Jackson, *Celtic Miscellany.*

18. Eugene O'Curry, *On the Manners and Customs of the Ancient Irish* (Dublin: Edmund Burke, 1996).

19. I. F. Grant, *Highland Folk Ways* (London: Routledge & Kegan Paul, 1961).

20. Margaret Fay Shaw, *Folksongs and Folklore of South Uist* (London: William Clowes and Son, 1955).

21. Julie Henigan, "Sean-nós in Donegal," *Ulster Folklife* 37 (1991).

22. Henigan, "Sean-nós."

23. Slightly adapted by Hilaire Wood.

24. Henigan, "Sean-nós."

OCTOBER

1. A. Rees and B. Rees, *Celtic Heritage* (London: Thames and Hudson, 1961).

2. Kuno Meyer, *Hibernica Minora* (New York: AMS Press, 1989).

3. Rees and Rees, *Celtic Heritage*.

4. J. F. Campbell, *Popular Tales of the West Highlands*, vol. 2 (Edinburgh: Birlinn, 1994).

5. Donald Mackenzie, *Scottish Folk-lore and Folk Life* (London and Glasgow: Blackie and Son, 1935).

6. Proinsias MacCana, *Celtic Mythology* (New York: Peter Bedrick Books, 1983).

7. Elizabeth A. Gray, *Cath Maige Tuired* (Kildare: Irish Texts Society, 1982).

8. F. Marian McNeill, *The Silver Bough*, vol. 3 (Glasgow: William MacLellan, 1959).

9. Available from Kilmartin House, Kilmartin, Argyll, Scotland, PA31 8RQ.

10. Ella Young, *The Tangle-Coated Horse* (Edinburgh: Flon's Books, 1991).

NOVEMBER

1. A. Rees and B. Rees, *Celtic Heritage* (London: Thames and Hudson, 1961).

2. Howard Patch, *The Other World, according to descriptions in medieval literature* (Cambridge: Harvard University Press, 1950).

3. Dennis Tedlock, *Breathe on the Mirror* (San Francisco: HarperSanFrancisco, 1993).

4. Rees and Rees, *Celtic Heritage*.

5. Edwin Muir, *An Autobiography* (London: Hogarth Press, 1954).

6. Adapted from Robin Moore, *Creating a Family Storytelling Tradition* (Little Rock: August House, 1999).

7. Rachel Bromwich, *The Welsh Triads* (Cardiff: University of Wales Press, 1978).

8. A good version of this story can be found in *Folktales of Ireland*, ed. Sean O'Sullivan (Chicago: University of Chicago Press, 1999).

9. Patrick K. Ford, *The Celtic Poets: Songs and Tales from Early Ireland and Wales* (Belmont, MA: Ford & Bailie, 1999).

10. Kevin Danaher, *The Year in Ireland* (Cork: Mercier Press, 1972).

11. W. Y. Evans-Wentz, *The Fairy-Faith in Celtic Countries* (Bucks: Colin Smythe, 1977).

DECEMBER

1. Ronald Hutton, *The Stations of the Sun* (London: Oxford University Press, 1996).

2. Quoted by F. Marian McNeill, *The Silver Bough*, vol. 3 (Glasgow: William MacLellan, 1959).

3. Kevin Danaher, *The Year in Ireland* (Cork: Mercier Press, 1972).

4. Alice Taylor, *An Irish Country Christmas* (New York: St. Martin's Press, 1994).

5. Danaher, *Year in Ireland*.

Breathnach, Breandán. *Folk Music and Dances of Ireland*. Cork: Mercier Press, 1971.

Brenneman, Walter L., and Mary G. Brenneman. *Crossing the Circle at the Holy Wells of Ireland*. Charlottesville: University Press of Virginia, 1995.

Briggs, Katharine M. *A Dictionary of British Folk-Tales*. Bloomington: Indiana University Press, 1970.

———. *An Encyclopedia of Fairies*. New York: Pantheon Books, 1976.

Cambrensis, Giraldus. *The History and Topography of Ireland*. Trans. John O'Meara. Portlaoise: Dolmen Press, 1951.

Campbell, J. F. *Popular Tales of the West Highlands*. Edinburgh: Birlinn, 1994.

Carmichael, Alexander. *Carmina Gadelica*. Vols. 1–6. Edinburgh: Oliver and Boyd, 1940.

Carney, James. *Medieval Irish Lyrics*. Berkeley and Los Angeles: University of California Press, 1967.

Child, Francis J. *English and Scottish Ballads*. Boston: Houghton and Mifflin, 1885.

Courtney, M. A. *Cornish Feasts and Folk-Lore*. N.p.: Penzance, Beare and Son, 1890.

Cross, Tom Peete, and Clark Harris Slover, eds. *Ancient Irish Tales*. Dublin: Figgis, 1936.

Cunliffe, Barry W. *The Celtic World*. New York: St. Martin's Press, 1993.

Danaher, Kevin. *Irish Country Households*. Cork: Mercier Press, 1985.

———. *The Year in Ireland*. Cork: Mercier Press, 1972.

Deane, T., and T. Shaw. *The Folklore of Cornwall*. London: Batsford, 1975.

Evans, E. Estyn. *Irish Folk Ways*. London: Routledge & Kegan Paul, 1957.

Evans-Wentz, W. Y. *The Fairy-Faith in Celtic Countries*. Buckinghamshire, England: Colin Smythe, 1977.

Flower, Robin. *The Irish Tradition*. London: Oxford University Press, 1947.

Ford, Patrick K. *The Celtic Poets*. Belmont, MA: Ford & Bailie, 1999.

———. *The Mabinogi and Other Welsh Tales*. Berkeley and Los Angeles: University of California Press, 1977.

Gailey, Alain, and Dáithi Ó hÓgáin, eds. *Gold Under the Furze*. Dublin: Glendale Press, 1982.

Gantz, Jeffrey. *Early Irish Myths and Sagas*. London: Penguin, 1981.

Grant, I. F. *Highland Folk Ways*. London: Routledge & Kegan Paul, 1961.

Gray, Elizabeth A. *Cath Maige Tuired*. Kildare: Irish Texts Society, 1982.

Green, Miranda. *Celtic Goddesses*. New York: George Braziller, 1995.

———. *Dictionary of Celtic Myth and Legend*. London: Thames and Hudson, 1992.

———. *The World of the Druids*. New York: Thames and Hudson, 1997.

Gregory, Lady Augusta. *A Book of Saints and Wonders*. London: John Murray, 1907.

Grigson, Geoffrey. *The Englishman's Flora*. London: Phoenix House, 1960.

Gwynn, Edward. *The Metrical Dindshenchas*. Dublin: Hodges, Figgis, 1924.

Harbison, Peter. *Pilgrimage in Ireland*. New York: Syracuse University Press, 1992.

Henderson, George. *Survivals in Belief Among the Celts*. Glasgow: MacLehose, 1911.

Hole, Christina. *British Folk Customs.* London: Hutchinson, 1976.

Hull, Eleanor. *Folklore of the British Isles.* London: Methuen, 1928.

Hutton, Ronald. *The Stations of the Sun.* London: Oxford University Press, 1996.

Jackson, Kenneth. *A Celtic Miscellany.* London: Penguin Books, 1971.

James, Simon. *The World of the Celts.* London: Thames and Hudson, 1993.

Kelly, Fergus. *Early Irish Farming.* Dublin: Dublin Institute of Advanced Studies, 1998.

Koch, John T., and John Carey. *The Celtic Heroic Age.* Maiden, MA: Celtic Studies Publications, 1995.

Livingstone, Sheila. *Scottish Customs.* Edinburgh: Birlinn, 1996.

MacCana, Proinsias. *Celtic Mythology.* New York: Peter Bedrick Books, 1983.

Mackenzie, Donald A. *Scottish Folk-lore and Folk-life.* London: Blackie, 1935.

———. *Wonder Tales from Scottish Myth & Legend.* London: Blackie, 1917.

MacKillop, James. *Dictionary of Celtic Mythology.* Oxford: Oxford University Press, 1998.

MacNeill, Máire. *The Festival of Lughnasa.* Dublin: University College, 1982.

Mahon, Bríd. *Land of Milk and Honey.* Dublin: Poolbeg, 1991.

McNeill, F. Marian. *The Silver Bough.* Vols. 1–4. Glasgow: William MacLellan, 1959.

Megaw, Ruth, and Vincent Megaw. *Celtic Art.* New York: Thames and Hudson, 1989.

Meyer, Kuno. *Selections from Ancient Irish Poetry.* London: Constable, 1928.

Nagy, Joseph Falaky. *The Wisdom of the Outlaw.* Berkeley and Los Angeles: University of California Press, 1985.

Ó Catháin, Séamas. *The Festival of Brigit.* Dublin: DBA Publications, 1995.

O Grady, Standish. *Silva Gadelica.* London and Edinburgh: Williams and Norgate, 1892.

Ó hÓgáin, Dáithi. *Irish Superstitions.* Dublin: Gill and Macmillan, 1995.

———. *Myth, Legend & Romance.* New York: Prentice-Hall, 1991.

———. *The Sacred Isle.* Cork: Collins Press, 1999.

Ó Súilleabháin, Seán. *Irish Folk Custom and Belief.* Cork: Mercier Press, 1967.

Owen, Trefor M. *The Customs and Traditions of Wales.* Cardiff: University of Wales Press, 1991.

———. *Welsh Folk Customs.* Llandysul: Gomer Press, 1994.

Patterson, Nerys. *Cattle Lords and Clansmen.* New York: Garland, 1991.

Pennick, Nigel. *Celtic Sacred Landscapes.* London: Thames and Hudson, 1996.

Rees, Alwyn, and Brinley Rees. *Celtic Heritage.* London: Thames and Hudson, 1961.

Rhys, Sir John. *Celtic Folklore, Welsh and Manx.* Oxford: Clarendon Press, 1901.

Ross, Anne. *Pagan Celtic Britain.* London: Routledge & Kegan Paul, 1967.

Sexton, Regina. *A Little History of Irish Food.* Dublin: Gill and Macmillan, 1998.

Sjoestedt, Marie-Louise. *Gods and Heroes of the Celts.* London: Methuen, 1949.

Stokes, Whitley. *The Lives of the Saints from The Book of Lismore.* Oxford: Clarendon Press, 1890.

———, ed. *Cormac's Glossary.* Dublin: Irish Archeological and Celtic Society, 1868.

Taylor, Alice. *An Irish Country Christmas.* New York: St. Martin's Press, 1994.

Tongue, Ruth L. *Forgotten Folk-tales of the English Counties.* London: Routledge & Kegan Paul, 1970.

Trevelyan, Marie. *Folk-lore and Folk-stories of Wales.* London: Elliott Stock, 1909.

Wilde, Lady Francesca. *Ancient Legends of Ireland.* London: Chatto & Windus, 1919.

Yeats, W. B. *Selected Poems and Two Plays.* New York: Macmillan, 1962.

ACKNOWLEDGMENTS

I am indebted to many people for their help in bringing this book to fruition: first, my agent, Carol Susan Roth, who opened the door and welcomed me warmly into the world of book publishing; Alexei Kondratiev, who provided invaluable guidance on linguistic and historical points; and Dennis King, who graciously allowed me to print his beautiful bilingual poems. I also want to thank my inner circle of supporters: my husband, David Watkins, for his enduring love and willingness to keep the hearth-fires burning while I was tethered to the computer, and for his hours of meticulous proofreading; Sidney Ramsden-Scott and Jacquelyn Smith, who not only offered their continuing friendship and support but also helped test and refine the recipes. A special word of thanks also to those who took the time to answer my questions and give suggestions: Conrad Bladey, Bob Breheny, Margie McArthur, Mary McLaughlin, Robin Moore, Ray Price, Miceal Ross, Professor Steve Sweeney-Turner, and Hilaire Wood.

In particular, I acknowledge with deep gratitude two very special contributors, without whom this book would never have been born:

Linda Carol Risso, for lending her expertise to the crafts and for creating such exquisite illustrations; and David Hennessy, my editor, whose intuition and sensitivity made him a veritable writer's dream.

Go raibh míle maith agaibh!

May you have a thousand good things = Many thanks to you all!

Mara Freeman
Carmel-by-the-Sea, California
Lughnasadh 2000

PERMISSIONS

Grateful acknowledgment is made to the following:

A&C Black (Publishers) Limited for permission to quote "The Rune of Hospitality" from *The Road to the Isles* by Kenneth MacLeod, 1943.

Rogers, Coleridge & White, Ltd., for "Love Epigram" from *The Silver Branch* by Sean O'Faolain, The Viking Press, 1938.

Oxford University Press for "Pangur Bán" and "The Ivy Crest" from *The Irish Tradition* by Robin Flower, 1947.

Scribner, a Division of Simon & Schuster, for "He Wishes for the Cloths of Heaven" from *The Collected Poems of W. B. Yeats,* Revised Second Edition by Richard J. Finneman, 1996.

Carcanet Press Limited for lines from "The White Goddess" by Robert Graves, Faber and Faber, 1948.

The O'Brien Press, Limited, for "My Hope, My Love," translated by Edward Walsh, from *Irish Love Poems,* ed. Norman A. Jeffares, Dublin, 1997.

Mr. Justice Paul Carney for "The Blackthorn Bush," translated by James Carney, in *Medieval Irish Lyrics,* University of California Press, 1967.

Fiona Davidson for lines from "The Serpent's Tale," *Dalriada Magazine,* 1986.

The Society of Authors for "Lob-Lie-by-the-Fire" by Walter de la Mare, from *The Complete Poems of Walter de la Mare,* Faber, 1969.

St. Martin's Press for lines from *An Irish Country Christmas* by Alice Taylor, 1994.

Northstone Publishing, Inc., for "An Act of Gratitude" from *Celtic Parables* by Robert Van de Weyer, SPCK 1997.

Taylor & Francis Books, Ltd., for poems "Winter and Summer" by Thomas Telynog Evans and "The Harp of Cnoc Í Chosgair" by Gofraidh Fionn Ó Dálaigh from *A Celtic Miscellany* by Kenneth Hurlstone Jackson, Penguin Books, Ltd., 1971.

Floris Books for lines from *The Tangle-Coated Horse* by Ella Young, 1991.

Ann C. Bauer for "Yule Round" from *Rounds Galore* by Sol Weber, 1992.

Hue Walker for "The Old God Sleeps" from *Journeys through Inner Space*, Pomegranate Art Books, 1995.

Patrick K. Ford for lines from "Secret Love" from *The Celtic Poets: Songs and Tales from Early Ireland and Wales,* Ford & Bailie, 1999.

Harcourt, Inc., for lines from *The Waste Land* by T. S. Eliot, London, Faber and Faber, Ltd., 1971.

Dennis King for *Deiseal/Sunwise, Mise Miach,* and *Altú/Grace.*